THE WILLIAMS-SONOMA COOKBOOK AND GUIDE TO KITCHENWARE

THE WILLIAMS-SONOMA COOKBOOK AND GUIDE TO KITCHENWARE

CHUCK WILLIAMS

RANDOM HOUSE NEW YORK

Published in the United States by Random House, Inc., New York, and
simultaneously in Canada by Random House of Canada Limited, Toronto.

Grateful acknowledgment is made to the following for permission to reprint recipes:
"Christmas Orange Bread" by Patrice Lenhoff Gunn, "Chocolate Cheesecake"
by Gino Cofacci, "English Lemon Tea Bread" by Evelyn R. Sullivan, "Sardine Butter,"
"Roquefort Creams" and "Fresh Fettucine with Chicken Liver and Lemon Sauce"
by Elizabeth David.

Library of Congress Cataloging-in-Publication Data
Williams, Chuck.
The Williams Sonoma cookbook and guide to kitchenware.

Includes index.
1. Cookery. 2. Kitchen utensils. I. Title.
TX715.W72174 1986 641.5 85-18366
ISBN 0-394-54411-0

Manufactured in the United States of America
24689753
First Edition

Credits

Photography by Pat Haverfield, Photographers, Inc.
Photography design by Carolyn Andres
Drawings by David Redmond
Book Design by Lilly Langotsky

To Mike Sharp for his faith,
support and devoted help to me
and to Williams-Sonoma in its growing years.

ACKNOWLEDGMENTS

All thanks first to Anne Mitchell Kupper for her love of and devotion to Williams-Sonoma, for her endless task of assembling material, for the testing and tasting of some of the recipes and for lighting the fire that got this book started in the first place. To Jackie Mallorca, whose prose has graced the pages of the Williams-Sonoma catalog from its inception (in fact she created the first one), for her work on this book, putting my ramblings and scribblings into proper English and for testing recipes and testing again when in doubt. To Elaine Anderson for her many typing hours and to my good friend Helen Kane, for tasting the results of my cooking and cleaning up the pots and pans afterwards.

A sincere thanks to all our loyal customers of the past thirty years, and especially those who have encouraged the writing of this book.

To all the employees of Williams-Sonoma, both past and present, a special thanks for their help in maintaining the company's integrity and making it grow. This includes Wade Bentson, who gave over seventeen years of his creative talents in helping to mold the character and personality of the business during its beginning years.

To David and Dennis Redmond for their illustrations of the cooking equipment, to Photographers, Inc., especially Pat Haverfield, who do our catalog photography, and did the photographs included in this book, and to Carolyn Andres and Peggy Hidell who design our catalogs and designed these photographs. Many thanks.

Much gratitude to Charlotte Mayerson, for wanting to do the book and be its editor, and to Lilly Langotsky for her superb book design.

Lastly, my sincere gratitude to my friend Elizabeth David, who has been such an inspiration to me in the cooking of good simple food over the past twenty-five years.

CONTENTS

INTRODUCTION

Chairman of the Board sounds like a pretty important job, but because of a flaw in my character, I'm still doing my own Xeroxing—probably for the same reason I swept the sidewalk in front of my first store every morning—secretly, I think I can do it better than anyone else. I know that the mark of a good executive is supposed to be the ability to delegate authority, but that's something I've never learned to do. Instead, I've a tendency to say, "Stand aside. Let me show you how it's done."

I no longer sweep the sidewalks, and we now have machines that seal packages so I don't have to tie them myself. Even so, at an advanced age, when most corporate executives are leaning back in their swivel chairs, I am still flying from one end of the earth to the other, finding merchandise for the Williams-Sonoma catalog and stores. I still supervise every detail of the design and production of our catalogs. I still insist on excellence.

Luckily for me, I have been able to combine this problematic character trait with a deep enthusiasm for food. The result has been a company that helped accomplish a revolution in the United States. Remember luncheon fare like "aspics," made of lime gelatine and canned string beans? The chicken "creamed" with canned condensed celery or mushroom soup? There is now an enormous public in this country that just laughs at that kind of eating. Modern Americans are intensely interested in fine-quality fresh food, well prepared and attractively presented. The transformation has been a modern miracle, and I like to think that we have been associated with it from its infancy.

I come by my knowledge of good food through the genes. My family was of hearty German-Welsh stock and there was no nonsense about what went on in the kitchen, and no nonsense about what went into it, either: good-quality, abundant fresh food was all they used. And my Dutch-German grandmother taught me the simple rewards of baking when most kids were still playing patty-cake.

When I took my first extended trip to Europe in 1952, I quickly dispensed with the museums and churches, and, with my eyes popping, walked my legs off in Paris, Brussels and Copenhagen, visiting the food stores, the shops that sold cookware, the inexpensive little restaurants that seemed to be everywhere. I had always treated the preparation, serving and eating of meals with care and enjoyment. Now I saw that in Europe such care was simply part of everyday life.

That trip to Europe lit a fire under me that still burns, but not only for "foreign" food. When I got back to Sonoma, California, where I lived, I began putting to use what I'd learned in Europe. True, I'd never served radishes with sweet butter before, but the taste, though slightly different from what I had had in France, was new and delicious. My version of *fraises des bois* with crème fraîche was even better, I thought, because I used wild blackberries, instead of strawberries, that I had picked myself.

I was lucky to be surrounded by a group of friends to whom cooking and eating, as well as talking about cooking and eating, was a passion. In those days, in the forties and fifties, good information was hard to come by. Good equipment was scarcer than the proverbial hen's tooth. And not much attention was given to the accouterments that added to the attractive presentation of a meal. But my friend Thérèse was authentically French, as were her grandmother's old copper pots (that badly needed retinning). I learned from her, among other things, the

French way with vegetables, like seasoning string beans with mace. Gordon Tevis, who was the first true gourmet in my life, and whose family had traveled the world, taught me how to take good American corn, fresh from the cob, and make it into a delicious custard. In Sabina Sebastiani's garden fountain grew watercress that seemed like a miracle to us. It was the only place I knew of in Sonoma where watercress grew, and I felt favored to know her. We ate Jean Miller's Cajun dishes one day and, then, on the next, learned to prepare the good classics of Italy from one or another of the many Italian families who lived in the valley.

Is it any wonder that in 1953 I turned a real estate venture into an opportunity to make a living out of the preparation of food? At that time I was a self-taught carpenter-contractor, as a result of my dreams of building a complete house with my own hands. I built that house in 1947, and then got my contractor's license. Years later I bought a commercial building containing a hardware store near the town square. It was a fantastically cluttered store, right out of a *Saturday Evening Post* cover by Norman Rockwell. Like it or not, I was forced to become its proprietor and, in the process, learned that there is nothing very stimulating about nuts and bolts and cans of redwood stain. Before long, the axes and saws disappeared from the front window and in their place appeared the tools of cooking. I sold off the hardware inventory and concentrated on the kitchenware. My collection of antique kitchen utensils was shifted from home to store, and I made trips to San Francisco, where I found sufficient merchandise to create a kitchenware shop with an unusual look. It rapidly became known in the Bay Area as a place to visit.

Eventually, in 1958, I took the plunge and rented a store in San Francisco on Sutter Street, a top location with a top rent. With the help of my friend, Mike Sharp, I brought the shelves and cabinets down from Sonoma and opened the door. My lifetime habit of buying all over the world—in Spain, Portugal, France, Denmark, Germany and Italy—began, and from that moment the venture was a success. We managed to do well both selling equipment and educating our customers. We also were learning a lot from them, too. Because the timing was so right, coinciding as it did with the growing interest in good cooking of the early 1960s, the store created a lot of interest. It became a headquarters and a clearing ground for people who needed information or wanted to discuss their own culinary interests or problems. At first most our customers were wealthy, trend-setting women, patrons of the elegant shops and clubs in our neighborhood. Later, word spread, and into Williams-Sonoma came young career people, serious food addicts and even some of San Francisco's 1960s commune generation. I found myself planning menus and discussing the techniques of constructing a *croquembouche* or plating a roast turkey with gold leaf. I began teaching people—and therefore having to think out carefully myself—such elementary procedures as making mayonnaise or a simple cheese soufflé. The store soon had a bulletin board filled with information on sources and on people related to cooking. The front counter seemed almost like a classroom, with discussions and teaching taking place every day, even though business was still being transacted.

The "greats" of American cooking—James Beard, Helen Evans Brown, Julia Child—would stop by and check in at the Williams-Sonoma store every time they came to San Francisco. All of this changed my life.

In 1973, we opened a store in Beverly Hills. It was at a time when Southern California had far fewer good restaurants than it does now, and though there were a lot of people who knew about good food, they had to learn how to cook it themselves. This is where we came in.

Since teaching was so important a part of our business at the time, we might have ended up with a school of gastronomy. I'm glad that didn't happen, because cooking classes and schools now abound in the United States. But I do think we have retained our unique position as a leader in the field of cookware. Which brings us back to where we started—to my own stubborn and persnickety interest in the best.

The concept of our business was to be "Purveyors of Equipment for the Preparation and Serving of Fine Food," but on my trips to Europe I couldn't resist bringing back things that caught my eye, though they had nothing much to do with our official title. For example, in

Paris I saw great French oyster baskets in front of restaurants and in food markets. I kept inquiring about them until we found the source: a farmer and his family in a tiny village north of Paris who made the baskets during the winter. I brought some to San Francisco and they sold—I suppose to people who were using them for wood baskets. Then the decorators—with Billy Baldwin first, as always—started using them for the ubiquitous plants that grew in everyone's living room in those days. Those oyster baskets are still doing duty today on Aubusson carpets in New York and on the slate floors of the modern houses in California. (Of course, they've since been copied and produced everywhere from Korea to Ireland.)

The Williams-Sonoma Company seemed to grow of its own accord. With the help of Edward Marcus of Neiman-Marcus we got started in 1973 on what is now the biggest part of the business—our mail-order catalogs. Then, with the experience of Howard Lester, who acquired the company, we opened more stores, we expanded, "went public"—but our basic interest remained the same: to help people achieve quality in the preparation and serving of food. By that I don't mean cluttering up your life with expensive equipment (we all know people who need a high price tag to be secure in their purchases) or serving complicated dishes in rich sauces. In fact, I don't really like sauces myself. What food, what service *do* I like? A little story from my own home will illustrate. When the great literary artist of the kitchen, Elizabeth David, came to San Francisco for the first time, I fixed a picnic lunch for her at my house. We had thinly sliced fresh fennel, celery and carrots served with a dressing made of lemon juice and good olive oil. Cold boiled beef was served in thin slices with a big round loaf of whole-wheat bread I had made that morning. We had good unsalted butter, of course, and fruit and cheese for dessert. Lunch was served on a mixture of Italian pottery plates, each one different. No attempt was made to "match" them; they were so lovely they made the food look better. Thin wine glasses, good but not pretentious silver, flowers from the garden on the table—Elizabeth loved it. It would have been silly to take such naturally delicious food and mask its true flavor with fancy preparation, just as it would have been stupid to try to impress my guest with "formal" service. Unless you have servants at your beck and call, it's impossible to be strictly formal anyhow.

And that philosophy—good, fresh (but not fancy) food, cooked with convenient and efficient equipment, served with beautiful things—is the answer to why, after all these years, I've decided to write a book. We have seen, in the growth of our business, how many people share our interests. There has been a continuing dialogue of learning and teaching between us and our customers from the time of the small Sonoma hardware store.

This book, then, is a compendium of advice about equipment, together with a collection of recipes that I have developed over the years. We present it with gratitude to our customers and our friends in the knowledge that a lot of what is to be found here developed out of our relationship and in the hope that the book is helpful and will give them pleasure.

PART I

EQUIPMENT

INTRODUCTION

In this section of the book we are going to try to help you select equipment for your kitchen in a way that coincides with your needs. We're going to do that, I hope, so that you understand the good qualities as well as the possible drawbacks. We're also going to tell you, where it's necessary, the best way to care for kitchen equipment.

We hope to give you the best possible advice—whether you're buying your equipment or learning to better understand what you already have. Though some of the recipes in this book were originally developed to use products that we were selling, not having a particular item doesn't mean you can't produce the desired result. You can, after all, make a delicious soufflé in a dog's dish.

You will see that we have illustrated the recipes with some of the special equipment that we use ourselves, but obviously you can, in many instances, make substitutions.

I've always tried to guide people in selecting the merchandise with which they will be most comfortable. To accomplish that, pick *each* item carefully. You wouldn't buy a "set" of living-room furniture, so why buy a "set" of pots and pans—or dishes, for that matter? Instead, buy one saucepan to try out. Even if it works well, you'll probably want a pan of another material for frying, and still another for slow cooking in the oven.

The next thing to consider is what you *really* need. Don't, for heaven's sake, buy anything until you're sure you're going to use it more than once. There are some things, of course, that you can't do without. If you're going to make Kugelhopf, you should have a Kugelhopf mold. And for ease in the preparation of food, you need good knives.

Which brings us to another question: cost. Good knives, for example, are expensive. They're also a pleasure to use. My own rule, for myself and for our customers, is to buy the best you can afford: quality is worth paying for. You should buy the best stove you can afford, but there's no point in having an elaborate "commercial"-type stove if you don't cook very much. I have to confess that I use a pretty modest four-burner stove I've had for years, though we sell more serious equipment.

I don't go in for too many gadgets myself, but there are some tools that, while not essential, do make life a lot easier. I don't always use my food processor for slicing and chopping: for me a good part of the fun and satisfaction of cooking is doing that kind of job myself. On the other hand, I do use a processor to make pasta dough and an electric pasta machine to roll and cut it. I'm afraid I'd never make pasta at all if I had to do it all by hand. And I do recognize that the food processor has stimulated a lot of people around the country to undertake formerly time-consuming preparations.

Before we go into the details of equipment, I want to say a word about serving food. I think it's a mistake to strive for too much formality and for the kind of "matching" we've discussed before. I don't mean you should use cheap plates and silver. Use good things, but informally. Don't be afraid to serve salad on plates different from those you used for the main course. Pick a dish that will show off your dessert, not necessarily on one that matches the rest of your service. Some foods look better served in the casserole in which they were cooked, so bring it right to the table and set it down proudly alongside your best glasses and silver. Try to get the feeling for displaying food in the most appropriate and natural way. I'm always impressed with the French and the Italians, who cleverly wrap cheese in leaves or serve berries in a twig basket. The Japanese, of course, are masters of the art of presentation, with their lacquered sushi trays and artfully cut vegetables and fish.

Certain items are basic to every kitchen—sharp knives, sturdy saucepans and skillets, a couple of casseroles, a few kitchen tools. Even a good cook can't work at his or her best with dull knives or flimsy pans. On the other hand, most of us can make do when we have to, as illustrated by this story James Beard once told me: Years ago, Jim found himself in a small Southern town where he was supposed to give a cooking demonstration. His hosts had scheduled him to prepare *steak au poivre* and *crêpes flambées,* but all he was provided with was a battered saucepan, a sheet-iron skillet and an electric warming plate. Jim panicked for a minute and then rushed to the nearest super-drugstore, where he bought a lightweight aluminum skillet, a couple of thin saucepans and two electric irons. Upending the irons to get some steady heat and flourishing his dollar pots, he got through the evening with the style and mastery that came to him as breathing does to the rest of us.

Obviously there are experts in both cuisine and cooking equipment. Still, I don't think anyone—even anyone at Williams-Sonoma—has the right to announce, "This is what the perfectly equipped kitchen should have. Here is your shopping list. Go out and buy everything on it." So much depends on personal taste, on the number of people you usually cook for, on the space you have and on the way you like to entertain. All we can do is to guide you to your own best choice. You'll need to know what is available, why certain utensils are made the way they are and why different materials are useful under different circumstances. You can then use that information to equip yourself with what you specifically need.

Your kitchen should express what you need and want, not what someone else has told you "everyone must have." Nor should you necessarily pick the most expensive merchandise. The highest price tag doesn't always mean you're getting the best item available.

At Williams-Sonoma we've been thinking about such matters for many years and I believe that we have as much expertise in guiding you as anyone else in the world. A home kitchen is a place where you can be nurturing and creative. It's a place to work in but also a place to talk to family or friends and maybe share a glass of wine while preparing dinner. It's a place to hang your collection of cookie molds or your child's drawings and it is still, even in this high-tech age, the center of many homes.

After looking around my kitchen and those of my friends who have a style of cooking similar to mine, I have put together a list of the most useful kitchen equipment. This list should be considered basic.

Knives
3- and 4-inch paring
8-inch chef's
10-inch slicing
Bread
Tomato
Sharpening steel

Wood chopping board
3 sizes mixing bowls

Tools
Vegetable peeler
Can opener
Corkscrew

Several wooden spoons
Stainless-steel cook's spoons
Stainless-steel slotted spoon
Strainer and colander
Fine mesh skimmer
Whisk
Rubber spatula
Lifting spatula
Pastry scraper
Ladle
Cook's fork
Grater

Measures
Measuring spoons
Liquid 2-cup measure
Set of dry measure cups

Thermometers: meat and fry

Baking
Rolling pin
Springform pan
Loose-bottom tart tin
Half-sheet pan
Bread pan and cloche
Layer-cake pans

Pots and Pans
12-inch sauté pan
8-inch skillet
1- and 2½-quart saucepans
4- and 6-quart casseroles
Gratin baking dish
Roast pan and rack
8-quart stock/pasta pot
Double boiler

Machines
Food processor
Mixer
Pasta machine
Juicer
Mouli julienne

GUIDELINES FOR POTS AND PANS

ITEM	*USE*	*MATERIAL*	*SIZES*
Skillet and Frying Pan	Quick-frying—eggs, potatoes, steaks, chops	Cast iron, enameled cast iron, anodized aluminum, stainless steel, cast aluminum, copper	6 to 12 inches
Sauté Pan	Sautéing meats, poultry and vegetables	Aluminum, anodized aluminum, stainless steel, copper, enamel on steel	8 to 14 inches
Saucepan with cover	Cooking vegetables, making sauces, heating liquids	Copper, anodized aluminum, stainless steel, enameled steel, enameled cast iron	1 pint to 5 quarts

ITEM	*USE*	*MATERIAL*	*SIZES*
Saucepot	Making soups, stews, cooking pastas	Enamel on iron, anodized aluminum, stainless steel	4 to 8 quarts
Low Saucepan	Sautéing meats, poultry and vegetables, cooking vegetables	Anodized aluminum, stainless steel, aluminum	8-inch diameter 3 inches deep
Fait Tout (Flared saucepan)	Making sauces and reducing liquids	Copper, aluminum	1½ to 2½ quarts
Stockpot	Soups, stocks, blanching, cooking corn, artichokes or lobsters	Anodized aluminum, stainless steel, enamel on steel, copper	8 to 20 quarts
Sugar Pan	Sugar syrups, caramel	Unlined copper	1½ to 2½ quarts
Zabaglione Pan	Sabayon, zabaglione	Unlined copper	1½ to 2½ quarts
Preserving Pan	Jams, jellies	Enameled steel, unlined copper	12 quarts
Omelet Pan	Omelets only	Cast aluminum, steel, anodized aluminum, copper	8- to 10-inch diameter
Crêpe Pan	Crêpes, pancakes	Steel, cast aluminum	5- to 8-inch diameter
Deep-Fat Fryer with basket	Deep-frying vegetables, fish, poultry, doughnuts	Aluminum, enameled steel	11- x 4-inch diameter, 5-quart capacity
Fish Poacher with rack	Poaching whole fish, boiling artichokes, corn, etc.	Stainless steel, aluminum, anodized aluminum, copper	20 to 26 inches x 4½ inches
Asparagus Steamer with rack	Cooking asparagus	Stainless steel, aluminum	
Vegetable Steamer	Steaming vegetables	Stainless steel, anodized aluminum, aluminum, copper	

ITEM	*USE*	*MATERIAL*	*SIZES*
Blanching Pot with steaming insert and blanching basket	Steaming and blanching vegetables, cooking pasta; use pot alone for soups	Stainless steel, aluminum	2 to 8 quarts
Couscousière	Couscous and other Moroccan dishes	Aluminum	
Wok with stand, cover, steamer plate	Stir-frying, steaming, Chinese dishes	Rolled steel, stainless steel	12 to 14 inches diameter
Chicken Fryer	Frying chicken, braising meats	Enamel on cast iron, cast iron	9 inch diameter
Paella Pan	Paella—Spanish and Portuguese stew dishes	Enameled steel, clay, copper	13 to 15 inch diameter
Pressure Cooker with 2 covers	Cooking fruit, vegetables, meats, preserves, etc., under pressure; use as stockpot with standard cover	Stainless steel with aluminum bottom	7½ quarts

THE MATERIALS

Pots and pans are now available in several basic materials. Don't buy a whole set of one type. It is far better to have a varied collection, with each pot chosen of the best material for its purpose.

Aluminum Alloy

Aluminum is one of the best conductors of heat, second only to copper. The heat spreads evenly throughout the entire pan and is transmitted rapidly to the food being cooked. The light weight of aluminum is another attractive feature, especially for large pots. Since pure aluminum is quite soft, most aluminum pans are alloyed with magnesium, copper or bronze for added strength.

There are two basic types of aluminum pans: sheet aluminum, which is spun or stamped, and the cast, seamless variety. Lightweight sheet aluminum is used for excellent stockpots, pasta pots, steamers, fish poachers and the like. Lightweight aluminum skillets lined with nonstick silicon are also available. Tough, thick, cast aluminum alloys are used for saucepans, Dutch ovens and roasters for virtually waterless cooking. Excellent aluminum pots and pans lined with stainless steel are also available, offering the heat conductivity of aluminum combined with the easy care and toughness of stainless steel. Thick (1/8 to 1/4 of an inch) aluminum alloy French restaurant ware—shaped just like the classic French copper pots and pans, with iron handles—can still be found, occasionally hammered like copper for additional strength. These pots give outstanding cooking results, but the bottoms can warp after long use over high heat.

The newest type of aluminum pots and pans are of anodized aluminum. They are subjected to an electrolytic process that seals the natural surface pores and the result is a smooth, tough surface that has been made an integral part of the pan. It will neither react with food nor crack or chip. Though most anodized aluminum is charcoal gray, you can get it in other colors.

Some vegetables, such as artichokes and asparagus, and sauces containing egg yolks, cause oxidation that discolors nonanodized aluminum pans. This harmless discoloration can be removed by scouring the pan with a fine steel wool or SOS pad, or by filling the pan with a solution of vinegar and water or two teaspoons of cream of tartar and water, and simmering for 10 minutes. Acidic foods absorb this oxidation, so it is advisable not to cook tomatoes or foods containing lemon or wine in a darkened pan. Do not let an aluminum pan soak overnight, as the chemicals in the water may cause pitting of the metal. For the same reason, do not leave food standing in an aluminum pan for any length of time. It is not advisable to put anodized aluminum pans in a dishwasher; the alkaline detergents usually stain the surface.

Stainless Steel

Stainless steel has many virtues: it is not easily dented, it resists corrosion, holds a high polish that will not scratch or pit, and does not react with either acidic or alkaline foods. However, stainless steel has one drawback—it is a poor conductor of heat. For this reason, better-quality stainless-steel pans are either sheathed in copper or aluminum to improve conductivity, or a core of one of these metals is sandwiched either into just the base or throughout the pan.

In order to be called "stainless steel," the metal must contain 11½ percent chromium. Eighteen parts chromium and 8 parts nickel (stamped 18/8 on the article) is adequate for kitchen tools, bowls, etc., but is not as good as the higher grade of stainless (stamped 18/10), which contains 10 parts nickel. The newest types of stainless-steel pots and pans are often of restaurant or commercial quality, which is to say they will stand up to a great deal of hard use. They are of a heavy gauge and 18/10 composition, with an extra heavy base that often extends partway up the sides of the pan. The base can be of 2-ply, 3-ply and even 5-ply construction, containing layers of pure aluminum, copper or even carbon steel. These pots and pans don't warp, and, unless the handles are of an unsuitable material, are ovenproof and dishwasher safe.

If food is burned onto a stainless-steel pan, soak and then scrub with a brush or nylon pad. If overheated, stainless steel can discolor or develop dark spots. These can usually be removed with any of the stainless-steel cleaners on the market.

Copper

Copper is by far the best conductor of heat. It heats rapidly and evenly, and cools as soon as it is removed from the heat, giving the cook maximum control. Copper pans never have hot spots; they promote even heat distribution that gently envelops the food, allowing the use of lower cooking temperatures.

Copper reacts with the natural minerals found in some foods. For this reason, it is lined with a nonreactive metal such as tin, nickel, stainless steel or, very rarely, silver. Some copper pans are hammered for greater strength, but this is becoming rarer due to laws governing noise pollution in the workplace.

Copper is extremely durable, and pans and molds are often passed down from generation to generation, refurbished occasionally with a new lining. The best-quality copper pans are of a heavy gauge (1/16 to 1/8 of an inch thick), and designed to be in perfect balance. (No good-quality pan should tip over because of the weight of its handle.) Very heavy professional or restaurant pans will usually have iron handles, while those for home use will be of brass. Either are perfectly safe in the oven. Many copper pieces are designed for oven-to-table use.

Copper is tin-lined, either by a block-tinning process or an electrolytic-plating process. Generally, block tinning yields a thicker coating that is firmly fused while the tin is molten and the copper is red-hot. It can be identified by the rough, uneven strokes that show it was done by hand. Electrolytic-plating gives a thinner coating that wears out more quickly. Nickel-plating is surprisingly hard-wearing, but be very careful not to abuse it as it is difficult to have it refurbished. A tin-lined copper pot can be retinned relatively easily, if at some expense. Old nickel is practically impossible to remove, and most retinners will not attempt it. A stainless-steel lining will last the life of a copper pan, but many cooks feel that the steel retards the extreme sensitivity of the copper's cooking properties. For best results the copper of a stainless-steel-lined pan should be extremely thick.

Tin-lined copper pots and pans should always be used on a relatively low flame and never placed empty over heat or the tin may begin to blister or even melt. Always use a wooden spoon; a metal one may scratch the tin lining. The tin lining will discolor slightly with normal use. This is harmless. Food should not be left standing for any length of time in tin-lined copper. Wash the pan after use in hot soapy water, using a sponge or bristle brush if necessary. Do not use scouring powders or abrasive cleaners, as this will wear the lining out. *Never put fine copper cookware in the dishwasher.* Any food that is stuck to the surface should come off with the briefest soaking.

Powder or liquid copper cleaners usually contain abrasives or chemicals for removing oxidation. They will either dull the finish or scratch it. To maintain the outside brilliance of buffed polished copper, use a soft cloth and a non-abrasive, nonchemical paste polish with a jewelers' rouge base. Copper preserving pans, zabaglione pans and sugar pans are traditionally unlined, as the high sugar content of jams, Italian wine custard and syrup retards any reaction with the metal. Use unlined copper for these purposes only. Clean the inside of the pans before use with half a lemon dipped in salt, or with a strong solution of water and vinegar. Then rinse and dry. Clean the outsides whenever necessary with nonabrasive polish.

Cast Iron

Cast-iron cookware and bakeware is extremely durable. It resists warping, denting and chipping. It conducts heat well but slowly, and distributes it evenly, holding heat extremely well long after the pot has been removed from the stove. It is ideal for browning meats or poultry and frying all types of foods. Do not use it to cook acidic foods or foods containing wine or lemon juice. The disadvantages of cast iron are that it is extremely heavy and if not preseasoned by the factory, it must be seasoned before being used for the first time. Should its protective coating be scrubbed off, it has to be reseasoned.

The surface of cast iron is porous, with microscopic jagged peaks. The seasoning process smooths this surface so that food does not stick to the pan. Seasoning also seals off the surface from water, helps prevent rusting and prevents the pan from imparting a metallic taste to the food.

Cast iron is used for frying pans, griddles and popover or muffin pans. Most cast-iron pans made today are either preseasoned or have a baked-on, nonrust or silicone finish. Some frying pans come with ovenproof glass lids. Read the manufacturer's instructions on individual pieces for use and care. (There are a few raw-iron muffin pans on the market which must be seasoned before being used.)

To season or reseason cast iron use a vegetable oil (safflower and corn oil are not recommended as they can leave a sticky residue). Thoroughly and evenly coat the interior of the pan with oil, using a pastry brush or paper towel. Wipe out excess. Place the pan upside down in a preheated 350° oven for one hour.

With continued use, the pan will become further seasoned. To maintain this seasoned surface, clean the pan with hot soapy water only. Detergents and abrasives will remove the seasoning. Dry cast iron thoroughly in a low oven before storing. Do not put cast iron in the dishwasher.

If at any time the pan shows signs of rusting, or if food is burned and stuck to the pan, scrub it well, using steel wool if necessary. Then reseason following the instructions given above.

Enameled Cast Iron or Steel

Enameled cast iron provides all the heat-conducting virtues of iron but does not require seasoning. The enameled surface will not interact with any type of food or impart any flavor to even the most delicate of sauces. The brilliant exterior colors of the pans are usually bonded to a matte black enamel finish which is fused to the pan to provide better bonding of the surface enamel. This also prevents rusting should the surface get chipped. Enameled cast-iron pots with buff interiors are more durable than white. Frying pans or skillets are another matter. Food does not brown well on light enameled surfaces, so these pans are usually lined with matte black enamel or a nonstick silicone material.

Some enameled cast-iron pans have their underneath surfaces milled smooth, exposing the iron for maximum heat absorption on electric elements.

Because enameled steel pans are thinner, they are vulnerable to chipping. They often have stainless-steel rims for added strength and chip-resistance, but such pans should not be banged, hit with hard objects or dropped. Care must be taken not to overheat an empty enameled steel pan as the porcelain surface can crack or chip.

Enameled cast-iron and steel pans should be cleaned with a soft pad or natural bristle brush. If food is stuck to the surface, it should be left to soak and then gently scrubbed with a nylon sponge. Never use steel wool or abrasives. Light enameled interiors may discolor slightly after long use. Do not be tempted to use bleach, as this will eat away at the enamel and make matters worse. The pan may not look brand-new, but it will perform just as well for many years.

GLASS, CERAMIC AND PORCELAIN

The virtue of glass, ceramic and porcelain cookware is that it will not react with food or impart any kind of flavor to it. None of these materials conduct or transmit heat well, but all retain heat efficiently.

A few beautiful laboratory-type glass and plain or decorated porcelain saucepans are made for stove-top use in Europe and the Orient. They must be treated with extreme care: always use a heat diffuser such as a thick asbestos pad or flame-tamer between such a pan and the source of heat, and always use low heat. Never subject these pans to extreme changes of temperature. Never put a hot glass or porcelain pan down on a cold or wet countertop; use a trivet. Wash pots and pans of this kind by hand with warm soapy water to minimize chances of breakage.

Modern glass ceramic cookware is especially treated and very sturdy. Most of it can go from freezer to oven to dishwasher without harm, and is safe in microwave ovens. It is not as efficient for frying or sauce-making, as the pans can heat unevenly. Food can be stored in them safely. Read the manufacturer's labels carefully to make sure that pans are stovetop as well as oven safe.

SHEET STEEL

Sheet steel is iron to which carbon or other elements have been added for extra strength. It is used to make cooking equipment with thin, strong, warp-resistant walls for rapid and efficient heat conductivity. It is an ideal material for such pans as Oriental woks and French omelet and crêpe pans. Unlike stainless steel, it can rust and must be seasoned before it is used. Special care must be taken to preserve the seasoned surface, and for this reason professional cooks will often keep a steel pan for a specific dish, such as omelets, and use it for nothing else. It is wiped out after use but not washed unless absolutely necessary, in which case only soapy water and a brush are used.

To season a carbon-steel pan before using for the first time, scour with steel wool, wash with soap and water, rinse and dry. Heat the pan for a few minutes and then coat with cooking oil. Remove from heat and let stand for several hours, then sprinkle with salt and rub vigorously with paper towels. Wipe clean. After use, wipe clean with paper towels and oil (removing any traces of salt) and store in a dry place. Do not put in the dishwasher. If necessary, or if the pan should rust, wash it with soap and water or scour with steel wool and then reseason.

HANDLES

Any pot or pan is only as good as its handle, so be sure that it is securely attached and cannot work loose, and that it affords a good comfortable grasp. Some handles are made of the same material as the pan, but most differ, as heat does not get transmitted as readily from one metal to another. Pot handles that are of hollow construction are always cooler to use. As a rule, stainless-steel handles are relatively cool, because this metal does not conduct heat well. Naturally, long handles are cooler at the end. Short, stubby handles heat up fast. Be careful when handling any hot pan. Even a wooden handle can burn you. Plastic composition handles sometimes have a metal rod running through them that terminates in a hanging ring or finial. These too can cause burns. It is a good idea to choose pots and pans with ovenproof handles, so that utensils can serve as casseroles or even simply keep their contents warm in the oven.

LIDS

Some pot lids match the pots and some differ. Stainless steel and heatproof glass are popular alternatives to lids of the same material. Look for a heavy lid that will stay in place over a boiling liquid. The cover should fit down into the pan tightly so that it can't be knocked off accidentally. Make sure that the handle of the lid is securely attached and easy to grasp through a potholder.

Saucepans. Saucepans are used for cooking vegetables, melting butter, boiling eggs, heating soup and even for making sauces. They are probably the most used pans in a home kitchen. Sizes range from 1 pint to 1, 1½, 2, 3 and 4 quarts. These pans should be deep and have tight-fitting covers. Saucepans are manipulated constantly, so be sure the ones you choose are well balanced, don't tip over and have handles at an angle comfortable to hold. Test the feel of the handle in your palm and make sure the pan can be lifted easily with one hand. If you plan to hang your pans for storage, the handles should have hanging holes. When selecting the material, bear in mind the kind of care the pan will require to maintain its appearance and extend its life. Some saucepans have pouring spouts. Saucepans come in copper, aluminum, anodized aluminum, stainless steel, enameled cast iron, enameled steel, ceramic and glass.

Low Saucepans. Low saucepans, about 3 inches deep, are new to the American market and to my way of thinking are among the most useful pans to have in a kitchen. Patterned after a French sauté pan, which is deeper than ours, they are extremely versatile. Because it has a wide diameter, this pan cooks vegetables rapidly in very little water. Chicken breasts can be sautéed or poached in minutes, cream and seasoning added, and the dish is done. A simple veal stew can be browned, assembled and simmered in the one pan. I have had a 2½-quart low saucepan for twenty-five years and I reach for it almost every time I cook. It measures 8 inches across, is 3 inches deep and the metal is ⅛ of an inch thick, a size suitable for two to six people, depending on what you are cooking. They are made in many sizes; of anodized aluminum and stainless steel.

Flare-sided Saucepan. Also known as a Windsor saucepan, or a "Fait Tout"—literally, "cooks all"—in France, this is a very versatile pan. It should be relatively thick and heavy. It is especially useful for heating milk or soup or for the reduction of liquids or sauces, as it has a wide surface area for rapid evaporation. A 1½- or 2½-quart size is probably the best for most home kitchens, thick anodized aluminum or tin-lined copper being the best choice in materials. This pan does not usually come with a cover.

Saucepots. Saucepots are large, useful saucepans with covers, usually with two handles. They can also be called ovens, casseroles, low marmites or low stockpots and their function is identical—to cook large quantities of vegetables, pasta and beans, and to make stock, soups and stews. Since the cooking

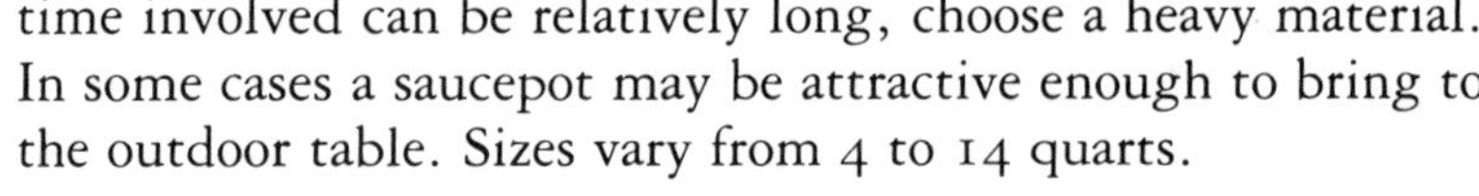

time involved can be relatively long, choose a heavy material. In some cases a saucepot may be attractive enough to bring to the outdoor table. Sizes vary from 4 to 14 quarts.

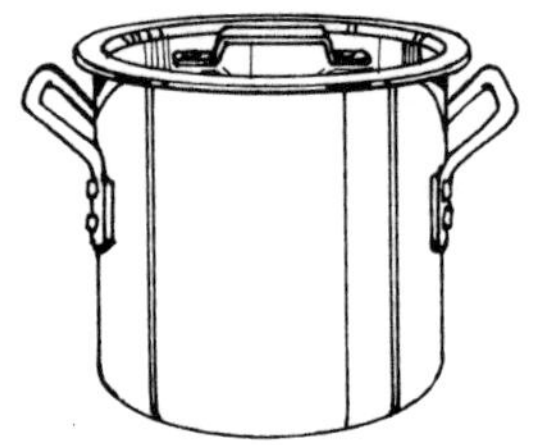

Stockpots. Used mainly for preparing soups and stocks, a stockpot should hold 8, 12 or even 20 quarts, depending on the quantity needed. A good stock can be made only when all the bones and meat and vegetables are completely submerged in water. A stockpot is also useful for cooking large quantities of pasta, lobster, ears of corn or artichokes. Most modern stockpots are made of aluminum, stainless steel or enameled steel.

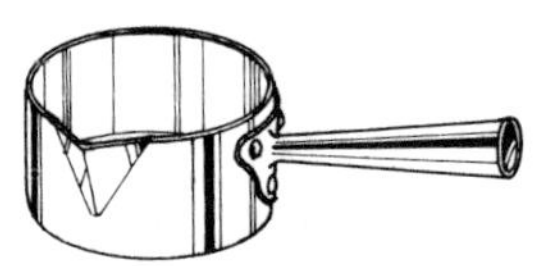

Unlined Copper Sugar Pot with Pouring Spout. Copper does not produce an adverse reaction with sugar, so these pots are traditionally left unlined. Since copper conducts heat so well, the sugar will melt evenly and the high temperatures of the syrup will be far easier to control. Sugar pots are made for professional use and are invariably of heavy-gauge unpolished copper with straight sides and a generous pouring spout. The handle should be large enough to grip firmly. Be sure to use a heavy pot holder as it gets very hot. Use *only* for cooking sugar syrup and for making sugar candy.

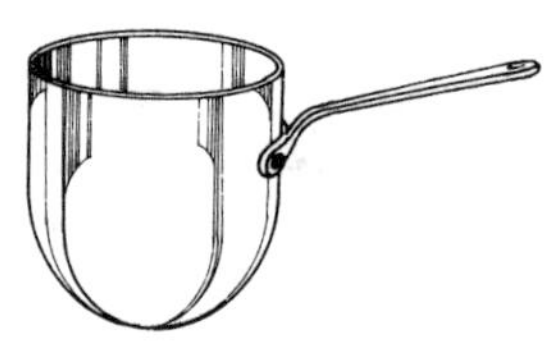

Unlined Copper Zabaglione Pot. Another special-purpose pot that is left unlined because the ingredients of the airy wine custard made in it (zabaglione in Italy, sabayon in France) do not react adversely with the metal. The pot is rounded on the bottom to allow easy whisking while being held by its handle over a flame or simmering water.

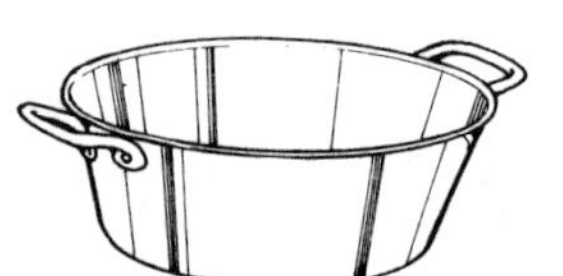

Unlined Copper Preserving Pan. Also known as confiture pans, these wide, low, capacious pans have double handles to help you lift them when they're full. They are unlined because of the the high sugar content in jams and jellies. Copper is such a good conductor of heat that it cooks preserves rapidly and evenly, helping to retain the fresh taste and bright color. These pans can be used for making sugar candies as well as preserves, but should not be used for other cooking purposes.

Sauté Pans. These wide pans have straight sides much higher than those of a skillet. Though they are the true workhorses of professional kitchens, their virtues are not widely known in home kitchens. Designed for the efficient browning of meats and poultry, they can also be used for many other tasks including stir-frying, lightly browning onions or other vegetables, quick stewing and poaching. Choose a heavy material that will not warp and make sure that the lid fits tightly. The most popular sizes for home kitchens are 10, 12 and 14 inches in diameter. Some sauté pans have a straight handle, others have handles that angle upward before following a straight line. A large sauté pan should have a loop handle opposite the straight one to help you lift it when it's full. Most sauté pans are made of thick copper or aluminum, anodized aluminum, stainless steel, aluminum lined with stainless steel, or enameled steel.

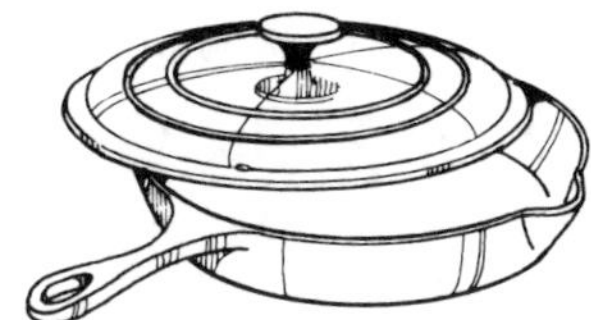

Skillets. Skillets are frying pans with sides that are gently sloped and quite low, so that condensed steam doesn't collect inside. Frying is done over high heat, so a good skillet should be thick, warp-proof and should transmit heat evenly. Some cooks swear by a well-seasoned iron skillet, others prefer a good-quality nonstick skillet with a silicone lining. It's best to have skillets in at least two or three different sizes, usually 8, 10 and 12 inches, to accommodate different amounts of food.

Omelet Pans. A good omelet pan is heavy so that the egg mixture doesn't cook too fast and get leathery, and it has gently curved sides to facilitate rolling and then sliding the cooked omelet onto a plate. The handle should be comfortable in the hand, with a good nonslip grip; it should be placed at an angle that makes it easy to maneuver the pan. A 3-egg omelet is best cooked in an 8-inch omelet pan. Bigger omelets

need increasingly larger pans. An old-fashioned black steel or thick aluminum omelet pan should be kept for cooking omelets only. Don't wash it. If you simply wipe it out after each use, the seasoning will get better and better. The smooth silicone nonstick surface inside some omelet pans does not require seasoning, and the pans can be washed and used for other cooking as well.

Crêpe Pans. At one time, crêpe pans were always made of thick black steel and reserved for this sole purpose so as not to disturb the all-important seasoning on the surface. Today they are also available in polished cast aluminum and silicone-lined aluminum. A good crêpe pan should have very low sides and be heavy enough to distribute heat evenly but light enough for the swirling and flipping that crêpe-making entails. The surface must be smooth so that the crêpes don't stick and the sides must slope so that the thin pancakes can slide out of the pan. Crêpe pans are measured by the size of the crêpes they produce, not by the top diameter of the pan: 5½ and 6 inches for dessert crêpes; 6½ and 7½ inches for entrees. Very small crêpe pans (3¾ inches) are called blini pans, and are used for making the thin buckwheat pancakes that are often served with sour cream and caviar.

In my experience, the best crêpe pans are made of black steel or thick aluminum. Stainless-steel crêpe pans are not very satisfactory, as crêpes tend to stick.

Covered Chicken Fryer. A chicken fryer is a deep frying pan with a short stubby handle and a domed lid, and is invariably solidly made, usually of cast iron or enameled cast iron. In the Deep South, one way of frying chicken is to first brown the chicken pieces, then cover the pan and steam the contents until the chicken is very well done and tender. For this you need a heavy, deep pan with a domed lid for self-basting. (Kentucky fried chicken is quite different. It is deep fried, quite quickly, in a batter coating. The same pan is used, but without the cover.) Even if you never cook chicken southern style, the pan is marvelous for any dish that requires browning and then braising.

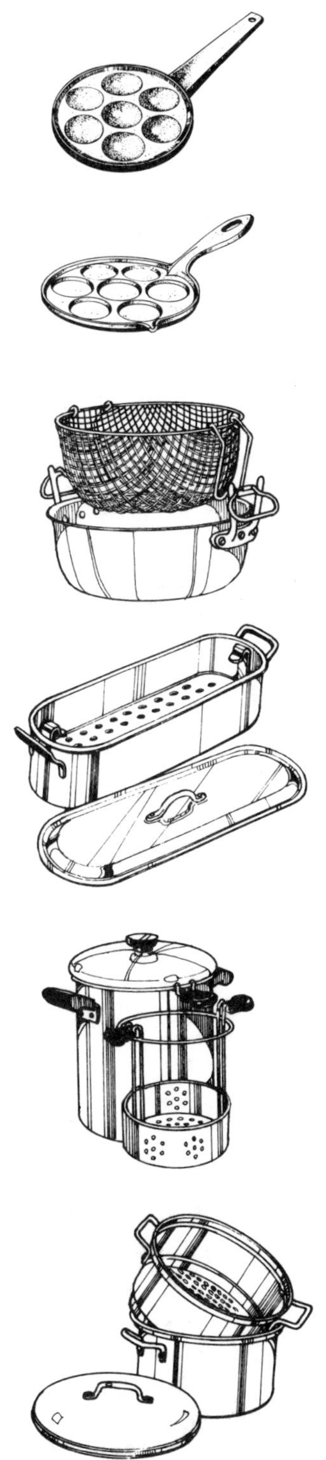

Danish Ebelskiver Pan. Made of cast iron with seven half-sphere depressions 2¼ inches in diameter, used for making this traditional Danish breakfast treat. The round puffs can be filled with fruit or preserves or served with syrup.

Plett Pan. Made of cast iron with seven round, shallow indentations 3 inches in diameter, used for making even-sized small pancakes. In Sweden these pancakes, called *plättar,* are served with lingonberries for dessert.

Deep-Fat Fryer. Essentially a deep, two-handled pot with gently curved or sloping sides and a wide surface area. It comes with a wire mesh basket that fits inside and doubles as a drainer; the handles of the basket clip onto the handles of the pan when draining. Plain steel, enameled steel or aluminum is very suitable for this kind of pan.

Fish Poacher with Rack. These pans are long and narrow so that a whole fish may be poached in a minimum amount of liquid. The perforated rack enables you to lift the cooked fish out in one piece. Very large fish poachers can be placed over two burners to maintain a slow simmer. They are available in two or three sizes and made of copper, aluminum and stainless steel.

Asparagus Steamer. This is a tall, cylindrical two-part pot with a cover. The perforated inner pot or wire basket holds the bunch of asparagus upright, so that the thick stalks simmer in water while the tender tips merely steam. Available in aluminum and stainless steel in several sizes.

Vegetable Steamer. This is a two-part pot with a cover, but the base of the upper pot is perforated and sits on top of simmering water in the lower pot. Vegetables placed in the upper pot cook in steam. These are available in many different shapes and sizes, in aluminum, stainless steel and enameled steel.

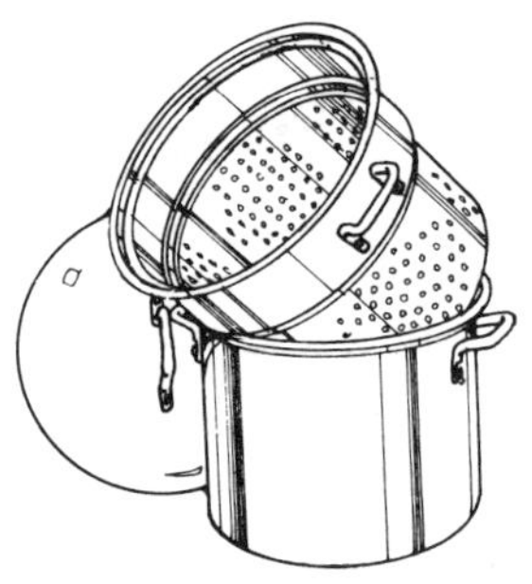

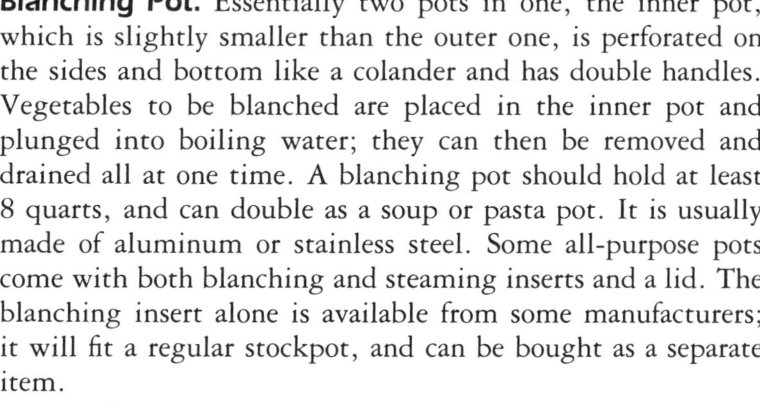

Blanching Pot. Essentially two pots in one, the inner pot, which is slightly smaller than the outer one, is perforated on the sides and bottom like a colander and has double handles. Vegetables to be blanched are placed in the inner pot and plunged into boiling water; they can then be removed and drained all at one time. A blanching pot should hold at least 8 quarts, and can double as a soup or pasta pot. It is usually made of aluminum or stainless steel. Some all-purpose pots come with both blanching and steaming inserts and a lid. The blanching insert alone is available from some manufacturers; it will fit a regular stockpot, and can be bought as a separate item.

Couscousière. This two-part aluminum pot is designed for cooking couscous, a type of semolina or granular wheat that is the national dish of much of North Africa. Both top and bottom are bulbous in shape, and the base of the upper pot is perforated. A stew of meat or poultry and vegetables goes in the bottom pot; the steam rising from it envelops and cooks the couscous placed in the upper pot. The lid of a *couscousière* is also perforated so that condensed steam does not drip back onto the grain, which should be dry and fluffy when cooked. An average *couscousière* is 12 inches high, 10 inches in diameter and the bottom pot will hold 8½ quarts. Other sizes are available.

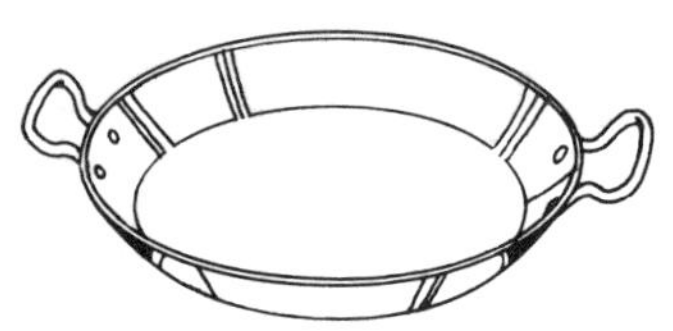

Paella Pan. The authentic Spanish pan is wide and shallow and generally made of enameled steel. It is used for cooking paella, a rice-based dish common to much of Spain. It has two handles to facilitate lifting, and is shallow so that the rice dries out when cooked. Paella is usually started on top of the stove; various ingredients are lightly sautéed or browned, and then the rice and the liquid are added and the dish is finished in the oven. Be sure that the pan is not too large to fit in your oven. Paella is a country dish and is usually served direct from the pan at the table. Deeper French or American paella pans are also available, made of aluminum, copper or stainless steel. The Spanish pan should be at least 13 inches in diameter.

Double Boilers. A double boiler consists of two pots made to fit together with one resting partway inside the other, and a cover that fits either pot. Simmering water in the lower pot gently heats the upper pot and its contents. Chocolate or custard sauces or anything that might suffer from too much direct heat benefits from being cooked in a double boiler. You can find double-boiler inserts that fit over a regular pot you may already own, or you can devise one yourself by resting a slightly larger pan with rounded sides over a smaller pan of simmering water. Most double boilers are designed so that they can be used separately as two individual saucepans. Those made of copper generally have a ceramic upper insert with a brass collar and handle, and are single-purpose, though very handsome. Double boilers come in many shapes and sizes and are made of various materials—aluminum, copper, enameled steel, stainless steel and heatproof glass.

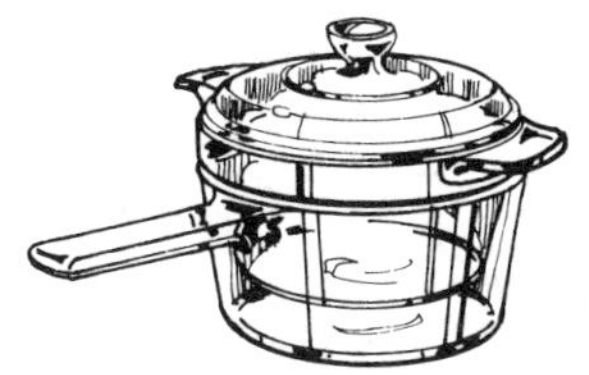

Pressure Cooker. Pressure cookers are still with us, but in far more sleek and attractive forms than those known to our grandmothers. The energy crisis has renewed interest in this type of cooking, since it takes about half the time of more conventional methods. The pots are made of polished aluminum or stainless steel, and at least one model comes with a regular lid as well as the pressure lid, so the cooker can double as a conventional pan. Food is cooked and tenderized under steam pressure; safety valves in the lid dissipate the steam safely. A clamp across the lid, held in place by two latches, is an additional safety device on the model shown here, which also comes with a useful wire basket insert. Pressure cookers range in size from 4 to 10 quarts, and can also be used for home canning.

Woks. Because the classic, round-bottomed Oriental wok was designed to cook food as quickly as possible, using a minimum of fuel, this kind of Oriental cooking has become increasingly popular in the United States. The traditional wok is made of rolled steel and affords extremely sensitive heat control. Ideal

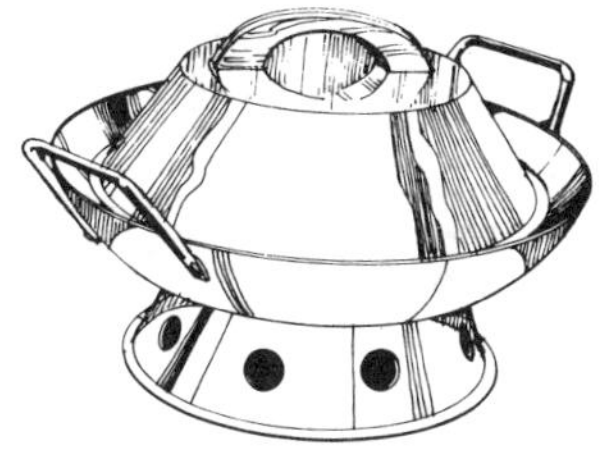

for stir-frying, a wok is also useful for steaming and braising. When it is used on a charcoal brazier or a commercial wok gas burner, the rounded bottom of this pan rests securely in an open grid. When used on gas and electric household stoves there are obvious problems. The solution has been a ring stand for the wok on gas stoves, and a flat-bottom wok for use on electric cooktops. Woks are available in sheet iron, anodized aluminum, stainless steel and even stainless steel with a copper bottom. Sheet steel and iron woks must be seasoned before the first use. (See pages 13-14 for instructions.) Woks come in many sizes. A 14-inch diameter wok is the most useful size for most home kitchens. Complete wok sets include a wok, a domed cover, a ring stand, cooking chopsticks and often a steamer rack, ladle and spatula.

Top-of-Stove Irons

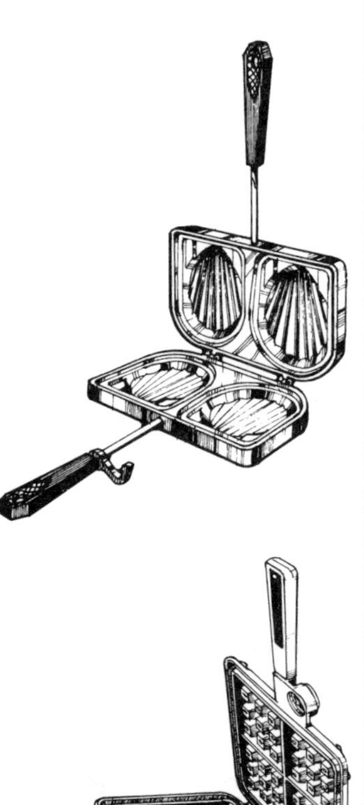

Sandwich Grilling Iron. This is called a "Croque Monsieur" in France, where it is made. It consists of two hinged, cast-aluminum plates with handles. The sandwich is placed between the plates, which have shell-shaped indentations, and the iron is then put on top of a heated burner for browning on both sides.

Waffle Iron. Made of cast aluminum, this consists of two hinged waffle-patterned forms with Bakelite handles. The interior surfaces of most irons have a nonstick surface. The iron is preheated on the stovetop, and the batter poured in, filling the waffle form. After a minute or so, the iron is turned over to bake on the other side. Some irons have a temperature gauge near the handle. There are, of course, many electric waffle irons available. Belgian type waffle irons are deeper than regular American waffle irons.

Pizelle Iron. This is used for the traditional thin, crisp, Italian cookies called *pizelle,* and is made of two round, cast-aluminum, embossed disks hinged together and attached to long handles for use on top of either gas or electric stoves. The iron is heated, and a special sweet dough is placed on the surface of one disk; the iron is closed and returned to the heat for baking. The cookie can be left flat, rolled or shaped into cups and either filled or eaten plain. Most pizelle irons are 5 inches in diameter, with 16½-inch handles. Many people prefer the electric version of the pizelle iron, which, of course, is more expensive.

Casseroles, Ovens and Roasters

Casseroles. Casseroles are made in sizes ranging from one pint to 8 or 10 quarts and are designed for slow cooking in an oven, although some can be used on top of the stove as well. You should always check the manufacturer's directions, but it is usually safe to assume that casseroles or ovens made of enameled cast iron, enameled steel, stainless steel, heavy anodized aluminum and tin-lined copper can also be used on a burner. Those made of earthenware, porcelain or glass can not. When choosing a casserole, remember that it will be hot when you take it out of the oven. Be sure that the casserole is easy to grasp securely with potholders and that the lid is easy to pick up. Casseroles are designed to be enveloped in heat, which penetrates through the top and sides of the cookware as well as the bottom. The lid should fit very securely, as this type of slow cooking relies on moisture.

Nonmetal casseroles can be of earthenware, stoneware, porcelain, heatproof glass or Pyroceram, a very hard ceramic glass that can resist extreme temperature changes. (It is used on the nose cones of space rockets.)

Earthenware, or terra-cotta, is very porous and breaks easily, but cooks extremely well, is attractive and relatively inexpensive. Some earthenware casseroles are fully glazed, others are glazed on the inside, unglazed on the outside. These should be washed by hand with soap and water. Stoneware is fired at a higher temperature than earthenware, is nonporous and is usually fully glazed. Porcelain is fired at a very high temperature and is extremely hard and long-wearing. Heat-resistant glass, generally known as Pyrex, will stand up to a lot of hard use but, like all traditional ceramic ware, should not be subjected to extreme temperature changes, or dropped. Pyroceram will stand up to just about anything.

Dutch Ovens. A cast-iron Dutch oven was standard equipment in American kitchens for at least a century or two, but it hit instant obsolescence when the "gourmet revolution" prompted people to make *boeuf bourguignon* and *coq au vin* in them instead of beef stew or pot roast. The wine took the precious seasoning right off the cast iron, and also made the stew taste odd. A cast-iron Dutch oven is a good pot, but don't try putting wine in it! It does have additional drawbacks as well. It has to be used frequently to maintain its seasoned quality and must be stored in a dry place to keep it from rusting. A European enameled cast-iron oven is more practical.

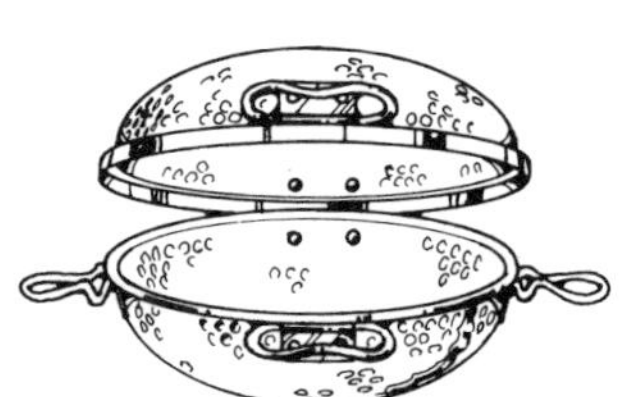

Portuguese Cataplana. This hinged double pan of tin-lined hammered copper looks like a fantastic sea shell. It is customarily used to steam seafood and vegetables, and is opened right at the table for a very dramatic—and aromatic—presentation.

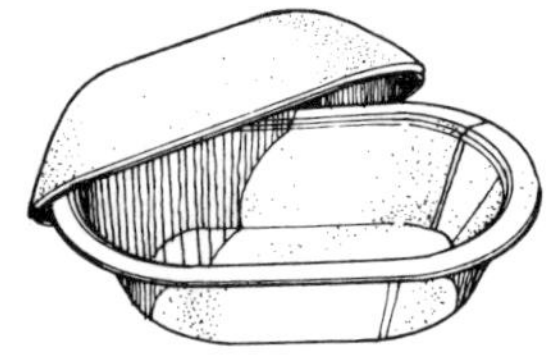

Clay Chicken Pot. An unglazed clay casserole of this type is first soaked in cold water for 15 minutes; the food then goes inside, and it is placed in a cold oven set to a very high heat. The hot steam from the wet clay helps to cook the contents and the "brick oven" effect further helps to tenderize the food. While most often used for chicken, a clay pot will also cook meats to a succulent tenderness. Do not subject a clay pot to abrupt changes in temperature. To clean, soak and then scour with a plastic scrubber and baking soda. Do not use soap or detergent, as the clay will harbor the taste, and do not put in the dishwasher. Available in various shapes and sizes.

Clay Cazuela. This rustic, shallow, natural earthenware terra-cotta casserole has no cover. It is glazed on the inside but left unglazed on the exterior, and is still the principal cooking utensil in much of rural Spain for stews and versions of paella. Do not subject to abrupt changes in temperature, and wash by hand with soap and water and air dry before storing. Advisable for oven use only, but if well seasoned and used over a flame-tamer, can be used on top of the stove over low heat.

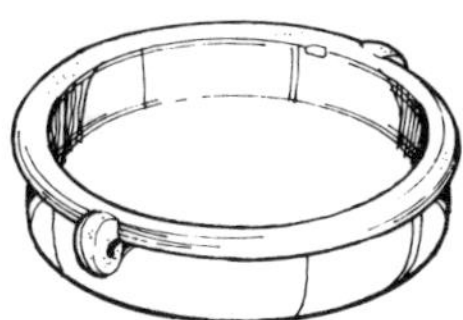

Clay Bean Pots. Clay bean pots, whether from New England or Tuscany, tend to have fat, rather round bodies and relatively narrow openings to minimize evaporation when beans are left to simmer in the oven. The lid should be close fitting, and the pot should have handles of a shape that permit safe lifting when it is hot. As with all clay pots, they should be treated gently and washed by hand, using a mild soap and water and air dried before storing.

Gratin Dishes. Gratins are browned on top and served in the dishes in which they are cooked. The dishes are therefore both shallow and ovenproof so that they can fit under a broiler or go on the top shelf of a hot oven. Oval or round, and ranging in size from individual to very large, they generally have twin handles, or rims that are extended on either side to form handles. Materials include tin-lined copper, porcelain, earthenware, glass, ceramic, enameled cast iron and stainless steel.

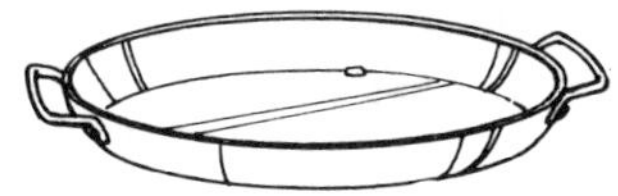

Bakers. Round, oval or rectangular, these are much like large gratin dishes but are deeper and usually do not have handles. They are used for layered casserole entrees, baked vegetables or baked fruit, puddings or custard desserts. If made of metal,

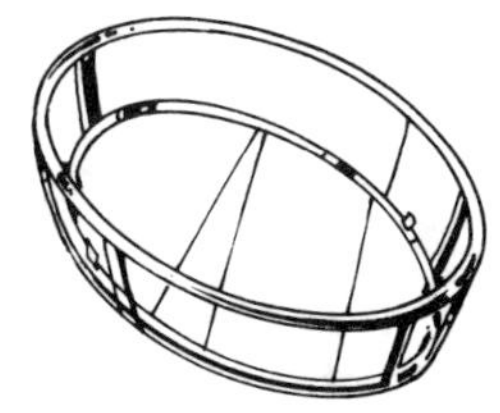

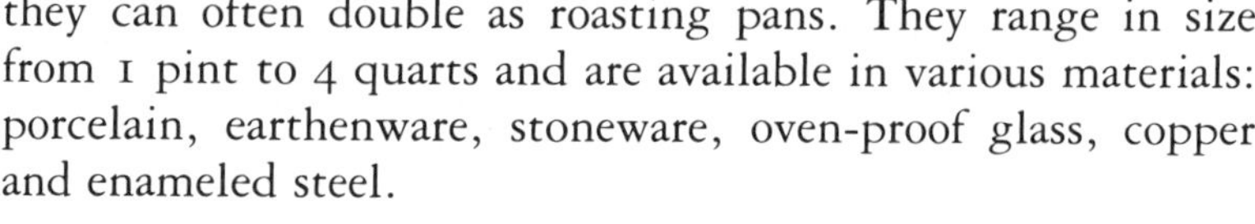

they can often double as roasting pans. They range in size from 1 pint to 4 quarts and are available in various materials: porcelain, earthenware, stoneware, oven-proof glass, copper and enameled steel.

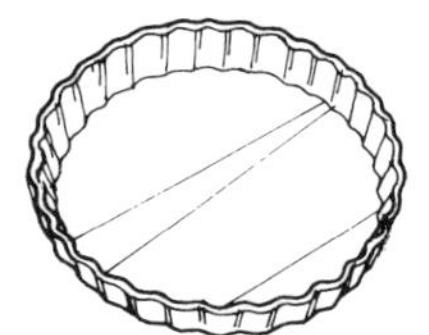

Shallow Porcelain Baker with Fluted Sides. Often mistakenly called a porcelain quiche dish, this decorative shallow baker is designed for the baking and serving of savory custards with or without pastry on top, baked fruits, fruit and custard desserts such as *clafouti* and the like.

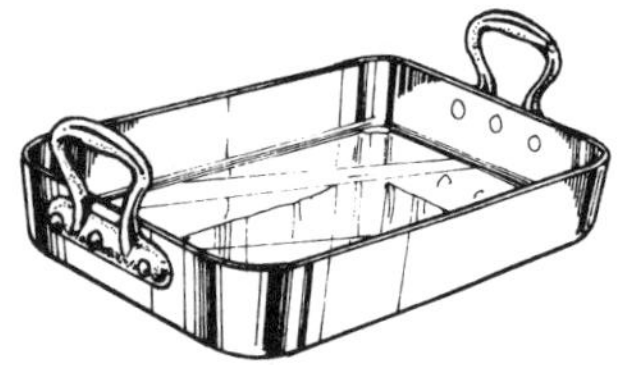

Roasting Pans. Roasting pans can be oval or rectangular, deep or shallow, open or covered. When choosing a roasting pan, remember that you will sometimes use it on top of the stove to make gravy, so get one heavy enough not to warp. The handles should be easy to grasp and firmly attached, and the pan itself should be sturdy—a good-sized turkey can weigh 20 pounds or more. Allow at least 2 inches of air circulation between the sides of the pan and the oven walls, and allow room for the handles.

Some cooks like covered roasters, which have vents in the lid. This gives a moister roast, but one that combines steaming with roasting.

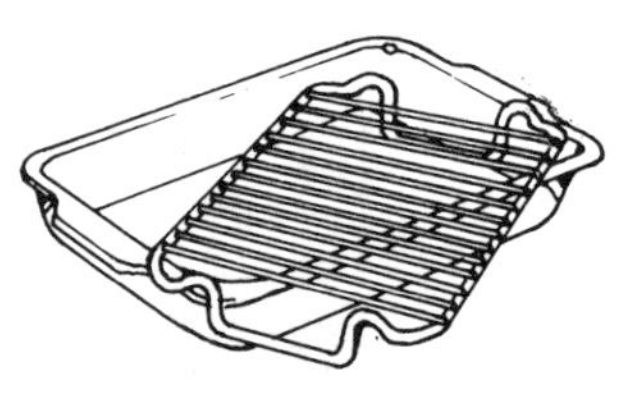

Use a fairly shallow roasting pan with a rack for the best air circulation around meat or poultry. A deeper roasting pan is invaluable for cooking custards. Put the dish or cups in the pan and then fill it with enough hot water to reach halfway up the sides of the dish. The custard then cooks very gently in its water bath.

Some roasting pans are handsome enough to double as bake-and-serve dishes. Roasting pans are available in light and heavy weight aluminum, stainless steel, tin-lined copper, enameled cast iron, enameled steel, ovenproof glass and ceramic materials.

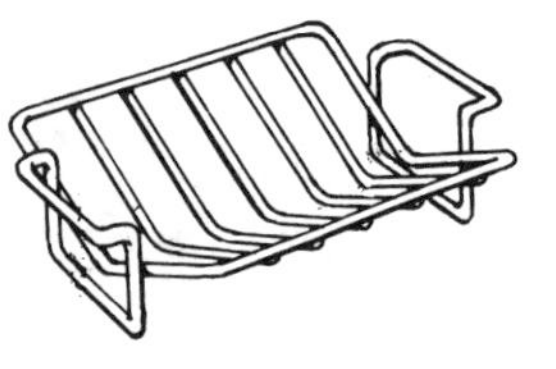

Roasting Racks. Roasts should always be placed on a rack to keep them clear of fat and roasting juices, and to permit good air circulation and browning. They are usually made of stainless steel or chromed steel, though some racks are coated with nonstick material. Racks can be flat or of the rigid V-shape, or the adjustable type that can be used both ways.

Molds and Terrines

Pâté en Croûte Molds. These tinned steel molds are made for baking pâtés that are like meat loaves in pastry crusts. They are not used for the mousse-type liver pâtés so popular in this country. The sides and base of this mold are of separate pieces, so the mold can be removed from the pâté. Wash by hand and thoroughly dry after use, and reassemble for storage so that the pins or clips that hold the pieces together don't get lost.

Rectangular Pâté en Croûte Mold. This mold has a herringbone pattern that imprints itself on the sides of the pastry-covered pâté when it is baked. L-shaped side pieces are held in place with two brass pins and slide on and off the base, which has turned-up edges on the long sides. These have a 1- to 2-quart capacity and are 10 to 14 inches long.

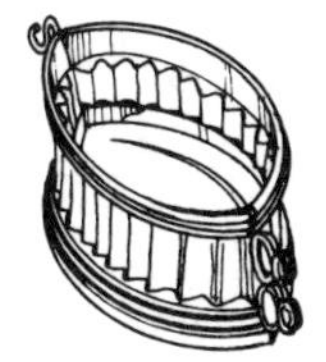

Oval Fluted Pâté en Croûte Mold. Traditionally used for layered meat and game pâtés, the sides of this mold are joined together with round wire clips and are held securely in place by the turned-up edges on the base. 1 pint to 1 quart capacity.

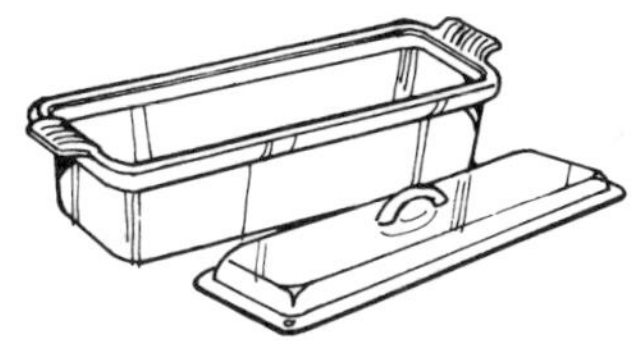

Enameled Cast Iron Pâté Terrine with Cover. This type of terrine is seen in every French country restaurant, filled with a savory pâté of coarsely chopped meat or game. The pâtés are always served from the terrine, and can be stored in it under refrigeration. Since it is heavy and a good conductor of heat, this terrine cooks pâtés slowly and thoroughly. The hole in the cover permits steam to escape. Available in several sizes, 1½ pints to 1½ quarts capacity.

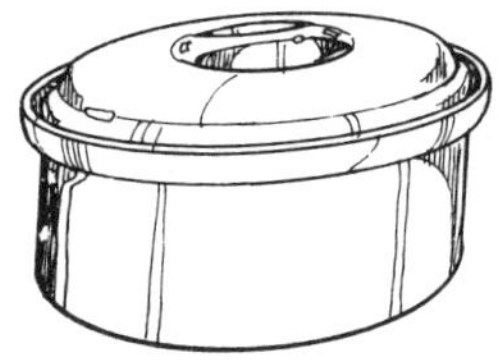

White Porcelain Oval Pâté Terrine with Cover. These come in a wide variety of sizes and make attractive bake-and-serve dishes for anything from a country pâté of pork and liver to a delicate mousse. The larger sizes can double as ovenproof casseroles.

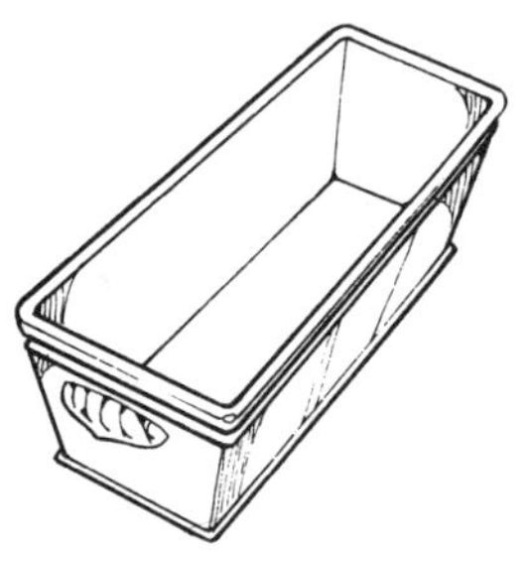

White Porcelain Galantine Mold. Open galantine molds of this type are perennial favorites with French *charcutiers,* who use them for preparing and then displaying artfully decorated spiced and herbed meats, poultry in aspic, pâtés, head cheese, parsleyed ham and the like. The contents are always served directly from this type of mold, which has slightly sloping sides and "lug" handles.

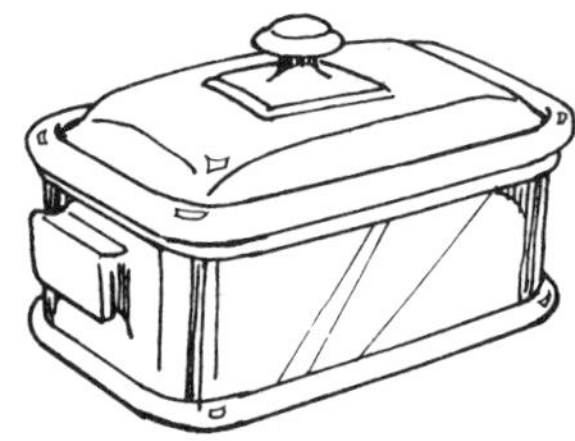

Earthenware Pâté Terrine. This country-style terrine lends itself perfectly to a simple country-type coarse meat pâté, or it will double as a small casserole. It is available in various sizes and shapes. Wash and dry by hand.

Hand-Decorated Porcelain Game Terrines. Cleverly molded and decorated to imitate a pastry crust, these terrines were originally designed and made for royalty and nobility in the eighteenth century, during one of France's flour shortages. Ovenproof, and with a glazed white interior, they were meant to be filled with pâtés of partridge, duck or hare, the bird or animal on the lid denoting the contents. Of course, any filling may be used. There is also a wide range of casseroles and baking dishes made in France with a crust finish reproduced from the original eighteenth-century models. It was an ingenious solution for pastryless tarts and pies—but only for the rich, of course.

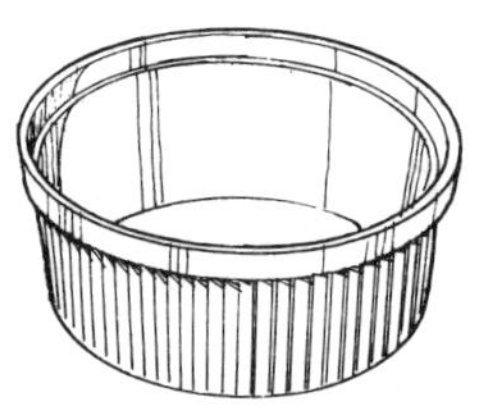

White Porcelain Soufflé Mold. This is the classic container for savory and sweet soufflés of all kinds. The ridged exterior duplicates the pleated paper collars used on plain molds by French chefs of the eighteenth and nineteenth centuries. The interior is perfectly smooth and straight, to encourage rising.

Three and a half to 5 ounces and 1-, 1½- and 2-quart sizes are probably the most useful. Most recipes are based on the 1½-quart size. These dishes are also useful for baking custards and casseroles, and can also be used as all-purpose serving dishes.

White Porcelain Ramekins. Ramekins are miniature versions of soufflé molds, usually of 4-ounce capacity, and are used for very rich egg dishes, fish and vegetable mousses and for desserts such as chocolate or lemon mousse.

Custard Cups. Usually made of glazed earthenware, porcelain or heatproof glass, custard cups generally hold about 4 to 5 ounces and can, of course, be used for other desserts and puddings.

Crème Brûlée Ramekins. These are wide, shallow 3-ounce ramekins, usually of ovenproof pottery or porcelain. A layer of dark-brown sugar is sprinkled over the cooked and chilled rich cream custards and then caramelized with the aid of a salamander (page 74) or under a broiler. In order to get as much of this thin crackly layer as possible, the ramekins have to be wider than usual. Crème brûlée can also be made in a large low porcelain baking dish.

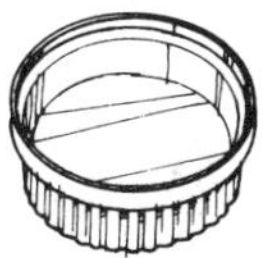

Oeufs en Gelée Molds. These are small oval molds of tinned steel, aluminum or porcelain, used for preparing poached eggs in a flavored and decorated aspic. They can also be used for molding small savory mousses.

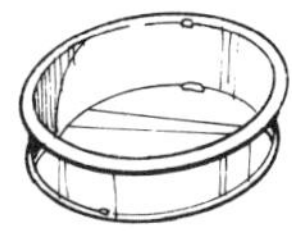

Timbale Molds. Timbale molds or darioles are round and slightly tapered for ease in unmolding, and come in sizes ranging from 2 to 7 ounces. They are used for small savory mousses and are usually made of tinned steel. The small ones are often used for baking babas au rhum.

Tinned Steel Steamed Pudding Mold with Cover. Although steamed pudding molds have been made in many shapes, bucket-shaped molds—plain or fluted on the sides—are the best, as they have a central tube to aid in cooking the pudding all the way through. The lid is fixed in place with clamps and has a handle. The bottom of the mold usually has a relief design that provides a decoration on top of the unmolded dessert.

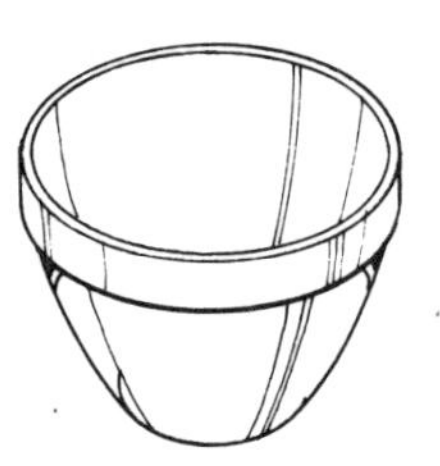

Steamed Pudding Basins. Of glazed earthenware, these basins have a deep rim so that a cloth or foil can be placed over the top and secured with string. Used in England for numberless steamed desserts like Christmas pudding and ginger pudding, they are also lined with suet pastry and filled with a savory steak-and-kidney mixture. These basins make excellent all-purpose mixing bowls, as their depth helps eliminate spatter.

Aspic or Gelatin Molds. Available in aluminum, tinned steel, tin-lined copper, earthenware, glass and plastic, these come in a huge variety of shapes and sizes, from turreted castles to rabbits. For clearly defined unmolded shapes, look for molds that are sharply modeled on the inside.

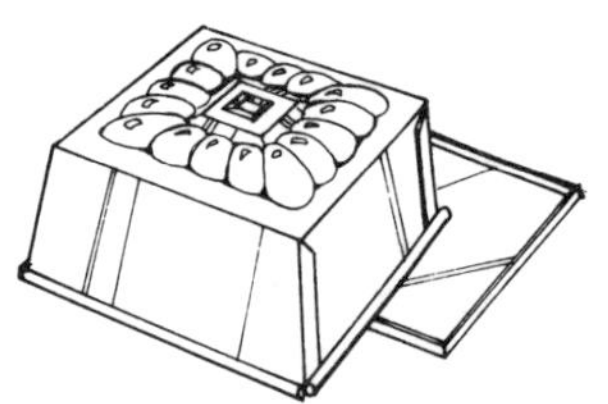

Ice Cream Molds. Usually made of tinned steel, stainless steel or plastic, these molds have covers and are made in various shapes and sizes. Classic ice cream *bombes* are made by lining an ice cream mold with one flavor of softened ice cream and filling it with another. Ice cream molding reached its peak of popularity in the latter part of the nineteenth century in both France and England as well as Italy. There were literally hundreds of fanciful shapes.

Chocolate/Candy Molds. In the past, chocolate/candy molds were usually made of lead, and tin-coated for safety. Today's flexible plastic molds, while they don't last indefinitely, are extremely easy to use and are available in plaques of various indented shapes. The melted chocolate is poured into the molds and then chilled for 20 minutes. The chocolate hardens and shrinks slightly, but holds the sharp patterns and is released by bending the sheets a little. There are many different kinds of stainless-steel molds for making solid or hollow chocolate animals. Mainly from Holland, they come in two parts, held together with clips.

Baking Pans

Most modern baking pans are made of tinned steel, black steel, stainless steel, aluminum alloy or anodized aluminum and heavy steel, coated with nonstick silicone, and generally conduct heat well. Some pie pans and bread-making equipment are made of clay and a few pans are made of cast iron or cast aluminum. Tinned steel and black steel pans should be treated carefully, because they can rust if scratched. Tinned steel darkens after continual use. This is harmless and actually improves the baking performance, because dark colors absorb heat instead of deflecting it. Silicone-coated pans must be treated with extra care to avoid damage to the surface.

Cookie Sheets. Also called baking sheets, these have many uses beyond baking cookies. You can bake many different types of pastries and free-form loaves on them, and they are often used to support small baking pans and tart pans. Choose the heaviest available of the largest size possible—it should fit in your oven with 2 inches of airspace all round. The pan should have a lip on one short side to aid in pulling it out of the oven. Some baking sheets have lips on both short sides to make them warp-resistant. While lightweight cookie sheets with nonstick surfaces are available, far better baking results are achieved with a heavyweight pan and a sheet of baking parchment (page 81). One exception is a new patented aluminum cookie sheet, which has a 3⁄16-inch airspace between two layers of aluminum. It bakes even more slowly than con-

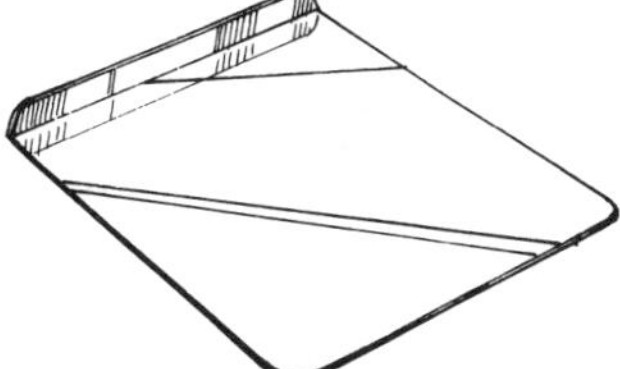

ventional heavy baking sheets and gives excellent results. Baking sheets are made of hardened aluminum alloy, anodized aluminum, tinplate steel, stainless steel and silicon-coated aluminum for non-sticking surfaces.

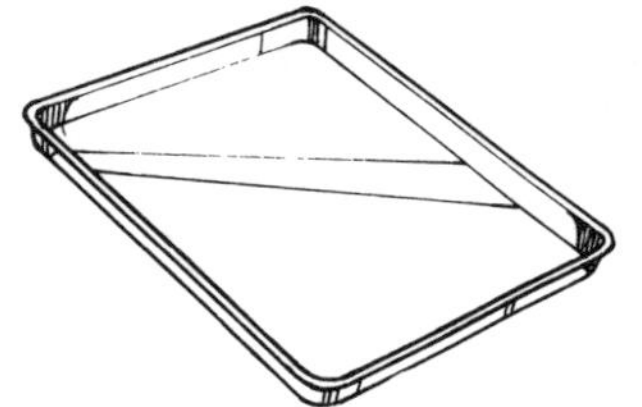

Half-Sheet Baking Pan. This is a professional baking pan that gets its name from the fact that it bakes a sheet cake half the size of a standard commercial sheet cake. It measures 18 x 13 x 1 inches, is made of heavy aluminum with a rolled rim, and is essential for baking sheet cakes, yeast rolls, cookies and pastries. This is of the maximum size that will fit in most domestic ovens.

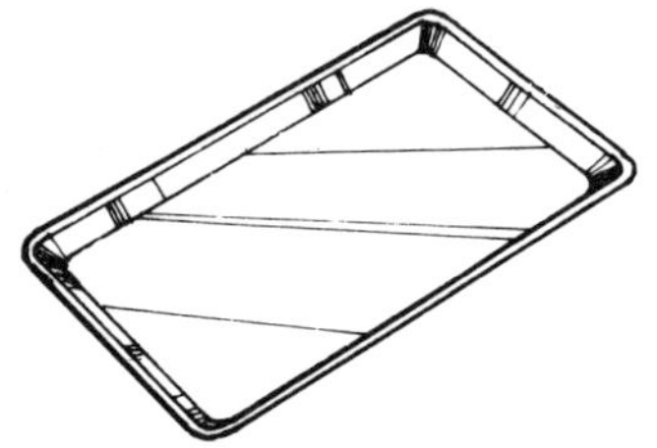

Jelly-Roll Pan. A jelly roll, before it is rolled up, is not the same as a sheet cake. It is smaller and thinner. Naturally, a very large jelly roll can be baked in a half-sheet baking pan, but a standard jelly-roll pan measures 12 x 7 x ¾ inches and most of those generally available today are made of aluminum with a nonstick lining or of tinned steel.

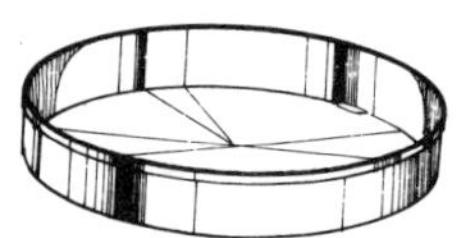

Round Cake Pans. These can be of one-piece construction or have a removable base. Aluminum is the favored material, though stainless steel and black steel are also available. Eight- and 9-inch diameters, with 1- to 1½-inch-high sides are most common. Professional quality layer-cake pans are available in tinned steel and in anodized aluminum.

Square Cake Pans. Usually of one-piece construction, square cake pans are used for unfilled cakes like gingerbread, and for cookies that are cut into squares after baking. The standard size is 8 inches square, and the pans are available in tinned steel, glass and plain or anodized aluminum.

Springform Pan. A springform pan has high sides of 2½ or 3 inches, and a clamp that releases the sides from the base. It is used for baking tortes and cheesecakes that are otherwise difficult to unmold. Some springform pans come with 3 interchangeable bottoms—one flat, one plain tube and one fluted with tube. The standard size has a 9- to 9½-inch diameter and it holds approximately 3 quarts. However, these pans are also made in sizes from 8 to 12 inches. Look for a heavy pan of tinned steel or silicone-coated steel with a completely flat base that fits accurately into the groove at the bottom of the sides. Also made in stainless steel and steel with a black baked-on enamel finish.

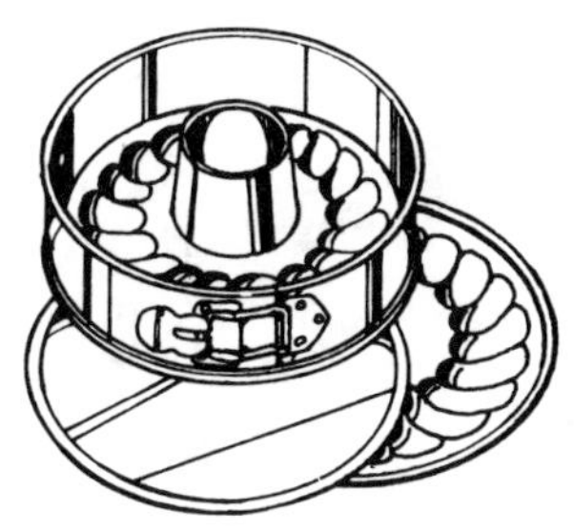

Bundt Pan. Very popular for making rather dense cakes of the pound-cake variety, these large fluted pans are usually made of cast aluminum with or without a nonstick lining. They always have a tube in the middle to promote even baking. The tube, incidentally, produces a cake that is easier to slice. Eight-and-a-half inches in diameter, with a 9-cup capacity, is standard.

Kugelhopf Pan. This pan is used for baking a raisin-studded, yeast-raised coffee cake that was supposedly invented by the Viennese when under siege by the Turks, and is a fanciful representation of a Turkish turban. All Kugelhopf pans have a central tube to assist in even baking. They were traditionally made of heavy tinned steel, but are now available in black steel, aluminum, and steel or aluminum with a nonstick lining. They vary in size from 1½ pints to 3-quarts capacity. A 9½-inch diameter pan with approximately 2½-quarts capacity is about average.

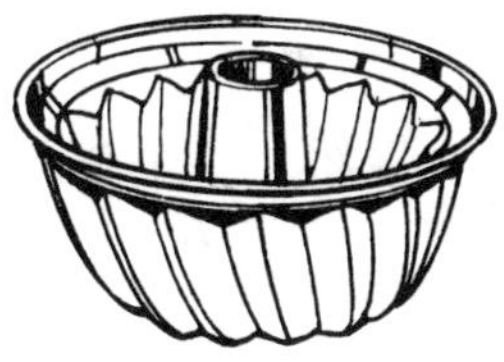

Tube Pan. Designed for baking angel food cake, which has lots of beaten egg whites but no fat in the batter, this pan has high sides and a removable bottom with a central tube to promote rapid rising and even baking. This cake is unusual in that it is always cooled upside down, so look for a tube pan with three small feet on the rim or a high central tube to allow air circulation. A 10-inch diameter, 9-cup capacity is average. Pans are usually of aluminum for home use, although tinned steel ones are made for professional bakeries.

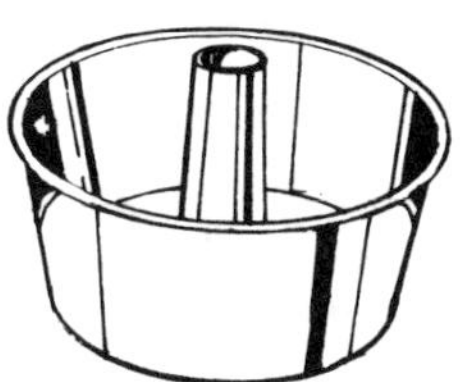

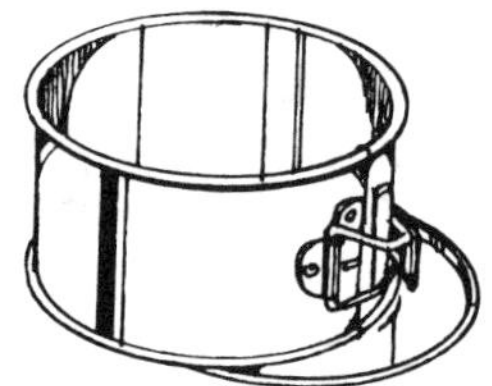

Panettone Pan. Imported from Italy, these tinned steel springform pans with extra-high sides are designed for baking the festive fruit bread of the same name. It is a light bread and needs support as it rises. The pan is traditionally 7½ inches in diameter, with 4-inch sides.

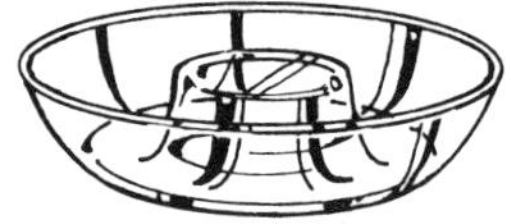

Savarin Mold. This shallow tinned-steel ring mold from France is designed for baking a yeast-raised cake known as a savarin, that is subsequently drenched in rum syrup and painted with an apricot glaze, producing a large rum baba. The pan has no seams and is reinforced with a beaded rim. The hole in the middle is quite small relative to the pan's size. This pan can also be used for baking a caramel custard. It is made in several sizes, with a diameter ranging from 7 to 9½ inches. A 6-cup capacity is average.

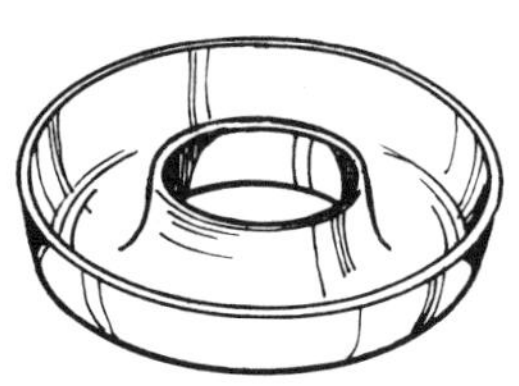

Ring Mold. Much deeper and larger than a savarin mold, and with a larger hole, a ring mold is meant for cakes or breads but can double as a gelatin mold if made of seamless aluminum. It is also known as a rice ring: mold a ring of hot cooked rice, turn it out and fill the center with creamed seafood or chicken. Made in tin-plated steel, aluminum or glass, it comes in various sizes, from 7 to 2 inches in diameter. An 8-cup capacity is average.

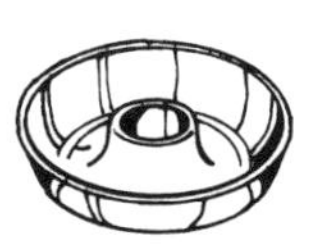

Baba Molds. These come in two basic shapes: small timbales or miniature ring molds. Sizes range from 2- to 6-ounce capacity. These molds are usually made of tinned steel or aluminum.

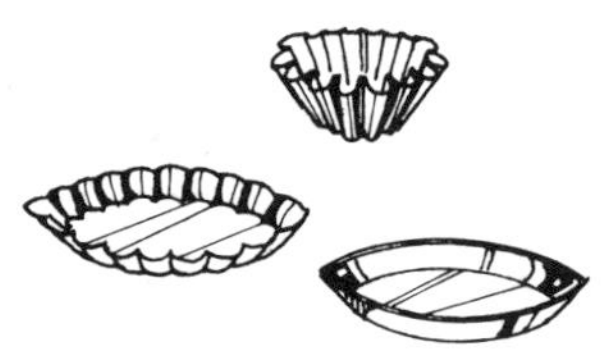

Tartelette Molds. Individual tartelette molds for small cakes and pastries are available in an enormous range of shapes and sizes, both plain and fluted, deep and shallow. Made of tinned steel, they are meant to be set on a baking sheet when placed in the oven. This slows down the baking (small items overbake easily) and makes it possible to get them in and out of the oven efficiently. Approximate sizes range from 2 to 4 inches.

Charlotte Mold. The traditional heavy tinned-steel charlotte mold has straight sides that flare out very slightly and two heart-shaped handles set slightly below the rim to aid in turning out desserts. Used for making hot apple charlottes and the chilled creams with an outer shell of ladyfingers or sponge cake known as *charlottes russes*. These pans are usually imported from France. Sizes range from 6- to 2-quart capacity.

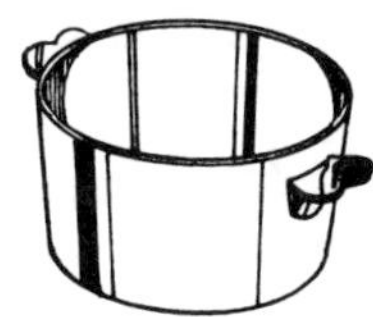

Brioche Pan. Good-quality brioche pans are stamped from a single sheet of tinned steel and shaped without seams, heavily fluted on the sides and flaring out from a small base. They range in size from individual ones 4 inches in diameter to larger, 9½-diameter ones.

German Loaf Cake Pan. Longer and not as wide as a bread pan, this pan is for pound cakes, fruit cakes of the lighter variety and some types of gingerbread. Made of tinned steel, aluminum and silicone-coated heavy steel, it measures from 8 to 12 inches long x 4 x 3 inches.

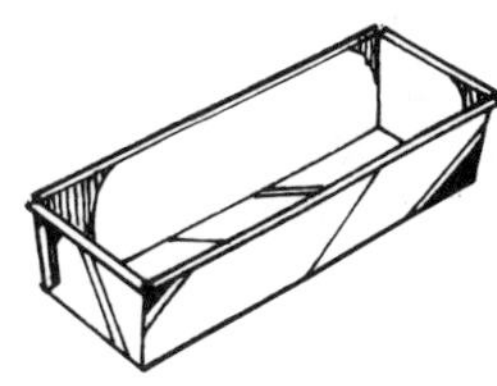

Indented Fruit Tart Mold. Popular in France and Germany, this pan is used for baking a shallow sponge cake that is subsequently turned upside down to form a shell, much like a pastry shell, for filling with pastry cream and fruit. The French ones are made of tinplated steel in sizes from 8 to 11 inches in diameter. A silicone-coated heavy steel version from Germany is the most satisfactory because a thin sponge cake can be difficult to unmold.

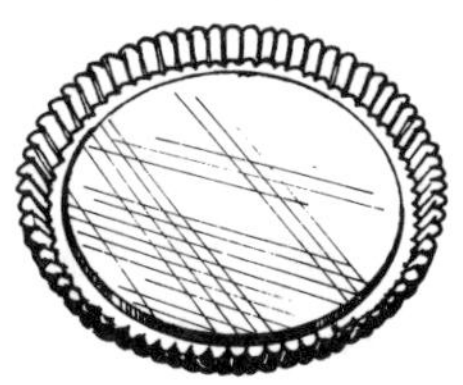

Pie Pans. Round pie pans are available in aluminum, black steel, tinned steel, terra-cotta, stoneware, heatproof glass and Pyroceram. Pastry bakes best in darkened metal. Since both black steel and tinned steel will rust if scratched, be careful when cutting the baked pies in the pan. For pies that have only a top crust, use ceramic pie dishes. Most pie pans are 8, 9 or 10 inches in diameter and 1 to 1¼ inches deep.

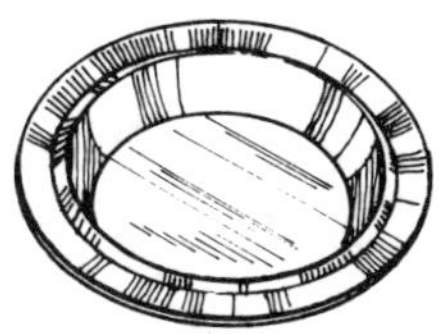

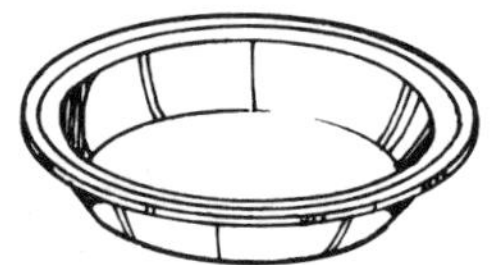

Deep Oval Pie Dish. The English traditionally made savory deep-dish pies with a top crust in an oval earthenware or porcelain pie dish. Rabbit, chicken and steak-and-kidney are favored ingredients, and the topping is usually of puff pastry, which is extended over the wide rim and sometimes scalloped round the edges. These oval pie dishes are very good for making deep dish fruit pies, too. Sizes range from 9 to 11 inches.

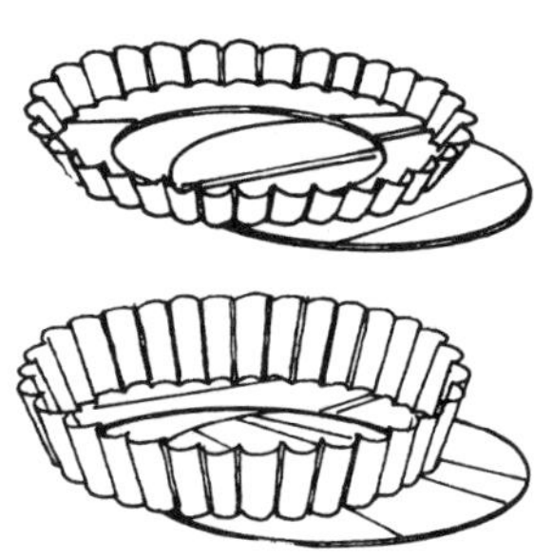

Fluted Tart/Quiche Pans. Tart or quiche pans with low fluted sides have either solid or removable bottoms. Those with solid bottoms are usually used for baking an empty tart shell. The ones with a removable bottom are for both filled tarts or empty shells.

These pans are generally available in 8, 9, 10 or up to 12 inches in diameter, as well as individual 4-inch-diameter sizes, and are made of tinned steel or black steel. To remove a baked tart from a pan with a removable bottom, set the pan on a coffee can and allow the sides to drop down. Slide the tart onto a serving plate, with or without the base. Fragile tarts and pastry shells are very easy to deal with this way. One- and 2-inch-deep sizes are available.

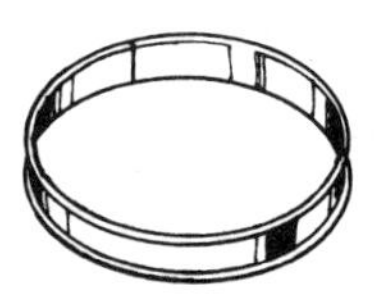

Flan Rings. Round, rectangular and square tinned-steel flan rings are simply 1-inch bands or collars of metal, usually reinforced with beaded rims, that are set on a baking sheet and lined with pastry to form shells for tarts and quiches. They come in a wide variety of sizes, from 8 to 12 inches in diameter for round ones to 14 inches long for rectangular types. Rectangular flan rings are used for glazed fruit bands, or pastries that are very easy to cut and serve.

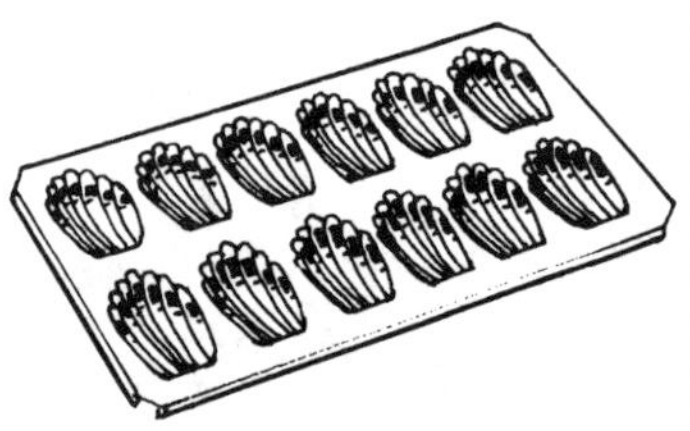

Madeleine Plaque. This rectangular tinned steel or aluminum plaque has 10 3-inch-long shallow, shell-shaped depressions for making the small sponge cakes known as madeleines. There are usually 12 to a plaque, though *madeleinette* plaques have 20 smaller depressions for 1½-inch cakes.

Cornstick Pan. Invariably made of cast iron, cornstick pans contain 7 molds shaped like ears of corn and are used to make a type of cornmeal muffin. A good heavy pan produces a nice light product, so these pans make sense.

Muffin Pan. A standard muffin pan holds either 6 or 12 2¾-inch muffins. The most common materials are aluminum, tinned steel, silicone-coated aluminum and cast iron. Each cup holds 3½ to 4 ounces, and the pan can be used for cupcakes as well as muffins. Miniature muffin pans, also known as gem pans, hold 12 or even up to 24 tiny muffins, usually 1½ inches in diameter.

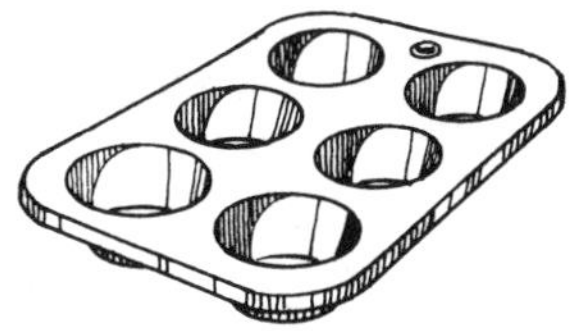

Popover Pan. Popover pans have extra-deep cups so that popovers can rise as high as possible. Up until a few years ago most popover pans were made of cast iron and had 11 cups. With the increased interest in American cooking, the pans are now being made with the molds set at a wide distance from one another in a wire frame which allows for excellent air circulation and efficient baking. Most of these are made in tinned or black steel. Overall size averages 15¾ x 9½ x 2¼ inches.

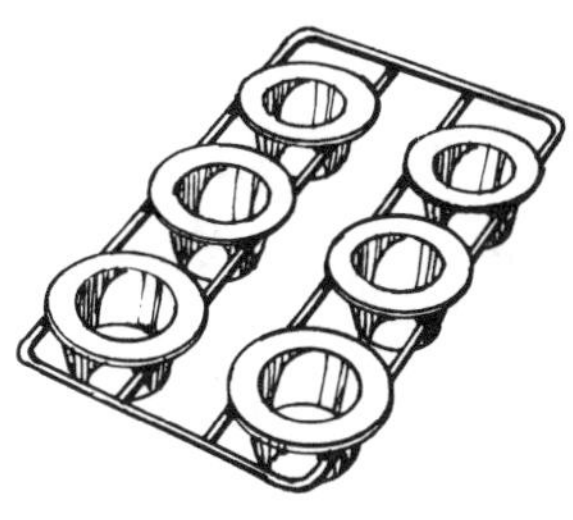

Bread Pans (Loaf Shape). These can be made of aluminum, tinned steel, black steel, terra-cotta or heatproof glass. The regular size, used for bread, measures 9 x 5 x 3 inches. The medium size, often used for quick breads, using baking powder, measures 8½ x 4½ x 2½ inches. Miniature bread pans come singly or on frames of 4, 6 or 8. Those on frames are much easier to handle in or out of the oven, and, of course, will not tip over.

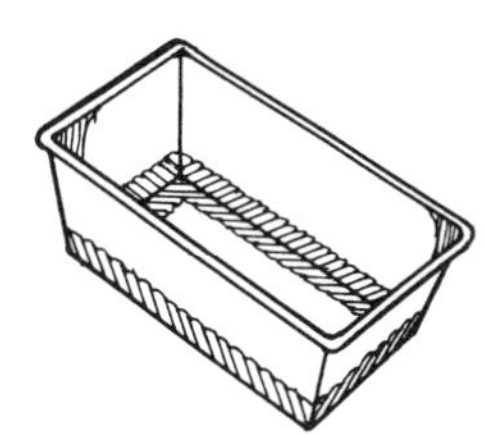

Earthenware Cloche. Also known as an instant brick oven, this consists of a stoneware bell or dome that fits over a wide, shallow dish with 2-inch-high sides. It is one of the most successful implements developed for home baking. Bread

dough is formed into a ball and placed inside the dome, resting on the cornmeal-covered base. When the dough has doubled in bulk, the cloche is placed in the oven. Hot steam forms inside the bell and helps the bread to rise so that it then forms a singularly crisp, thin, crackly crust. The resulting loaf looks and tastes as though it had been made in an old-fashioned brick bread oven. Base is 11½ inches in diameter, dome cover is 10 inches high. Do not subject to extremes of temperature. Wipe clean with a cloth when cool; do not wash.

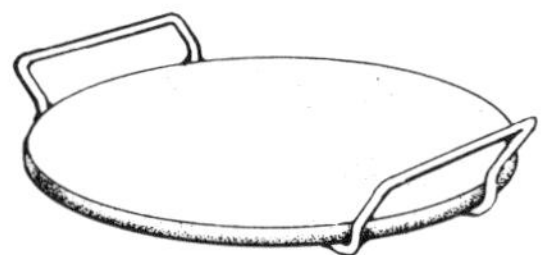

Pizza Brick. This dense stoneware plaque, either round or rectangular, conducts heat like the floor of a brick oven, thus producing crustier pizza doughs and lighter freeform breads. The surface is smooth and requires little care, but it should not be subjected to sudden changes of temperature. Most pizza bricks come with a chromed steel rack to make them easier to handle. The round plaques are usually 12 to 13 inches in diameter and ½ an inch thick. Wipe clean with a damp cloth. Do not put in dishwasher.

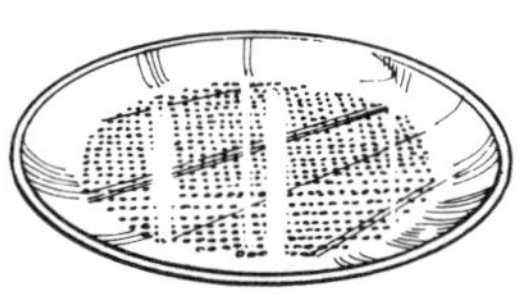

Pizza Pan. Available in aluminum or steel, this 12¾-inch round pan has hundreds of small or large holes which allows heat to penetrate the dough rapidly and expel moisture. This process promotes a crisp brown crust that rises evenly. Some pans have solid rims which prevent the pizza edges from overbrowning.

Baguette Pan. This extra-heavy black steel pan is made in France in the form of a double trough joined by a slotted center band which promotes air circulation in the oven. The pan is 18 inches long with 2-inch-wide troughs. A half-baguette pan, which holds 4 8½-inch loaves, is also available.

Pullman Pan. This pan is used for baking a very firm, close-textured milk bread known as a Pullman loaf or *pain de mie.* The pan has a sliding cover and the bread is baked in a tightly closed space. This makes it completely rectangular and gives the bread a soft, light crust. The bread is especially suitable for canapés, rolled sandwiches, regular sandwiches and toast. Available in tinned steel or black steel, pans vary in size; the most useful is 13 x 4 x 4 inches.

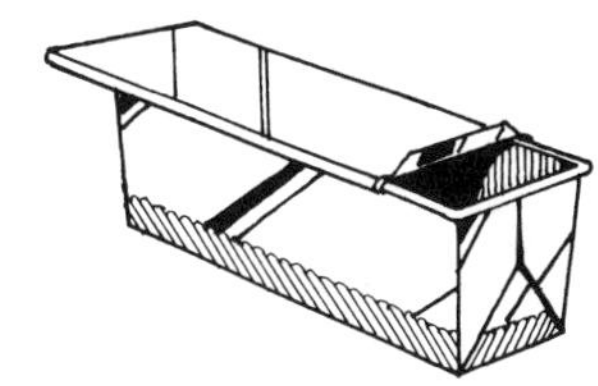

Banneton. This is not a pan, but a bread-rising basket made of coiled reeds whose pattern imprints itself on the dough. When baked, the reeded pattern remains on the surface of the round loaf, giving it the appearance of an old-fashioned beehive. Bannetons probably originated in Germany. The usual size is 8 inches in diameter and 3 inches deep, but, of course, the final rising in the oven produces a much larger loaf.

Electric Machines

Food Processor. First introduced to the United States home market from France in the early 1970s, this multipurpose machine became an overnight success. It chops, slices, shreds, grinds and purées all kinds of foods at high speed and with great efficiency. It can knead bread and make good short-crust pastry and cookie dough; with different attachments, some models can even cut French fries or slice whole fruits and vegetables. In the best models, a quiet, powerful, constant-speed induction motor is housed in a plastic-covered base that can be as small as 6 inches square. A virtually unbreakable, though not scratch-proof, Lexan-covered work bowl fits over the direct-drive motor shaft. The bowl has a feed tube through which ingredients can be added. These machines come with a set of basic tools including a chopping knife, a dough blade and disc cutters for grating and slicing. The tools fit over the drive shaft inside the work bowl, and both tools and bowl are dishwasher safe. Some food processors have a wide range of attachments for specific culinary tasks such as extra-fine slicing, julienne cutting or even extruding pasta. Motor capacity

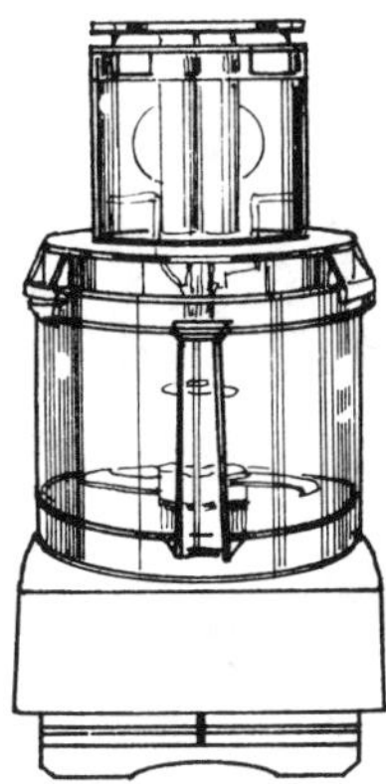

and bowl sizes vary. Most food processors are quite heavy and will not "walk" in operation. All models come with instructions and recipe booklets.

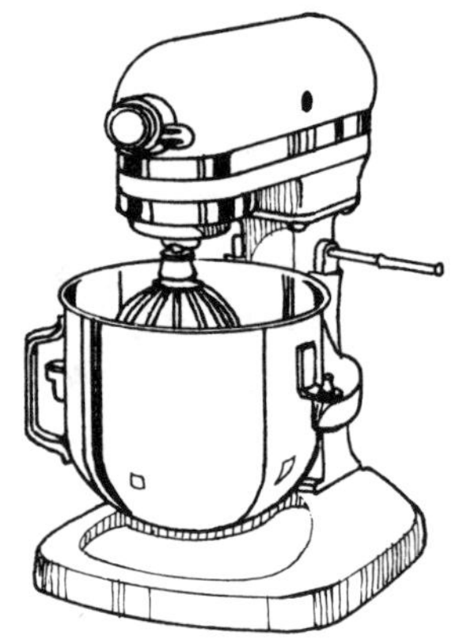

Stand Mixer. A heavy-duty stand mixer requires a lot of counter space, but it takes all the hard work out of beating, mixing, whipping and kneading large amounts of batter, egg whites and bread dough. The best American model has an extremely powerful variable-speed motor housed in an enameled steel stand with a large, heavy-gauge stainless-steel bowl securely held in place. It has a large balloon wire whisk, a flat beater and a dough hook. A good machine will have a wide range of optional attachments, from a citrus juicer to a grain mill.

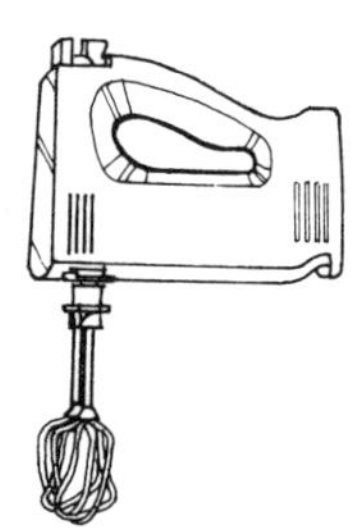

Hand-Held Mixer. The great advantage of a hand-held mixer is its portability and ease of storage. It is useful for beating egg whites, cake mixtures, cream sauces, whipping cream and making mayonnaise in any kind of bowl or pan. Look for a heavy-duty mixer that weighs 2 to 3 pounds but is well-balanced, with most of the weight in front of the handle. Some portable mixers have optional stands with bowl and attachments.

Blender. Used mainly for making purées, smooth soups, sauces, batters and frothy drinks, chopping a few nuts or making breadcrumbs, a good quality blender has not been altogether replaced by the food processor. In fact, many people who gave away their blenders when they acquired a food processor subsequently regretted it. A blender liquefies soft foods extremely well. The motor is housed in a plastic or steel base; the tall goblet that fits on top is made of glass, stainless steel or heavy plastic. Four blades, shaped like propellers, rotate at high speed, cutting and recutting food as it falls back from the sides of the goblet. Some good-quality blenders have a special attachment for making mayonnaise. A fairly large goblet, holding 3 to 4 pints, is desirable. Many blenders have variable speeds, but a simple on-off switch is perfectly adequate and less likely to malfunction.

Citrus Juicer. A good citrus juicer should have an all-purpose ridged cone that will accommodate limes, lemons and grapefruit as well as oranges. In most models, the motor is activated when gentle pressure is exerted on fruit placed over the cone. The machine should separate juice from pulp and seeds. Look for one that doesn't drip. Some juicers have spouts that close automatically with finger-tip touch. Generally made of heavy-duty plastic, juicers are more or less cylindrical, with the motor in the base. The juicer should come with a cover to keep the cone dust-free when not in use.

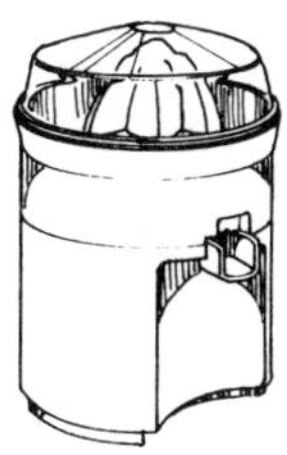

Grain Mill. This compact Lexan-and-stainless-steel flour mill micronizes grains such as wheat, corn, rye and oats into flour at 25,000 rpm, or at the rate of about a pound per minute. The temperature of the self-cleaning milling chamber remains very low, allowing all the nutrients of the grains to be preserved. Just-milled flour is both very fresh and very flavorful. In fact, the difference in taste between a newly baked loaf of bread made with freshly milled flour and one made with regularly available commercial flour is astonishing. Whole grains keep well, whereas wholemeal flour goes stale quickly, so if you are a serious bread maker this machine is a good investment. The machine measures 10 x 8 x 10 inches when in use, but only 10 x 8 x 5 inches when stored, as the flour bin reverses to act as a cover. Its only drawback is that it's noisy.

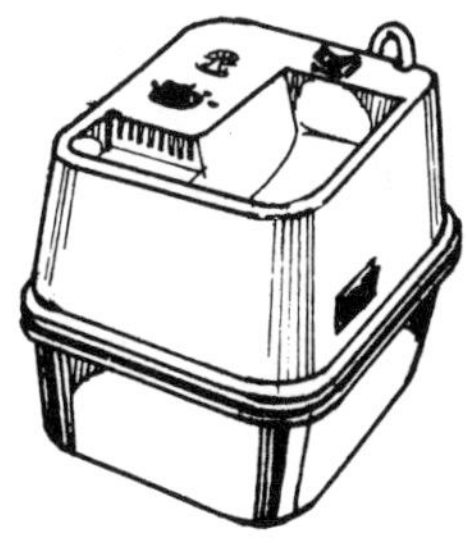

Pasta Machines. Electric pasta machines come in two types: the one with rollers and the extruder variety. The roller pasta machine is extremely fast and efficient to use. The heavy-duty motor is housed in a sturdy plastic L-shaped base. Three roller attachments come with the machine: a smooth pair for kneading and rolling the pasta dough and two notched pairs for cutting wide or narrow noodles. If the pasta dough is mixed in a food processor, the whole performance, from raw egg and flour to finished noodles, takes about the same time as boiling a pot of water in which to cook the pasta. Extruder machines make pasta on a different principle. Dough is mixed inside the machine, then forced out through perforated plates as solid or hollow pasta of various dimensions. The consistency of the dough has to be judged very carefully for successful results.

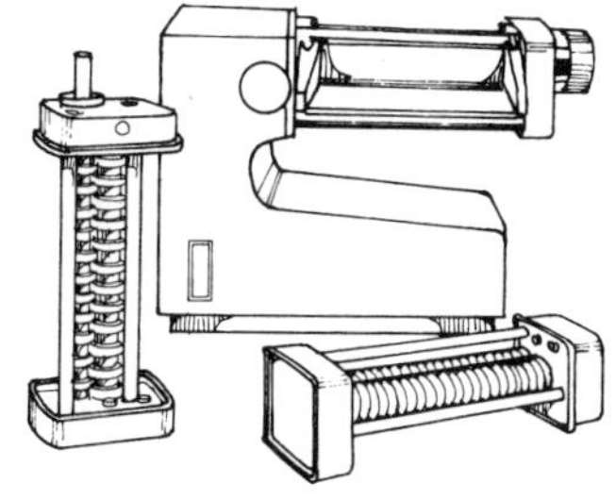

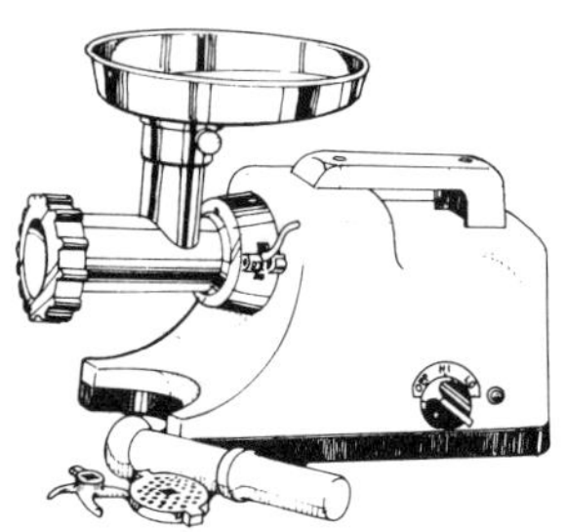

Meat Grinder. All meat grinders work on the same principle, forcing pieces of meat through cutting blades and a perforated plate. A heavy-duty electric grinder will reduce even tough cuts of beef into good hamburger. Professional chefs almost always use a meat grinder for grinding fish and chicken when making quenelles and forcemeats because other types of machines reduce this delicate flesh to paste. Make sure that the grinder you choose is rustproof and easy to disassemble and clean properly. A sausage-making attachment should be available. Homemade sausages are satisfying to make and wonderful to eat.

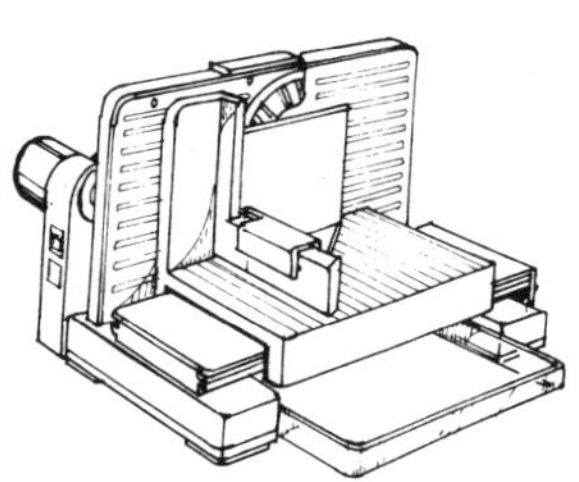

Meat Slicer. There is a wide range of small household electric slicing machines on the market. The newest and best slicers have an electronically controlled stainless-steel blade that automatically adjusts speed according to the density of the food being cut. All of the machines, however, have a circular blade, usually serrated. It will cut through cold meats, cheese and bread, and should be adjustable to cut at a 45° angle for oval slices; slice thickness should also have a wide range of adjustments, from paper thin to about 1½ inches thick.

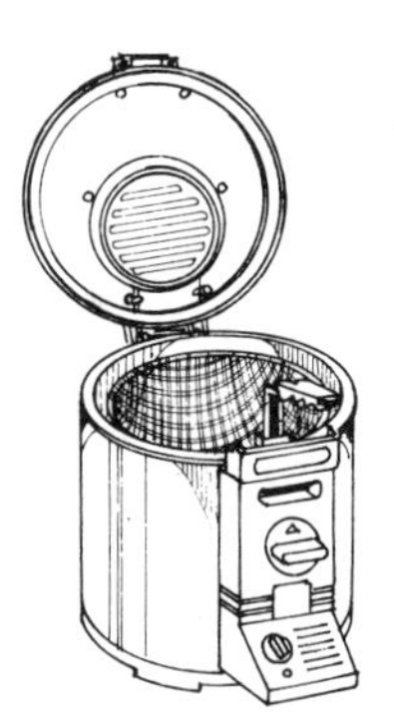

Enclosed Deep-Fat Fryer. An electric, enclosed deep-fat fryer allows you to enjoy the results of deep-fat frying without the disadvantages. Food is cooked within a sealed container. Only steam escapes through the replaceable charcoal filter in the cover. A thermostat controls the temperature, and the frying basket, which has a removable handle, is raised and lowered by an outside lever when the pot is closed. Made of stainless steel and plastic.

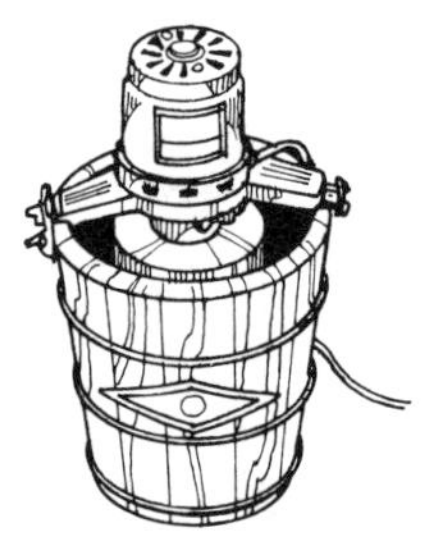

Ice Cream Machines. Broadly speaking, there are two types of quality electric ice cream machines on the market: the old-fashioned wooden bucket type that requires ice and rock salt, and the compact countertop type that stirs and chills frozen desserts automatically, the refrigeration unit being integral with the machine. Naturally, the latter are more expensive.

The bucket-type ice cream machine usually has a pine tub reinforced with metal bands. The motor unit rests across the top. The ice cream mixture is poured into a tin-plated steel 4- or 6-quart can that is placed in the tub and surrounded with crushed ice and rock salt. Beechwood dashers attached to the motor unit stir the ice cream, which solidifies in about 30 to 40 minutes. There are also various small inexpensive electric ice cream makers employing refrigerator ice cubes and rock salt, and machines that go into the freezing compartment of a refrigerator or deep freeze. Most of these small machines make 1 pint or 1 quart.

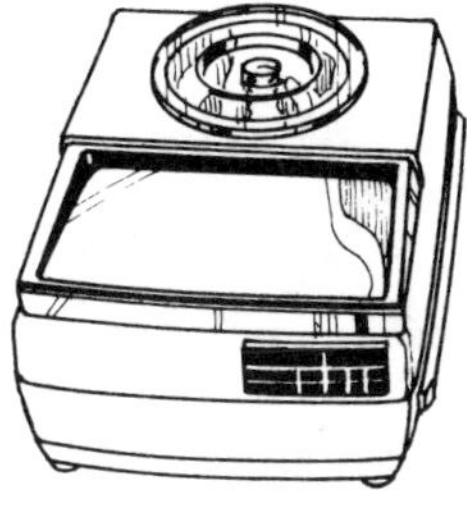

Compact countertop electric ice cream machines generally housed in plastic make 1 or 1½ quarts of frozen dessert at a time. Ice cream or sorbet mixtures are poured into a stainless steel fixed container with stirring blades and the machine is switched on. The dessert is made automatically in 20 to 25 minutes.

Micro/digital timers and temperature controls with three-phase operation—precooling, freezing and storing—are featured on a few machines. All of the machines have Freon refrigeration with electric, motor-driven stirring paddles, either direct, gear or belt driven.

Knives

Fine-quality kitchen knives are one of the best long-term investments. The finest knives available are made of stain-resistant high-carbon alloys containing molybdenum and vanadium as well as chrome for protection against rust and discoloration. These knives hold a keen edge, and yet are soft enough to be sharpened, unlike the stainless-steel knives of 15 to 20 years ago. Carbon steel knives are the easiest of all to sharpen, but they discolor and rust.

The process of making a good knife begins with a single piece of metal which is stamped out, cut or, best of all, hot forged. It is then shaped to taper evenly from the spine to the cutting edge and from the handle to the tip. The knife is further ground to a fine finish either by hand or machine.

A knife is said to have a "full tang" when the metal of which the blade is formed extends the entire length of the handle and follows its shape. Light-duty knives such as bread, boning and some specialty slicing knives do not require a full tang to work well. They may have partial tangs or a metal portion that runs halfway down the handle. Sometimes a rattail tang, a narrow shaft that runs through the length of the handle, is used to keep a knife from being too heavy and at the same time to provide the necessary strength. Generally speaking, most superior knives have a full tang or rattail tang for balance and weight.

A heavy-duty knife, such as a chef's knife, will have extra reinforcement (known as the "bolster"—*see illustration*) in the area between the handle and the blade. This makes the knife comfortable to use, adds balance and protects the fingers from the blade when chopping and mincing. The correct way to hold a knife is to center the grip over the bolster with three fingers around the handle, using the thumb and forefinger to grip the blade. This provides maximum control and leverage, as it is the balance point of the knife. Using a knife in this manner is less tiring when doing large amounts of chopping or mincing.

The blade of a good knife is made to last a long time and so is the handle. For this reason, certain hardwoods are treated with an infusion of plastic and firmly riveted to the tang in three places; molded polypropylene handles are permanently bonded to the entire tang without seams or gaps. Very few handles are made of natural wood, but if they are, extremely hard and close-grained woods are used, such as Brazilian ironwood and rosewood. The best-made handles are shaped for comfort and ground flush to the sides of the knife. If rivets are used, these too are ground flush to eliminate any crevices.

Contrary to popular belief, *a sharp knife is actually safer to use than a dull one.* Because greater force is required to work with a dull knife, it is more likely to slip and hurt the user. A dull knife will also squash and tear food instead of cutting it.

Never put good cutlery in the dishwasher. The intense heat and radical temperature changes will affect the temper of the steel, the sharpened edge can be nicked or gouged and the handle may deteriorate and split. Some knives are advertised as having dishwasher-safe handles. However, for the protection and long life of the blade, even these knives should be washed by hand.

After use, wipe the knife dry or wash it in warm, soapy water. Never leave knives to soak, even with the handles and bolsters above water level. Always dry the blade from the spine side to avoid accidentally running a finger along the cutting edge. To test the sharpness of a knife, draw the blade lightly over a tomato. A sharp knife will cut the skin by its own weight; a dull knife will slide over it.

Paring Knife. The all-purpose paring or utility knife is handy for anything from trimming and peeling vegetables to small chopping and slicing jobs. The most useful sizes have a 3- or 4-inch blade.

Chef's Knife. The professional cook's most widely used knife, this is primarily for chopping, in a rapid repeat motion, or for slicing vegetables. It should be strongly made, with a bolster or collar, and have a wide, rigid blade. Most home cooks use an 8- or 10-inch blade.

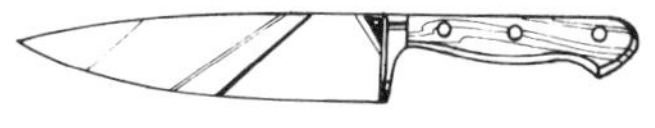

Slicing Knife. Slicing knives have thin, flexible blades and are designed to cut through hot or cold cooked meats of all kinds. The most popular sizes have 6- 8- and 10-inch blades.

Serrated Knives. These scalloped-edge knives do not need resharpening once they have left the factory. Those with a 7½-inch blade are generally used for bread; the serrated knife edge has a sawing action which does not squash the crumb. The 4½-inch blade is invaluable for slicing tomatoes and citrus fruit cleanly and evenly. Be aware that some knives with serrated blades are beveled on the right side only, which makes them primarily for right-handed users. They do not work as well for a left-handed person.

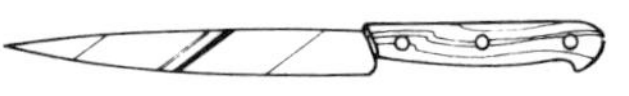

Fish-Filleting Knife. This knife has an exceptionally thin, narrow, flexible blade for following the contours of raw fish, between the bones and the flesh, once the outer skin has been removed. The average blade is ½ an inch wide by 6 inches long and sharply pointed.

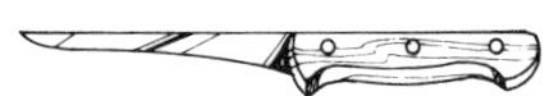

Boning Knife. Boning knives used in most home kitchens have 3- or 5-inch blades that are curved inward on the cutting edge. A better shape for the task than a paring knife, a good boning knife is particularly useful for getting the bones out of chicken, cutting through tendons at the joints, and so forth.

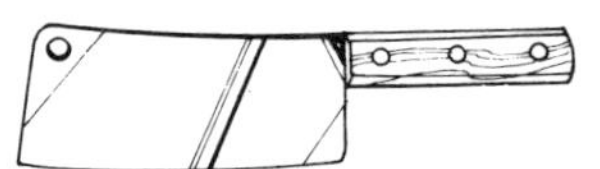

Meat Cleaver. A good meat cleaver should be blade heavy—choose one even heavier than you think feels comfortable at first—so that it does all the work of splitting bones and cartilage with one downward swing.

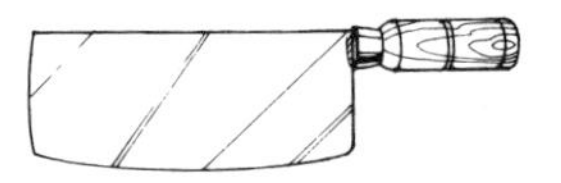

Oriental Chef's Knife. Although a wide-bladed Oriental chef's knife may look like a meat cleaver, it is in fact a finely edged, beautifully balanced cutting tool and should never be wielded like a sledgehammer. In the hands of an experienced practitioner, this type of knife can perform all kinds of cutting, mincing and slicing tasks at high speed—and the blade can then be turned sideways to act as a scoop.

Oriental Slicing Knife. Beautifully balanced and beveled, these knives are used mainly for cutting paper-thin slices of raw fish, or sushi, though they can be utilized for slicing western-style meats, tomatoes and bread. Be aware that most of them are sharpened for right-handed use.

Now that children are no longer forced to be right-handed, whether they were born that way or not, beveled knife manufacturers—in Japan as elsewhere—are discovering that they have hitherto unthought-of problems. We can only assume that, in the past, left-handed children did not train to be sushi chefs!

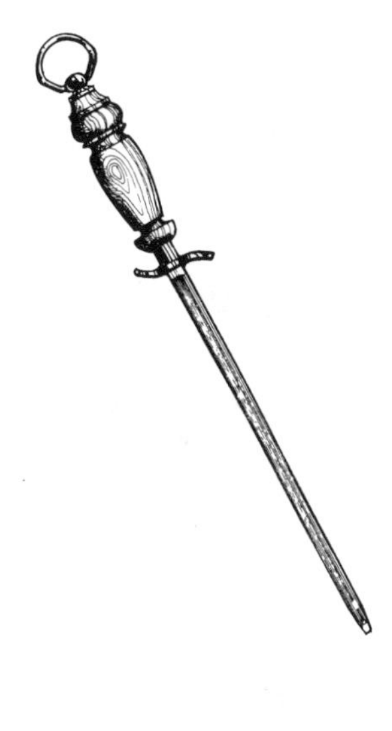

Butcher's Steel. A butcher's steel is for keeping a sharp knife sharp. A whetstone is for sharpening a dull knife. For the regular maintenance of a fine edge on a sharp knife, use a butcher's steel frequently, preferably every time the knife is used. The steel is a long, narrow, round shaft of super-hardened, magnetized steel, finely grooved and tapered toward the end. It is securely attached to a handle with a guard to protect your hand from the knife blade that is being sharpened. Steels usually have a hanging ring and should be kept within easy reach. To use, hold the blade to be sharpened at no greater than a 20° angle to the steel and draw the entire cutting edge toward you 5 or 6 times on each side of the blade. Clean grooves in steel with a fine brass brush occasionally. Do not wash.

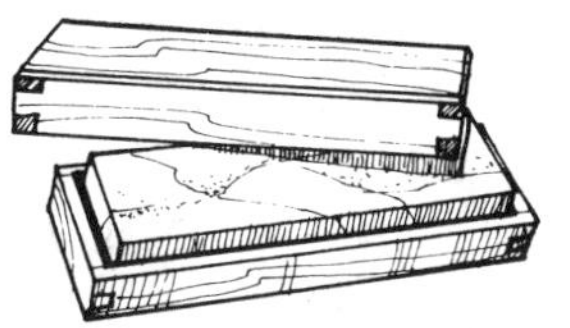

Whetstone. A traditional carborundum stone is an abrasive block, harder than molybdenum steel or carbon steel, that will put a fine sharp edge on a knife. As with the butcher's steel, the knife blade is drawn across it at a 20° angle, 5 or 6 times on each side.

The use of electric or other automatic knife sharpeners is not recommended; they tend to spoil the edge of the blade.

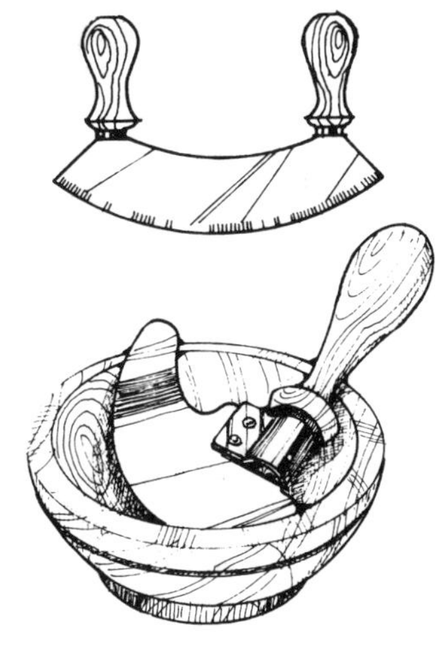

Mezzaluna or Crescent Cutter. These curved "half-moon"-shaped steel blades, which can be single or double, are attached to knob handles with collars. A heavy-duty chopping tool, it is swiftly rocked from side to side for chopping and mincing on a wooden cutting board.

Wooden Chopping Bowl and Curved Chopper. A favorite tool in French kitchens, the single-handled crescent cutter is curved to match the bottom-heavy wooden bowl. It provides an efficient way to chop small quantities of parsley, a clove or two of garlic or a shallot, because the item being chopped stays in one place.

Grills and Portable Ovens

Grilling is a method of cooking over a source of heat. This source can be wood, charcoal, gas, electric or butane. For grilling meats, fish or fowl the heat produced should be intense enough to sear the surface, keeping the interior moist.

Outdoor Grills come in many sizes, from the small portable "hibachi" to the large stationary gas-fired type. Some are on wheels with hoods attached for roasting or smoking. Whichever you choose, make sure the fire pan and grill can withstand the intense heat required for grilling.

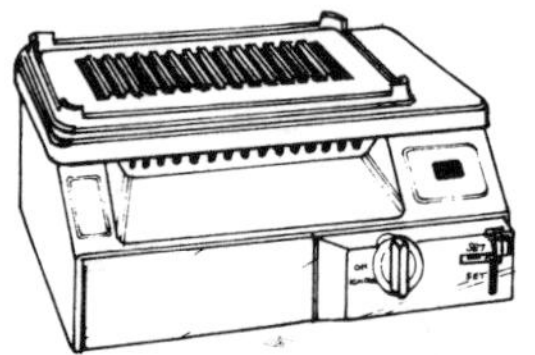

Tabletop Grill. Compact grills fired by canisters of butane gas or by electricity are now available. Some produce infrared heat, the same intense heat that you get from charcoal embers, which grills meat, fish and poultry very successfully.

Portable Barbecue Pit Smoker. Constructed like an upright drum on legs with a high, domed cover, smokers are usually made of cold rolled steel and finished with an anti-rust undercoat and heat-resistant enamel. The base unit holds charcoal and can be used as a charcoal grill. Put the cover in place and it becomes an oven. Add hardwood chips to the charcoal and a pan of water and you get smoke as well as heat for smoked foods. Some smokers are heated by electricity instead of charcoal.

Ridged Stovetop Grill. A cross between a frying pan and a griddle, this solid cast-iron grill has a ridged cooking surface that allows fat that drips from cooking meat to run off and collect in the shallow channel around the perimeter. The fat can then be poured off through a spout. Most grills are coated with baked-on matte black finish to resist rust and sticking.

The ridged grill can be made very hot, which seals meat or poultry successfully without added fat.

Portable Convection Ovens. As heat is circulated by an interior fan, foods are cooked very evenly. Convection ovens do an outstanding job of baking breads, cakes and pastries that are particularly sensitive to uneven heat.

Hand-powered Machines

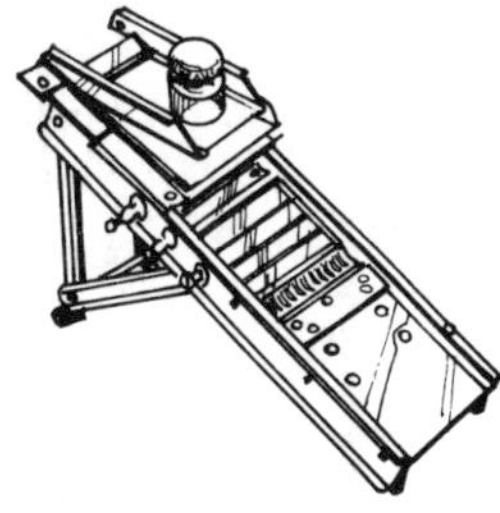

Stainless-Steel Mandoline. A first-rate slicer that is found in most professional kitchens, this machine cuts with precision and versatility. Of heavy gauge stainless steel with stainless-steel blades, it is made in the form of a 15½ x 4½-inch rectangle with folding legs that can be screwed down to a tabletop if desired. Hard vegetables such as potatoes, beets, cucumbers and cabbage are passed over the adjustable blades for thick and thin slicing, julienne cutting, waffle cutting and French-fry cutting. A metal carriage on guides holds the food, so there is no danger to fingers.

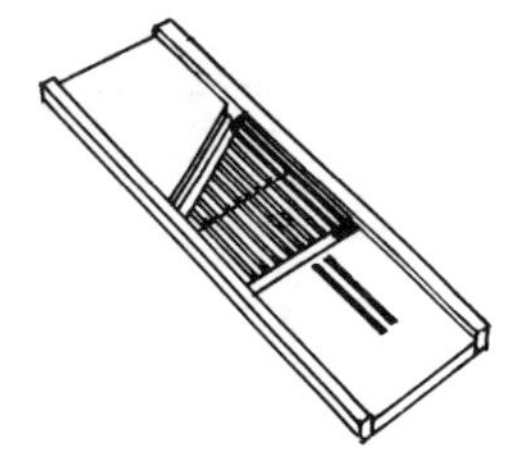

Wooden Mandoline. This smoothly sanded hardwood frame has two stainless-steel slicing blades set into it; one straight and one corrugated. The angle of the blades can be adjusted with wing nuts. Not as efficient as the stainless-steel mandoline, it is nevertheless a fast and consistent cutting machine.

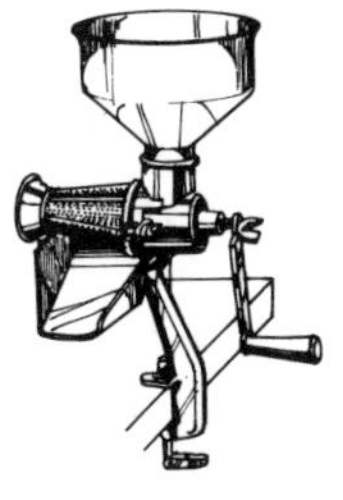

Tomato Press. Usually made of stainless steel and plastic, a tomato press forces quartered tomatoes through a perforated stainless steel cone, ejecting the juice and pulp from one chute and skins and seed from another. It has a clamp or a suction cup for attaching it to the table. These machines are usually about 11 inches high and come apart for cleaning.

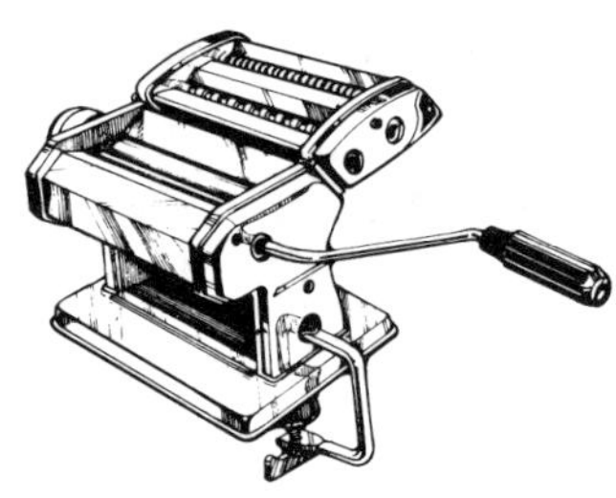

Pasta Machine. The hand-cranked pasta machine kneads and cuts dough by means of plain and notched rollers. It is a quick and convenient way of making pasta. The machine clamps to a work table and comes with plain rollers for kneading and rolling the pasta dough, and two sets of notched rollers, one wide and one narrow, for cutting it. Extra attachments can be obtained for making ravioli or crinkle-edged strips of pasta for lasagne and spaghetti. Hand-cranked pasta machines measure about 5½ x 7½ x 5½ inches, and are made of chromed steel with nickel steel rollers and cutters.

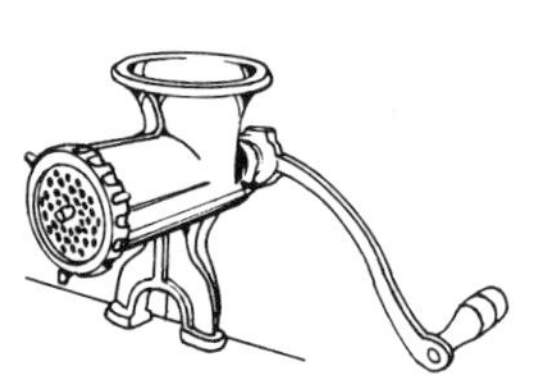

Meat Grinder. Choose a hand-operated cast-iron meat grinder that will resist rust and corrosion. The best-quality ones are double-dipped in zinc and the steel attachments are zinc-plated or chromed. The cutting edges of the rotary "worm" or screw should be of hardened steel. Additional perforated cutting plates and a sausage-stuffing horn are usually available. Be sure to wash and dry the component parts carefully after use.

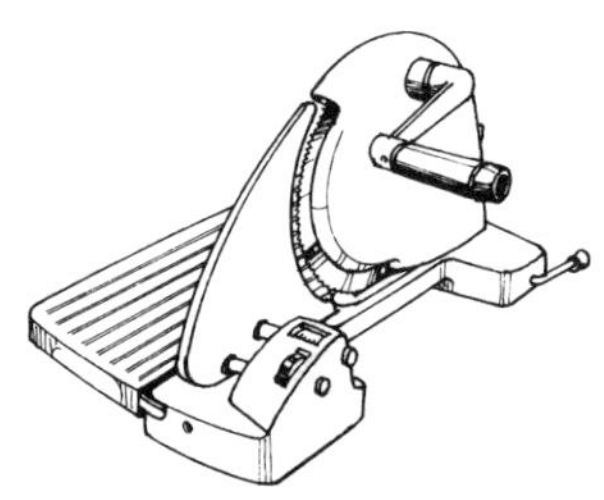

Meat Slicer. Hand-operated meat slicers consist of a flat platform with a circular blade set parallel to it in a housing that has a handle attached. Hold the food to be sliced against the guard with one hand and turn the handle with the other. The food will pass through to the other side in slices. The blade opening, which is adjustable, determines the thickness of the slices. Usually made of enameled cast aluminum or chromed steel and plastic with a stainless-steel blade, these machines are attached to the work surface with a clamp or suction cups. Some models have plastic carriages that hold the food to be cut and slide to and fro on the base of the machine. Most slicers measure about 14 x 10 x 8 inches.

Ice Cream Maker. A hand-powered ice cream machine should have a heavy tin-coated freezing container with metal and wood paddles for stirring. The outer bucket should be constructed of wood with metal bands or of sturdy plastic. The gear drive should be securely mounted across the top and easily locked into place and should be smooth-running and easy to crank. There should be ample space for ice and rock salt. Available in several sizes from 2 to 6 quarts, these machines may have an old-fashioned charm but they are a lot less than convenient to use.

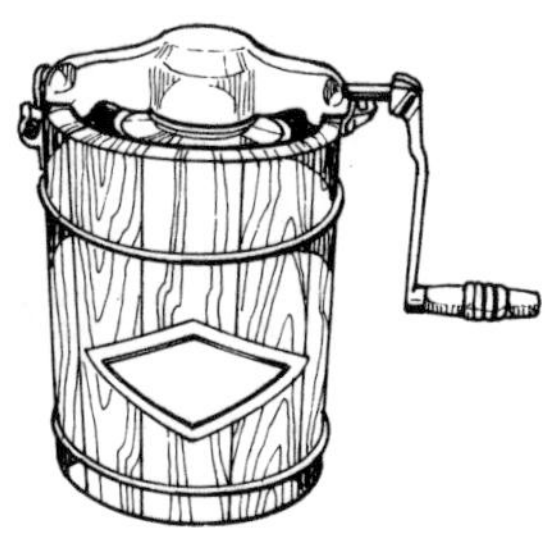

Bowls and Measures

Bowls come in a variety of shapes and sizes for mixing, beating, marinating, storing and serving, and in different materials for different uses. You should have 4 to 5 bowls in various sizes.

Sphere-Shaped Bowls. These usually come in sets of 3 or 4 graduated sizes, ranging from 1½ to 6½ quarts. Use them for all-purpose mixing, stirring and beating. An English bowl, also known as a "Gripstand," is probably the best designed. It has a flattened area on one side so that the bowl can be tilted securely on the counter while you're beating, and its outside surface has a raised pattern that makes it easier to grip securely.

Some bowls have pouring lips, others have sloping sides or flat inside bottoms; some are deep, others shallow. They are made in various materials such as porcelain, earthenware, stoneware, glass, stainless steel and plastic. Choose bowls that are easy to pick up and hold, that are smooth on the inside and can safely be put in the oven.

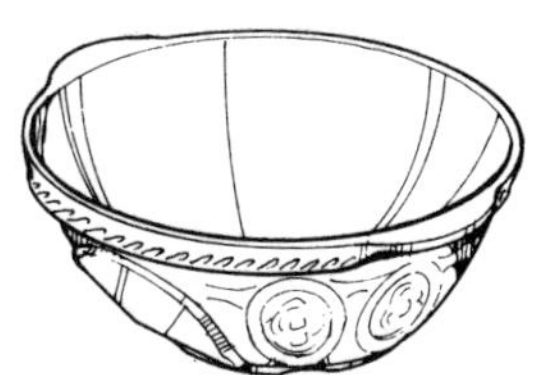

Batter Bowls. Batter or mix-and-measure bowls are made of glass, heavy plastic or earthenware. Usually of a 2-quart capacity, they have a handle and spout with liquid measuring amounts marked on the side. Deep bowls of this type are good for whipping cream or egg whites because they eliminate spat-

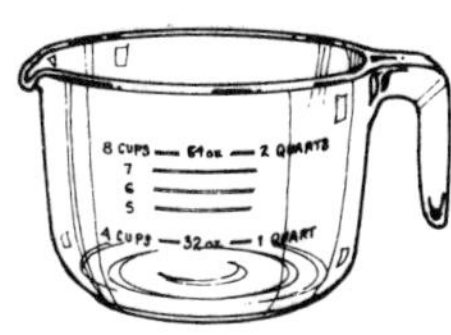

ter. If you prefer a plastic bowl, choose one with a rubber ring on the bottom to ensure a secure footing. Deep batter bowls usually come in a set of 3 or 4, in graduated sizes.

Unlined Copper Bowl. Egg whites should increase 7 to 8 times their volume when beaten. This is best attained by using a balloon whisk and an unlined copper bowl. Copper has a harmless chemical property that binds with the albumen in the egg white, making a more stable foam that is less likely to deflate. Let the bowl pivot on its rounded bottom as you whisk the egg whites, or hold the bowl in the crook of your arm against your body. Steady the bowl by putting your thumb through the attached ring. Always clean the inside of the bowl just before use with half a lemon dipped in salt or a strong solution of vinegar and water to clean off oxidation, then rinse and dry. Bowls range in size from 9 to 14 inches in diameter. The most practical is either 10 or 12 inches in diameter.

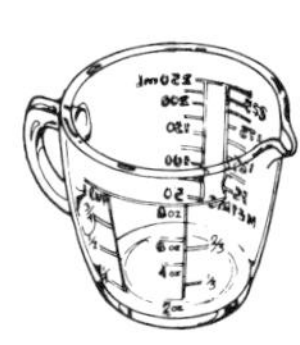

Glass Cup Measures. Made of heatproof glass, these cups are intended for measuring liquids only. They won't give you an accurate measure for dry ingredients. Designed for pouring with a handle and a spout, most are now marked in milliliters as well as ounces. Usual sizes are 1- , 2- and 4-cup capacity. Buy one of each.

Dry Measure Cups. With a true level rim for accurately measuring dry ingredients, these cups are generally made of aluminum, stainless steel or plastic. They usually come in sets of four for ¼, ⅓, ½ and 1 cup, though a 2-cup measure is also available.

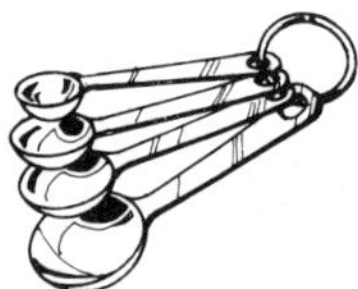

Measuring Spoons. Usually designed with round or oval bowls, measuring spoons almost always come in sets of 4, on a ring, to measure ¼, ½ and 1 teaspoon, and 1 tablespoon. Aluminum, plastic and stainless steel are the most common materials. Every kitchen needs a set of these spoons.

Scales and Thermometers

Baking is an exact science, and professional bakers use scales to ensure consistent results. Scales are also useful for weighing meats to estimate cooking times and for portion control. Old-fashioned balance scales with weights are accurate but take up a great deal of counter space. Many scales are now digital.

Spring Scales. Most spring-balance scales are calibrated in both gram and ounce measures, but make sure the total weight capacity suits your needs. The dial registers the amount of weight placed in the pan according to the degree by which the spring is depressed. Easy to use and easy to read, the disadvantage of this type of scale is that the spring may eventually weaken and give inaccurate measurements. However, its accuracy can always be monitored with a standard weight such as a pound of butter. In some spring scales, the pan folds up against the dial and hangs on the wall much like a clock. In the countertop version, the pan may reverse to form a cover.

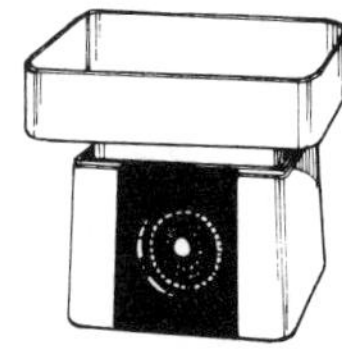

Bowl Scales. This spring-balance scale has a fairly large capacity bowl instead of a pan, and the dial can be reset to zero after the addition of each ingredient called for in a recipe. The scale also will work with a plate or another bowl. Most are marked in both ounce and gram measure, though the total weight capacity varies.

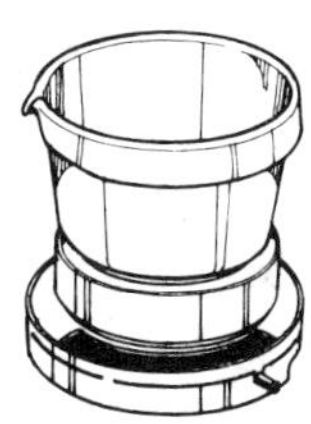

Beam Balance Scales. These scales are a little more difficult to read but are very accurate: some will weigh anything from a tablespoon of salt to a 22-pound turkey. The item to be weighed is placed on the removable tray and two weights are pushed along the bar—one for ounces/grams, the other for pounds/kilos—until the bar balances.

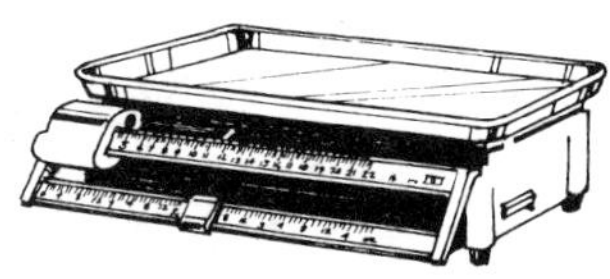

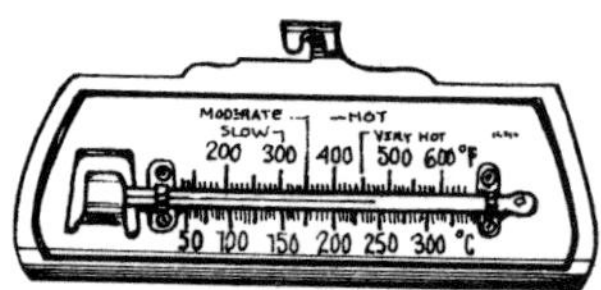

Oven Thermometer. Even the most expensive ovens may have faulty thermostats, so it makes sense to have an oven thermometer on the oven shelf to double-check the temperatures. Insulation also can vary, so move the thermometer around to see if different parts of the oven are hotter than others and situate pans accordingly. Choose a stainless steel stand with a glass mercury thermometer that measures from 100° to 650° F.

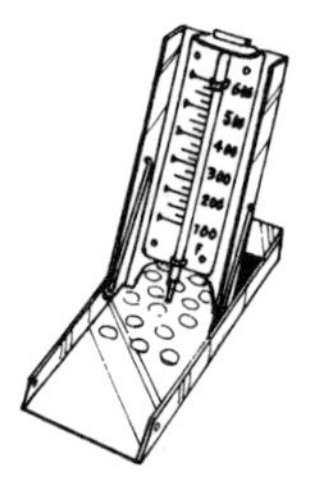

Folding Oven Thermometer. Not meant to be left in the oven, this easy-to-read glass mercury thermometer is used to spot check oven heat by professional chefs and service mechanics. The stainless-steel folding case forms a stand and the thermometer is mounted on a white enameled steel face. It measures from 100° to 600° F. and is extremely accurate.

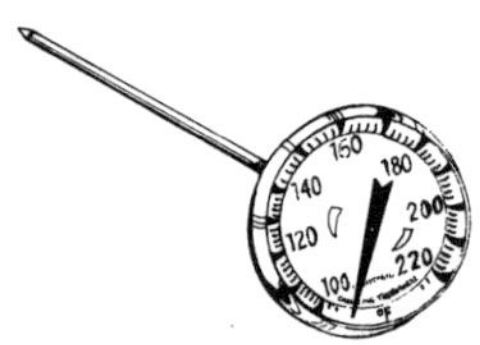

Meat Thermometer. The old-style meat thermometer is rather thick and is designed to be stuck in the meat and left there until the needle in the dial climbs to the appropriate doneness. If you use this kind of thermometer, be sure that your idea of rare, medium and well done coincides with that of the manufacturer. Most home cooks today prefer an instant meat thermometer that is inserted in the meat or poultry for an instant reading and then immediately taken out. The probe is slender, and doesn't make large holes that juices can run out of, and the dial is easy to read. Two different sizes are available: the 1-inch dial measures 0° to 220°; the 2-inch dial measures 100° to 220°. You should have one meat thermometer among your cooking equipment.

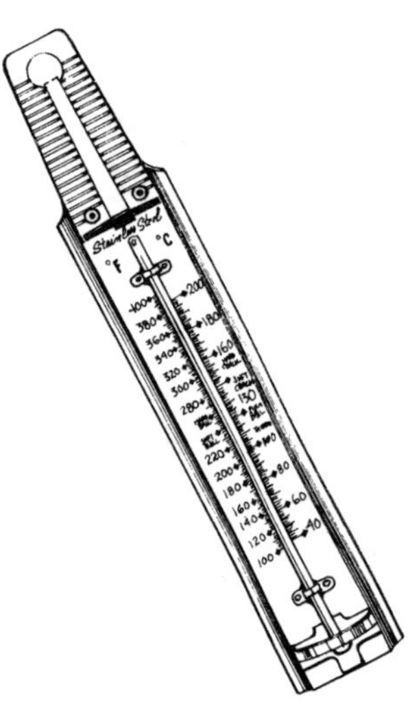

Candy/Deep-Fat Thermometer. Sugar syrup passes through distinct stages as it heats from a simple syrup of 215° F. to hard crack and caramel at 310°. Doughnuts and onion rings are deep fried at an oil temperature of 350° F., whereas French fries are cooked at 370° to 390° F. Overheated fat makes the kitchen smell, so it makes good sense to monitor it carefully. Choose a dual-purpose thermometer that registers from 100°

up to 400° and is both easy to read and mounted on a stainless-steel frame with a plastic handle at the top. Some models have an adjustable hook on the back for attaching to the side of the pan.

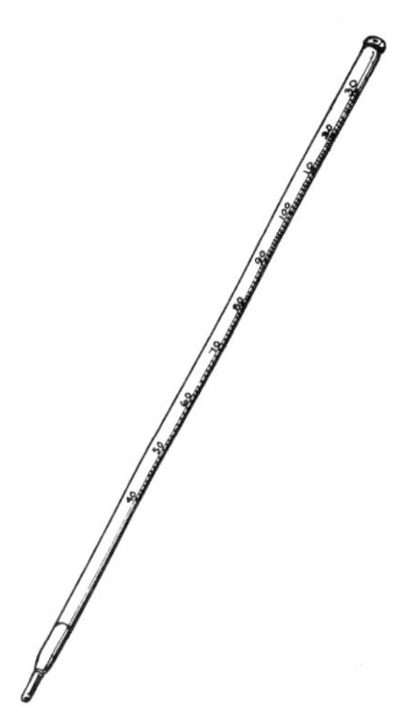

Chocolate Thermometer. In order to temper chocolate successfully so that it cools to a hard sheen it must be heated and cooled very precisely at temperatures ranging from 80° to 122° F. A glass mercury chocolate thermometer is really a piece of professional equipment, but it's a good investment for the home cook who is interested in making professional-looking candies and *pâtisserie.* It should measure temperatures from about 50° to 140°, in wide, one-degree gradations that are easy to read.

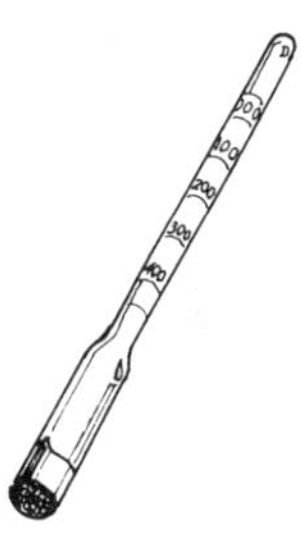

Saccharimeter. Also known as a *pèse-sirop,* this device measures the density of sugar syrup, important when you're making ice cream, sorbet or fruit syrups. The weighted glass tube floats upright at a level determined by the sugar density, and is marked from 0 to 40 on the Baumé scale. It is simple to use: You put some of the prepared syrup mixture in a tall glass and drop in the saccharimeter. Check the scale and add more sugar or water as necessary. (Too much sugar in a frozen dessert will inhibit freezing; too much water promotes ice crystals.) Instructions for use should be included with the instrument.

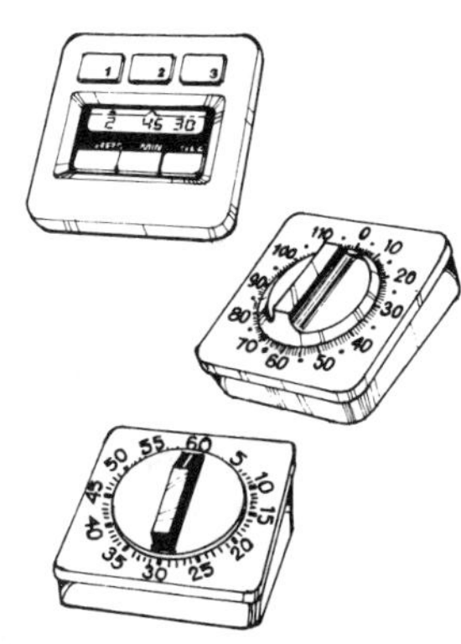

Timers. Modern kitchen alarm timers, as opposed to the old-fashioned hourglass type, are available in two basic models. The simple spring type looks like a small alarm clock, a low drum or even an egg. It can be set for up to 60 minutes usually, though there is one on the market that registers up to 120 minutes. When the allotted time has ticked away, the bell rings. Digital timers can have up to three circuits for three different simultaneous activities and run silently until the buzzer sounds. Some digital timers measure in seconds as well as minutes, still others can be used as a stopwatch.

Equipment for Preparing Tea and Coffee

Tea. Connoisseurs agree that the best tea is made by pouring freshly boiling water over loose tea leaves in a heated ceramic or glass teapot. It should steep for three to five minutes and then be poured into china cups.

To make good tea you need a kettle for boiling the water, a teapot in which to brew it, and a tea strainer so that you don't get leaves in your cup. Some people like to use a tea bell or infuser that can be removed from the teapot when the tea is brewed. Some teapots have perforated inserts for tea leaves which can be removed when the tea is ready. And there is at least one automatic tea-brewing machine on the market that will make tea for you, all timed scientifically, in the same way that an electric coffeemaker brews coffee.

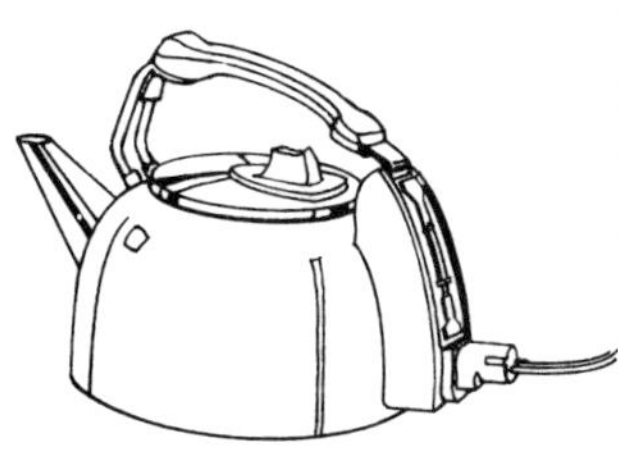

Teakettles. Stove-top teakettles are available in tin-lined copper, aluminum, stainless steel, enameled steel and chromed steel or chrome-plated copper. Electric teakettles, less common here than in Britain, can be of copper, aluminum, stainless steel and even heat-resistant plastic.

When choosing a teakettle, make sure that the handle is heatproof and easy to grasp. Avoid handles that fold down. They get very hot when the water is boiled as they invariably lie against the metal. Steam vents should not endanger your hand when boiling water is poured. Some teakettles are filled through the large spout, in others you must remove the lid. Since most teakettles eventually build up mineral deposits from tap water, use a decalcifier, a small disc-shaped brush with natural bristles that attract mineral deposits. A whistle on the spout is also a convenient reminder that you should never let a kettle boil dry, especially a copper one. Always use fresh water for tea or coffee and use bottled water if your tap water has a chemical taste.

Tea Infusers. Spherical or bell-shaped tea infusers have a metal chain and a hook for attaching to the side of the teapot. When the tea is brewed, the infuser can then be retrieved easily. These pot infusers are made of perforated chromed steel, porcelain, silver or stainless steel. Individual tea infusers are shaped like a teaspoon with two bowls that clip together, facing each other. They are filled with loose tea, placed in a teacup and covered with boiling water. They are generally made of perforated stainless steel or chrome-plated steel.

Tea Strainer. Usually made of wire mesh or perforated stainless steel, silverplate and sterling silver, these small strainers have a handle and a hook on the opposite side for resting over a teacup to catch loose leaves as the tea is poured.

Teapots. Teapots come in many shapes, sizes and materials. Georgian silver, for example, is beautiful but may give its flavor to the tea. Ceramic, glazed earthenware or porcelain are best for brewing tea. Choose a pot with a good, nondrip pouring spout and a handle large enough to keep your hand away from the heated pot. Don't rely on the cover of a pot remaining in place on its own when pouring. Always hold the cover with your hand. Clean the inside of a teapot from time to time with baking soda and water and then rinse well. Tea tends to leave a tannin deposit which can build up and impart a bitter flavor.

Glass Teapot. Some people believe that the best tea is steeped in glass. Glass teapots are made of thin laboratory glass and have removable, central perforated containers of generous capacity for holding the tea leaves. This enables fast, complete steeping. A warming stand that holds a candle is also available.

Automatic Tea Machine. This electric teamaker has a stainless-steel water chamber that releases bubbling water into the large tea-steeping chamber for a controlled length of time.

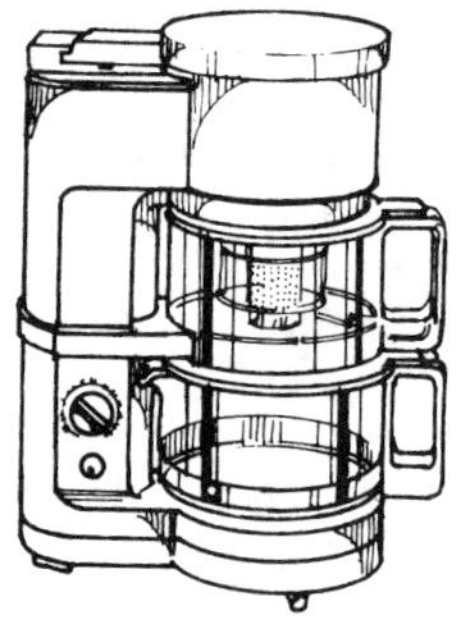

Once the tea is brewed, it descends to the preheated glass carafe below, where it is kept at just the right serving temperature. It is sleekly designed in plastic and heat-resistant laboratory glass. Capacity is 8 cups (36 ounces).

Coffee. The choice of coffee makers is almost infinite. Percolators have largely been replaced by drip and filter coffee makers and espresso machines. Remember that any kind of coffee is only as good as the freshly roasted beans from which it is made. It is really best to grind your own, as ground coffee quickly loses its flavor and aroma unless it has been vacuum packed immediately after roasting. Some roasted coffee is packed in bags with one-way valves that expel the nitrogen build-up in the bag but do not admit oxygen from the outside. This preserves the freshness of the packaged roasted coffee for 6 to 12 months.

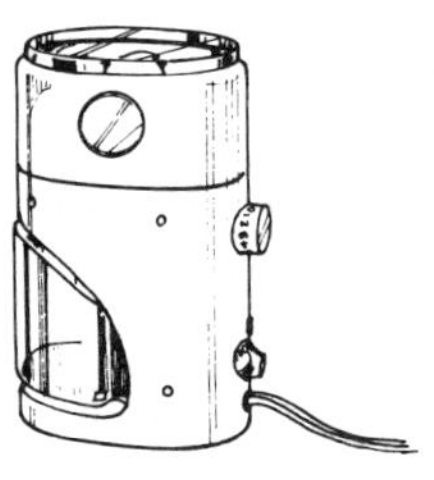

Electric Coffee Grinder. The best type of electric coffee grinders have a disc-type grinding system that mills the beans evenly and with no heat buildup. They usually have a detachable beaker for the ground coffee and a receptacle for the coffee beans. They are adjustable for coarse to fine grinds. The housing is usually of plastic.

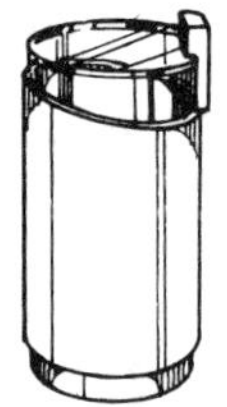

Electric Coffee Mill. A coffee mill has stainless-steel cutting blades that chop or pulverize the beans from coarse to rather fine. Controlled by a push button, this mill can also be used to chop shelled nuts, grains and spices. The disadvantage to this machine is that it pulverizes the beans unevenly and is apt to burn the coffee if ground too fine, releasing the bitter oils.

Electric Drip Coffee Maker. At its most simple, an electric drip coffee maker heats water that has been poured into the water chamber and allows it to drip over coffee grounds placed in a cone paper filter. The infused coffee drips into a carafe that sits on a warming plate.

Look for a machine that allows easy access to the water chamber and the filter holder. The hot water, which should be at approximately 203° for maximum brewing efficiency, should soak all the coffee grounds for several minutes, not just wet those at the center of the filter. A "drip trip" is a convenient feature. The brewing coffee ceases to drip for a few seconds if the carafe is removed, instead of splashing onto the warming plate. Some machines have two brewing cycles; one for up to 3 or 4 cups of coffee, the other for up to 8 or 12 cups, so that smaller amounts are not brewed so fast that they are weak.

French Porcelain Drip Coffee Pot. Still the favorite of many coffee connoisseurs, this pot produces coffee with absolutely no taste added to mar the flavor. Ground coffee goes into the two-handled perforated cylinder that is placed on the pot. The porcelain strainer is then set on top of the cylinder and the appropriate amount of hot water poured through to distribute the water evenly over the coffee. The lid is then set in place. The water filters slowly through the ground coffee in the porcelain cylinder and into the pot below. The entire pot is made of high-fired porcelain and can be kept warm on the stove with a heat diffuser. Dishwasher safe, these pots are available in sizes from 3- to 8-cup capacity.

Infusion Coffee Pot. This is the filter coffee pot that you see in many French restaurants around the world. Ground coffee is measured into the glass beaker, hot water is added, and the cover, with its stainless-steel filter disc and plunger rod attached, is set in place. Infusion takes place in 3 to 5 minutes, and then the plunger and filter are depressed through the liquid, trapping the coffee grounds at the bottom of the pot with a very fine mesh screen. Pots are available in 3- to 9-cup capacity.

Electric Espresso Machine. In these machines, water is heated to several degrees below boiling, the pump is activated and it forces the water through the finely ground coffee. The

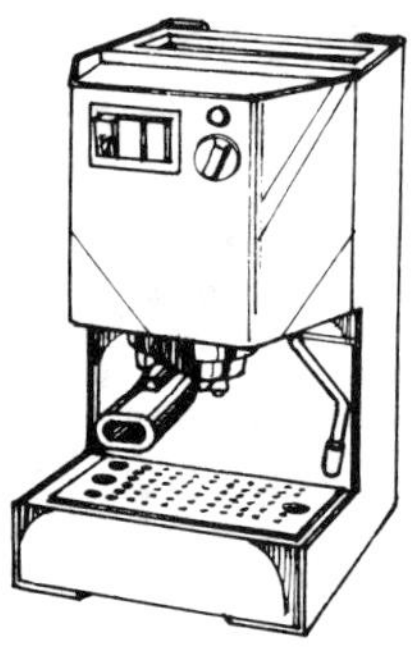

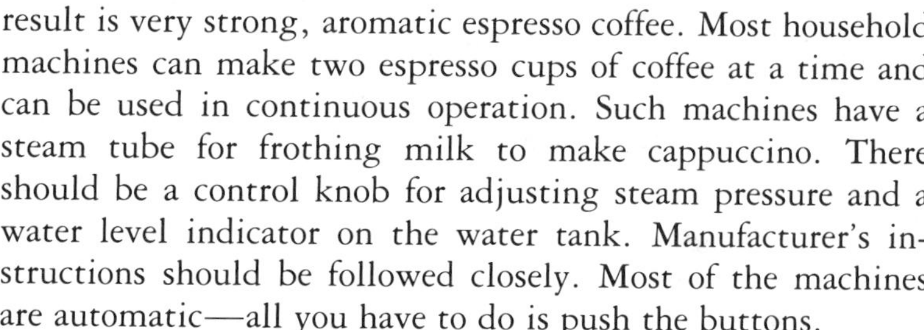

result is very strong, aromatic espresso coffee. Most household machines can make two espresso cups of coffee at a time and can be used in continuous operation. Such machines have a steam tube for frothing milk to make cappuccino. There should be a control knob for adjusting steam pressure and a water level indicator on the water tank. Manufacturer's instructions should be followed closely. Most of the machines are automatic—all you have to do is push the buttons.

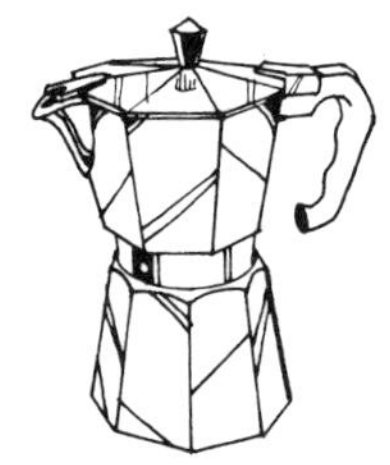

Stovetop Espresso Pot. You can't froth milk for cappuccino with most of these pots, but they make excellent espresso coffee. Water goes in the base, the basket is filled with finely ground coffee and then the top and the bottom parts of the narrow-waisted pot are screwed together. The pot is placed over low heat and as the water heats, pressure is created, forcing the water up through the coffee via a central tube into the top part of the pot. It emerges as richly flavored espresso. A space-saving and very inexpensive alternative to an electric espresso machine, it is made of heavy cast aluminum or stainless steel and has a safety valve. Available in 3- to 12-cup sizes.

Sieves, Graters, Shredders and Mills

Wire Mesh Strainers. These can be used for straining solids from liquids or for sifting dry ingredients such as flour and confectioners' sugar. As the mesh is relatively fragile, look for a strainer with a strong frame and handle, and make sure it has "ears" or hooks for resting over a bowl. A fine- or medium-mesh strainer does a good job of straining and sifting, but may be damaged when you press solids through it. Some strainers are therefore reinforced with narrow cross-bands around the bowl; others have double mesh, the outside being very coarse. The best are made of extra-fine stainless-steel mesh with polished stainless-steel frames and handles. It is a good idea to have at least three strainers: small, medium and large.

The smallest is handy for straining tea, the medium size for general-purpose tasks and the largest is invaluable for straining stock. A large coarse-mesh strainer will do double duty as a colander and is useful for such tasks as straining strips of lemon peel out of custard and making coarse purées of soft food. Strainers are manufactured in tinned steel, stainless steel, aluminum and nylon. Handles can be of the same material or of wood or plastic. Stainless-steel sieves are recommended and every kitchen should have a fine, medium and coarse mesh strainer.

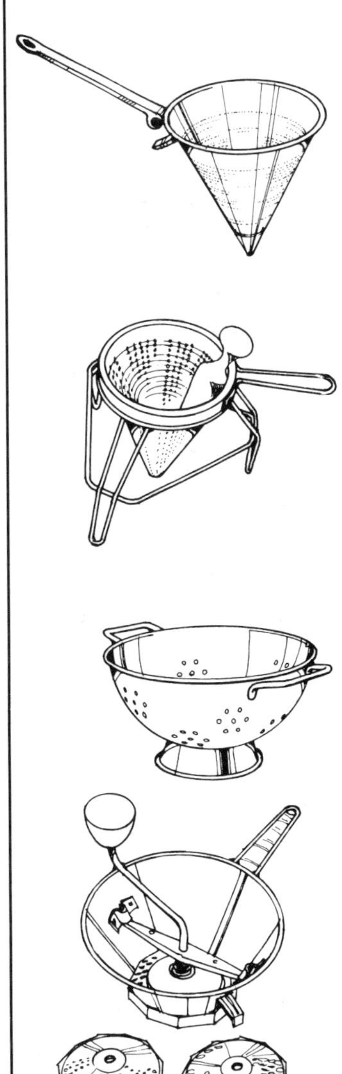

Conical Bouillon Strainer. Also known as a chinois, this cone-shaped strainer has a very tightly woven mesh that ensures a really clear result—every last impurity is strained from bouillon or fish stock. Usually of tin-plated steel and at least 7½ inches wide and 7 inches deep.

Conical Perforated Sieve with Pestle. Another chinois, this one is made of solid aluminum, tin-plated steel or stainless steel perforated with tiny holes. The pointed wooden pestle is swiftly rotated inside it, pushing food through the holes to form a purée. The one illustrated here has a clip on the handle so that it can be attached to a pot. Made for professional use, this type of sieve is usually at least 8 inches deep. Some come on sturdy metal stands.

Colander. A colander is invaluable for draining cooked pasta and vegetables and rinsing foods under running water. It is simply a large perforated bowl set on legs or a ring stand for stability. Some resemble a sieve, with a single handle and hook, for straining over a pot. Colanders are made of stainless steel, aluminum, enameled steel, tin-lined copper, plastic or even porcelain or earthenware. You should have at least one.

Food Mill. A food mill is a mechanical sieve that produces an even-textured purée while eliminating seeds, fibers and skins. Cooked vegetables or fruits are pushed against the holes in the bottom by a hand-cranked paddle fitted with a tension spring; solids are forced through holes; the seeds, skins and fibers stay in the food mill. Some mills have interchangeable fine, medium or coarse plates. The mill is easy to disassemble for cleaning, and the legs may fold for storage. These mills are usually made of tinned steel, stainless steel or tinned steel and plastic. A food mill is one of the essentials for your kitchen.

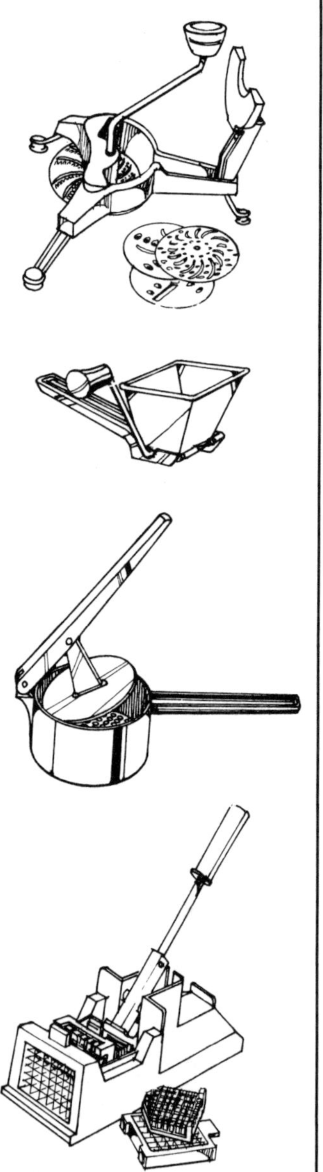

Salad Shredder. These mechanical shredders work on the same principle as a food mill to cut shreds of vegetables. Vegetables are placed in a hopper and are held in place by a hinged lid. There are several interchangeable discs or cones. Salad shredders are in tinned steel, stainless steel, cast aluminum or tinned steel and plastic, and come made in many designs and shapes. The Mouli julienne is the best known.

Parsley Mincer. Parsley, chives and other fresh herbs are minced automatically when the crank is turned on this cutter. It has four rows of sharpened teeth at the base of the hopper and is made of tinned steel or stainless steel and plastic.

Potato Ricer. Any boiled vegetable—carrots, parsnips, turnips or potatoes—can be pushed through this device to emerge as little ricelike pieces. The mixture is then easily transformed into a smooth purée by beating, usually with the addition of butter, cream and various seasonings. Place the cooked vegetable into the perforated cylinder, then squeeze the long handles together to push the contents out through the holes. Ricers are available in various shapes and are usually made of chromed steel, enameled steel or cast aluminum. As it is not necessary to peel the potatoes, a ricer is a time saver.

French-Fry Cutter. Bringing down the handle on this plastic cutter forces a potato out through the stainless-steel cutting grid. It takes a little force, but the resultant French fries are ejected with uniform precision—square cut and identical—which means they all cook in the same length of time. Be sure to choose a heavy-duty model.

Graters. There are three types of graters. In the first, a sheet of metal is punctured with rough-edged round holes which form a rasplike surface for grating cheeses, dry bread, etc. In the second, the metal is perforated with holes that have a raised cutting edge on one side only. This type shreds food into strips or strings as opposed to reducing it to crumbs. The third type has grating, shredding and slicing slits. Tinned steel tends to rust, so choose stainless steel. Graters are found in flat, cylindrical or box shapes. The latter two have handles across the top for a good grip. You will want at least one stainless-steel grater/shredder.

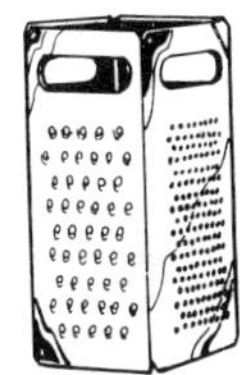

Cheese Grater. This 7½-inch hand-held grater is easy to use and is excellent for grating small amounts of cheese directly over a dish. It can be made entirely of stainless steel or of plastic and stainless steel. At one end of the lower handle is a hinged hopper enclosing a grating drum with a crank for turning. At the end of the upper handle is a curved plate which holds the cheese against the drum. The handles are gripped in one hand while the crank is turned to grate the cheese. The best known of these cheese mills is the Mouli grater.

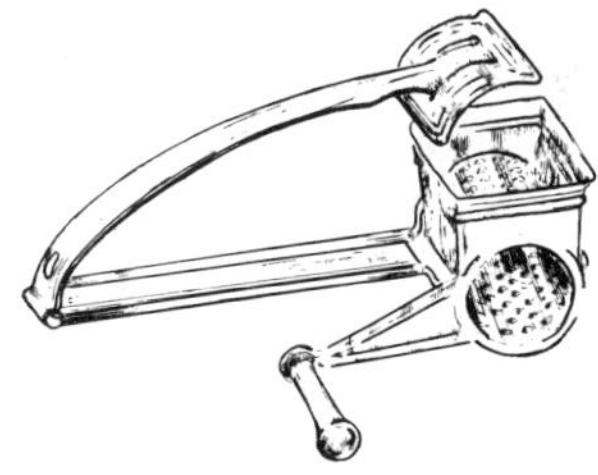

Ginger Graters. These flat porcelain graters are made in the Orient for grating fresh ginger root and daikon radishes, and have rows of pointed porcelain teeth. They work surprisingly well for their intended purpose and are easy to clean.

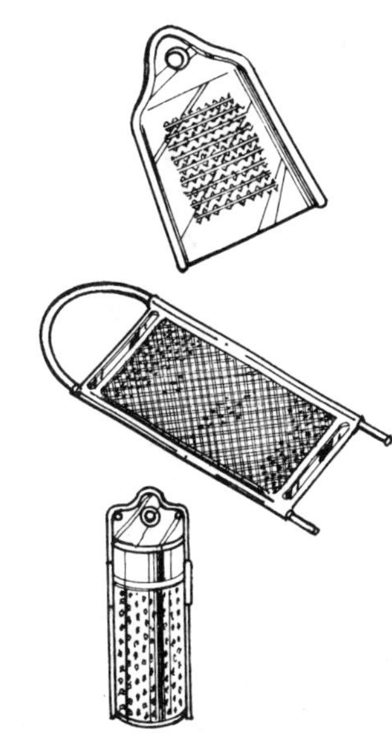

Lemon Graters. Lemon graters, which can be flat or slightly convex, are simply small versions of regular-size flat graters. They have fine rasp surfaces that remove only the outer skin of lemons or oranges.

Nutmeg Graters. These are made of tin-plated or stainless steel, and always come equipped with a fine rasp surface. They are usually formed into a small tapered cylinder with a small enclosure for storing whole nutmegs. Be careful of your knuckles when you use this grater.

Nutmeg Mill. Much easier to use and more efficient than a grater, a nutmeg mill is made of wood and looks somewhat like a pepper grinder. The nutmeg is held in place over the steel cutting edge at the base of the mill by a spring-loaded shaft with handle. When the handle is turned, fine granules of nutmeg fall from the bottom of the mill. Your money would be well invested in this item.

Pepper Mills. Peppercorns have far more aroma and flavor if ground just before use. Pepper mills can be made of wood, aluminum, stainless steel, brass, acrylic, porcelain or even ivory and silver. The grinding mechanism inside is the most important part. There are many inferior pepper grinders on the market. Look for a well-known one. It should be made of superhardened or stainless steel. A good pepper mill should be adjustable for fine to a very coarse grind and should also be easy to fill. Many cooks like to keep two pepper mills in the kitchen, one of light and one of dark wood, for white and black peppercorns. You certainly should have at least one.

Salt Mill. To make it free flowing, ordinary table salt contains chemical additives which can be quite noticeable. The alternative is to use sea salt, which comes in coarse granules. (Coarse kosher salt, incidentally, is pure. If this sounds like nonsense, try tasting iodized or plain table salt, kosher salt and sea salt at the same time.) A salt mill grinds the granules in much the same way that a pepper mill grinds peppercorns. Salt mills are usually of wood or acrylic, and often come in matched pairs with pepper mills. The stainless steel or nylon grinding mechanism of a salt mill is slightly different from that of a pepper mill. Never use a pepper mill for grinding salt. Salt is corrosive and induces oxidation of vulnerable metals, so the grinding burrs could become damaged.

Nut Mill. Electrical graters, blenders and food processors chop nuts into uneven fine granules and also release the nut oil. An essential piece of equipment for pastry cooks, a nut mill produces a soft cloud of nut flour for light cakes and cookies. The mill is attached to a countertop with a clamp, and shelled nuts are placed in the hopper. They are pressed against the grating drum that is rotated by a hand crank. A nut mill is old-fashioned, but quick and simple to use. Available in enameled cast iron with tinned steel grater.

Mortar and Pestle. Before pepper mills were invented, peppercorns—and all other spices and dried herbs—were ground in a mortar with a pestle. These are extremely fast and easy to use: seeds and dried berries are first cracked with the end of the pestle, which is then rotated very fast around the mortar to obtain a fine powder. The aroma and flavor of freshly ground spices is unbelievable when compared to the pre-ground spices generally available. Larger-sized mortars and pestles can be used to make purées of garlic, nut pastes, bean pastes and the like with complete control and lack of waste. Mortars are made of marble, porcelain, stoneware, pottery and wood. Pestles either match or are made of hardwood.

Small Kitchen Tools

Wooden Spoons and Spatulas. Hard and finely grained woods such as beechwood, boxwood, cherry, olive and hard rock maple are used to make a vast array of kitchen tools. Good quality wooden implements will not split and will last much longer than those made of softer woods like pine. Wooden spoons and spatulas will not scratch and are recommended for stirring foods in metal pots and pans, particularly tin-lined copper or enameled cast-iron pans, which scratch easily. Since wood absorbs some flavors from food, it is best to keep separately identified tools for special uses, otherwise the

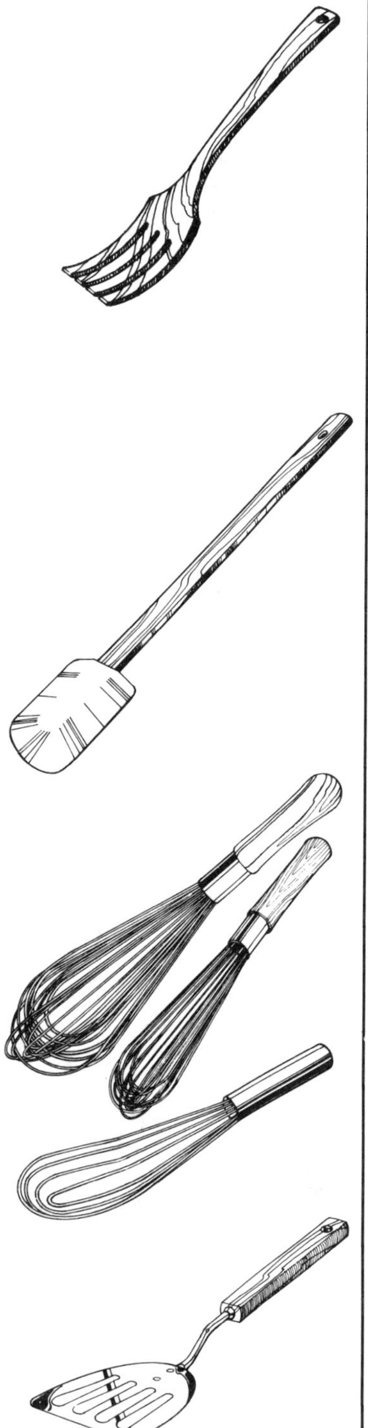

garlic in yesterday's pasta sauce could end up flavoring today's custard.

Clean all wooden tools with a damp cloth or rinse quickly under running hot water. Never soak them in water or put in a dishwasher; the natural oils will dry out and the wood will absorb detergent. Spoons and spatulas come in a large variety of sizes and lengths. Try to find ones that are comfortable for you to hold, and invest in several sizes and shapes.

Rubber and Plastic Spatulas. Pliable rubber and plastic spatulas with wood or hard plastic handles are designed for scraping bowls and folding cake and soufflé batters. They should never be used for stirring foods over heat because plastic softens in hot food, and rubber can slowly melt.

Whisks. Whisks come in different shapes and sizes for different purposes. Rust-free stainless steel is recommended, and it is best to choose whisks with large-diameter wood or steel handles that fit comfortably in the hand. A *balloon whisk,* with approximately 10 very flexible wires, is sphere-shaped for incorporating as much air as possible into beaten egg whites. A *pastry/sauce whisk* has approximately 8 flexible wires formed into narrow loops. It cuts through and mixes custards, pastry creams and sauces without incorporating air. A *flat whisk,* with 6 or 8 heavy looped wire tines, will rest on the bottom of a pan so that any thickened portions of sauce or gravy can be incorporated, resulting in a lump-free mixture.

Turners. These come in convenient sizes for flipping pancakes, turning fish, bacon or hashed browned potatoes, removing cookies from baking sheets, etc. They should be of stainless steel with comfortable wood or composition handles. The blades can be flexible or rigid depending on size and use.

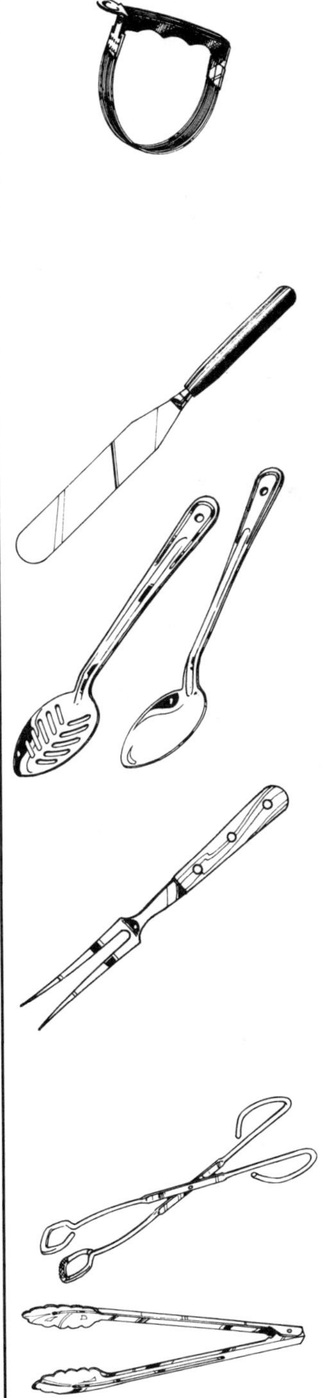

Pastry Blender. A pastry blender is used to cut cold fat into flour when making pastry dough. The steel wires, which are attached to either side of the handle, cut through the fat as you chop down, distributing rice-size pieces throughout the flour. This makes it easy to form the dough into a ball when it is moistened with water. Be sure to choose a blender with wires firmly attached to the handle.

Pastry Spatula. Also called an icing spatula, the straight, narrow blade is used for applying smooth coatings of glaze or frosting to the tops and sides of cakes, and for slicing and then filling layer cakes. The best are of flexible stainless steel with composition handles and a comfortable grip. They come in several lengths (a 9-inch blade is average), including a short 4-inch blade for delicate work.

Cook's Spoons. Choose long-handled spoons with large bowls, in heavy quality, rigid stainless steel. Spoons with solid bowls are used for serving in the kitchen; those with slotted bowls are invaluable for removing foods from liquids.

Two-Pronged Cook's Fork. Choose rigid all-stainless steel that will not bend. This fork's principal function is for turning large pieces of meat, retrieving poached chicken from hot broth and holding meat or poultry steady while carving. Precision-made cook's forks are also made by the cutlery manufacturers who make fine knives. These are constructed of forged, hardened, stain-resistant steel with thick shanks, and full tangs with riveted hard-composition handles.

Cook's Tongs. An all-purpose retrieval tool, tongs don't pierce foods and let the juices escape. There are two types available—those with a heavy wire scissor-action and those with a spring. Both are made in either stainless steel or chromed steel. Stainless steel is recommended.

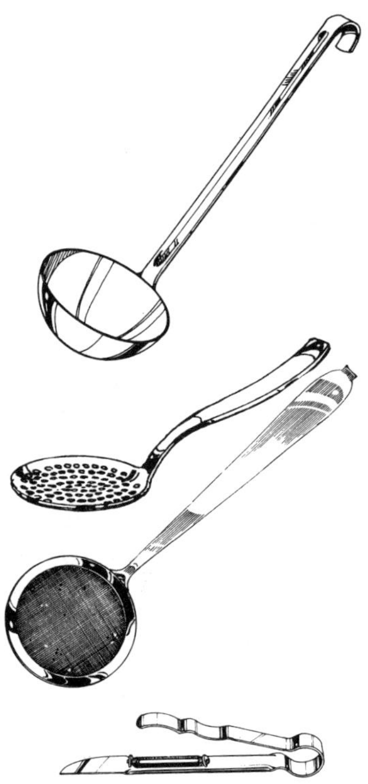

Cook's Ladle. Ladles come in stainless steel, tough cast-aluminum alloy or acrylic. A deep-bowled ladle is used for serving soups and stews, the long handle effectively keeping the cook's hand away from the hot liquid. Use a pierced ladle to remove vegetables and pieces of meat from soup or stock. Both come in several sizes.

Skimmers. Made in tough cast aluminum or stainless steel, the most useful skimmers come in two types: a slightly concave, wide metal disc pierced with small holes for skimming coagulated scum, vegetables and herbs from broths; and a fine-mesh type (in stainless steel only), which is used for lifting all of the frothy scum that forms in the initial stages of cooking broths and preserves.

Asparagus Peeler. This tool, made of chrome-plated steel, is designed to hold asparagus stalks steady while the black steel swivel blade removes a very fine layer of asparagus skin. Just enough skin is removed to let the stalks cook in the same length of time as the tips. It is 6¾ inches long.

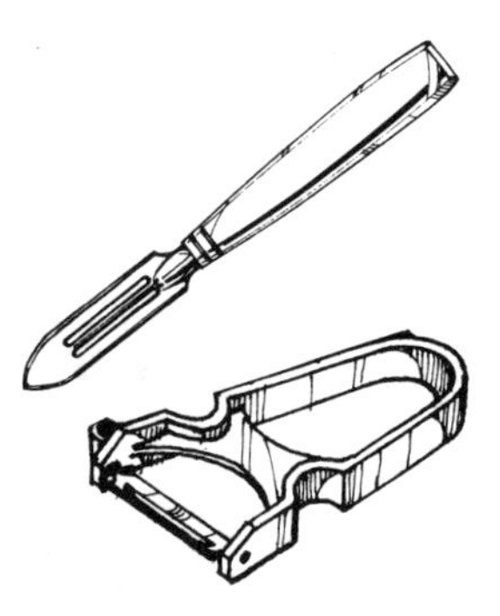

Vegetable Peeler. There are many types to choose from: swivel-action blades that follow the contour of the vegetable being peeled, or rigid blades; double-bladed peelers for right- or left-handed use, or single-bladed for right-hand use only; a straight type with handles of wood, plastic or metal. Blades can be of carbon or blue steel, which will rust if not taken care of, or of stainless steel. There are superior peelers made with a plastic harp frame and a very sharp single swivel blade designed to remove a minimum paring of outer skin. Try several types until you find one that suits you.

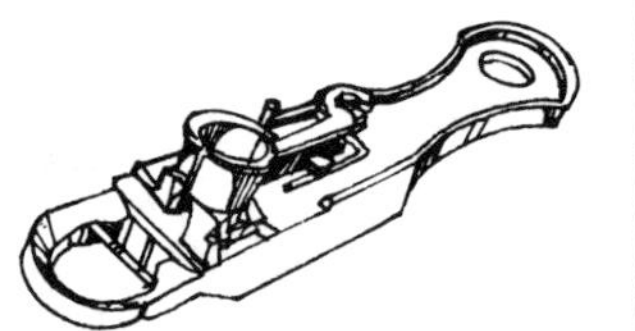

Bean Slicer. Green beans must be crisp for this tool to do its work. Then it is a simple matter to push the bean through the grid of razor-sharp blades and get thin, even, lengthwise slices.

Rolling Mincer. Five or more stainless-steel circular blades are set into a plastic housing with an integrated handle for rolling back and forth across parsley, onion, garlic, etc., for fine mincing.

Garlic Press. Pump-type action forces a clove of garlic in a finely minced form out through the perforated face of the tool. Most garlic presses are of cast aluminum, but some are made in stainless steel or strong nylon plastic. To eliminate cleaning the holes it is best not to peel the garlic clove. Newer models have a self-cleaning arrangement built in.

Folding Vegetable Steamer. The folding steamer has perforated, overlapping petals that can be opened and expanded to fit into pots up to approximately 9½ inches wide. Short legs keep the base above water, and a separate, central post forms a handle for removing steamer and contents from pot. The best folding steamers are made of stainless steel.

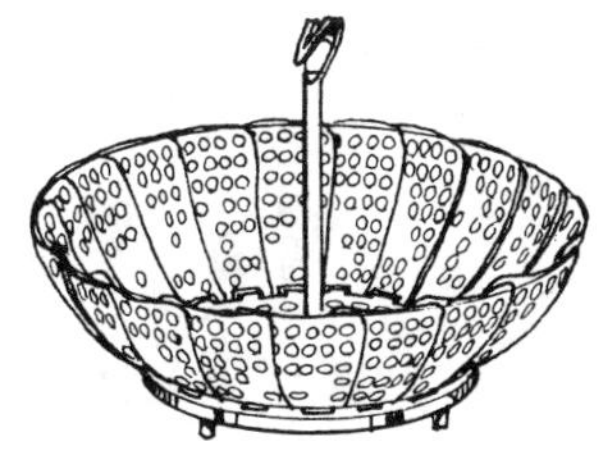

Salad Spinner. Freshly washed salad greens or herbs go in the inner, perforated drum, which is set inside the outer container. By turning the handle set into the lid or by pulling a cord, the drum rotates at high speed. The contents are spun dry by centrifugal force and the water is thrown off into the outer container. The spinner is handy, too, for drying thinly sliced and well-rinsed potatoes when preparing gratins of potato or a fried potato cake. All models on the market are made in plastic.

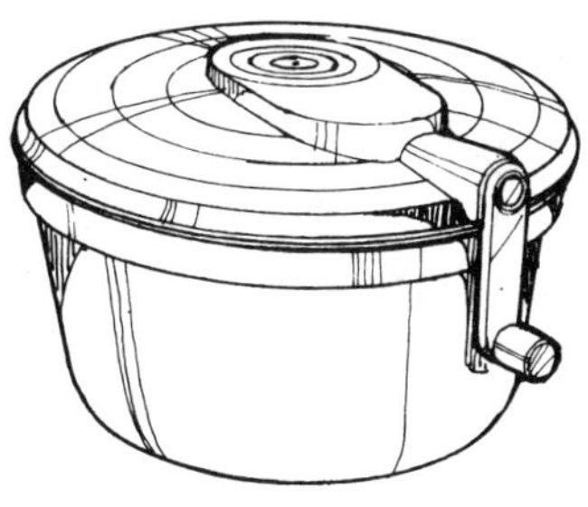

Lemon Zester. The cutting edges of the five small holes at the end of this stainless-steel tool removes tiny strips of only the colored outer layer of lemons or oranges. You get more satisfactory results than if you grate the peel off, as none of the bitter taste of the pith is transferred to the food. The cutting action of the zester releases the citrus oil, so it is a good idea to work over the dish to be flavored. Blade is of stainless steel with plastic or wood handles.

Lemon Stripper. The stripper produces thin strips or spirals of lemon or orange peel that are very useful in cooking as well as in beverages. Use it also for notching lemons, cucumbers and other vegetables when slicing for garnishes—the cut slices will have a scalloped edge. Blades are of stainless steel with plastic or wood handles.

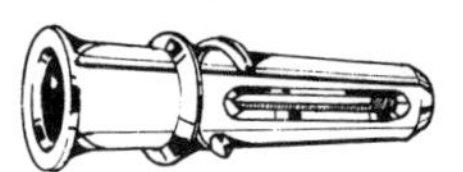

Lemon Spout. Screw this spout into the stem end of a lemon and then squeeze the fruit to pour off seed-free juice. Made of either plastic or cast-aluminum alloy, this spout is practical when you need small amounts of juice. Store lemon, with spout in place, in refrigerator between uses.

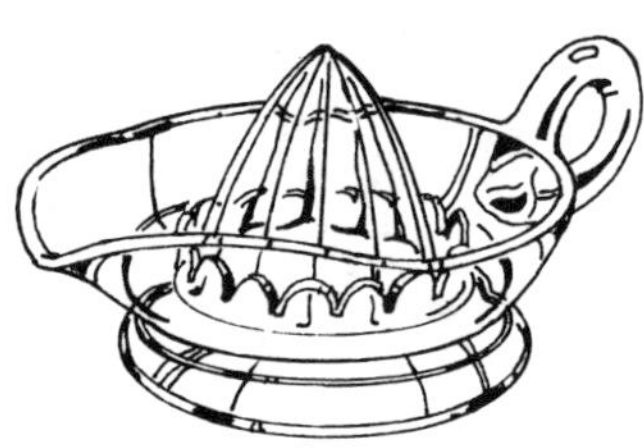

Lemon Juicer. Halved lemons or oranges are rotated on the cone of this type of citrus juicer. Convenient when the juice of only one or two lemons is needed. Usually made of glass or ceramic, though there are some available in plastic or aluminum.

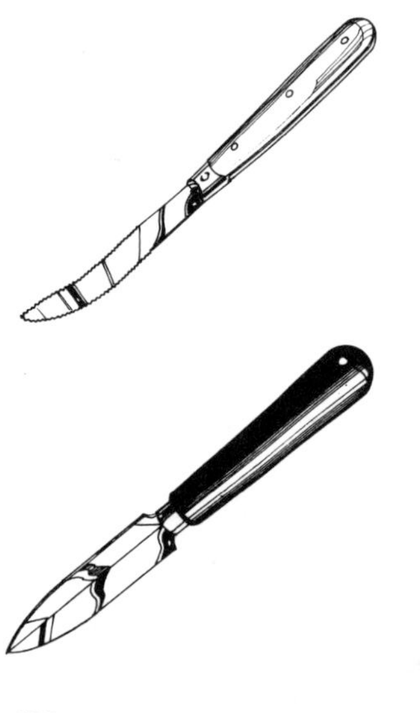

Grapefruit Knife. The curved and flexible blade of a good grapefruit knife should be of stainless steel, which is impervious to the fruit's acidity. The best ones have thin blades with sharp, tiny teeth or serrations on both edges for right- or left-hand use. Insert knife between the flesh and skin of a halved grapefruit to free it from the shell. The individual fruit segments can then be freed from their side membranes with a downward cut of a paring knife.

V-Shaped Melon Cutter. The V-shaped blade of this tool is inserted with each cut touching the next, around the "equator" of a ripe melon. When separated, the two halves will have an attractive zigzag edging. Choose one with a stainless steel blade and plastic or wood handle.

Melon Ballers. These small, bowl-shaped cutting tools come in round or oval shapes and can be used for melons as well as papayas, apples, pears, carrots, potatoes, zucchini, turnips, cucumbers and beets. The edges of the bowl should be sharp. The round ballers come in several sizes, from pea size to 1 inch. Get rigidly constructed ones of stainless steel, with wood or plastic handles.

Meat Pounder. Also known as a meat bat, this tool is used to flatten a slice of meat to a uniform thinness, and the heavier it is, the better. The pounder breaks down the meat fibers, tenderizing the meat and permitting even cooking. Use a heavier blow on veal, a lighter pressure on breast of chicken. Place the meat between two sheets of plastic wrap so that it doesn't tear easily or stick to the pounder and press outward as well as downward to spread the meat out evenly. Pounders come in many shapes and sizes: mallet shaped in wood or metal with smooth and ridged ends; round, flat, heavy disc type with vertical handle in stainless steel or brass; and round or square disc type with horizontal handle.

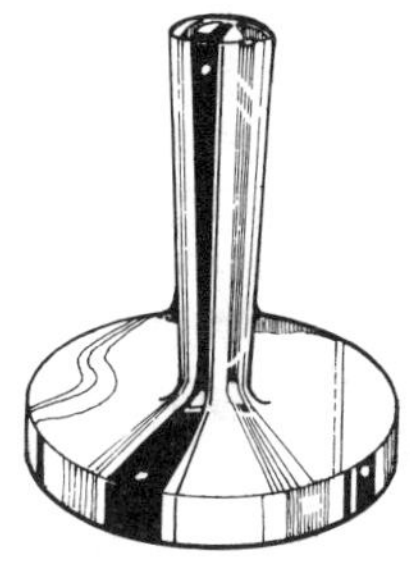

Poultry Lacers. These tiny stainless-steel skewers are pinned through the skin of a fowl to close the cavity. The twine is laced back and forth between the skewers and then pulled tight. The ends have loops so that they can be pulled out of the hot roasted bird with the tines of a fork. Poultry lacers can also be used to hold stuffed meats, and they make good cake testers.

Butcher's Twine. Butcher's twine is used for trussing poultry, tying rolled roasts and the like. Buy strong linen string which doesn't char in a hot oven.

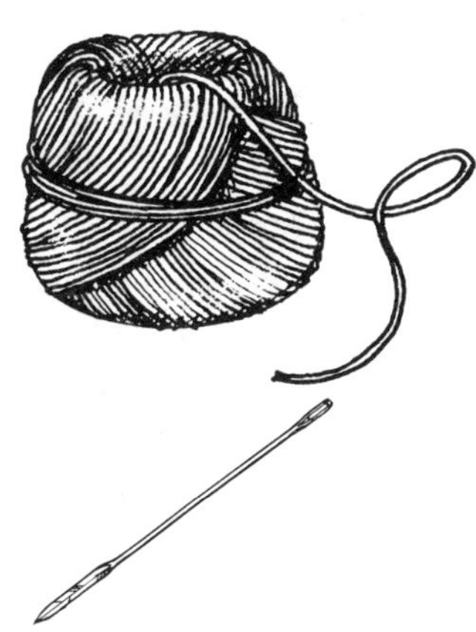

Trussing Needles. These long, stainless-steel needles come in various lengths. They are threaded with butcher's twine for trussing through poultry and boneless meat so that it stays compact during cooking, and therefore cooks evenly. Trussing is more efficient than simply tying string around the outside of roasts. Trussing needles are 4 to 10 inches in length.

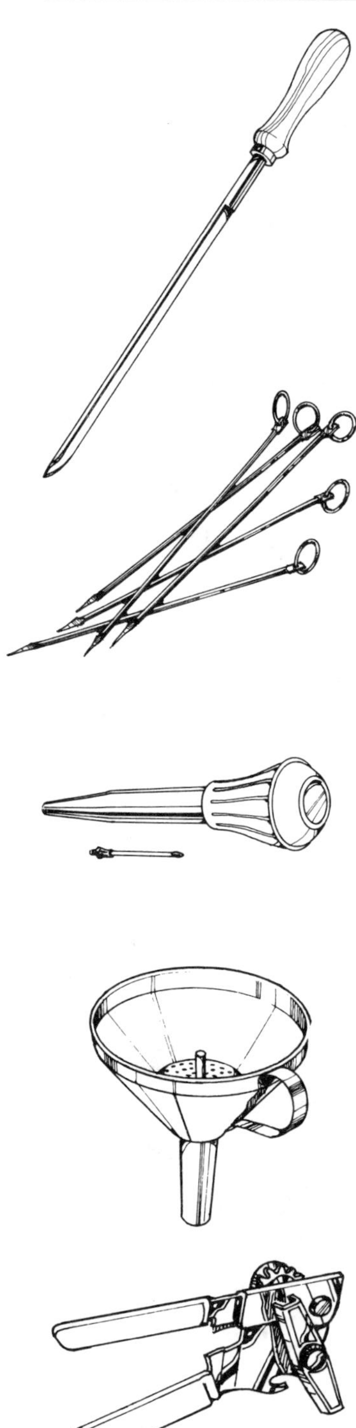

Larding Needle. Also known as a *boeuf à la mode* needle, this consists of a 10-inch stainless-steel trough attached to a wooden handle. A strip of seasoned pork fat is laid in the trough and, going with the grain, the needle is pushed and turned through the length of meat. When the needle is withdrawn, the fat is left in the meat. If you do this at 1½- to 2-inch intervals, lean meat will be basted and tenderized internally as it cooks.

Kebab Skewers. The most desirable skewers are stainless steel, moderately thick and square-sided or flat so that the meat, poultry or vegetables being grilled stick to the skewers as they are turned. Ring-shaped ends are best because they can be grasped securely while removing the food. Use a knife blade as a stop guard, put a fork through the ring, or hold with a napkin, and pull.

Bulb Basters. Far easier to use for basting a roast than a spoon, a good bulb baster has a heavy rubber bulb; those of plastic tend to split. Basters with stainless-steel shafts are easy to keep clean but you can't see how much liquid is being taken up. Nylon shafts are transparent, but they may melt if the tip is brought into contact with a hot surface. They also can harbor flavors. Some stainless-steel bulb basters have injecting needles that can be screwed into the tip for internal basting of meats.

Funnels. Plain funnels of stainless steel or plastic in various sizes are used for transferring liquids into narrow-mouthed containers. Funnels with a perforated removable screen inside perform double duty: they clear liquid of small particles and are invaluable when straining cooking oil for use another time.

Can Opener. Essential in every kitchen, even for cooks who make everything "from scratch," the best hand-operated can opener is of heavy stainless steel, with twin handles. It clamps onto a can and cuts around the top perimeter effortlessly with the turn of a wing screw.

Shrimp Deveiner. The curved, serrated tip of this tool follows the arc of a shrimp's shell. As you push from the head toward the tail, the ridged edge removes the intestinal vein while the upper edge cuts the shell. Deveiners are made of stainless steel with plastic handles.

Fish Scaler. This stainless-steel double-bladed knife has a deeply serrated, curved blade that swiftly removes fish scales and a pointed blade sharpened on both sides for gutting.

Oyster Knife. This short-bladed knife is inserted and then twisted to open well-armored oysters. There are various oyster knives on the market; most of them have short, thick, stainless-steel blades with wood or plastic handles and with or without guards. One or two have a notch in the blade as a guide for breaking off a bit of shell to get started.

Clam Openers. These have serrated ridges inside the curved "bowl" to hold the clam steady, and the straight blade slices through the clam, forcing it open.

Potato-Nest Basket. This handy gadget consists of two long-handled tinned-steel wire baskets. Line the larger one with shredded raw potato, then place the smaller basket inside. Submerge in hot fat for a minute or two and the result is a crunchy, golden container for vegetables. Potato nests can be made in advance and reheated. They come in several sizes, but the most useful basket is approximately 4 inches in diameter.

Tortilla-Basket Fryer. Like the potato-nest basket, this chromed steel tool consists of two nested, long-handled wire baskets. A tortilla is placed in the larger one, the smaller basket is fitted inside, and the tortilla is deep-fried. In a few seconds, a crisp cup is formed for holding salad, chili, refried beans, braised meat or guacamole.

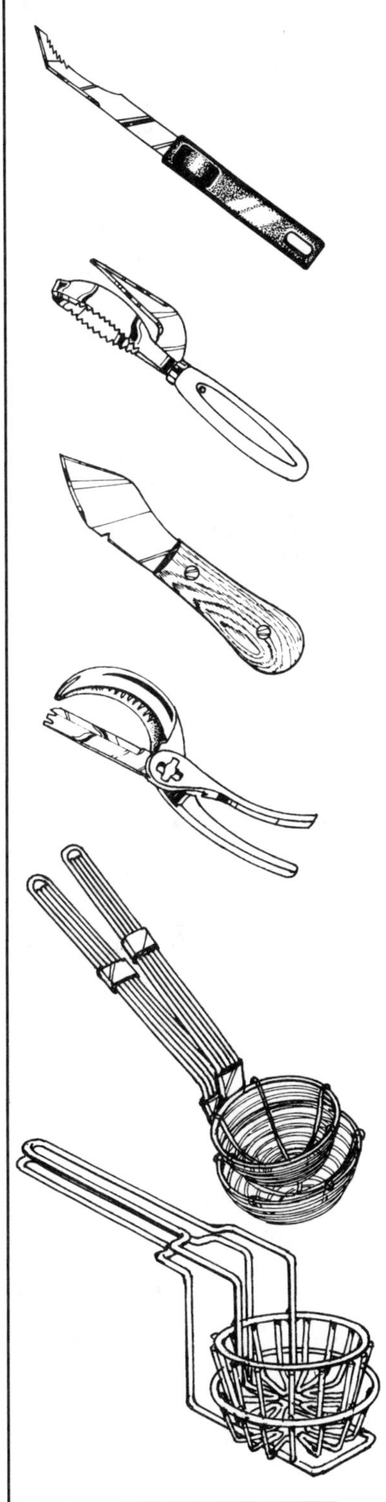

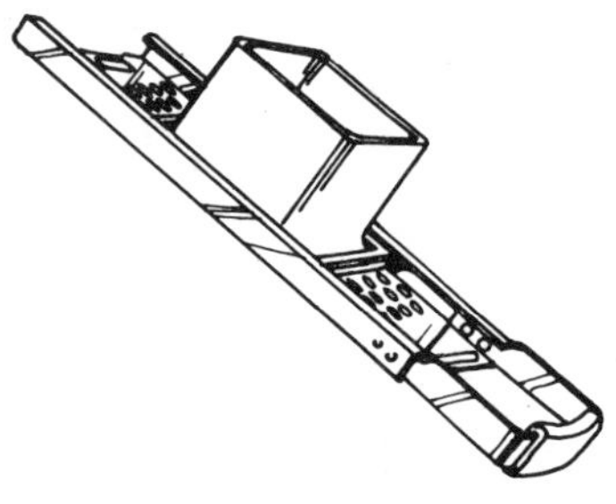

Spätzle Maker. A good alternative to pasta, spätzle are tiny, quickly prepared dumplings of East European origin. The perforated rectangle of this spätzle maker looks much like a flat shredder. It is rested over a pot of boiling water and a sliding box filled with batter is pushed back and forth along runners at the sides of the grater. The batter is forced through the holes to form teardrop-shaped dumplings, which cook in seconds. Most spätzle makers are made of stainless steel and rigid plastic.

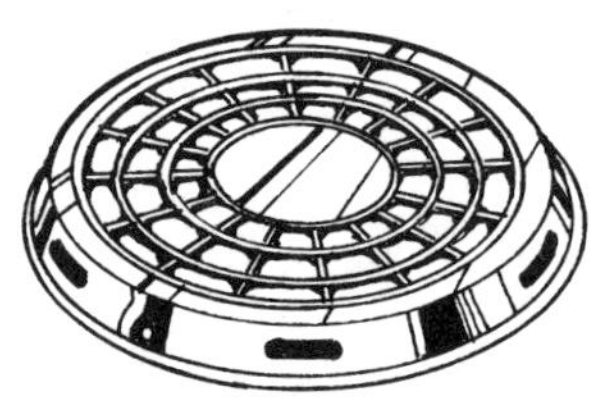

Heat Diffusers. Burners on electric stoves cannot be adjusted to achieve slow, even cooking; low gas flames tend to blow out. These diffusers are effective in separating a pot of food from the source of heat to achieve a very slow simmer. A diffuser or "Flame-Tamer" has a hollow disc shape with about 1 inch of airspace. It is made of chromed steel, and diffuses the heat over an 8-inch spread. The solid-iron diffuser is unobtrusive on a gas stove, sits in place on a burner and spreads the heat from a small flame out over the 7-inch plate. The adjustable diffuser, of enameled steel with a wood handle, can be raised or lowered so that the bottom of a pot is 2 or 3 inches above the top of the flame.

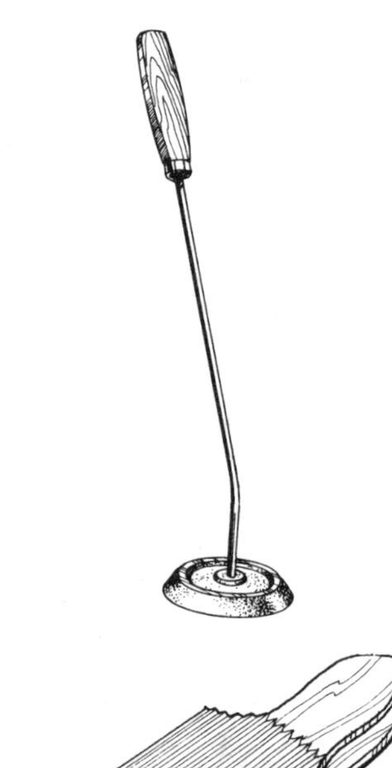

Salamander. Professional ranges often have grill-type ovens called salamanders for browning the tops of dishes. This tool has the same name and performs the same function. The heavy iron head is heated to red hot on a stovetop burner, then passed closely over the dish to be browned—for example, cheese and breadcrumb-topped tomatoes, or custard covered with a layer of brown sugar. The heat will brown the crumbs or caramelize the sugar in seconds and is very easy to control. The red-hot head is at a safe distance from the wooden handle and the cook's hand.

Wooden Butter Paddles. To achieve round, decorative butter balls, soak the paddles in ice water. Place a small lump of cold butter between the ridged surfaces of the two paddles. Rotate lightly, holding paddles so that the ridges are at right angles to each other. The butter will form itself into a ball with a crisscross pattern. The balls should be ½ to ¾ of an inch in diameter. Use unsalted butter and store in ice water.

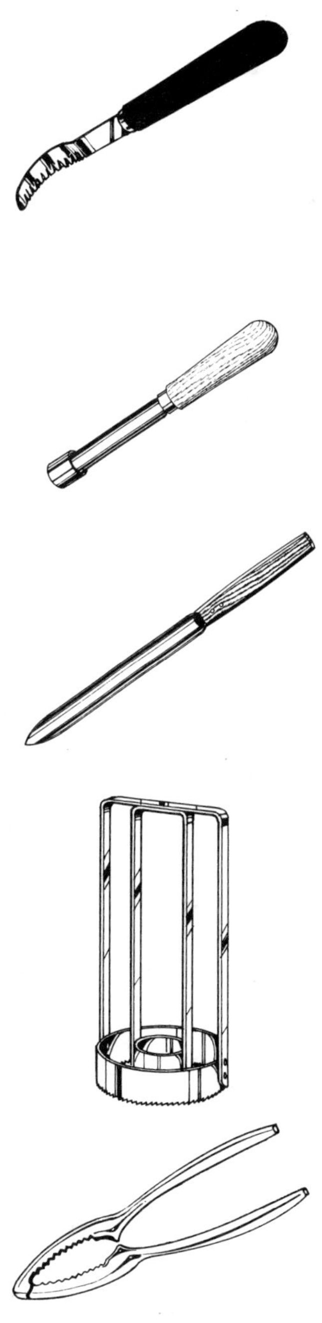

Butter Curler. The curved and serrated stainless-steel blade produces shell-like curls of butter. Dip the blade in warm water and pull firmly along the top of a block of cold but not hard butter and the shell will form itself. Serve over shaved ice. Use unsalted butter.

Apple Corer. The most efficient apple corer is designed to cut apples all the way through. The trough of the tool retains the core, which you can pull back through the apple to de-core it. Corer should be wide enough to remove all the seeds and sharp enough to cut through easily. The best are of heavy stainless steel with a wood handle. Some types have a peeler built in, but they are usually too short and not very sharp.

Zucchini Corer. The trough-shaped, pointed blade is inserted into the zucchini and rotated to remove the seeds and central core, leaving a hollow tube for stuffing. (Cut zucchini in even lengths to fit corer.) Made of heavy stainless steel with a wood or plastic handle.

Pineapple Corer. This stainless-steel tool is designed to cut the core and peel from a pineapple in one action. Two serrated circular cutters are held together, doughnut-cutter fashion, by 6-inch-high arched handles. The top and bottom of the pineapple is sliced off, and the tool inserted from the top down to the base of the fruit, using a circular motion. This tool is not adjustable, so the pineapple has to be about a half-inch larger than the diameter of the outer cutting blade.

Nutcracker. The common variety is made of stainless steel or nickel steel with a ridged interior surface for holding nuts steady. A simple press action cracks the shells of most nuts. It can also be used effectively in cracking crab or lobster claws. There are also various nutcrackers available for specific nuts that release whole nuts or whole halves intact.

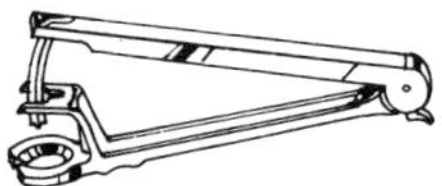

Olive/Cherry Pitter. A simple combination tool, shaped like spring-release pliers, it efficiently punches out the pits from cherries or olives. The fruit is placed in the small ring and as the jaws are closed, the punch goes through it, and the pit drops free. Made of a cast-aluminum alloy.

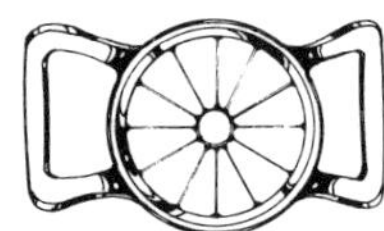

Divisorex. This wheel-shaped cutter with cast-aluminum frame has stainless-steel blades that radiate, spoke fashion, from the hub. When pressed on top of apples or pears it cuts the fruit into twelve even segments and cuts out the core at the same time. The 4-inch diameter is large enough to cut most moderately sized apples or pears.

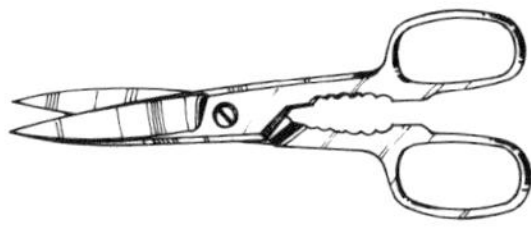

Kitchen Shears. Good kitchen/household shears should have a good "heft" to them, feel comfortable in the hand, and have really sharp stainless-steel blades so they will not rust. They are useful for anything from cutting butcher's twine to snipping chives or bacon.

Poultry Shears. Poultry shears with slip-proof handles, a stout spring mechanism and sharp, semi-curved blades make short work of cutting a duck into four portions—a bird that is notoriously difficult to carve. These shears are also invaluable for snipping the backbone out of chickens destined to be grilled flat, and for cutting up poultry carcasses for stock. Most poultry shears have been made of chromed steel; however, more are appearing in stainless steel. It is important that one of the blades has a notch for cutting bones and be serrated on the edge to grip flesh while cutting.

Rotary Egg Beater. The most efficient beater has round wire loops instead of flat blades, to duplicate the aerating abilities of a whisk. A gear-driven egg beater is fast and easy to use and invaluable for whipping cream or beating small amounts of eggs, pancake or crêpe batter. Available in combinations of stainless steel, cast aluminum, chromed steel and plastic, the most durable and smooth-running are of stainless steel with nylon gears and bushings.

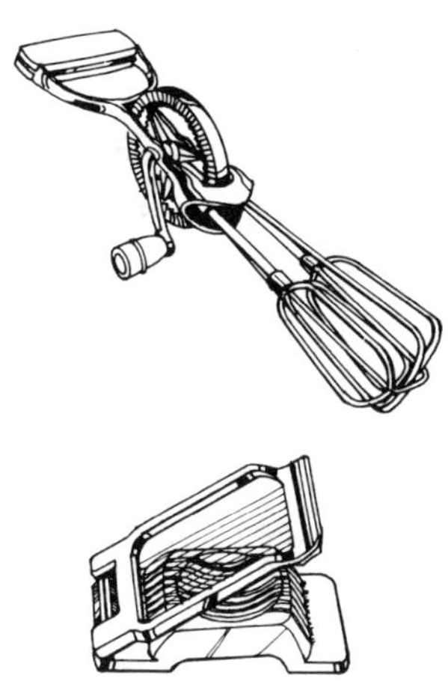

Egg Slicer. The hinged upper portion of a typical egg slicer is tautly strung with stainless-steel wires. The base has an oval depression with slats that mesh with the wires. A hard-cooked egg is placed in the base, the upper portion is brought down and the egg is cut into neat, even slices. Frame can be of a cast-aluminum alloy or stainless steel.

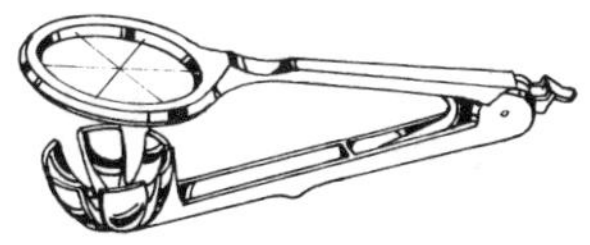

Egg Wedger. An egg wedger is designed on the same principle as an egg slicer, but this time the egg is set on its end and sliced into even wedges. It has a cast-aluminum alloy frame with stainless-steel wires.

Egg Separator. Generally of glazed ceramic or aluminum, this device is made in the form of a small saucer with a slot running midway around the perimeter. Break an egg into it, and the white slides through the slot while the yolk remains in the center compartment.

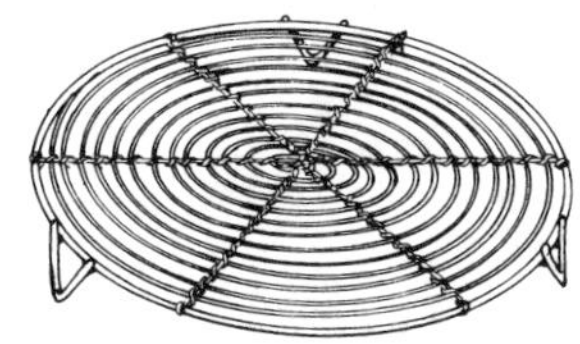

Baker's Cooling Racks. Breads, cookies and most cakes should be cooled on wire racks when they come out of the oven. Air circulation underneath is very important so that baked goods don't get soggy on the bottom. A good rack should be of heavy-quality tinned wire or stainless steel, with feet to raise it up off the counter. The wires should have a reasonably smooth surface and be closely set for optimum support and so that small cookies don't slip through. Racks should be of sufficiently strong wire to avoid sag (it is important that surface is level; large racks should have additional feet in center). It is as well to have two large rectangular racks for cooling batches of cookies, and three round ones for layer cakes.

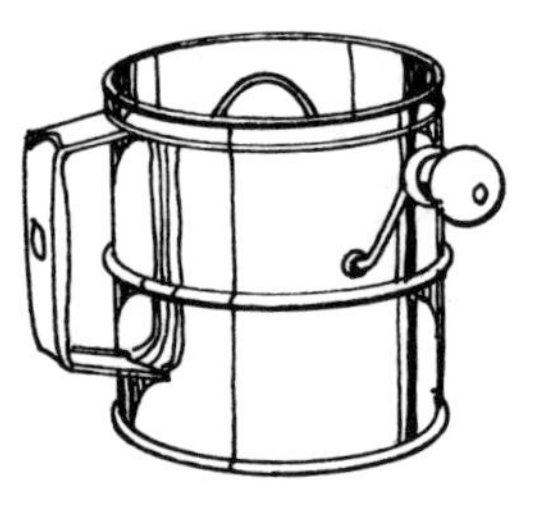

Flour Sifter. To achieve feather-light cakes, even pre-sifted flour should be sifted again. A stainless-steel sifter with rotary crank mechanism, moderately fine mesh and at least a two-cup capacity is recommended, though there are many other types of sifters available: triple action, battery operated, etc.

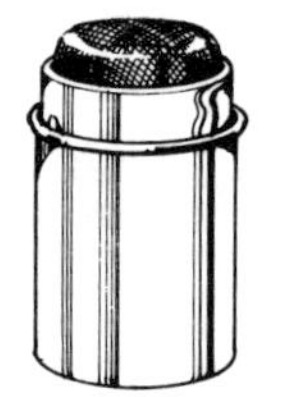

Confectioners' Sugar Dredger. A drum-shaped container with a screw-on lid of wire mesh set in a collar, this provides an efficient method of sifting confectioners' sugar over cakes and cookies. It is far easier to control than a mesh strainer. A small stainless-steel dredger is best for home use.

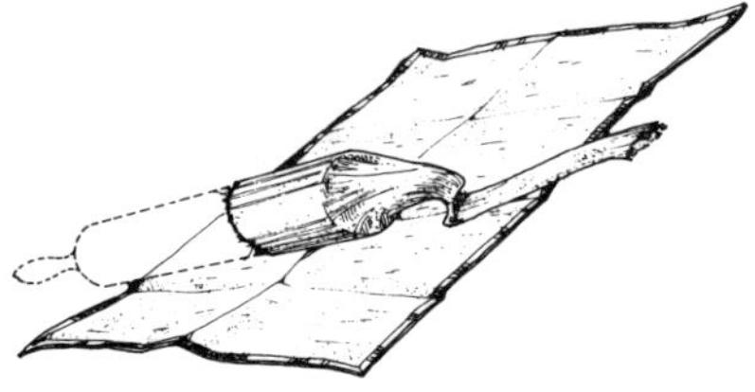

Pastry Cloth. A canvas pastry cloth provides a good surface for rolling out dough. Rub flour down into the weave as well as on the surface. The cloth should be shaken out and aired before storing, but if it needs a thorough cleaning, lay it flat, scrub with a brush and soapy water, and rinse very well before hanging to dry.

Pastry Bags. These cone-shaped bags, when fitted with a metal tip, are for decorating cakes and pastries and for forming cookies, choux paste shapes, quenelles, borders of mashed potatoes and the like. They are available in various sizes in nylon or plastic-coated cotton. After use they should be thoroughly rinsed and air-dried.

Pastry and Decorating Tips or Tubes. Made of tinned or chromed steel, these cone-shaped nozzles in several sizes have a variety of openings: plain round, star-shaped, and slit in various ways for piping icing decorations and forming cookies. The small decorating tips are attached to the pastry bag by means of a plastic screw collar and coupling. They can be changed when decorating cakes, say from a rose tip to a writing tip. The larger tips, for pastry, whipped cream or mashed potatoes, are placed inside the bag without a coupling.

Pastry Brushes for Glazing. Pastry brushes designed for glazing breads and pastries should be of sterilized natural bristles, fine nylon bristles or goose feathers. Natural and nylon bristle brushes should be thin or round, like artists' brushes but with flat ends. The collar that is set around the bristles and attaches them to the wooden handle should be of stainless steel and tightly fixed so that bristles don't work loose. Goose-feather brushes are made up of six or eight sterilized goose feathers, with the quills braided together to form a handle. These are best for egg glazes, as they lay a very thin, even coating. All pastry brushes should be washed with soapy water and well rinsed immediately after use so that fruit glazes, egg washes and sweet milk glazes don't coagulate. Air dry thoroughly before storing. They should not be interchanged with brushes used for basting meats and poultry.

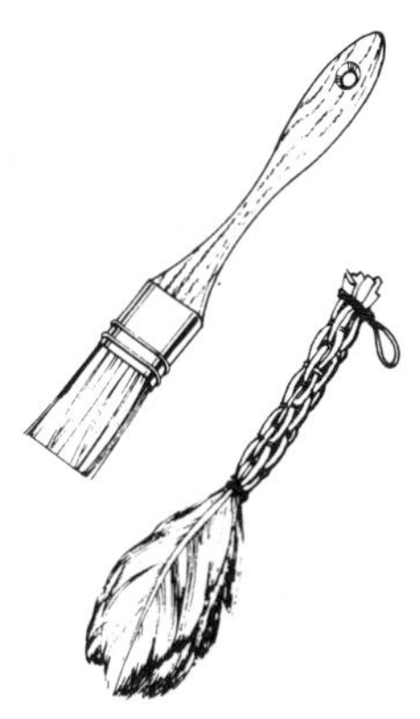

Basting Brushes. Basting meat and poultry as it roasts or is barbecued keeps it from drying out and adds an appetizing glaze. The best basting brushes are made of sterilized natural bristles or fine nylon bristles, fixed with a stainless-steel or nylon collar to a wooden handle. Barbecue basting brushes should be moderately thick and have long handles, for obvious reasons. The brushes will absorb fats and cooking flavors as they are used, so it is essential to wash them in hot soapy water and rinse well before hanging to dry.

Rolling Pins. Rolling pins have been around for hundreds of years. They are available in glass, porcelain, ceramic, marble, brass, copper, plastic and, of course, wood. The hardwood rolling pin is the one that has endured the test of time and the one widely used throughout the world. The heavier the rolling pin is, the better it will perform. The most efficient is a baker's rolling pin, made of dense hardwood with a steel rod running through it, and mounted on heavy-duty ball bearings, with sturdy handles. It is 15 inches long, 3½ inches in diameter. Hardwood rolling pins should never be submerged in water (much less put in the dishwasher!) but wiping with a damp cloth and rubbing dry with a kitchen towel is absolutely necessary.

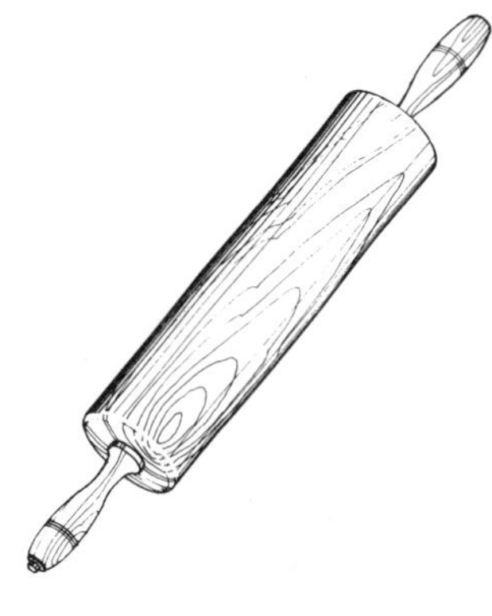

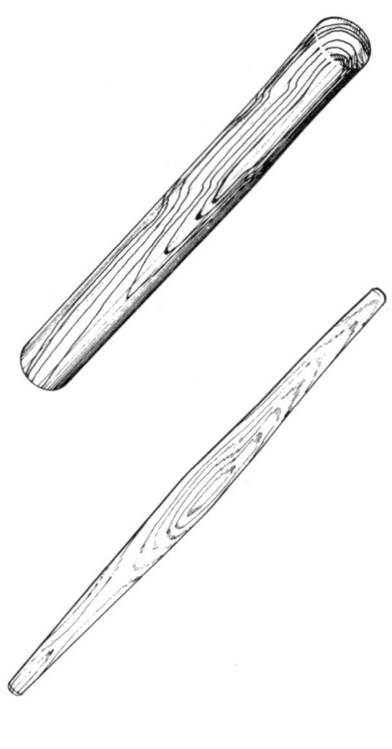

Straight Rolling Pin. This straight French rolling pin, preferred by many professional pastry chefs, is of dense boxwood or mahogany and has no handles. You roll it under your palms, which gives you an excellent "feel" of the dough. These pins are usually 2 inches in diameter and 19 inches long.

Tapered Rolling Pin. Light in weight and tapered from the center to both ends, this rolling pin can be rotated while rolling so that it forms a neat circle of dough. The thickened section in the middle of the pin makes this possible. Many nonprofessional cooks find it handy for getting the center portion of a sheet of pastry dough flat before using a heavy straight pin. Of French origin, they usually are 1½ inches diameter by 18 inches long, and made of beechwood.

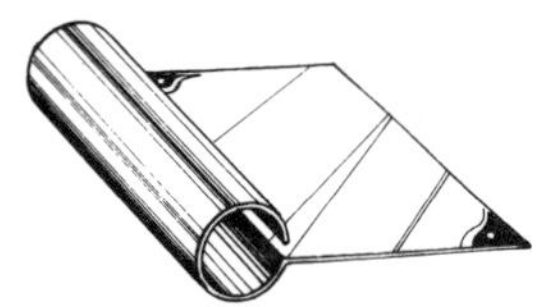

Pastry/Dough Scraper. This handy tool fashioned from a rectangle of stainless steel, which is either rolled over on one edge to form a handle or riveted to a wood handle, is indispensable for lifting and turning sticky bread doughs when they are still too soft to knead by hand. It is also essential for keeping wooden boards scraped clean. Dough scrapers made of hard plastic are also good for lifting and turning dough.

Pastry Crimper. A pastry crimper is shaped like a broad-ended tweezer. With a little practice, it can be used to make professional-looking crimped borders on open-faced tarts. It both crimps and seals the edges of double-crust pies. Made of hardened chromed steel.

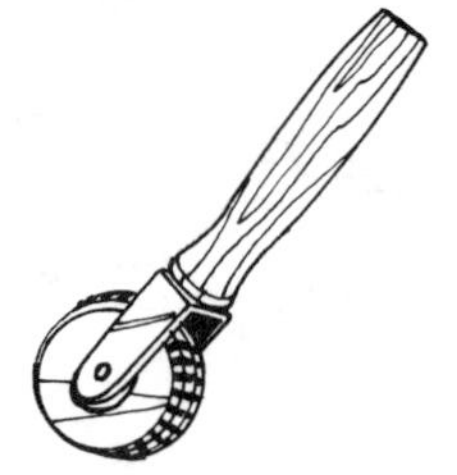

Pastry Crimper and Sealer. This tool has two separate crimping discs, axle-mounted on a wooden handle. It is run round the edges of small pies and turnovers to crimp and seal them; also to crimp, seal and separate sheets of ravioli, which are subsequently cut apart with a knife. Usually made of aluminum.

Pastry and Pasta Wheels. These are sharp cutting wheels mounted on an axle and attached to a wooden handle. They come in various sizes; the small, plain ones are used for marking and cutting pastry, the larger ones for cutting pizza. Fluted pastry wheels, also known as jaggers, leave an edge on pastry similar to that made by pinking shears on cloth. They are sometimes used to cut the strips of pastry for decorative latticework on open-faced pies. They are also used for cutting ravioli apart, leaving the pasta packages with a zigzag edge. Usually made of chromed steel, and sometimes of brass, with wood handles.

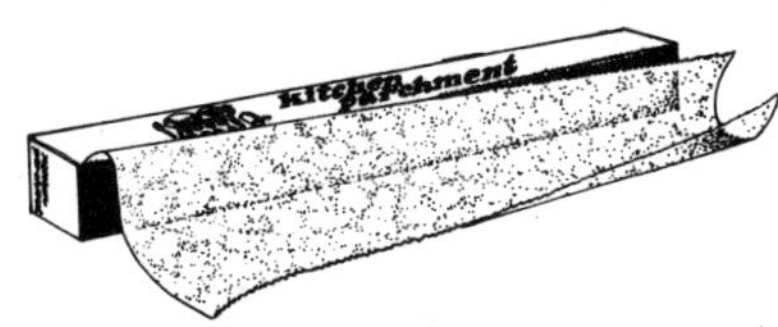

Baking Parchment. Sold in rolls like plastic wrap or in folded sheets, this paper is sometimes available in pre-cut circles for lining cake pans. Baking parchment is specially treated for use in the oven, and some is being treated with silicone for non-stick baking. Cookies won't stick to it, so it is used to line baking sheets, which saves buttering, flouring and subsequent clean-up of pans. It can be cut into shapes suitable for lining all types of cake pans; cakes will then unmold without trouble. It is also designed for baking tender foods such as fish and other seafood in parchment packages *(en papillote),* thus concentrating all the aromas and flavors.

Cookie Cutters. Cookie cutters come in a wonderful variety of shapes and sizes: plain or scalloped rounds and ovals, animals and gingerbread men, hearts and flowers. To be efficient, they must be strong enough to retain their shape, but thin and sharp enough at the cutting edge to slice through cookie dough cleanly. Some have handles, some have rolled or beaded edges. Cutters are available singly or in sets, and are made of stainless steel or tin-plated steel.

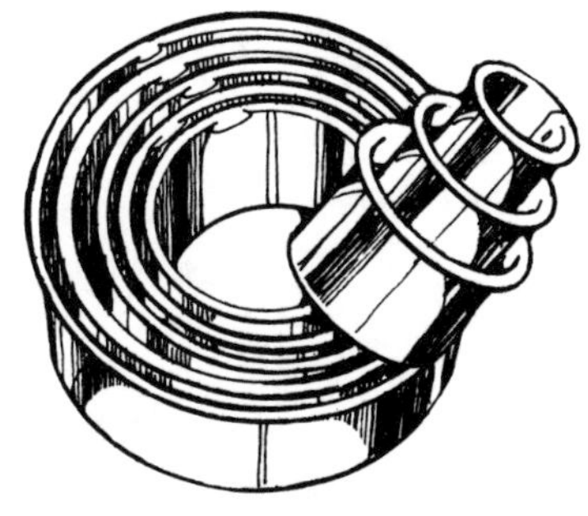

Pastry Cutters. Professional pastry-cutter sets are precisely made, by hand, of heavy tinned steel. They come boxed in a graded range of about 10 sizes, and can be either fluted or

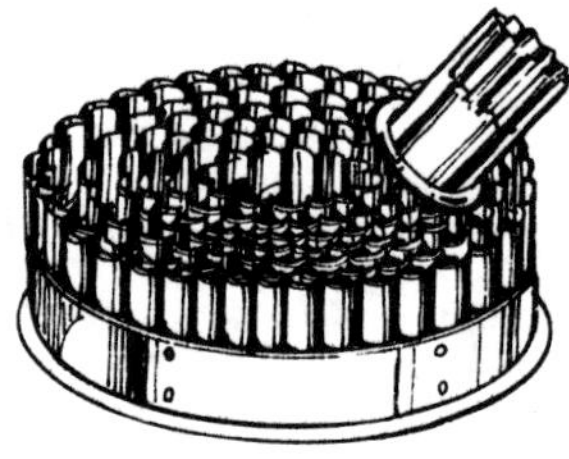

plain. Sets are round, square, oval or boat-shaped, and the cutters are used for everything from small pastry decorations to *vol-au-vent* cases and cookies of every dimension.

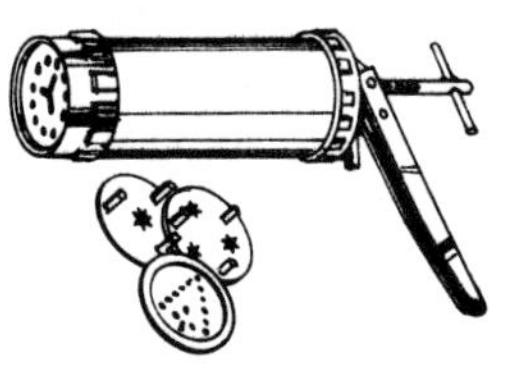

Cookie Gun. Professional-looking, evenly sized butter cookies can be obtained by ejecting a fairly soft dough through a cookie gun fitted with a decorative nozzle or plate. The one shown here works on a ratchet mechanism to ensure even size, and comes with about 20 different plates for making cookies of different shapes. There are also cookie guns with a screw mechanism. Most are made of hardened anodized aluminum.

Rolling Cookie Cutter. Designed as an axle-mounted drum on a wooden handle, this type of cutter is rolled across the dough heavily enough to cut through it. The raised design on the drum cuts a pattern like a simple jigsaw puzzle. All the pieces form differently shaped cookies without any wasted dough. Usually made of cast aluminum.

Cookie Stamps. Usually round or square, cookie stamps are made of wood, glass or ceramic. Decorative designs are cut into them in reverse, so that when the stamp is pressed onto a small ball of dough, it will both flatten and imprint a relief design. They are dipped in flour when used, to prevent the cookie dough from sticking to them.

PART II

THE RECIPES

INTRODUCTION

This section of the book had its beginnings in our catalog, where I included recipes for a specific piece of equipment. Many of those recipes are included here for people who didn't see them or who may have lost them or who wish to have them in a more convenient form.

When I started to review and improve the catalog recipes in preparation for this book, I realized that the recipes had already been tested by tens of thousands of cooks—and that if there was ever anything not quite right, we certainly would have heard about it and fixed it up. Sometimes, too, when we print a recipe we get a letter saying, "I tried your muffins and I thought you'd like to know that I think mine are better. Enclosed is the recipe—try it." Often they are right.

I haven't attempted a comprehensive cookbook that rivals Fanny Farmer's, but I have included, along with the recipes from the catalog, recipes from our readers and from friends, as well as many new ones from my own kitchen. I like good, classic, rather simple food and that bias, I suspect, is strongly reflected in this book. For the most part, the recipes are simple and rely on fresh ingredients—a dish of blue mussels steamed with saffron and orange topped with a beurre blanc sauce and toasted pine nuts is all very well, but I'm not going to make it and you won't catch me opening a can of truffles at 8:15 on a Tuesday night. On the other hand, I've never settled for tuna casserole and I don't subscribe to meals-in-a-minute. Some of the recipes—my mother's caramel crunch cake, for example—do take quite a bit of doing, but they're worth the trouble since most of us don't eat desserts every day and we want them to be special when we do.

I do have some favorite ingredients that might be considered a little out of the ordinary, but if I use such things it's because they're good, not because they're fashionable!

I always use unsalted butter, for example, because it has a good fresh taste and I like to control the amount of salt that goes into my food. (Salt is a preservative after all, and salted butter can sit around in storage for quite a long time.) I use standard grade AA large eggs throughout this book, regular milk and heavy cream. I don't insist on free-range chickens delivered to my door. The fresh kind you buy in a good poultry market are fine by me, but I am finicky about fish being very fresh.

The list below contains a few special items that you'll find in any specialty food shop in major U.S. cities. And of course you can always shop by mail.

Before You Start Cooking . . .

Aceto Balsamico. Also called balsamic vinegar, this is a very well-aged wine vinegar made only in the Italian city of Modena. Decanted into smaller and smaller kegs of different kinds of wood over a long period of time, sometimes twenty-five years or more, the resulting condiment is very richly flavored and not at all sharp. You can add a few drops to bubbling cream and get a better sauce than many chefs achieve after working at it for hours, and it does great things for sautéed vegetables, salads, meat and poultry.

Arborio Rice. This is a very short-grain rice grown in Northern Italy. It's the only kind to use when making Italian risotto, as the grains stay separate, firm and yet creamy when cooked. Regular raw rice, whether long or pearl grain, gets mushy when used in this dish. Arborio rice, or a similar type grown in Spain, is really best for paella too, though you can use regular short-grain rice grown in this country if you're careful not to overcook it.

Bay Leaves. I prefer leaves imported from France or Italy. They're milder than California bay, and very aromatic. Bay can be overpoweringly strong and acrid if overused.

Cooking Oils. My favorites are French, Italian and Spanish olive oils, preferably the mild, fruity ones from Provence, Tuscany and Cataluña. "Extra virgin, first pressing cold" means that an olive oil is low in acid; and it's also mild because the first pressing of the fruit does not involve heat or crushing the pits, which have a bitter flavor. Olive oils are produced in most of the Mediterranean countries, and in California.

Hazelnut oil and walnut oil are simply oils pressed from hazelnuts or walnuts. They come from France as a rule, and should be refrigerated after opening. Both are used in salad dressings and in some baking. Sweet or toasted almond oil is pressed from almonds and is used chiefly for oiling dessert molds and in baking. Avocado oil, made from avocados, of course, is used both in cooking and as a salad dressing.

When I want a neutral oil for general cooking or for deep-fat frying, I usually prefer peanut oil, although many cooks favor corn oil, safflower oil or unspecified vegetable oil.

Chocolate and Cocoa. I find that it pays to use the best-quality chocolate, whether unsweetened, bittersweet or semisweet. Try to get one with a high cocoa and cocoa-butter content, because it melts smoothly and dries to a high sheen. It's the best kind to use when making truffles, dipped candies or cake glazes. Milk chocolate is fine for eating but less satisfactory when used in the kitchen, as it is too soft. White chocolate isn't really chocolate at all, although one or two brands have a little cocoa butter added for flavor, but it is excellent for dipping as it dries to a high gloss. It is also fine for use in white chocolate mousses and the like. When buying cocoa, look for the unsweetened Dutch process variety. Top-quality chocolate and cocoa is imported from Belgium, France and Switzerland, and some very good products are made in this country, too.

Couscous. This is a kind of semolina granule made from hard durum wheat. In North Africa it is used in place of rice, potatoes or pasta as the staple starch. The kind generally available here has been precooked, and can be prepared in 5 minutes. Look for the unflavored, medium-grain type, which is usually packed in small boxes and imported from France.

Flours. I use all-purpose flour for almost everything except some bread baking. Low-gluten cake flour does help to achieve lighter results in cake baking, and high-gluten unbleached white or whole-wheat flour definitely makes the best bread. Dedicated bread makers will usually seek out health-food stores that carry more unusual flours, such as oat, rye or millet, or even grind their own from whole grains. I do buy stoneground cornmeal when I can find it, as I think it has a better texture and flavor.

Hard durum-wheat pasta flour is available for making homemade pasta, but be sure that you buy the very finely ground variety, which looks like coarse flour. Granular semolina, which is sometimes packaged as pasta flour, is much too difficult to work with for a pasta dough. However, you can make it into a fairly fine flour in a food processor. Tomato flour and spinach flour, packaged for pasta makers, are meant to be added to regular flour and not used alone, as they are simply dehydrated powdered vegetables.

Herbs. I use fresh herbs whenever I can get them. If I can't, I use herbs that have been dried on the stalk or branch, and then crumble the leaves in the palm of one hand with my thumb to release the oils. Powdered herbs tend to lose their pungency if kept for long, so if you buy this type be sure to get them at a store with a rapid turnover and buy small tins.

Vanilla. I find that it makes sense to use the very best quality pure vanilla extract, which is made from well-aged and properly cured vanilla beans and mixed with alcohol. It should have a true vanilla flavor. When buying whole beans, usually sold in glass tubes, go for plump moist ones, not old, dried-up beans that look like shoelaces.

Vinegars. For dressing salads, I prefer a white wine vinegar made by natural fermentation and not over-processed. (Wine vinegar made from champagne grapes is one of the best!) Red wine vinegars can be very mellow and good, but usually are stronger in flavor. Many white wine vinegars contain herbs, such as tarragon or thyme, which is a good way to get extra flavor into salads or sauces. Wine vinegars will often throw a sediment, like some wines. This is normal in vinegars made by a natural process and not too finely filtered; it is not harmful, but it's best to filter it through a fine cloth into a clean bottle. Raspberry vinegar is simply white wine vinegar with an infusion of fresh raspberry essence. It can have a wonderful flavor and I find that I need far less salt when I use it in cooking. Avoid the cheap brands that are made with artificial raspberry flavoring. Predictably, they have an odd taste, like a raspberry soda.

Cider vinegar is made at least in part from apples, and the best brands have a nice crisp, clean taste. Pear vinegar is also available in some specialty food shops. It is quite expensive and usually tastes agreeably fruity.

The Orientals use rice vinegar, and the British favor distilled malt vinegar. Malt vinegar is just what's needed to sprinkle on fish and chips. Years ago, when I was hunting for antiques in the English countryside, I'd stop for fish and chips and eat them in the van. It always seemed to be freezing or raining, but the food was always hot, the newspaper wrapping added a certain something and the malt vinegar was delicious. You probably have to be young, cold and hungry to enjoy this meal to its fullest (or even at all), but it certainly tasted good at the time.

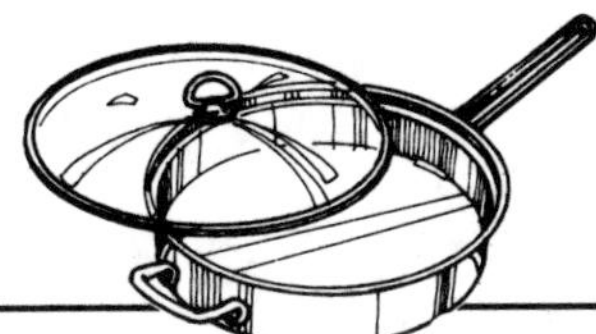

One final word about pots and pans to use in these recipes. You don't have to use a 9-inch sauté pan or a 2-quart rectangular baker just because it's illustrated. You can substitute another pan that holds more or less the same amount. (Using too large a pan usually means you'll either dry the food out or end up with far too much liquid.)

Bon appétit!

FIRST

COURSES

Braised Fennel

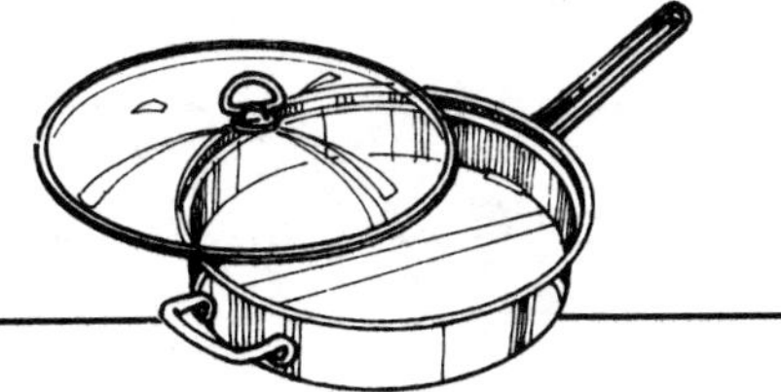
10-INCH SAUTÉ PAN

If you are not familiar with this rather strange-looking, bulbous white vegetable, I urge you to try it. It has a slight flavor of anise, but don't expect licorice candy, it's not like that! This is one of my favorite Italian dishes. It can be served as a first course or as a vegetable with a simple entree. Fennel is also delicious raw, thinly sliced and dressed with olive oil and lemon juice.

2 to 3 heads (2 pounds) fennel
3 tablespoons butter
½ cup water
Salt
Freshly ground pepper
¼ cup Parmesan cheese, freshly grated

Trim heads of fennel by cutting off tops close to the bulbous part and removing any discolored or tough-looking outer leaves. Cut lengthways into ¼-inch slices.

Melt butter in sauté pan, add fennel in 1 or 2 layers, then pour in the water. Partially cover pan and simmer over moderately low heat for 10 minutes. Uncover and cook for 10 to 15 minutes more, until tender. Check water level occasionally to make sure that pan does not boil dry, and add more water if necessary. However, fennel should have absorbed most of the liquid when done. Remove from heat and let cool for 10 minutes.

Preheat oven to 400°. Transfer fennel and any juice to a shallow ovenproof dish and season with salt and pepper. Sprinkle with the Parmesan cheese and bake for 20 minutes, until lightly browned on top.

Serves 4 to 6.

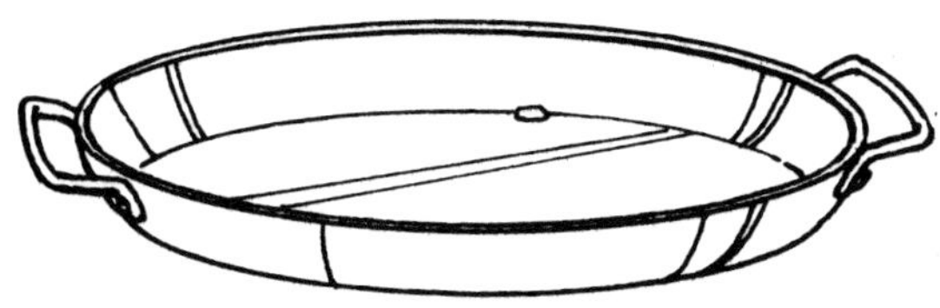
2-QUART SHALLOW OVENPROOF DISH

Button Mushrooms with Aceto Balsamico

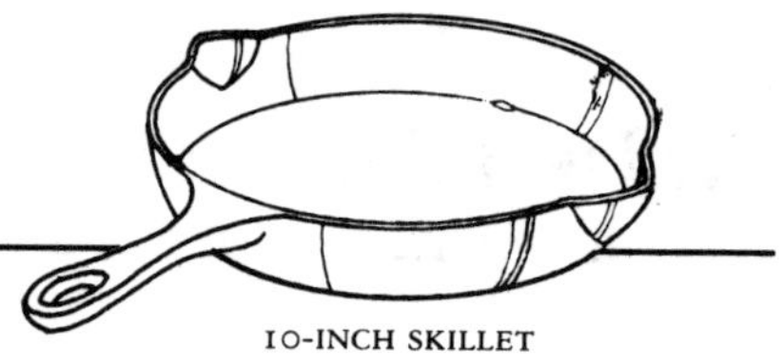

It is important to use very fresh white mushrooms that haven't opened up to show the brown gills under the cap. This is a great addition to a selection for antipasto.

1 pound, small firm white button mushrooms
⅓ cup good Italian olive oil, preferably Tuscan
3 cloves garlic, finely chopped
2 to 3 tablespoons Aceto Balsamico (see page 86)
3 tablespoons dry white wine
Salt
Pepper

Clean mushrooms with a soft brush or damp cloth and trim bottom of stems. Cut vertically into ¼-inch slices. Heat oil in skillet and cook garlic over moderate heat for 1 minute. Do not brown. Add mushrooms and sauté for 3 to 4 minutes, stirring and tossing. Add Aceto Balsamico and white wine and cook for 2 minutes. Season with a little salt and pepper. Serve hot or allow to cool and serve at room temperature.

Serves 4 as a hot first course; 6 to 8 as part of a mixed hors d'oeuvre.

Chinese Vegetable Pickles

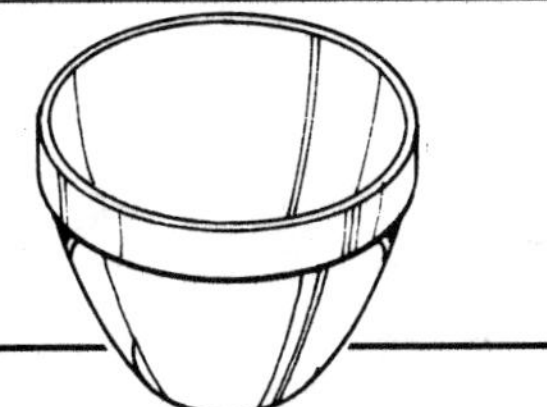
2-QUART GLAZED EARTHENWARE PUDDING BASIN

When I visited China last year for the first time, I was intrigued by the delicious fresh vegetable pickles that appeared before every meal, usually accompanied by fresh roasted peanuts. I discovered that Chinese cooks make them in a special pickle jar of glazed earthenware with a bowl-shaped lid that is reversed and used as a serving dish; but of course any 2-quart glass or glazed ceramic bowl will do. Any combination of fresh vegetables may be used.

1 cup white cider vinegar
1 cup sugar
1 cup water
2 medium carrots, peeled and sliced
½ red bell pepper, core and seeds removed, diced into 1½-inch pieces
1 cup cauliflower flowerets, sliced
1 cup seedless cucumber, sliced
2-inch piece of fresh ginger root, peeled and sliced thin

Combine the vinegar, sugar and water in a glazed earthenware or glass bowl. Stir until sugar is completely dissolved. Add the vegetables, including the ginger root, to liquid and cover tightly. Place in the refrigerator for 24 to 36 hours. Pickles may be kept refrigerated for about a week. Remove with a slotted spoon and serve with other hors d'oeuvres as a first course or as an accompaniment to cold meats or fish.

Makes about 3 cups.

SLOTTED SPOON

Leeks à la Grecque

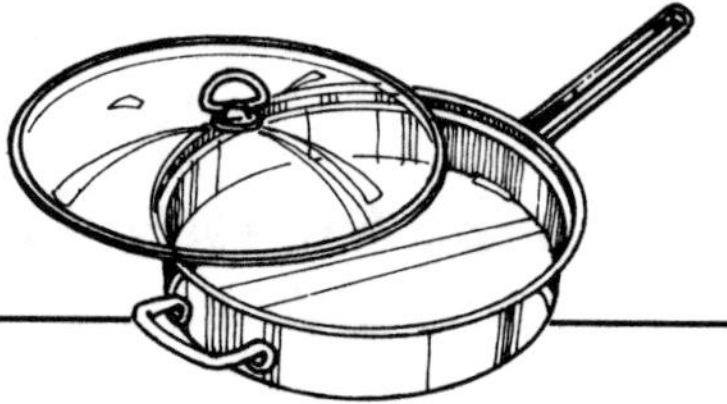

10-INCH SAUTÉ PAN

It's important to barely simmer the leeks—just a bubble or two should rise at a time. If they cook too fast, they'll fall apart and won't develop a good flavor.

4 to 6 slender young leeks
8 tiny white onions
4 French bay leaves (page 86)
1 teaspoon black peppercorns
3/4 cup chicken stock (page 107)
6 tablespoons white wine
3 tablespoons olive oil
1 tablespoon tomato paste
Paprika

Trim leeks, leaving some of the green, and wash very carefully to remove any sand trapped between the leaves. Slice leeks lengthways from top end to within half an inch of the root end, but do not sever completely. Fill pan with water, bring to a boil, add the leeks and blanch for 5 minutes. Drain and finish cutting leeks in half. Return to pan and arrange halves in one layer.

Put onions in a small bowl and cover with boiling water. Let stand for 30 seconds, then drain. Cool under running water and slip off skins. Cut a cross in the root end to prevent onions from coming apart while cooking. Add to pan. Tuck bay leaves under leeks and sprinkle peppercorns evenly on top. In a bowl, combine the chicken stock, wine, olive oil and tomato paste. Mix well and pour over leeks. Return pan to heat and barely simmer, uncovered, for 45 minutes. Remove leeks to a serving dish with a slotted spoon, discarding bay leaves. There should be about a half cup of liquid remaining. If you have too much, reduce by rapid boiling. Pour over leeks, chill, and serve sprinkled with paprika.

Serves 4.

Pâté Maison (Country-style pâté)

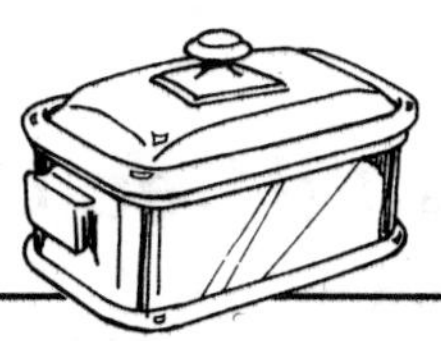

1-QUART RECTANGULAR TERRINE WITH COVER

About twenty years ago, Elizabeth David designed a brown-and-cream glazed earthenware pâté terrine for her shop in London, and we were subsequently able to get it for Williams-Sonoma. I came up with this recipe in which to use it. It's an authentic, French country-style pâté—the kind you get in good country restaurants. It's seasoned with *quatre épices,* a mixture that's used a lot in France, and which is available in some specialty food shops in this country. You'll find a recipe for it below.

- *1 pound ground pork shoulder, with fat*
- *1 pound ground lean veal*
- *1 pound pork or beef liver, finely chopped*
- *2 tablespoons brandy*
- *1 egg*
- *1 clove garlic, finely chopped*
- *1 teaspoon* quatre épices
- *2 teaspoons salt*
- *3 strips bacon, diced*
- *1 bay leaf*
- *½ tablespoon plain gelatin*
- *1 cup beef stock (page 105)*

In bowl, mix together thoroughly the pork, veal, liver, brandy, egg, garlic, *quatre épices,* salt and bacon. Let stand for 2 or 3 hours for flavors to develop.

Preheat oven to 350°. Pack mixture into terrine and place bay leaf on top. Cover with lid and place in baking pan, adding enough water to reach halfway up the sides of the terrine. Bake for 1¼ to 1½ hours, until juices run clear.

Remove terrine from baking pan. Let cool to lukewarm, then pour off fat and cooking juices. In a small saucepan, combine the cold beef stock and the gelatin and let stand for 5 minutes. Heat gently until gelatin is dissolved, then pour into terrine to fill space around pâté. Chill before serving. Serves 10 to 12.

Quatre Épices

- *2 teaspoons ground white pepper*
- *¼ teaspoon ground cloves*
- *½ teaspoon ground ginger*
- *½ teaspoon ground nutmeg*

Combine the spices well and store in an airtight container.

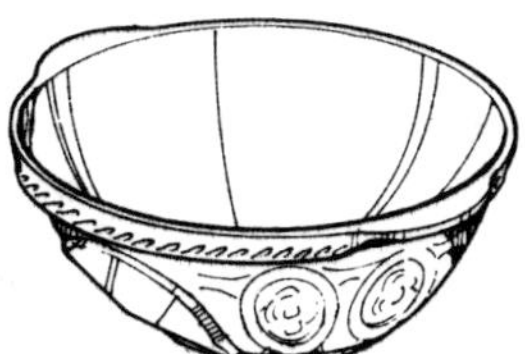

LARGE MIXING BOWL

Roasted Red Bell Peppers

1-QUART SHALLOW BAKING DISH

The Italians serve this dish at room temperature, but I prefer it hot, with plenty of crusty bread for mopping up the good juices.

4 red bell peppers (about 1 pound)
2 cloves garlic, finely chopped
Salt
Freshly ground black pepper
¼ cup good quality olive oil
2 teaspoons chopped parsley

Preheat oven to 400°. Put peppers on upper shelf and place a sheet of aluminum foil on lower shelf under peppers to catch any juice. Roast for 1 to 1¼ hours, turning twice, until skins are evenly puffed and blackened. Remove peppers from oven with tongs and immerse in cold water. Drain and then pierce peppers with a knife, catching the juice in the baking dish. Peel peppers—skin should come off easily—remove core, ribs and seeds and slice into thin strips. Arrange the strips in the baking dish, sprinkle with the garlic, salt and pepper and drizzle with the olive oil. Bake for 15 to 20 minutes until bubbling. Sprinkle with the chopped parsley. Serve hot or at room temperature.

Serves 4.

Roquefort Creams

RAMEKINS

4 ounces Roquefort cheese
3 tablespoons heavy cream
2 eggs
4 tablespoons milk
Freshly ground black pepper
Freshly grated nutmeg
Pinch salt

Preheat oven to 350° and butter the ramekins.

Put Roquefort cheese in bowl and mash to a paste with a fork. Add the cream and stir gently until blended. Beat the eggs and milk together and add to the Roquefort mixture. Add pepper, nutmeg and salt. Stir carefully—do not overmix.

Fill ramekins with mixture and place them in baking pan. Pour enough hot water in pan to come two-thirds of the way up the ramekins. Bake for 25 to 30 minutes, until tops of creams are puffy and pale golden brown. Serve immediately.

Serves 4.

Sardine Butter

RAMEKINS

Elizabeth David gave me this recipe to include in an illustrated newsletter we began publishing for our customers back in 1974. The newsletter turned out to be too expensive and time-consuming, so we eventually discontinued it, but I understand that back issues are now collectors' items. Elizabeth called this an old-fashioned fish paste or "potted" fish, and she says it's best made from French or Portuguese olive-oil-packed sardines, if possible. It makes a delicious and very easy first course that can be prepared one day and served the next.

2 4-ounce cans sardines
4 ounces (1 stick) unsalted butter, softened
2 teaspoons lemon juice
Pinch cayenne pepper
Salt (optional)
Lemon wedges
Hot whole-wheat toast

Drain the oil from the sardines and discard. Remove as many of the bones and as much of the skin as possible. Put the sardines and butter in a bowl and mash with a fork, working both together thoroughly into a paste. Season lightly with the lemon juice and cayenne, and add a little salt if desired. Pack into ramekins or terrine. Cover with plastic wrap and refrigerate overnight. Serve with lemon wedges and plenty of hot toast.

Serves 4.

Tortilla Baskets

TORTILLA BASKET FRIER

Make sure that the tortilla-basket fryer can be completely submerged in your deep-fat fryer, if you have one, or use a deep saucepan. Tortilla baskets can be filled with guacamole (see page 101), marinated shrimp and scallops, salad or chili, and can be served as an hors d'oeuvre, a first course or as an accompaniment to an entree. Be sure the tortillas are fresh and pliable, otherwise they will break while handling. If they are too dry, dampen slightly and steam for a few seconds in the oven, wrapped in aluminum foil.

Vegetable oil
6 to 8 ready-made tortillas

Fill deep-fat fryer or saucepan with enough vegetable oil to submerge the tortilla basket fryer. Heat to 350°. Place a tortilla in the larger basket and fit the smaller basket inside. Holding the two baskets firmly together by the long handles, lower into the hot oil. Do this gently to avoid splattering. Cook for just a few seconds, until crisp. Unmold and drain upside down on paper towels. Repeat procedure for desired number of baskets.

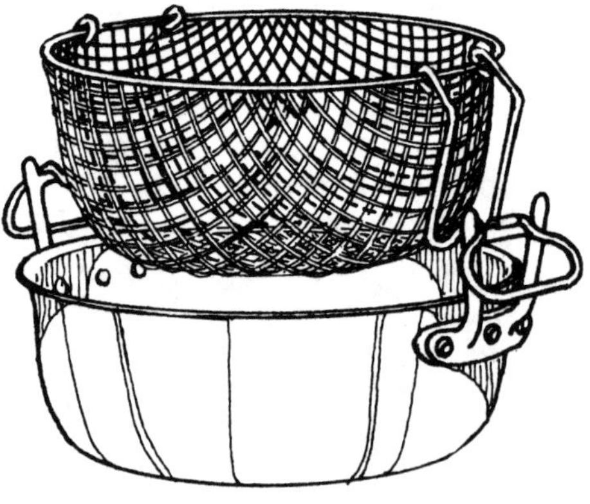

DEEP-FAT FRYER

Guacamole

Guacamole will discolor if you keep it very long, so plan to serve it as soon as possible after mixing. Use serrano chilies with discretion; they are quite hot. One or two is enough for most people.

- 2 *tomatoes*
- 2 *ripe avocados*
- 1 *teaspoon lemon juice*
- 3 *to* 4 *scallions, white part only, finely chopped*
- 1 *to* 2 *fresh serrano chilies, seeded and finely chopped*
- 5 *sprigs cilantro (coriander), chopped*
- *Salt*

Core the tomatoes and make a small cross at the blossom end. Dip in boiling water for 5 seconds to loosen skin. Peel, cut in half crossways and gently squeeze out seeds. Chop tomatoes fairly fine. Cut avocados in half and remove pits. Spoon out the flesh and place in mixing bowl. Add the lemon juice, and mash coarsely. Add the scallions, chilies, cilantro, tomatoes and a pinch of salt. Mix well and taste for seasoning.

Makes about 3 cups, enough to fill 6 to 8 tortilla baskets.

SOUPS

Beef Stock

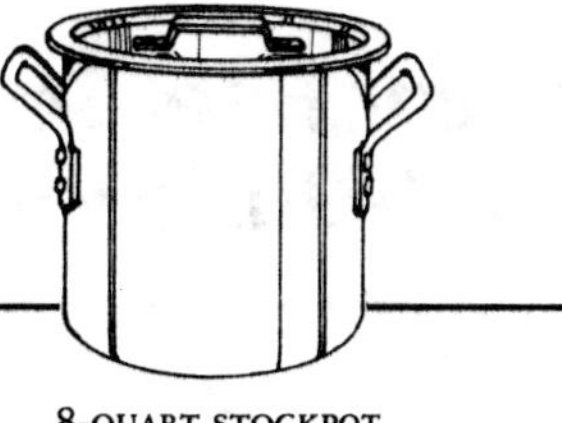
8-QUART STOCKPOT

1½ pounds veal or beef knucklebones
2 pounds beef shin, cut up
3 tablespoons vegetable oil
2 medium onions, sliced
2 medium carrots, sliced
2 stalks celery, in 2-inch pieces
1 cup boiling water
1 bay leaf
3 whole cloves
3 sprigs fresh thyme or ½ teaspoon dried
1 medium tomato, cored and chopped
1 clove garlic
3 sprigs parsley
2 teaspoons salt
3 quarts water
4 black peppercorns, crushed

Preheat oven to 475°. Brush the pieces of meat and bones with the oil. Place in roasting pan in one layer and put pan on top rack of oven. Brown meat on all sides, turning pieces frequently for about 20 minutes. Add onions, carrots and celery to pan and let brown for 10 minutes, stirring so they do not burn.

With tongs and slotted spoon, transfer meat and vegetables to stockpot. Pour off grease from roasting pan and add the boiling water. Loosen any browned bits of cooking residue with a wooden spoon and add to stockpot. Add the bay leaf, cloves, thyme, tomato, garlic, parlsey, salt and water. Bring to a boil, and after 3 or 4 minutes of cooking skim any scum from the surface. Reduce heat, partially cover and let simmer very slowly for 3 hours. Add peppercorns, check seasoning and simmer for 30 minutes more. Line strainer with several thicknesses of dampened cheesecloth and place over bowl. Strain broth into bowl and refrigerate. When well chilled, remove fat from surface. Use within 2 days, or freeze.

Makes 8 to 9 cups stock.

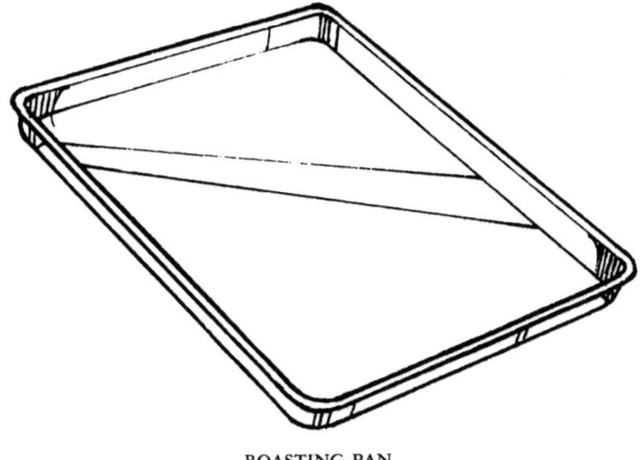
ROASTING PAN

Clear Beef Soup with Julienned Vegetables

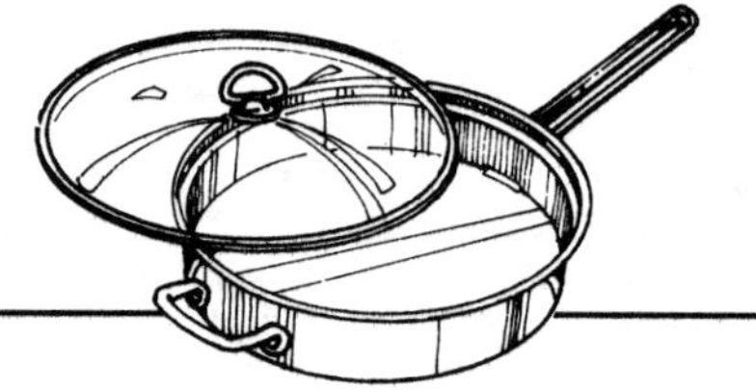

10-INCH SAUTÉ PAN

1 medium leek
2 medium carrots
1 medium turnip
2 tablespoons unsalted butter
Pinch salt
Freshly ground black pepper
4 cups beef stock (see recipe, p. 105)
1 tablespoon parsley, chopped

Trim leek, leaving some of the green, and wash very carefully to remove any sand trapped between the leaves. Cut into strips the size of matchsticks. Trim and peel carrots and turnip and cut into matchsticks.

Heat butter, and sauté the vegetables over gentle heat for 5 minutes, stirring occasionally. Do not let brown. Season lightly with salt and pepper. Add stock, bring to a boil and then simmer slowly for 5 minutes. Serve at once, sprinkled with parsley.

Serves 4.

Chicken Stock

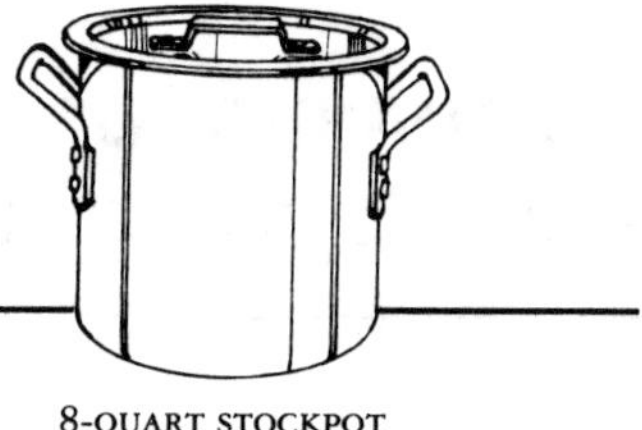

8-QUART STOCKPOT

Throughout this book you'll find chicken stock listed under recipe ingredients. Canned stock really isn't as good as homemade, and this recipe is very little trouble to prepare. If you want a stronger broth, either poach a whole chicken in the prepared, finished broth, or reduce it by boiling. However, reducing it means you lose the fresh flavor.

3 pounds chicken wings, necks and backs
2½ quarts water
2 stalks celery, cut in 2-inch pieces
1 onion, chopped
2 whole cloves
1 clove garlic, chopped
1 bay leaf
3 sprigs fresh thyme or ½ teaspoon dried
3 sprigs parsley
2 1½- x ½-inch strips lemon peel, colored part only
2 teaspoons salt
6 black peppercorns, crushed

Wash chicken parts well and place in stockpot. Add the water and bring to a boil. After 2 or 3 minutes of cooking, skim any scum from surface. Add all other ingredients except peppercorns. Reduce heat to a simmer, partially cover, and let simmer for 1½ hours. Add peppercorns and check for seasoning, adding more salt or thyme if necessary. Simmer 30 minutes more.

Line sieve with several thicknesses of dampened cheesecloth and place over bowl. Strain broth into bowl and refrigerate. When ready to use, remove the fat from the surface. Use within 2 days, or freeze.

Makes 8 cups stock.

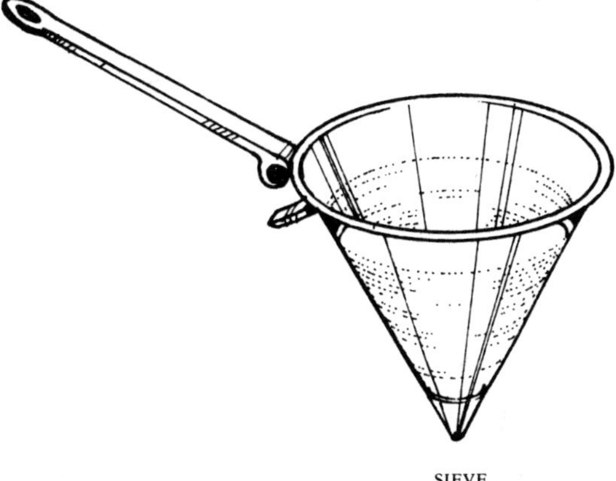

SIEVE

Avgolemono (Greek egg-and-lemon soup)

BALLOON WHISK

4 cups chicken stock (page 107)
1/4 cup uncooked rice
1 egg yolk
Juice of 1/2 lemon

Bring chicken stock to a boil in a stockpot and add rice. Reduce heat and simmer for 20 minutes, until rice is tender.

In a bowl, beat egg yolk with lemon juice and stir in 1/2 cup of the hot stock. Pour this mixture back into the pot, stirring with a whisk. Reheat but do not let boil.

Serves 4.

Cauliflower Soup

4-QUART DUTCH OVEN

When I first visited the famous 150-year-old Herend porcelain factory in Hungary, we were served lunch in the directors' dining room. It was a splendid lunch served on beautiful Herend porcelain, every piece in a different pattern, with crystal wineglasses and handsome silver. The first course was a delicious cauliflower soup. This recipe is as close as I can get to the Hungarian original.

2 quarts milk
1 cup onion, chopped
1 cup carrot, chopped
6 ounces cooked ham, diced
1 medium-sized head cauliflower
1/2 cup sour cream
2 teaspoons salt
Freshly ground white pepper

In a saucepan, bring milk to a boil and then strain through a fine sieve into Dutch oven. Add onion, carrot and ham. Simmer partially covered, over moderate heat, for 10 minutes. Be careful it does not boil over.

Remove cauliflower flowerets from head of cauliflower and chop; there should be about 4 cups. Add to the soup and let simmer for 15 minutes more. Mix a little of the hot soup with the sour cream and stir until smooth. Add this to remaining soup and season with salt and pepper. Stir well and check seasoning.

Serves 4 to 6.

Cream of Mushroom Soup with Brie

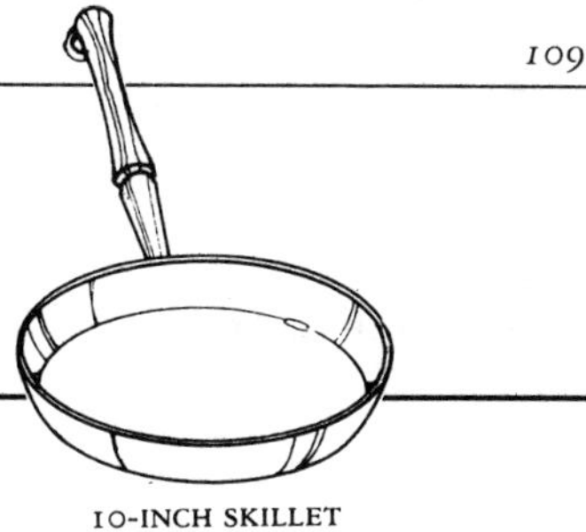
10-INCH SKILLET

This dish was served to me by my good friend Cheryl Schultz, the manager of our Dallas stores and an excellent cook.

2 ounces (½ stick) unsalted butter
1 pound fresh mushrooms, coarsely chopped
1 shallot, finely chopped
½ medium onion, finely chopped
2 tablespoons flour
1½ cups chicken stock (see page 107)
¾ cup port wine
1 cup heavy cream
Freshly ground nutmeg
Freshly ground black pepper
Salt
4 ounces firm Brie cheese

Melt the butter in a skillet, add the mushrooms, shallot and onion, and sauté over medium heat until mushrooms begin to wilt and give up some juice and onion begins to turn translucent.

Add the flour and stir until evenly blended. Add the chicken stock and port. Bring to a boil and cook for 2 minutes, stirring until thickened and smooth.

Reduce heat to low and simmer for 15 minutes. Add the cream, season with nutmeg, pepper and salt, and stir until well blended and slightly thickened. Cut the Brie into ¼-inch slices. Place on top of the soup and let the heat of the soup melt the cheese. Serve immediately.

Serves 4.

Fish Stew

12-INCH SAUTÉ PAN

Any white-fleshed fish works well in this recipe, and a combination of two or three works best.

2 carrots
1 potato
2 stalks celery
3 small leeks
1 cucumber
4 cups water
2 teaspoons salt
6 peppercorns, crushed
3 sprigs of parsley with stems
3 stalks fresh or dried fennel or ½ teaspoon fennel seeds
2 pounds of white fish fillets: sole, halibut, red snapper, etc.
Chopped parsley

Peel and trim carrots and potato into ¼-inch by 2-inch julienne strips. Cut celery into 2 pieces and slice thin lengthwise. Trim and wash leeks well and cut into 1-inch pieces, using only the white part. Peel cucumber and cut in half lengthways. Scoop out seeds and cut each half lengthways into 4 strips, then cut into 2-inch pieces. After preparation, there should be about one cup of vegetable.

Put water, carrots, potato, celery and leeks in sauté pan. Add salt. Wrap peppercorns, parsley and fennel stalks or seeds in a cheesecloth bundle. Add to pan. Simmer over moderate heat for 20 minutes. Add cucumber and cook for 5 minutes more. Remove vegetables with a slotted spoon and set aside. Cut the fish into 3-inch serving pieces and place in the simmering broth. Rapidly bring back to simmer, cover and cook gently for 10 to 15 minutes until fish is just cooked. Remove cheesecloth bag, and return vegetables to pot. Let stew cook for a few seconds until just heated through. Check seasoning and serve immediately, garnished with the chopped parsley.

Serves 4.

PARING KNIFE

Indian Lentil Soup

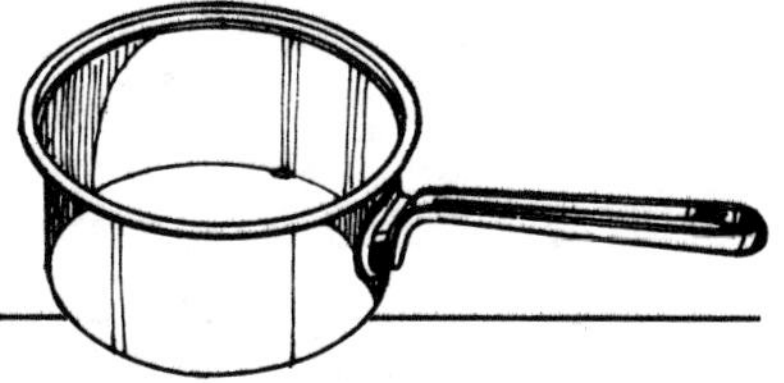

2½-QUART SAUCEPAN

I spent some time in India years ago and discovered, like most visitors, that Indian food can be more subtle and spicy than fiery hot. It is mainly a matter of whereabouts in India you are—in the south, where the weather is hot, the food is hot. Curry powder as we know it isn't used in India, though they do export it for the foreign market. Instead, an Indian cook blends a mixture of carefully selected spices for each dish, grinding each one by hand. Naturally this tastes far better than a commercial blend that, more often than not, has been on the shelf for so long that it has lost much of its flavor. I find that I can grind and blend my own spices with a mortar and pestle in seconds, and the aroma is marvelous. If you can obtain whole spices, use them; otherwise blend recently purchased (not stale!) ground spices.

½ cup lentils
6 cups water
1 bay leaf
1 medium tomato
¼ teaspoon ground cinnamon
⅛ teaspoon ground cardamom
⅛ teaspoon ground coriander
¼ teaspoon ground ginger
½ teaspoon ground turmeric
¼ teaspoon ground cumin
½ teaspoon ground cayenne pepper
2 tablespoons unsalted butter
1 medium onion, finely chopped
1 clove garlic, finely chopped
1 tablespoon freshly squeezed lemon juice
1 teaspoon salt

Wash and drain lentils and place in saucepan. Add the water and bay leaf. Bring to a boil, lower heat and simmer for 45 minutes.

Core the tomato and make a small cross at the blossom end. Dip in boiling water for 5 seconds to loosen skin. Peel, cut in half crossways and gently squeeze out seeds. Chop tomato and reserve.

Blend together the cinnamon, cardamom, coriander, ginger, turmeric, cumin and cayenne pepper. When lentils are almost ready, melt the butter in a skillet. Add spices and let cook over low heat for 1 minute to bring out flavors. Add the onion and garlic and sauté, stirring, until onion is transparent, about 3 minutes. Add onion mixture to lentils. Stir in tomato, lemon juice and salt and simmer soup for 15 minutes more. Taste for seasoning and discard bay leaf.

Purée lightly in food processor or blender (do not reduce to a completely smooth purée) and return to pan. Reheat and then serve.

Serves 4.

Oxtail Soup

6-QUART DUTCH OVEN

2 tablespoons olive oil
1 teaspoon salt
2 pounds oxtails, sliced at joints
Flour
1 small onion, sliced
1 clove garlic, peeled
2 stalks celery, sliced
2 whole cloves
3 sprigs parsley
1 bay leaf
2 to 3 sprigs fresh marjoram or ½ teaspoon dried
2½ quarts boiling water
1 medium carrot, sliced
1 medium leek (white part only), well washed and sliced
1 medium turnip, chopped
Freshly ground black pepper
2 to 3 tablespoons Madeira

Heat the olive oil in the Dutch oven. Salt the oxtail pieces and roll in flour, shaking off excess. Brown in the oil on all sides. Remove with slotted spoon and set aside. (It may be necessary to do this in 2 batches.) Add onion, garlic and half the celery to pot and sauté, stirring, for 3 minutes, until onions are transparent. Return meat to pot, add cloves, parsley, bay leaf and marjoram. Pour in the boiling water, return to a boil and then reduce to a simmer. Cover and simmer for 2½ hours or until meat is tender.

Remove meat from pot with a slotted spoon. When cool enough to handle, separate meat from bones, discarding any fat and the bones. Set aside. Remove grease from top of broth and pour broth through a fine mesh strainer into a large bowl. Rinse pot. Measure the broth. You should have 2 quarts. If not, add water. Return broth to pot and add the meat, carrot, leek, turnip and remaining celery. Season with pepper and more salt if required, bring to a boil, reduce heat and simmer, partially covered, for another 20 to 30 minutes or until vegetables are tender. Check seasoning and add Madeira.

Serves 4 to 6.

FINE MESH STRAINER

Tuscan Beans

6-QUART CASSEROLE WITH COVER

Soup stews, like this one, are really one-dish meals when served with salad and good crusty bread. In Tuscany it is traditional to use an unglazed earthenware bean pot, but the dish can be made in any ovenproof casserole or even in a Dutch oven on top of the stove. To get the flavors as authentic as possible, try to find Tuscan olive oil, sun-ripened Italian-type plum tomatoes and fresh sage.

1 pound dried white beans, large size preferred
4 quarts water
2 bay leaves
6 sprigs parsley
4 cloves garlic, unpeeled
1 tablespoon salt
½ cup Italian olive oil
2 medium-sized onions, chopped
2½ pounds ripe tomatoes
1 teaspoon fresh sage leaves, chopped, or ½ teaspoon dried
4 tablespoons tomato paste
Pinch salt
Freshly ground black pepper
4 tablespoons parsley, chopped

Soak beans overnight in enough cold water to cover.

Preheat oven to 350°. Drain beans and put in casserole. Add the water, bay leaves, parsley and garlic. Cover casserole and bake for 2 hours. Stir in salt and cook for 30 minutes more, or until beans are tender. (Do not add salt at the beginning; it makes the beans hard.)

Heat olive oil in saucepan. Add onions and sauté until transparent, about 3 minutes. Do not let brown.

Core the tomatoes and make a small cross at the blossom end. Dip in boiling water for 5 seconds to loosen skin. Peel, cut in half crossways and gently squeeze out seeds. Chop tomatoes and add to onions. Stir in sage and tomato paste and let simmer for 20 minutes. Season with salt and pepper. Drain beans, discarding bay leaves, parsley sprigs and garlic. Combine with tomato mixture and add chopped parsley. Return to casserole and bake for 20 minutes so that beans can absorb flavors.

Serves 8 to 10.

SAUCEPAN

Vegetable Soup

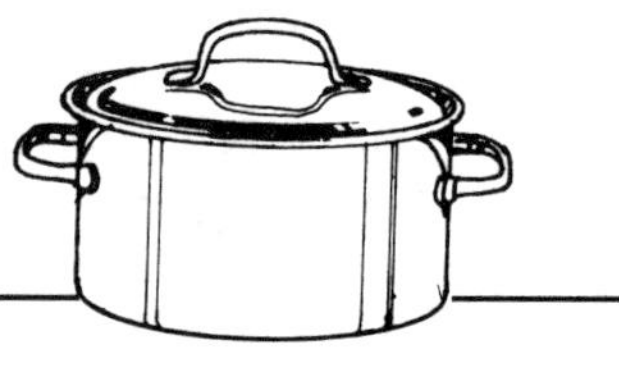
4-QUART STOCKPOT

All the vegetables in this fresh-tasting soup should be diced the same size, about ⅜ of an inch. Be careful in timing the cooking of the vegetables so that the individual flavors and textures come through, and the vegetables don't get overcooked.

4 medium tomatoes
2 tablespoons unsalted butter
1 medium onion, diced
2 quarts water
2 teaspoons salt
2 medium carrots, diced
2 large potatoes, diced
2 stalks celery, diced
1 green bell pepper, seeded, cored and diced
20 string beans, trimmed and cut into ½-inch lengths
2 7-inch-long zucchini, diced
Freshly ground black pepper
Freshly grated Parmesan cheese

Core the tomatoes and make a small cross at the blossom end. Dip in boiling water for 5 seconds to loosen skin. Peel, cut in half crossways and gently squeeze out seeds. Dice and reserve.

Melt the butter in the pan, add onion and sauté until softened but not browned, about 3 minutes. Add the water, salt, carrots, potatoes and celery. Bring to a simmer and cook for 10 minutes. Add the bell pepper, tomatoes and string beans and simmer for 5 minutes more. Add zucchini and cook for another 5 minutes. Add freshly ground black pepper and check seasoning. Serve with grated cheese to sprinkle on top.

Serves 8 as a first course, 4 as a supper dish, accompanied by crusty bread.

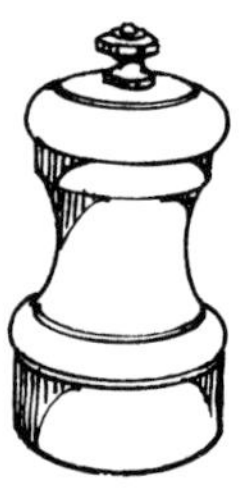
PEPPER MILL

EGGS

AND CHEESE

Baked Eggs and Cheese

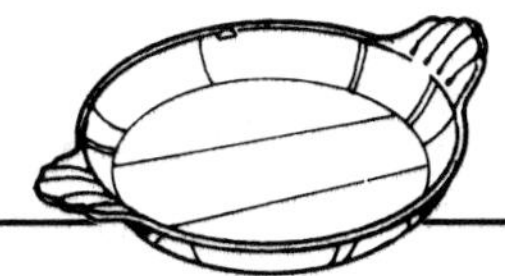

OVENPROOF BAKING DISH

2 strips bacon, diced
8 ounces Gruyère cheese, coarsely shredded
4 eggs
1 teaspoon chives or scallions, chopped
Freshly ground black pepper
1/4 cup fresh breadcrumbs

Preheat oven to 300° and butter baking dish.

In skillet, fry bacon until just cooked and reserve. Spread half the cheese on the baking dish. Break eggs over cheese, spacing evenly. Sprinkle with bacon and chives, and cover with remaining cheese. Season with pepper and sprinkle with the breadcrumbs. Bake until eggs are lightly set, about 15 minutes. Crumbs should be slightly browned; if they're not, slide dish under hot broiler for 1 or 2 minutes. Serve at once with crusty bread and chutney.

Serves 2 or 4, depending on appetites.

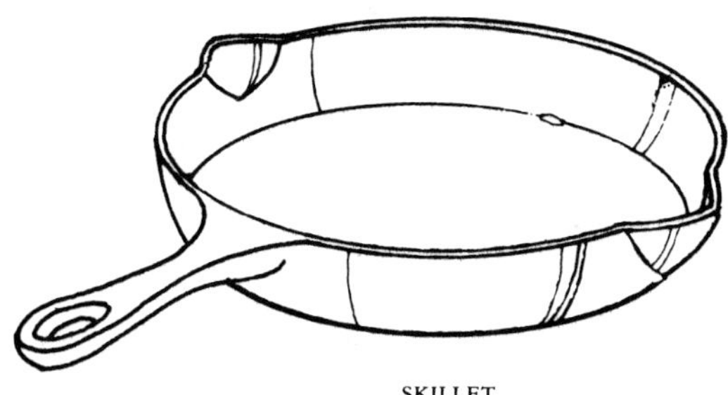

SKILLET

Crustless Broccoli and Ham Quiche

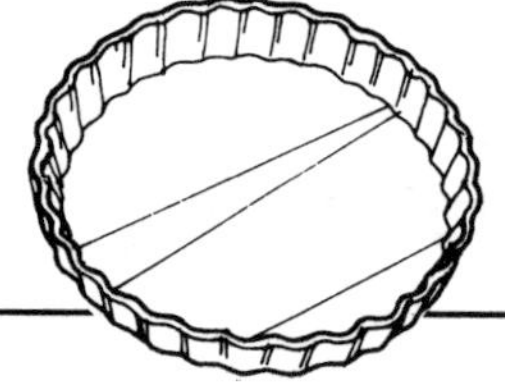

SHALLOW 2-QUART PORCELAIN BAKING DISH

There are some quiche mixtures that are really better served without a pastry crust. This is one of them. The combination of broccoli, prosciutto, Gruyère and Parmesan cheese in a delicate custard is really sufficient.

2 cups broccoli flowerets, cut into small pieces
Salt
1 cup heavy cream
1 cup milk
4 eggs
½ cup ham, chopped
¾ cup Gruyère, coarsely shredded
2 teaspoons lemon juice
Freshly ground black pepper
Dash freshly grated nutmeg
¼ cup freshly grated Parmesan

Preheat oven to 375° and butter the baking dish. Bring pot of water to boil, add a little salt and blanch broccoli for 2 minutes. Drain, cool and chop coarsely. (Do not purée.) Whisk together cream, milk and eggs. Add broccoli, ham, Gruyère and lemon juice. Season with salt, pepper and nutmeg.

Pour mixture into prepared dish and sprinkle with Parmesan cheese. Bake for 30 minutes, until custard is set (a knife inserted in center should come out clean) and brown on top. Let rest for a few minutes before serving.

Serves 6 to 8.

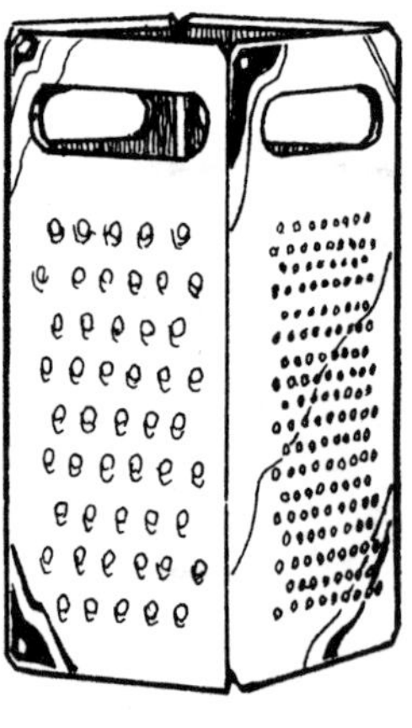

GRATER

English Buttered Eggs

DOUBLE BOILER

The French call this *Oeufs Brouillés* or jumbled eggs. It's one of the best dishes I know for serving at a weekend brunch: It doesn't spoil if it has to wait around! Be patient when cooking eggs this way. It's a slow process and must be watched constantly. Make sure that water does not touch top part of double boiler, and use very low heat, or all will be lost.

8 ounces (2 sticks) unsalted butter
12 eggs
1 teaspoon salt
Freshly ground white pepper
½ cup heavy cream
Hot toast

Melt 4 ounces of the butter in top of double boiler set over simmering water. In bowl, beat eggs well and season with the salt and pepper. Add to melted butter and stir continuously with a wooden spoon, over simmering water, until smooth and creamy. This will take 15 to 20 minutes. Cut remaining butter into small cubes. Once eggs start thickening and have absorbed the melted butter, start adding cubed butter. Let each cube be absorbed before adding the next, stirring constantly. Stir in cream.

After eggs have reached the desired creamy consistency, they may be kept warm in the double boiler over (not touching) hot (not simmering) water. Serve on toast.

Serves 4 to 6.

Leek and Shrimp Frittata

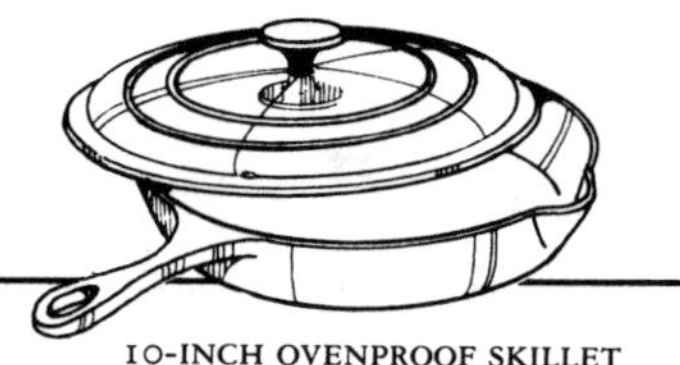
10-INCH OVENPROOF SKILLET

1 leek
½ pound fresh medium shrimp
4 tablespoons unsalted butter
1 teaspoon fresh tarragon, chopped, or ½ teaspoon dried
6 eggs
1 tablespoon Madeira
Salt
Freshly ground black pepper

Preheat broiler. Trim the leek, discarding green top. Wash well and slice into ½-inch pieces. Shell the shrimp and cut into ½-inch pieces. Melt 2 tablespoons of the butter in the skillet, add the leek and tarragon, and toss to coat well with the butter. Cover and let sweat over low heat for 2 minutes. Do not allow to brown. Uncover pan and add the shrimp. Stir and cook until shrimp turn pink, about 1 to 2 minutes. Remove shrimp and leek and set aside.

In a bowl, beat the eggs until well blended. Add the leek, shrimp and Madeira, and season with salt and pepper. Add remaining butter to skillet and return to heat. When bubbling, pour in egg mixture, reduce heat to low, shake pan to level ingredients and let cook gently until eggs are just set, about 5 minutes. Bottom should be golden brown. Put under broiler and let top brown lightly. Cut in wedges to serve.

Serves 4.

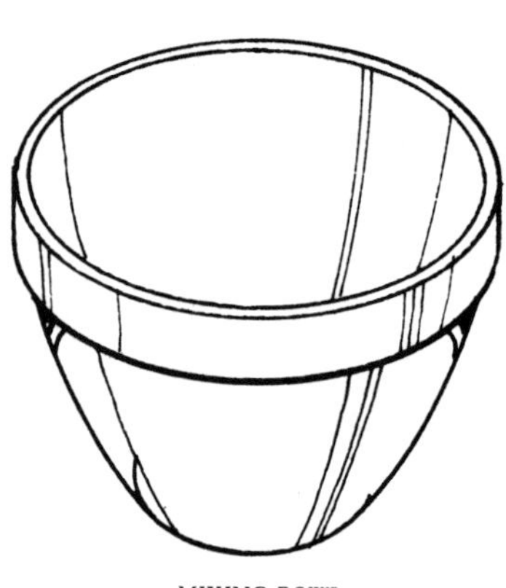
MIXING BOWL

Mediterranean Eggs

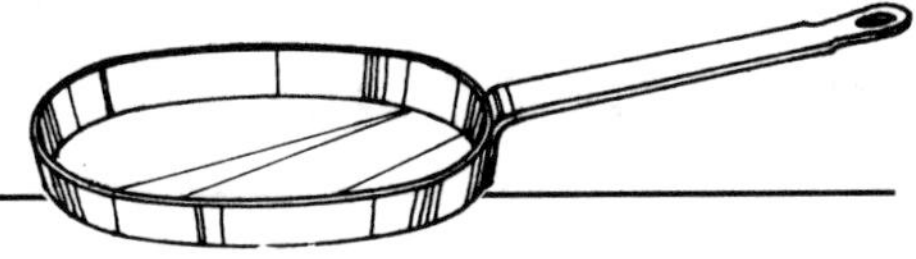

10-INCH OVENPROOF SKILLET

3 ripe tomatoes (about 1 pound)
2 tablespoons olive oil
1 small onion, diced
1 clove garlic, chopped
2 tablespoons fresh basil, chopped
Salt
Freshly ground black pepper
4 eggs
4 mushrooms, sliced
4 teaspoons grated Parmesan cheese
4 slices hot toast

Preheat broiler. Core the tomatoes and make a small cross at the blossom end. Dip in boiling water for 5 seconds to loosen skin. Peel, cut in half crossways, gently squeeze out seeds and chop. Set aside.

Heat the oil in an ovenproof skillet, add the onion and garlic and let cook over low heat for 2 minutes until transparent. Do not allow to brown. Add the tomatoes and basil, season with salt and pepper and let cook for 5 to 6 minutes more. Remove from heat, make 4 deep indentations in the tomato sauce with a spoon, and break an egg into each. Arrange the mushroom slices around the eggs on the tomato sauce. Cover and return to heat. Let steam over low heat for 5 to 6 minutes or until whites of eggs are just set and yolks are still soft. Remove from heat. Sprinkle 1 teaspoon of the cheese over each egg.

Place pan under broiler for a few seconds to brown cheese. Put the toast on 4 serving plates, and transfer the eggs and tomato sauce to the toast with a large spoon. Serve at once.

Serves 4.

COOKING SPOON

Sonoma Soufflé

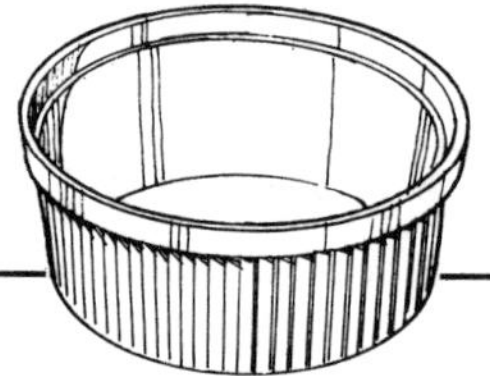

1½-QUART SOUFFLÉ DISH

When I was living in Sonoma, thirty years ago, I made a great many soufflés. It was considered quite a feat back then, though now many home cooks have their own "secrets" for a perfect soufflé. In this recipe I have used 1 cup of shrimp meat, but you may substitute crabmeat or chopped cooked chicken. In fact, I add all kinds of things, depending on what's in the kitchen when the mood hits. By the way, the Madeira is important. The alcohol vaporizes and helps the soufflé to rise without fail. It also leaves behind a wonderful flavor.

The best way to beat egg whites for a soufflé is with a balloon whisk and in an unlined copper bowl. Due to a harmless chemical interaction (egg whites adhere to copper, so more air can be beaten in), you'll get up to a third more volume, and therefore a higher soufflé. The whites should be beaten to "soft peaks." The way to tell if you've achieved this is to lift the whisk straight out of the bowl and invert. The peaks on the whisk should remain standing upright, with just a slight bend at the tips. (If the whites are too soft they won't hold the soufflé up; if too stiff you won't be able to combine them with the sauce. Soft peaks blend right in.)

½ cup heavy cream
½ cup milk
2 tablespoons unsalted butter
2 tablespoons all-purpose flour
4 egg yolks
1 cup shrimp meat, cooked and finely chopped
½ teaspoon salt
Freshly ground black pepper
Pinch cayenne pepper
1 tablespoon Madeira
1 tablespoon lemon juice
5 egg whites

Preheat oven to 350°. Make a baking parchment or aluminum foil collar that extends 2 inches above the outside rim of the soufflé dish. Secure it with a pin or paper clip, or tie with string. Do not butter dish.

In saucepan, combine cream and milk. Heat and set aside. In separate saucepan, melt butter over moderate heat and stir in flour. Cook for 2 minutes, stirring vigorously with a wooden spoon or whisk. Add cream and milk mixture and cook, while stirring, over low heat until smooth and thick, about 2 to 3 minutes. Remove from heat and let cool for 5 minutes.

Beat egg yolks lightly and stir in a little of the

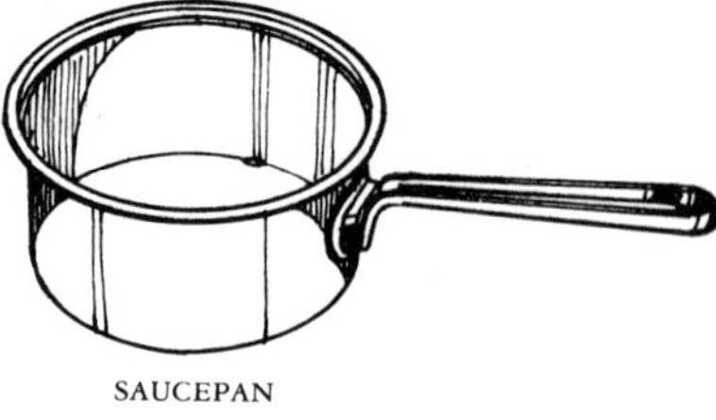

SAUCEPAN

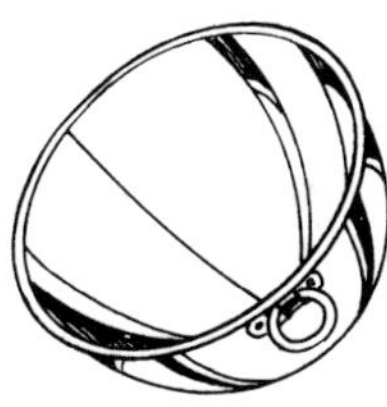

COPPER BOWL

sauce, then combine with remaining sauce. Stir in shrimp and season with salt, pepper, cayenne, Madeira and lemon juice. Beat egg whites to soft peaks and stir a quarter of them into the sauce. Fold sauce gently into remaining egg whites. Pour into prepared soufflé dish and bake for 35 minutes, until just done in center and lightly browned. Carefully remove collar and serve at once.

Serves 4.

SALADS

Blacksmith Salad

VEGETABLE PEELER

This salad is served in the Fini Restaurant in Modena, the Tuscan town famous for its aged wine vinegar, Aceto Balsamico. It's a wonderful salad, but you have to use this special vinegar (Fiui Aceto Balsamico if possible) and the most expensive Parmesan cheese (Parmigiano Reggiano) for it to come off. And try to get Tuscan olive oil.

1 large head butter lettuce or 2 small ones
3 ounces Parmesan cheese
2 tablespoons Aceto Balsamico (page 86)
Pinch salt
1/3 cup good quality Italian olive oil

Chill the salad bowl, but don't get it too cold or the lettuce leaves will stick to it. Separate the leaves of the lettuce, discarding any tough or discolored outer ones. Wash and dry thoroughly, tearing large leaves in half, and place in prepared bowl. Slice Parmesan into very thin chips, using a vegetable peeler and scatter over lettuce. Sprinkle with Balsamic vinegar and salt, and toss well. Dribble with oil and toss again. Serve immediately.

Serves 6.

COLANDER

Dressy Salad

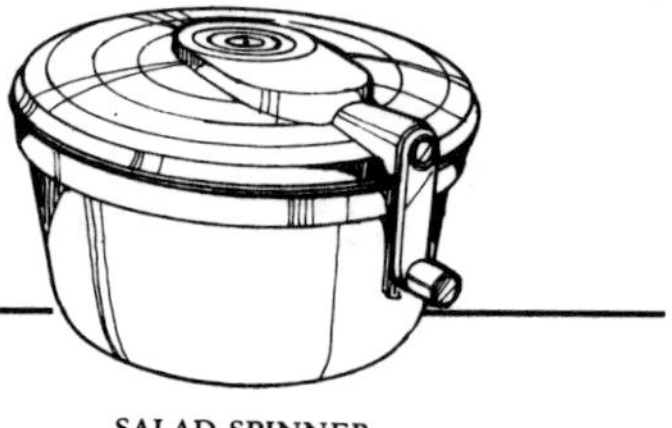
SALAD SPINNER

I have had a longstanding love affair with tiny Pacific bay shrimp ever since I first tasted them. This salad was always known as "Dressy Salad" in Sonoma because it has a "real" dressing, otherwise known as mayonnaise! Be sure to use very fresh shrimp and do make your own dill mayonnaise.

1 head romaine lettuce
1 bunch watercress
3 scallions, chopped
2 stalks celery, diced
½ cucumber, peeled, seeded and diced
½ green bell pepper, seeded and diced
½ pound tiny bay shrimp (cooked and peeled)
2 tablespoons capers
Pinch salt
Freshly ground black pepper
Dill mayonnaise (see recipe below)

Discard any tough or discolored outer leaves of the lettuce. Wash and thoroughly dry, then tear leaves into bite-sized pieces and place in salad bowl. Wash and dry watercress, discarding discolored leaves and large stems. Break into small sprigs and add to bowl. Add the scallions, celery, cucumber, green pepper, shrimp and capers. Season lightly with salt and pepper and toss lightly. Spoon the mayonnaise on top and mix well. Taste for seasoning, and serve at once.

Serves 4.

Dill Mayonnaise

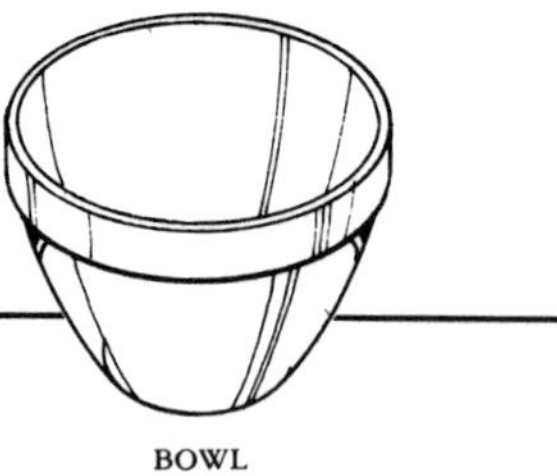
BOWL

The trick to making successful mayonnaise is to have all the ingredients at room temperature, and to beat in the first tablespoon of oil vigorously. This sets the mixture—from then on the oil can be added steadily.

1 egg yolk
1/4 teaspoon Dijon mustard
1 tablespoon lemon juice
1/8 teaspoon salt
Freshly ground black pepper
1/2 teaspoon fresh dill, chopped, or 1/4 teaspoon dried
1/4 cup mild olive oil (page 87)
1/4 cup salad oil

Combine egg yolk, mustard, lemon juice, salt and pepper in bowl. Rub the dill in the palm of one hand with your thumb to bring out the flavor and add to bowl. Whisk vigorously. Add 1 tablespoon of the olive oil and whisk vigorously again until well incorporated. Continue whisking and add the remaining olive oil, a little at a time. By this time the mixture should have thickened. Incorporate the salad oil in a thin stream, still whisking. Check seasoning.

Makes approximately 3/4 of a cup.

Green Bean and Fresh Basil Salad

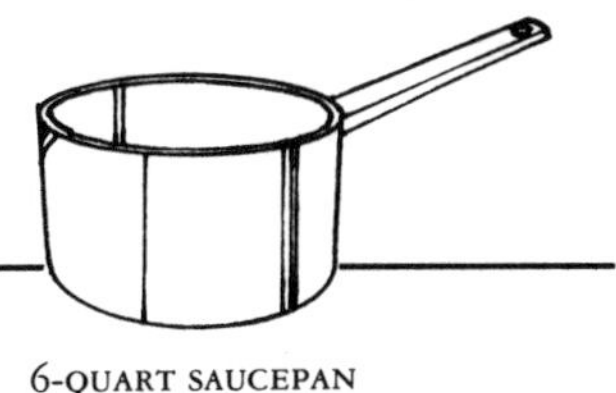

6-QUART SAUCEPAN

This is an outstanding salad to serve when tiny Blue Lake beans or *harticots verts* and fresh basil are in season. Don't bother making it with dried basil! Baby Blue Lakes, if you can get them, often vary in size. As you trim them, sort them into small, medium and large. Add the largest to the boiling water first, wait a minute or so before adding the medium ones, and put the tiny ones in last. The only way to tell if green beans are cooked is to bite into one.

1 pound crisp, tiny green beans
4 quarts water
2 tablespoons plus 1 pinch salt
1 tablespoon white wine vinegar
2 tablespoons fresh basil leaves, chopped
1 clove garlic, finely chopped
2 scallions, finely chopped
4 tablespoons olive oil
2 tablespoons freshly grated Parmesan cheese

Trim the beans and bring the water to a boil. Add 2 tablespoons salt and the trimmed beans. Cook at a rapid boil until beans are tender but still crisp, from 3 to 10 minutes depending on size. Drain in colander and run under cold water to stop cooking. Drain again and let cool. Place in bowl.

In another bowl dissolve a pinch of salt in the vinegar and add the basil, garlic, scallions, oil and cheese. Mix until well blended and taste for seasoning. Pour over beans and toss well. Serve at room temperature.

Serves 6.

Hot Potato Salad with Scallions

NEST OF BOWLS

This is the way good French cooks prepare potato salad. It's a long way from the average deli potato salad drowned in bottled mayonnaise!

1 pound red or white new potatoes
1/4 cup parsley, finely chopped
4 scallions, finely chopped
4 tablespoons olive oil
1 tablespoon lemon juice
Pinch salt

Boil potatoes until just done, about 15 to 20 minutes. Drain, then peel and slice while still hot. Place in bowl and add parsley and scallions. In separate small bowl, whisk together oil, lemon juice and salt until blended. Combine with hot potatoes and mix carefully, adding more lemon juice or salt if necessary. Serve warm.

Serves 3 or 4.

Hot Three-Squash Salad

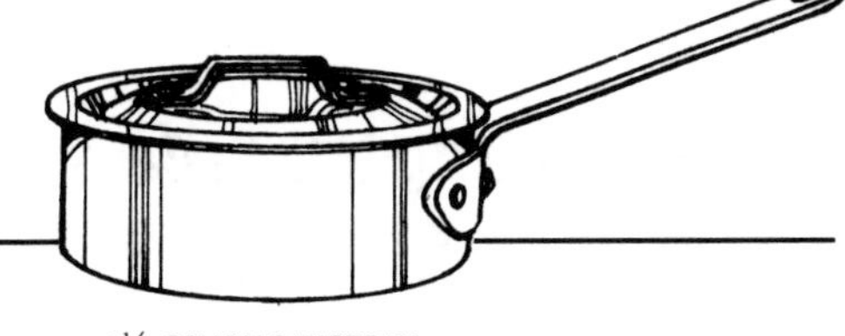

2½-QUART SAUCEPAN

This is a warm salad that's at its best eaten with European-type sausages, such as bratwurst, bockwurst, kielbasa or mild pork sausage.

2 medium zucchini
2 medium yellow squash
2 medium patty pan (summer) squash
½ large red bell pepper
¾ cup water
5 tablespoons olive oil
4 to 5 scallions, sliced
2 teaspoons fresh dill, chopped, or 1½ teaspoons dried
2 tablespoons red wine vinegar
Salt
Freshly ground black pepper

Trim the three kinds of squash, then quarter the zucchini and yellow squash lengthways and cut into ⅝-inch pieces. Cut the patty pan squash into cubes approximately same size as the other squash. There should be about 2 cups of each squash. Cut the bell pepper into ½-inch dice.

Heat the water in the pan, add squash and bell pepper. Cover and cook over moderately high heat for 3 to 4 minutes. Do not let boil dry. Drain and set aside. In same pan, heat the olive oil, add the scallions and cook over moderate heat for 1 minute. Stir in the chopped dill and vinegar, add the vegetables, mix and toss. Season with salt and pepper and toss again. Serve warm.

Serves 4.

Mediterranean Salad

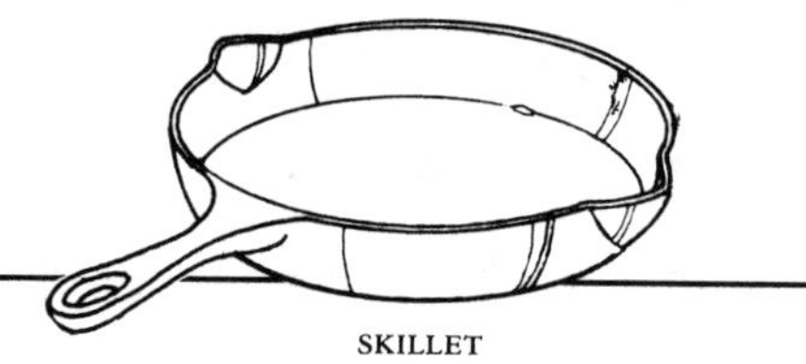
SKILLET

¼ cup pine nuts (pignoli)
1 head crisp Romaine lettuce
4 ounces feta cheese, diced
½ cup seedless green grapes, cut in half
Pinch salt
3 tablespoons white wine vinegar
½ cup good quality olive oil
Freshly ground black pepper

Put pine nuts in a heavy skillet and brown until golden over medium heat, stirring continuously, about 2 minutes. Set aside.

Separate the leaves of the lettuce, discarding any tough or discolored outer ones. Wash and dry thoroughly, then tear into bite-sized pieces. Place in bowl and sprinkle with the pine nuts, feta cheese and grapes. In a separate bowl, dissolve the salt in the vinegar. Whisk in the oil and season to taste with pepper. Taste for seasoning, then dribble over salad and serve at once. Toss at the table.

Serves 4 to 6.

Walnut-Apple Salad

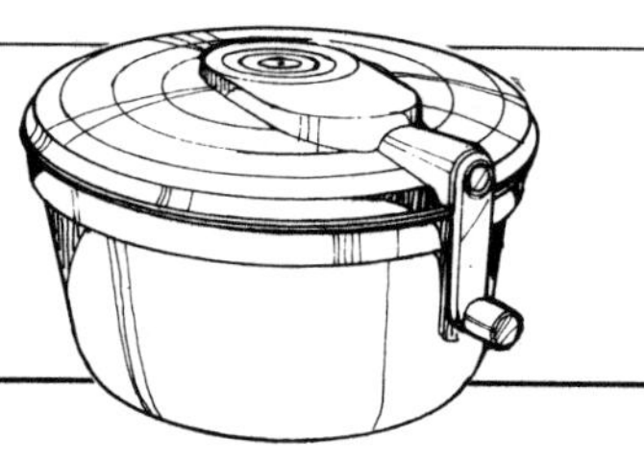
SALAD SPINNER

1 head crisp Romaine lettuce
½ cup walnuts, coarsely chopped
1 tart apple, peeled, quartered and thinly sliced
¼ cup seedless raisins
Pinch salt
1½ tablespoons mild white wine vinegar
4 tablespoons walnut oil or olive oil
Freshly ground black pepper

Separate the leaves of the lettuce, discarding any tough or discolored outer ones. Wash and dry thoroughly, then tear into bite-sized pieces and place in bowl. Add walnuts, apple and raisins. In separate bowl, dissolve the salt in the vinegar and whisk in the oil and black pepper—about two twists of the mill. Taste for seasoning and adjust if necessary. Pour dressing over greens and toss well. Serve immediately.

Serves 4.

VEGETABLES

Baked Beets

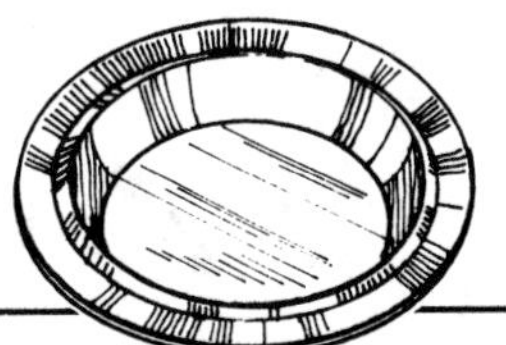
ALUMINUM FOIL DISPOSABLE PAN

In France, you always buy beets ready baked in the vegetable markets. I've found that even people who claim they don't like beets enjoy them done this way. Baked beets can also be served cold with oil and vinegar.

4 to 6 medium to small beets
2 tablespoons unsalted butter
Salt
Freshly ground black pepper

Preheat oven to 450°. Cut tops off beets, leaving about half an inch of stem. Do not trim off the root end or the beets will "bleed" while cooking. Put in pan and cover tightly with a sheet of aluminum foil. Make 2 or 3 slits in top of foil to let steam escape. (You can also wrap beets in a large sheet of foil, folding the seams well to make a tight package, and making slits for steam.) Bake for 1¼ to 1½ hours, depending on size of beets. Uncover and let cool slightly. Peel and slice beets. Melt the butter in sauté pan, add beets and heat through. Season with salt and pepper.

Serves 4 to 6.

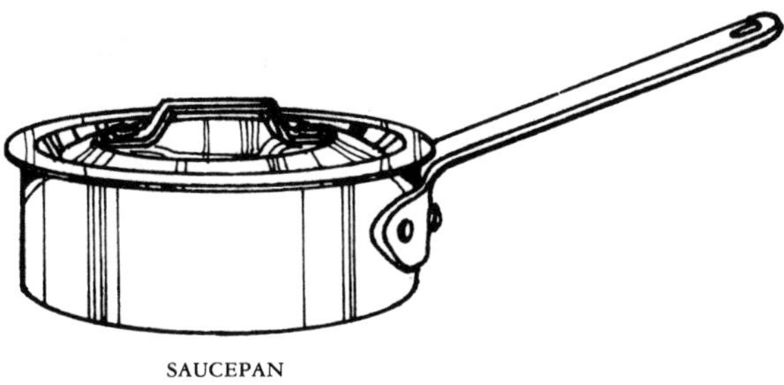
SAUCEPAN

Baked Bicycle Corn

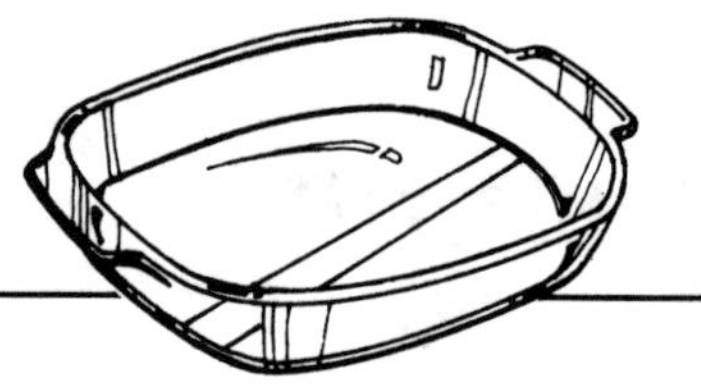
SHALLOW 1-QUART BAKING DISH

I first had this dish at Gordon Tevis's house in Sonoma. The Tevis family has lived in California for years and years, and in fact a very famous 100-mile cross-country horse race is still run every year called the Tevis Cup. The winning rider gets an engraved silver belt buckle that would deflect a cannon ball. I don't know what the horse gets. Sore feet, probably. Anyway, this was Gordon's favorite dish, and he was very fussy about the corn that went into it. (It's a kind of custard, but it doesn't need eggs because milky fresh corn thickens it.) He'd buy his corn in only one place. In those days, there was a large field next to the Sonoma high school, where an old man with two sons raised corn. You told them how many ears you wanted, and one of the sons would get on his bicycle and race off through the field to pick it for you. Naturally, it became known as Bicycle Corn, and it doesn't come any fresher than that.

4 to 5 ears very fresh corn
1/3 cup heavy cream
Salt
Freshly ground black pepper
Freshly grated nutmeg

Preheat oven to 375° and butter the baking dish. Shuck the corn, remove all silk and wipe cobs clean with a paper towel. Working over a wide shallow bowl or dish so as to catch all the liquid, and using a very sharp knife, make a cut lengthways down the middle of each row of kernels. Hold ear of corn at an angle and carefully scrape all the pulp out of the kernels with the back of the knife. There should be approximately 2 cups. Stir in the cream and season with salt, pepper and nutmeg. Blend well. Transfer mixture to baking dish and bake for 30 to 35 minutes until corn is thickened and puffed up slightly and lightly browned across the surface. Serve immediately.

Serves 4.

PARING KNIFE

Baked Onions with Raspberry Vinegar

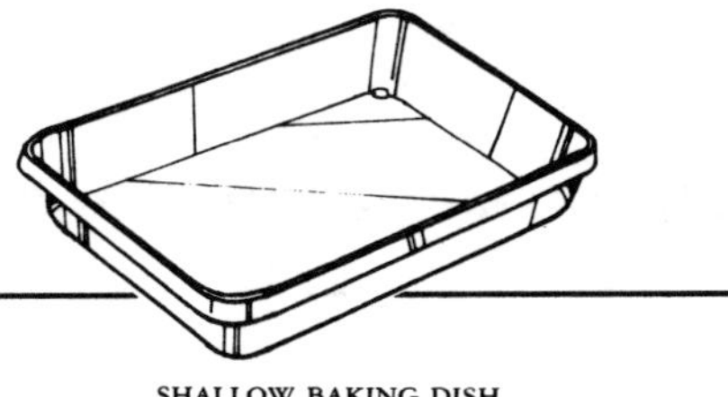

SHALLOW BAKING DISH

Used with discretion, raspberry vinegar is an excellent seasoning, and I find that I need far less salt when I use it. You can also use it to season zucchini and other vegetables.

4 medium brown-skinned onions
2 tablespoons sugar
2 tablespoons raspberry vinegar (page 88)
1/4 cup water
1 tablespoon unsalted butter, diced
Salt
Freshly ground black pepper

Preheat oven to 350° and butter the baking dish. Peel onions, trimming as little as possible off the root end. Put into a pot of boiling, salted water and cook for 10 minutes. Drain. When cool enough to handle, cut each onion in half vertically. Place in baking dish cut side down. Dissolve sugar in vinegar and water and pour over onions. Dot with butter, season with salt and pepper, and bake for 30 to 40 minutes or until tender, basting often.

Serves 4.

Brussels Sprouts with Mustard

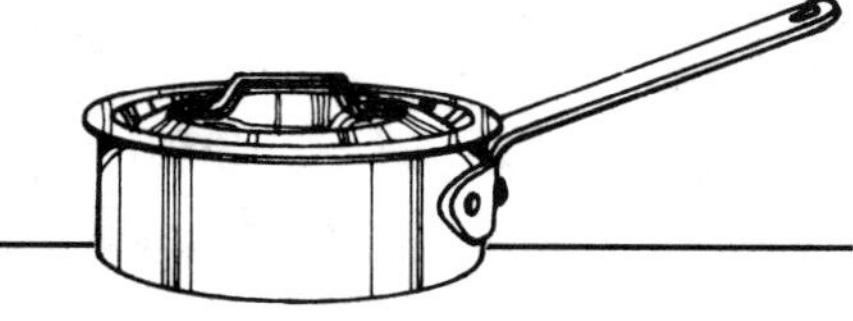

2-QUART SAUCEPAN WITH COVER

1 pound Brussels sprouts
4 cups water
1 tablespoon salt
2 tablespoons Dijon mustard
2 tablespoons sour cream

Trim stems and remove any wilted or yellow leaves from the Brussels sprouts. Cut a cross in the stem end and let soak for 15 minutes in enough cold water to cover well. Put the 4 cups of water in saucepan, bring to a boil and add salt. Drain sprouts and put into the boiling water. Partially cover and cook for 10 minutes or until just tender. Drain well and return to saucepan. Combine the mustard and sour cream, add to the sprouts and toss until well coated. Serve immediately.

Serves 4.

Cucumbers with Dill

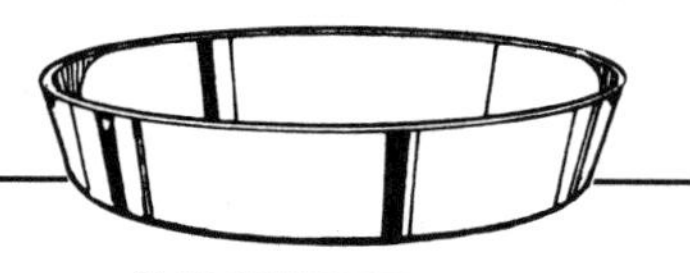

FLAT-BOTTOMED DISH

2 cucumbers
Salt
6 tablespoons sour cream
½ to 1 teaspoon dried dill

Peel cucumbers, cut in half lengthwise and scoop out seeds; then thinly slice to about the thickness of a quarter. Layer slices in the dish, sprinkling each layer with salt. Place a smaller dish on top of the slices and weight down with a heavy can or wrapped brick, in order to press out excess liquid. Let stand in refrigerator for 2 to 3 hours. Drain off juice and dry slices between paper towels.

Place cucumber slices in bowl and add the sour cream. Rub dill in the palm of your hand to release oil, and combine with cucumber and sour cream, mixing well. Serve chilled as an accompaniment to fish.

Serves 4 to 6.

Eggplant and Tomatoes

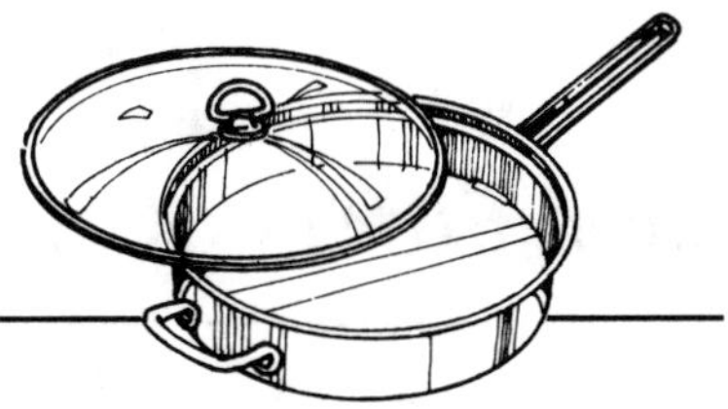

12-INCH SAUTÉ PAN

Eggplant is a delicious vegetable, but you have to salt it before cooking to drain off some of the liquid, which is bitter and will also make the dish watery. Be sure the slices have enough room to drain. Just piling them on top of each other in a colander won't do the job.

1 large eggplant (about 2 pounds)
Salt
3 medium tomatoes
6 to 8 tablespoons olive oil
Flour
1 small onion, chopped
1 clove garlic, chopped
1 tablespoon capers
½ teaspoon salt
Freshly ground black pepper
1 teaspoon fresh oregano, chopped, or ½ teaspoon dried
¼ cup vermouth

Trim and cut the eggplant into ⅜-inch slices. Sprinkle with salt on both sides and place in colander, overlapping as little as possible. Let drain for 1 hour. Rinse and blot dry with paper towels.

Core the tomatoes and make a small cross at the blossom end. Dip in boiling water for 5 seconds to loosen skin. Peel, cut in half crossways and gently squeeze out seeds. Chop and reserve. Heat 4 tablespoons of the olive oil in sauté pan. Dust eggplant slices with flour, shaking off any excess. Sauté, a few slices at a time, for 1 or 2 minutes on each side until golden, adding more olive oil as needed. Remove with slotted spoon and drain on paper towels.

In saucepan, heat 2 tablespoons of the oil. Add onion and garlic and cook over gentle heat until transparent, about 3 minutes. Add tomatoes, capers, salt, pepper, oregano and vermouth. Stir and cook gently for 5 minutes. Wipe out sauté pan with paper towels. Return eggplant to pan and arrange in an overlapping pattern. Pour tomato mixture on top, partially cover pan and heat to bubbling. Cook for 1 minute and serve immediately.

Serves 4.

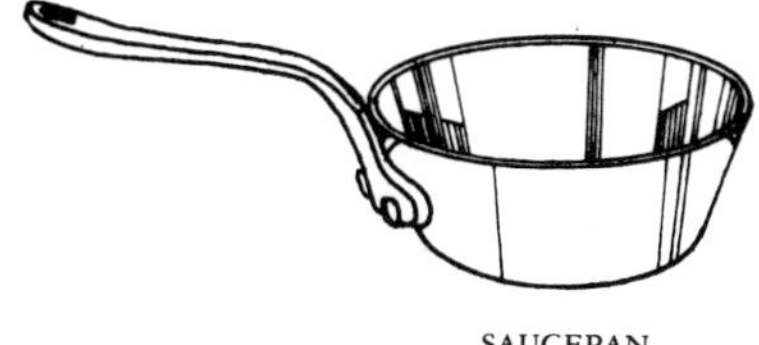

SAUCEPAN

Glen Ellen Potato Cake

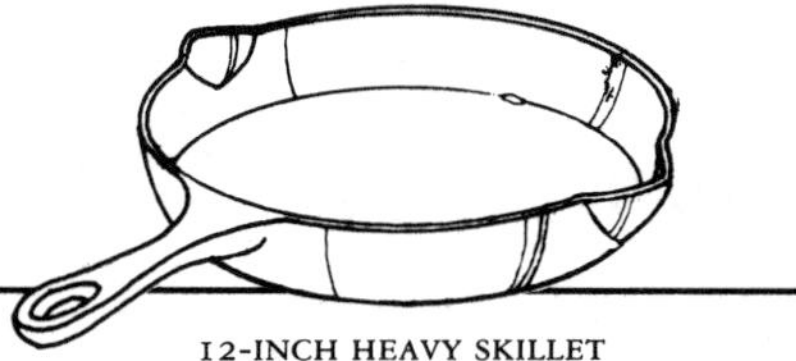

12-INCH HEAVY SKILLET

Glen Ellen is a small community a few miles from the wine country town of Sonoma, where I opened the first Williams-Sonoma store. I had a French neighbor and friend, an exceptionally good cook, who used to make this potato cake. When I asked her what it was called, she said, "Pommes Glen Ellen, I suppose, since I live here." And Glen Ellen Potato Cake it has remained. She always cooked it in an old, well-seasoned black iron skillet, but I find that a heavy aluminum skillet with rounded sides also works well. Don't try shredding the potatoes with the grating disc of a food processor. It shreds too finely for this dish. The medium disc of a Mouli julienne shredder works best, but a mandoline or the shredding side of a square or conical grater will also do the job.

1 ½ pounds all-purpose potatoes
4 tablespoons unsalted butter
Salt
Freshly ground black pepper

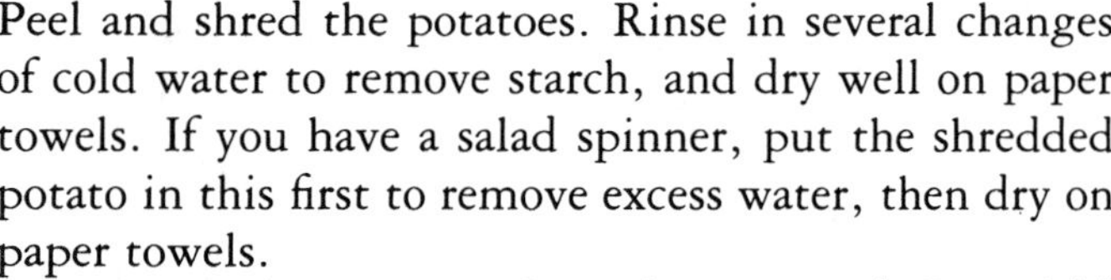

Peel and shred the potatoes. Rinse in several changes of cold water to remove starch, and dry well on paper towels. If you have a salad spinner, put the shredded potato in this first to remove excess water, then dry on paper towels.

Heat 2 tablespoons of the butter in skillet. Add potatoes and pack down well into a cake about 1-inch thick. Cook over medium to low heat for 15 minutes. If unable to turn with a spatula, loosen edges of potato cake and invert a plate on top of skillet. Holding plate and pan together, turn over completely. Lift off skillet and return to burner. Add rest of butter to pan, allow to melt, and slide potato cake on top, brown side up. Cook second side for 15 minutes, until crisp and golden brown. Season with salt and pepper and serve at once, cut into wedges.

Serves 4.

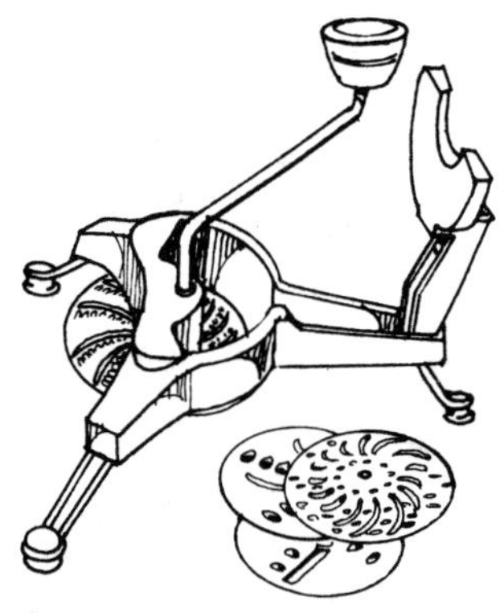

SALAD SHREDDER

Poached Plum Tomatoes

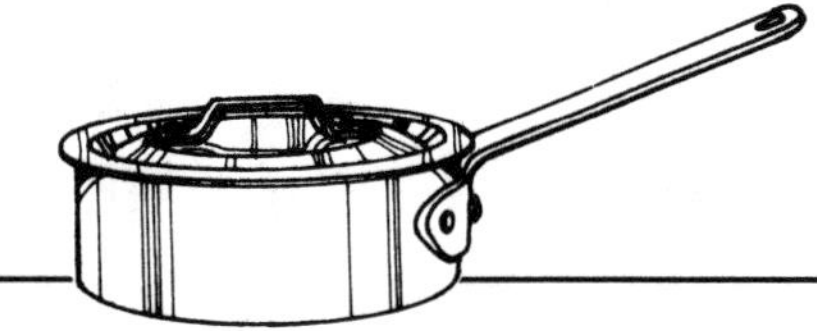

2½-QUART SAUCEPAN WITH COVER

People don't cook tomatoes often, but they're marvelous prepared this way. Make sure they're not cooked for too long—you don't want stewed tomatoes. I like to serve them on toast because it absorbs the juices.

12 to 16 ripe oval Italian-type plum tomatoes
1½ tablespoons fresh basil, chopped
Salt
2 tablespoons water
2 tablespoons unsalted butter

Core the tomatoes, making as small a conical cut as possible, and make a small cross at the blossom end. Dip in boiling water for 5 seconds to loosen skins. Peel, and cut a very tiny slice off the core end of each tomato so that it will stand upright, but the juices won't leak out. Sprinkle half the basil on the bottom of saucepan and arrange tomatoes in one layer, cut side down. Sprinkle with salt and remaining basil and add the water. Cover pan and bring to a simmer. Simmer over very low heat until tomatoes are just tender, about 5 minutes. (Time depends on ripeness of tomatoes.) Remove to a serving dish. Add butter to liquid in pan and let boil for a minute or two, then pour over tomatoes.

Serves 4 to 6.

Potato Nests

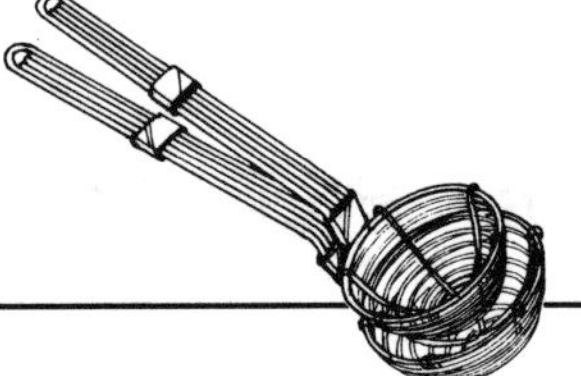
POTATO-NEST BASKET

Use waxy-type potatoes for this recipe. They should be 3½- to 4-inches long, as you need long strips for the baskets to hold together properly. Don't wash the shredded potato: the starch also helps to hold the deep-fried nests together. If your shredded potato discolors a bit, don't worry. It will look fine once it hits the hot fat. You can expect to get 6 to 8 baskets out of 3 large potatoes.

Vegetable oil
3 large potatoes
Salt

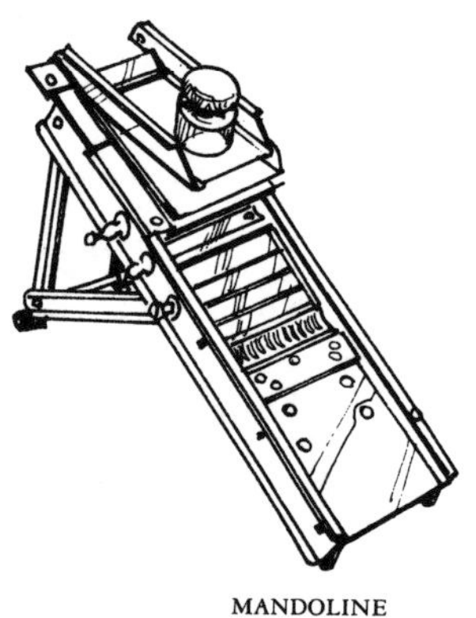
MANDOLINE

Fill deep-fat fryer or deep saucepan with enough vegetable oil to completely submerge the potato-nest basket fryer. Heat oil to 350° or 360°.

Peel the potatoes and shred into long julienne strips on a mandoline equipped with julienne blade, or a Mouli julienne, or cut into julienne strips by hand. If preparing by hand, cut potatoes lengthways into thin slices. Then stack several slices together and slice into matchstick strips. Dry between paper towels.

Dip the potato-nest basket fryer in the hot oil for a few seconds, then line the larger basket with approximately ½ a cup of shredded potato. Start by placing long strips upright or angled around the basket, then crisscross other strips on top until you have almost a solid pattern of potato. Place the smaller basket inside. Holding the two baskets firmly together by the long handles, lower slowly into the hot oil. When potatoes start to turn color, after about 1 minute, loosen the inner basket free of the potatoes by wiggling or twisting it slightly from side to side. Continue to cook until potatoes are crisp and golden brown, about 2 to 3 minutes.

Unmold potato nest (the tip of a paring knife can be helpful) and drain on paper towels. Sprinkle lightly with salt. Potato nests can be made ahead and reheated. Fill with cooked vegetables such as peas, carrots, mushrooms, tiny pearl onions, broccoli or cauliflower and serve with meat or poultry entrees.

Puréed Broccoli Flowerets with Cream

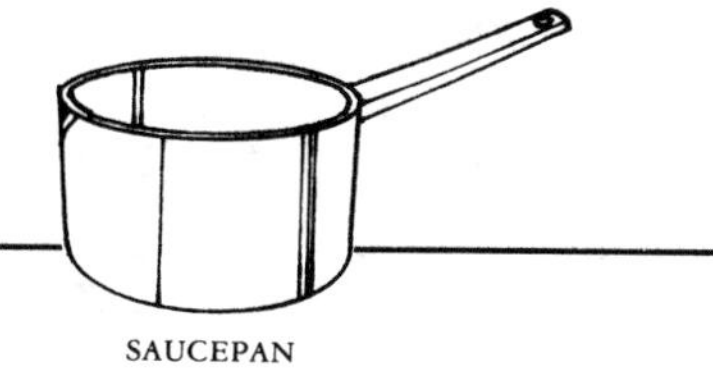

SAUCEPAN

Be sure that broccoli is drained of all liquid before puréeing, otherwise it will be too watery. After draining the flowerets, I put them back in the pan and shake over heat for a few seconds until all liquid has boiled off.

2 bunches broccoli, about 2 pounds
Salt
⅔ to 1 cup heavy cream
Freshly grated nutmeg
Freshly ground black pepper

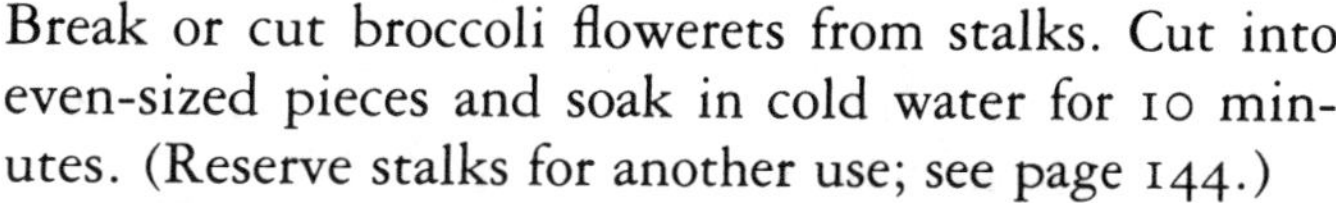

Break or cut broccoli flowerets from stalks. Cut into even-sized pieces and soak in cold water for 10 minutes. (Reserve stalks for another use; see page 144.)

Bring plenty of water to a boil in saucepan, add salt and broccoli and cook uncovered for 1½ to 2 minutes, until JUST tender. Drain well and purée in food processor, using on-off pulses and scraping down sides of bowl to obtain an even purée.

When ready to serve, put the purée in heavy saucepan, heat for a minute or two until bubbly, stirring constantly. Add as much of the cream as the broccoli will absorb without getting too thin and season to taste with nutmeg, salt and pepper. The purée should be bright green and very fresh tasting. Serve at once.

Serves 6 to 8.

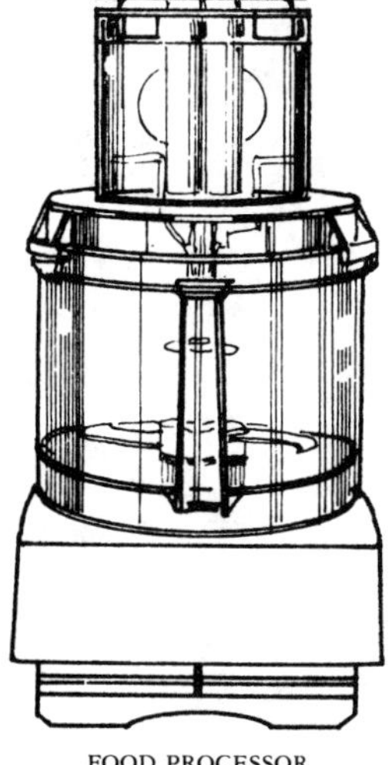

FOOD PROCESSOR

Sautéed Broccoli Stems

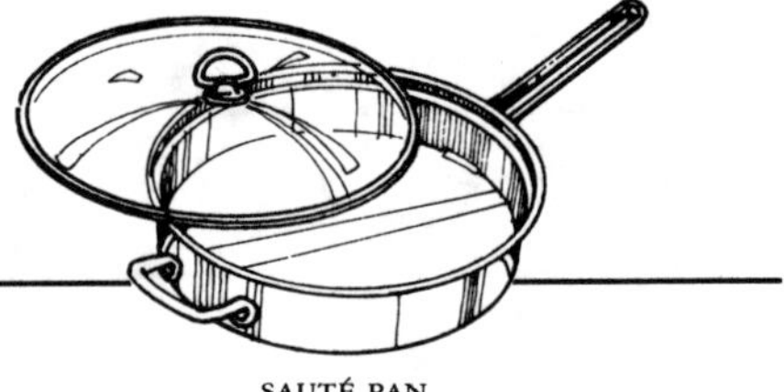

SAUTÉ PAN

This is a good way to get extra mileage out of a bunch of broccoli. Unsuspecting guests can never decide what this interesting new vegetable is! Use the flowerets at another meal.

2 bunches broccoli with large *stems*
2 tablespoons unsalted butter
Freshly grated nutmeg
Salt
Freshly ground black pepper
Pimiento strips for garnish

Cut the flowerets from the broccoli stems and save for another use. See page 143. Peel the stems carefully and cut into ¼- x 2-inch-long julienne strips. Put in cold water and let crisp for 30 minutes in refrigerator. Bring a pot of salted water to the boil, add broccoli stems, bring back to a boil and let blanch for 1 minute. Immediately drain and plunge into cold water to keep stems crisp and green. Drain again.

When ready to serve, melt butter in a sauté pan, add a little nutmeg, then add broccoli. Toss until well coated with butter and heated through—1 to 2 minutes. Add salt and pepper if desired. Serve immediately in neat piles, garnished with pimiento strips.

Serves 4.

Chinese Vegetable Pickles

Kitchen gadgets: top row (left to right): apple corer, asparagus peeler, zucchini corer, egg slicer; bottom row: butter curler, vegetable peeler, lemon zester.

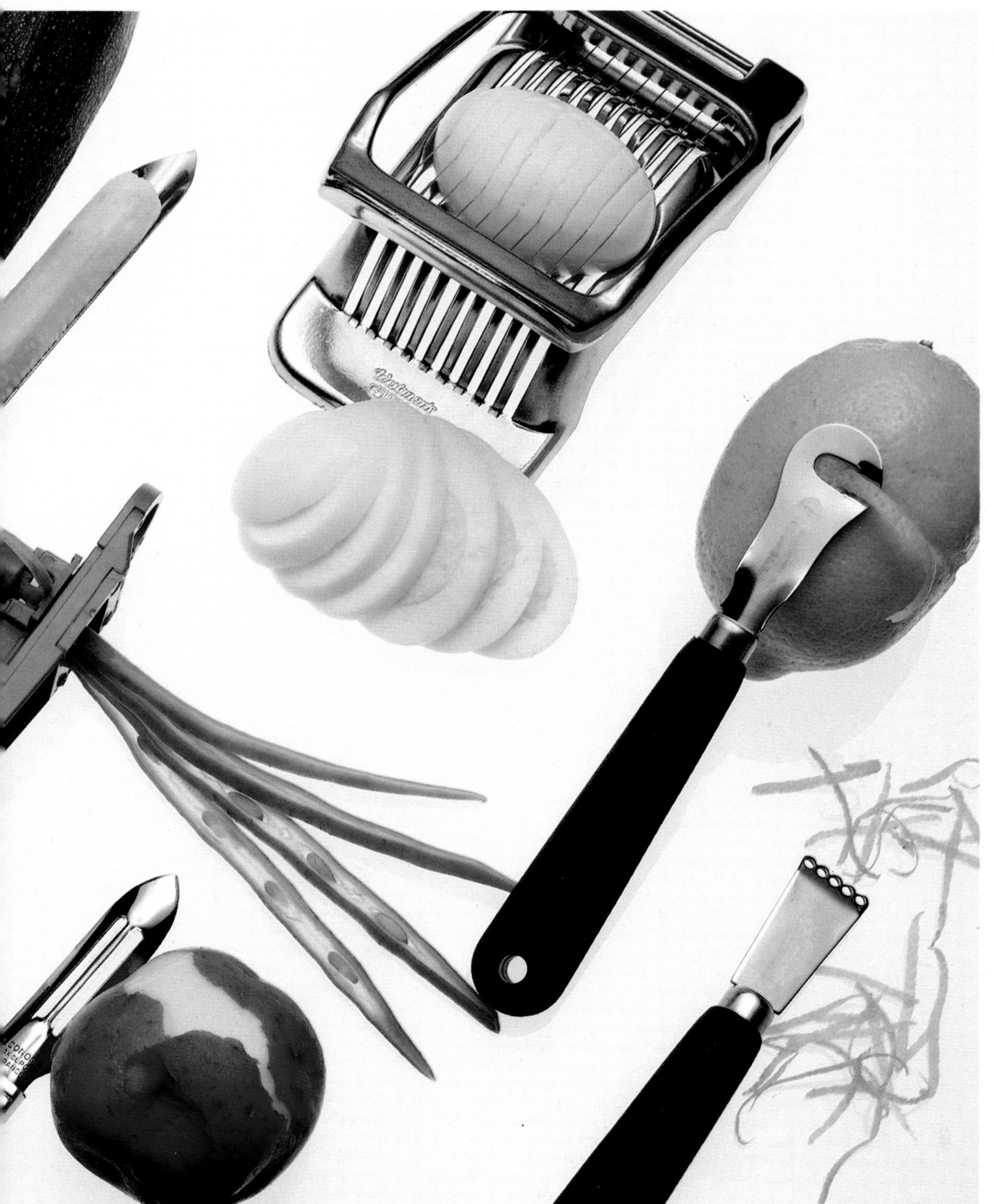

middle row: shrimp peeler and deveiner, bean slicer, lemon stripper;

Vegetable Soup

Opposite: Tortilla Baskets

Baked Cornmeal with Parmesan

Opposite: Hot Three-Squash Salad

Fresh Fettuccine with Tomato and Shrimp

Shredded Cabbage with Cream and Raspberry Vinegar

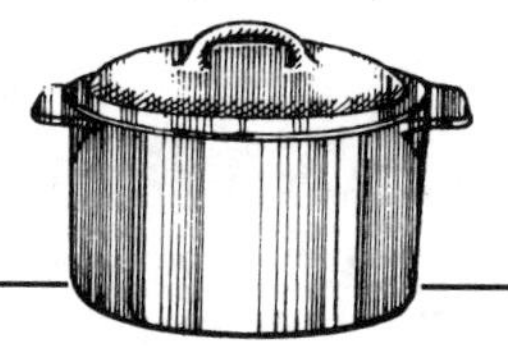

SAUCEPOT

½ head medium-sized green cabbage
½ cup heavy cream
2 tablespoons raspberry vinegar (page 88)
½ teaspoon cracked peppercorns
Salt

Trim cabbage of any coarse outside leaves and remove core. Cut into medium shreds and soak in cold water for 30 minutes.

Bring pot of water to boil. Add cabbage, bring back to boil and blanch for 1 to 2 minutes. It should remain crisp. Drain well.

In heavy saucepan, heat cream and let boil for 3 minutes to reduce slightly. Stir in raspberry vinegar and add cracked pepper and salt to taste. Remove from heat and add drained warm cabbage. Toss well and serve immediately.

Serves 4.

String Beans and Turnips

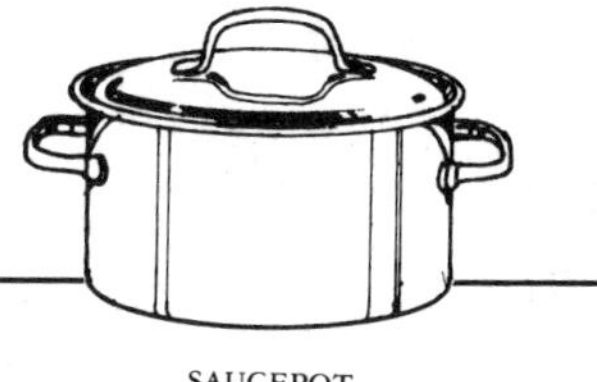

SAUCEPOT

1 pound tender young string beans
4 small young turnips
1 small white onion
3 quarts water
2 tablespoons salt
4 tablespoons unsalted butter, at room temperature
Freshly grated nutmeg
Salt
Freshly ground black pepper

Trim beans, cut in half or thirds if long, and soak in cold water for 20 minutes to crisp. Peel turnips and cut into ½-inch julienne strips. Peel and thinly slice the onion. Put 3 quarts cold water in saucepan and heat to a vigorous boil. Add salt. Drain beans and add to the boiling water, together with turnips and onion. Cook uncovered for 6 to 8 minutes, until vegetables are just tender. Drain, return to pan and add butter, nutmeg, salt and pepper to taste. Stir, toss and serve immediately.

Serves 4.

Squash Trio

10-INCH SAUTÉ PAN

This colorful and fresh-tasting dish was considered very daring and innovative when I first made it thirty years ago in Sonoma. At that time summer squash was just not fashionable, and red bell peppers were practically unknown.

8 small white boiling onions
2 yellow crookneck squash
2 zucchini
2 summer squash
1 red bell pepper
Salt
1 cup boiling water
3 tablespoons unsalted butter, diced
½ cup shredded Gruyère cheese

Preheat oven to 400°. Peel the onions and make a small cross at the root end to keep them from coming apart while cooking. Bring saucepan of water to boil and simmer onions until tender, about 10 minutes. Drain and set aside.

Trim and cut the 3 types of squash into equal-size pieces, about 2 inches across. Cut bell pepper into strips, discarding ribs and seeds. Place in sauté pan with the squash. Add salt to taste and pour in the boiling water. Cover and cook over high heat 4 to 5 minutes, until just tender. Check to make sure that vegetables do not boil dry. Add more water if necessary. Do not overcook. Drain.

Arrange the squash, peppers and onions in baking dish and top evenly with the butter and cheese. Bake for about 5 minutes until cheese begins to melt. Serve at once.

Serves 4 to 6.

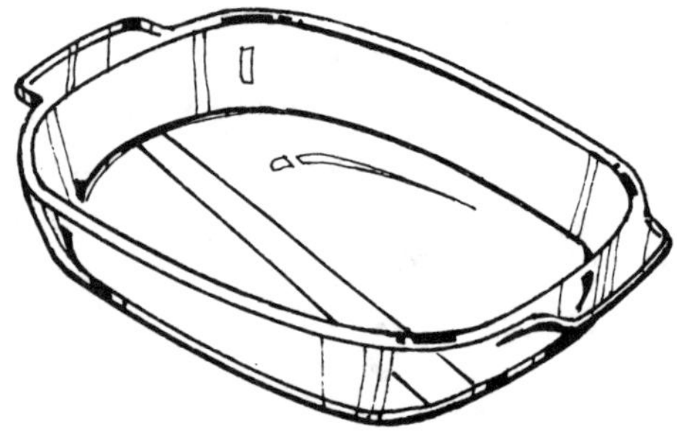

2-QUART BAKING DISH

Stuffed Whole Zucchini

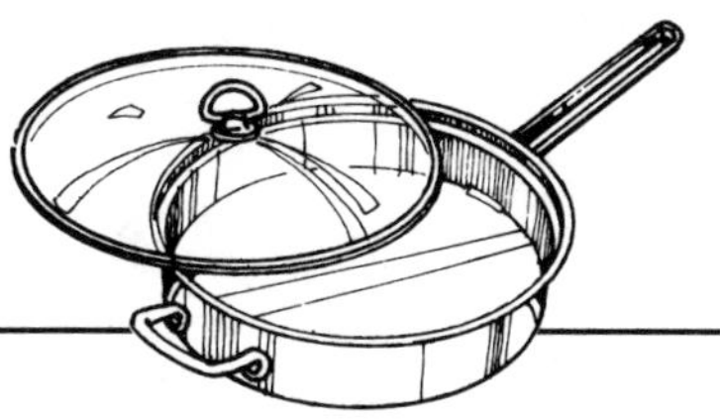
12-INCH SAUTÉ PAN

Italian cooks use a zucchini corer to get the seeds out of zucchini, leaving the vegetable whole. They are available in this country in specialty cookware shops. You can also hollow zucchini out with an apple corer, working it in from both ends, but be careful not to break the skin, or the zucchini will fall apart while cooking.

8 to 10 zucchini, 6 inches long, 1½ inches in diameter
½ pound ground veal
1 egg
4 tablespoons grated Parmesan cheese
½ cup fresh white breadcrumbs
3 tablespoons cooked ham, finely chopped
Freshly ground black pepper
1 teaspoon fresh oregano, chopped, or ½ teaspoon dried
2 tablespoons unsalted butter
1 tablespoon olive oil
1 medium onion, chopped
1 tablespoon parsley, chopped
2 tablespoons tomato paste
1 cup water
1 bay leaf

Cut a slice from both ends of zucchini, making them all the same length, approximately 5½ inches. Carefully hollow out centers of zucchini with zucchini corer, working from both ends if necessary, leaving vegetable whole. Combine veal, egg, cheese, breadcrumbs, ham, pepper and oregano. Mix well and stuff the zucchini with this mixture.

Melt butter and oil in sauté pan. Add onion and cook over moderate heat until transparent, about 3 minutes. Stir in parsley, tomato paste and water. Add bay leaf and simmer for 5 minutes. Add zucchini in one layer, cover and simmer for 40 minutes, turning the zucchini once. Serve topped with juices from pan, discarding bay leaf.

Serves 4.

GRAINS

Baked Cornmeal with Parmesan

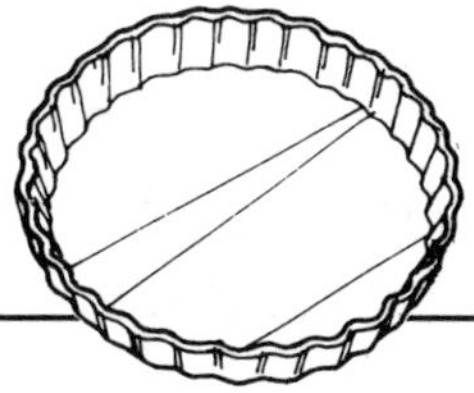
2-QUART BAKING DISH

Italians would recognize this dish as polenta, Roman style. It's simpler to make it with cornmeal than to try and find the traditional Italian semolina, and I think it's almost as good. Allow enough time to first roast the bell peppers and then chill the cornmeal mixture so that it's firm enough to cut into rounds.

1 red bell pepper
1 quart milk
½ teaspoon salt
¼ teaspoon freshly grated nutmeg
¼ teaspoon freshly ground black pepper
1¼ cups yellow cornmeal
2 eggs
1 cup imported Parmesan cheese, grated
4 ounces (1 stick) unsalted butter, melted

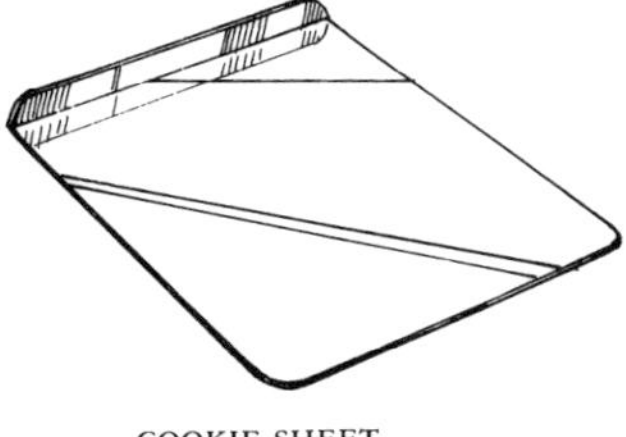
COOKIE SHEET

Roast the bell pepper for 1 to 1¼ hours, then peel, seed and chop into ¼-inch dice. (See page 98 for directions.)

Butter a cookie sheet and set aside. Put the milk in the deep saucepan and add salt, nutmeg and black pepper. Bring just to a boil and gradually sprinkle in the cornmeal, stirring constantly. Do this carefully to avoid lumps. Let mixture boil and continue to stir vigorously for 6 to 8 minutes, until very thick. *(Do not undercook.)* Remove from heat. Beat the eggs and combine with ¾ cup of the cheese and the chopped bell pepper. Gradually stir into cornmeal. Spread evenly ½ inch thick on the cookie sheet. Refrigerate for 1 hour or until very firm.

Preheat oven to 450° and butter the baking dish. Cut the cornmeal mixture into 1¼-inch rounds with a cookie cutter and arrange in one layer in overlapping rows, or in circles if using a round dish. Dribble the melted butter on top and sprinkle with remaining cheese. Bake for 15 to 20 minutes, until crisp, browned and bubbly.

Serves 6 as a first course, 4 as a luncheon dish with salad.

Barley and Bacon Casserole

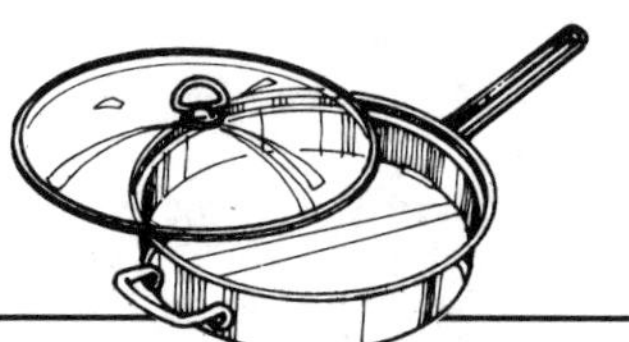

12-INCH SAUTÉ PAN WITH COVER

Barley is a grain that most people encounter only in soup. It has such a good nutty flavor and interesting texture that I like it in a casserole or as a side dish.

2 ounces (½ stick) unsalted butter
1 medium carrot, diced
1 medium onion, finely chopped
1 cup pearl barley
2 cups chicken stock, heated (page 107)
Salt
Freshly ground black pepper
1 stalk celery, very finely chopped
6 to 8 strips thick-cut lean bacon, broiled or fried

In sauté pan, melt butter and cook carrot and onion until softened but not browned, about 3 minutes. Add barley and stir until grain turns golden, about 5 minutes. Add warm chicken stock and season to taste with salt and pepper. Bring to a boil, cover and simmer over low heat for 1 hour—the barley should be tender but not mushy. Stir in celery and taste for seasoning. Let stand, uncovered, for 5 minutes. Serve topped with hot bacon.

Serves 4 to 6.

Lamb and Vegetable Stew with Couscous

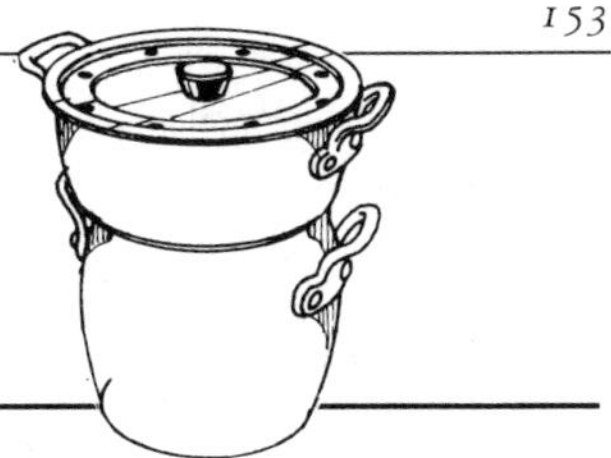

8-QUART *COUSCOUSIÈRE*

Couscous is the national dish of much of North Africa. The word can refer to the grain itself, a type of semolina, or to the complete meal of steamed grain, lamb or chicken, and vegetables. It is cooked in a special 2-part pot, a *couscousière.* The meat and vegetables simmer in the lower part; the grain cooks in a colander that fits on top, enveloped in the aromatic steam that rises from the stew. The lid of a *couscousière* is also pierced, so that condensed steam does not drip back onto the grain and make it soggy. In Morocco and Algeria, a searingly hot condiment called Harissa sauce is served with couscous. It's available in this country in specialty food shops or you can make a somewhat milder version yourself. The meat and vegetables should be well seasoned with freshly ground black pepper or according to your taste.

3 pounds lean boneless lamb shoulder
2 medium onions
4 tablespoons unsalted butter
1 teaspoon ground ginger
1 teaspoon ground turmeric
2 whole cloves
freshly ground black pepper
5 to 6 sprigs parsley
3½ quarts water
2 red bell peppers
2 medium tomatoes
5 medium carrots
4 medium turnips
2½ teaspoons salt
1 pound (3 cups) couscous
½ pound string beans
5 medium zucchini
2 cups cooked or canned chickpeas, rinsed and drained
Imported Harissa sauce (optional)

Trim fat from lamb and cut in 1-inch pieces. Set aside. Peel onions, quarter and slice lengthways. Melt the butter in the bottom of *coucousière.* Add onions, ginger, turmeric, cloves and a generous grinding of black pepper. Cook and stir for a few seconds until onion begins to wilt. Add the lamb and stir for 2 minutes so that the onions, spices and meat are well mixed. Add parsley and 3 quarts of the water and bring to a boil. Reduce to a simmer, cover and cook for 1 hour.

Roast the bell peppers over a gas burner or under broiler until blackened on all sides. Hold with tongs under cold running water and remove skins. Remove seeds and slice peppers into thin strips. Cut core from tomatoes and make a small cross at the blossom end. Dip in boiling water for 5 seconds to loosen skin. Peel, cut in half crossways and gently squeeze out seeds. Dice tomatoes. Peel and slice carrots into ½-inch-thick diagonal pieces. Peel and cut turnips into 1½-inch cubes. Stir ½ teaspoon of the salt into remaining water. Put the couscous in a large bowl and, while stirring, dribble in the salted water. Let stand for a few minutes until water is completely absorbed. Line the top (colander) part of the *couscousière* with a double

Or

½ cup stew liquid
2 tablespoons tomato paste
½ teaspoon cayenne pepper

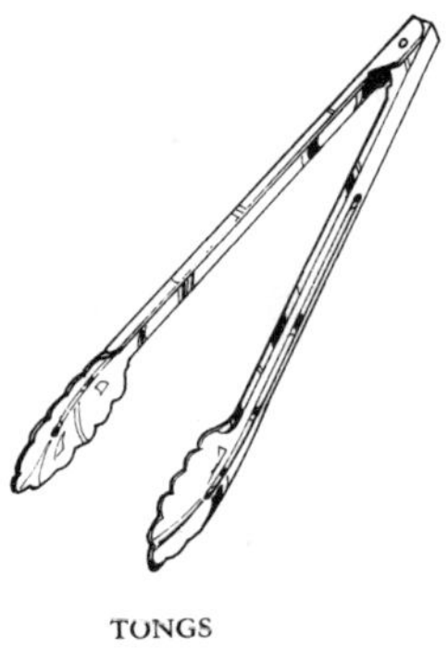

TONGS

thickness of dampened cheesecloth. Stir couscous with your hands to break up any lumps and pile loosely into the lined colander.

Add the remaining salt to the stew and stir in the bell peppers, carrots, tomatoes and turnips. Bring back to a simmer and set couscous-filled colander in place on top of pot. Cover and let cook for 25 minutes. Loosen up the couscous with a fork twice during cooking. Remove colander and turn couscous out into a large pan. Spread out and loosen up grains completely, breaking up any lumps. Return couscous to colander.

Trim string beans and cut into 2-inch pieces. Trim and cut zucchini into ½-inch-thick slices. Add beans and zucchini to stew, and stir in chickpeas. Replace colander on top of pot, cover and cook for 15 to 20 minutes more. Check seasoning of stew.

To serve, mound the couscous in the center of a large warmed platter. Arrange the vegetables and meat around the couscous and put the broth in a separate bowl to serve as a sauce. Accompany with Harissa sauce or make a hot sauce by combining ½ cup of the stew liquid with tomato paste and cayenne pepper.

Serves 6 to 8.

Paella

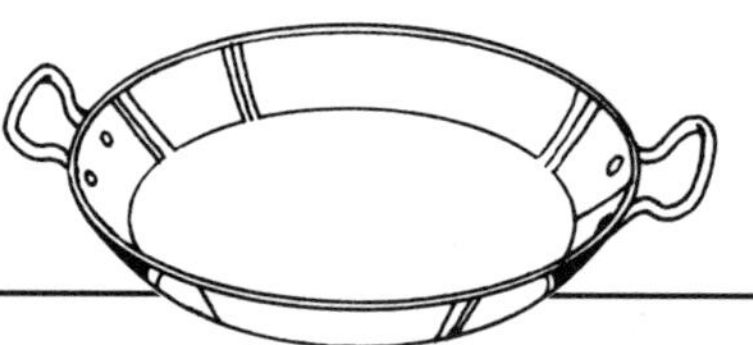

14–16-INCH SHALLOW PAELLA PAN

Paella might be called the national dish of Spain, though it differs a great deal from region to region. The rice may be mixed with rabbit and snails in one area; clams and tomato in another. Often, paella gets started on top of the stove and finished in the oven, so if you don't have a traditional paella pan, use an ovenproof skillet. Using a paella pan is not just an affectation: because it is very shallow, the rice cooks quickly and remains dry instead of getting steamed and mushy. This recipe may sound a bit long and complicated, but in fact the dish can be made in about an hour and a quarter, from start to finish. The secret is to have all the ingredients measured out and prepared before you start.

½ pound medium-sized shrimp (prawns)
1 tablespoon lemon juice
6 pieces chicken—legs, thighs or halved breasts
1 medium onion
2 cloves garlic
¼ pound ham
2 large tomatoes
2 red bell peppers
1 cup shelled peas
3½ cups chicken stock (page 107)
½ cup dry white vermouth
4 to 5 tablespoons olive oil
2 cups short-grain rice (American or Italian Arborio)
Salt
Freshly ground black pepper
Chopped parsley for garnish

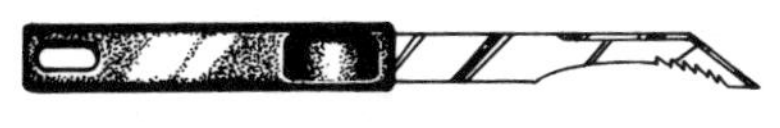

SHRIMP DEVEINER

PREPARE THE FOLLOWING BEFORE ASSEMBLING THE PAELLA

Peel shrimp and combine with lemon juice in a bowl. Skin chicken and trim off any fat. Peel and chop the onion and garlic. Dice the ham. Cut core from tomatoes and make a small cross at the blossom end. Dip in boiling water for 5 seconds to loosen skin. Peel, cut in half crossways and gently squeeze out seeds. Chop tomato. Roast the peppers over a gas burner or under broiler until blackened on all sides. Hold with tongs under cold running water and remove skins. Remove core and seeds from peppers and cut into small dice. Shell or defrost peas. Combine chicken stock and vermouth and heat.

Preheat oven to 350°. Heat the olive oil in paella pan. Season chicken pieces with a little salt and sauté on all sides for about 10 minutes, until golden. Remove and reserve. Add onion, garlic and ham to pan and cook for 3 minutes, until onion is transparent. Add tomatoes and bell peppers, stir and cook for 2 minutes more. Add shrimp with lemon juice and cook for 2 minutes, until pink. Remove shrimp and reserve. Add rice and stir until grains are coated with oil and opaque, about 3 minutes. Add fresh peas and then carefully stir in the hot chicken broth. (If peas are frozen, add just before placing in the oven.) Check seasoning and add salt and pepper if needed. Cook over moderate heat, uncovered, for 8 minutes, stirring occasionally. Most of the liquid should be absorbed, but mixture should not dry out. Check seasoning again. Arrange the shrimp and chicken pieces over the rice, burying shrimp and pushing chicken halfway under. Place pan in oven and bake uncovered for 15 minutes. Remove from oven, cover loosely with aluminum foil and let rest for 5 minutes to finish cooking. Garnish with chopped parsley and serve at once.

Serves 6.

Risotto with Zucchini

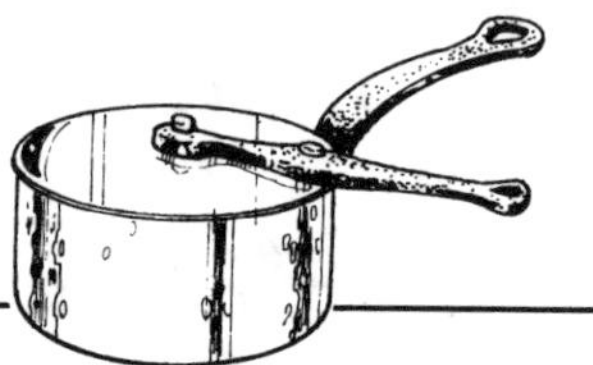

3-QUART SAUCEPAN

The zucchini in this dish develops concentrated flavor and a good chewy texture after the salting process, and makes a really good combination with the creamy rice. You *must* use imported Italian Arborio rice to get the authentic texture: the grains separate, yet creamy.

1 pound small zucchini
Salt
4 cups chicken stock (page 105)
4 ounces (1 stick) unsalted butter
1 medium onion, finely chopped
1 clove garlic, finely chopped
1 cup Arborio rice
½ cup dry white wine, heated
½ cup grated Parmesan cheese
Additional Parmesan cheese to serve at table (optional)

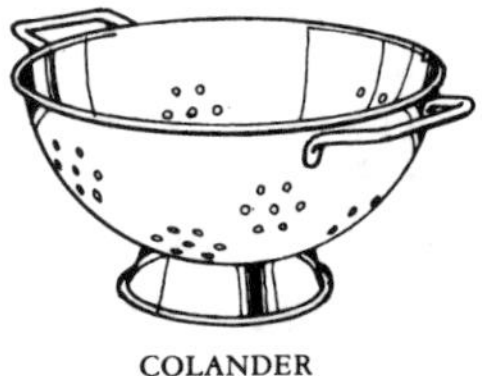

COLANDER

Trim both ends and cut zucchini into ¼-inch julienne strips 2½-inches long. Place in a colander, sprinkle well with salt and let drain for 1 hour. Rinse and pat dry on paper towels.

Heat stock and keep warm at a very low simmer. In a separate saucepan, melt 2 ounces of the butter and gently sauté onion until softened but not browned, about 3 minutes. Add garlic and stir in rice. Continue stirring until grains are transparent, about 2 minutes. Add heated wine and cook slowly, stirring, until liquid is absorbed. Then add 1 cup of the warm stock and cook until absorbed. Add the zucchini and keep stirring in remaining stock a half cup at a time—the rice should become neither dry nor soupy. This should take about 25 minutes; the rice should be creamy. Just before rice is ready, stir in cheese and mix. When ready to serve, stir in remaining butter. Serve with additional cheese if desired.

Serves 4.

Spätzle

SPÄTZLE MAKER

A pleasant change from potatoes or rice, and very fast to make, spätzle is a kind of tiny dumpling. If you don't have a spätzle sieve, push the mixture through the holes of a colander with a rubber spatula. It will separate into small teardrop shapes.

1 1/2 teaspoons salt
2 eggs
1/2 cup water
1 1/2 cups all-purpose flour
Pinch nutmeg
1/4 teaspoon baking powder
4 tablespoons grated Parmesan cheese
4 tablespoons unsalted butter, melted

Fill saucepan two-thirds full of water, add 1 teaspoon of the salt and bring to a boil.

In the meantime, beat the eggs in a large bowl. Add the water, flour, nutmeg, baking powder and remaining salt. Beat well, then push through spätzle sieve into the boiling water. Stir the spätzle to prevent them from sticking together and let boil for 3 minutes, until tender. The spätzle will swell and rise to the surface. Drain thoroughly and toss with the cheese and melted butter.

Serves 4.

Spoon Bread

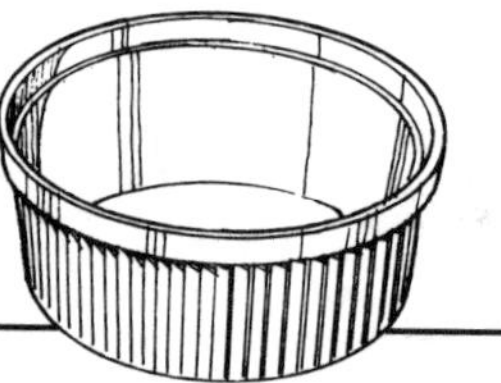
1½-QUART SOUFFLÉ DISH

This is really a kind of cornmeal soufflé that's delicious with pot roast or any entree that has lots of good gravy.

1½ cups milk
Freshly grated nutmeg
1 teaspoon salt
¾ cup yellow cornmeal
2 tablespoons unsalted butter, melted
3 egg yolks
1 teaspoon baking powder
2 tablespoons freshly grated Parmesan cheese
4 egg whites

Preheat oven to 425° and butter the soufflé dish. Put milk into saucepan, add a little nutmeg and the salt and bring to a boil. Remove from heat and gradually add the cornmeal, stirring vigorously to avoid lumps. Stir in the egg yolks, baking powder and grated cheese. Blend well. Beat the egg whites until soft peaks form and gently fold into cornmeal mixture. Pour into soufflé dish and bake for 10 minutes. Reduce heat to 375° and bake for 20 minutes more, until top is golden.

Serves 4.

BALLOON WHISK

Vegetables, Ham and Couscous

4-QUART SAUCEPOT

The French have used couscous as a substitute for rice for many years. I was introduced to it about twenty-eight years ago by my friend Mademoiselle Hermamse Ponposi, at her flat on the Boulevard St-Germain in Paris. It is too bad that the grain—actually it is semolina—has not caught on in this country. It takes only about 5 minutes to prepare and can be used in many ways—in desserts, casseroles, or as an accompaniment to meats, vegetables or stews. Incidentally, if the tomatoes in this recipe don't give off enough liquid, the dish may be too dry. Just add a little chicken stock in that case.

2 pounds tomatoes
3 tablespoons olive oil
2 medium onions, thinly sliced
2 cloves garlic, chopped
1 to 1¼ pounds cooked ham, in 1-inch dice
2 teaspoons Herbes de Provence *(page 175)*
3 stalks celery, sliced
1 green bell pepper, cored, seeded and sliced
1 pound summer or yellow squash, sliced
Salt
Freshly ground black pepper
2 cups couscous
1½ cups chicken stock (page 107), heated to boiling
1 tablespoon lemon juice
4 tablespoons unsalted butter

8-INCH SAUTÉ PAN

Fill saucepan with water and bring to a boil. Core the tomatoes and make a small cross at the blossom end. Dip in boiling water for 5 seconds to loosen skin. Peel, cut in half crossways and gently squeeze out seeds. Cut tomatoes in pieces and set aside. Heat the olive oil in the saucepot, add onions and garlic and sauté over gentle heat for 2 minutes, until transparent. Do not allow to brown. Add ham and herbs, stir and cook for 1 minute. Add the celery and tomatoes and cook over moderate heat for 10 minutes, stirring occasionally. Add the green pepper and squash and cook for another 5 minutes. Taste for seasoning and add salt and pepper if necessary.

Put couscous into a bowl, add the boiling chicken stock, lemon juice and 2 ounces of the butter. Stir, cover and let stand for 2 to 3 minutes until broth is absorbed. Melt remaining butter in the sauté pan, add the couscous, stir and cover. Let steam over low heat for 2 to 3 minutes, stirring several times. Do not let brown.

Spoon couscous onto warmed serving plates and add vegetables, ham and broth.

Serves 4.

POULTRY

Chicken with Eggplant and Marsala

10-INCH SAUTÉ PAN WITH COVER

I first had this dish in a small country hotel near Perugia, north of Rome. The motherly woman in the kitchen obligingly wrote down the ingredients for me and I figured out how to cook it when I got back to San Francisco, weeks later.

1 small eggplant, about ½ pound
Salt
2 medium tomatoes
3-pound chicken
2 strips lean bacon, diced
1 tablespoon unsalted butter
1 red bell pepper, cored, seeded and chopped
1 stalk celery, finely chopped
1 clove garlic, finely chopped
1 teaspoon fresh thyme, chopped, or ½ teaspoon dried
Freshly ground black pepper
½ cup Marsala

Cut eggplant, unpeeled, into 1-inch cubes. Put in colander, sprinkle well with salt and let drain for 1 hour. Rinse and blot dry with paper towels.

Core the tomatoes and make a small cross at the blossom end. Dip in boiling water for 5 seconds to loosen skin. Peel, cut in half crossways and gently squeeze out seeds. Chop tomatoes and reserve.

Wash and dry chicken and cut into serving pieces, discarding back. In sauté pan, fry bacon until almost crisp, remove with slotted spoon and set aside. Add butter to bacon fat in pan, heat and brown chicken on all sides, about 10 minutes. Push chicken pieces to edge of pan and add eggplant, bell pepper and celery, and sauté for 5 minutes. Stir in tomatoes and garlic and return bacon to pan. Season with thyme, salt and pepper. Add Marsala, reduce heat and partially cover pan. Simmer for 20 to 25 minutes until chicken is tender, turning pieces once. Check seasoning and serve immediately.

Serves 4.

COOKING FORK

Chicken and Ham Hash

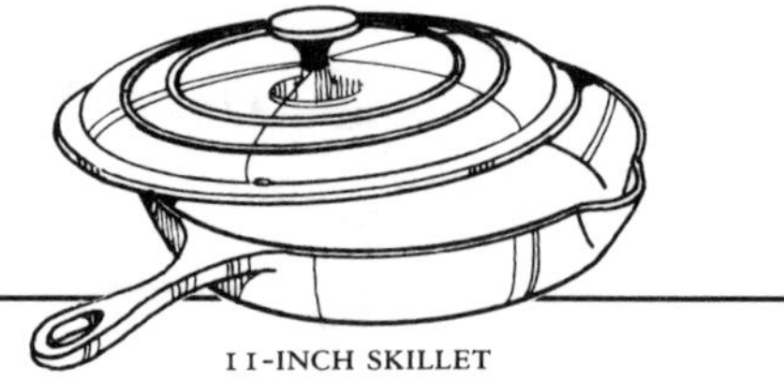

11-INCH SKILLET

A well-seasoned heavy skillet or a heavy one with a nonstick finish is best for this dish. You want the hash to brown but not stick.

4 tablespoons unsalted butter
1 medium onion, diced
1 stalk celery, diced
1/3 cup whole roasted canned pimiento, diced
2 cups boiled potato, diced
3/4 cup cooked ham, diced
2 1/2 cups poached or roasted boneless chicken, diced
1 teaspoon fresh marjoram, chopped, or 1/2 teaspoon dried
1 tablespoon lemon juice
Salt
Freshly ground black pepper

Melt 1 tablespoon of the butter in skillet, add onion, cover and cook gently for 2 minutes. Do not let brown. In a bowl, combine the celery, pimiento, potato, ham, chicken, marjoram and lemon juice. Add the onion, season with a little salt and pepper and mix well.

Melt remaining butter in skillet and add mixture. Pat down into a cake, partially cover and cook over low heat 10 to 15 minutes, until bottom is golden brown. With a spatula, turn mixture over a section at a time, pat down and brown the other side, about 10 minutes. Check seasoning and sprinkle with more salt and pepper if necessary.

Serves 4.

Chicken Breasts with Raspberry Vinegar

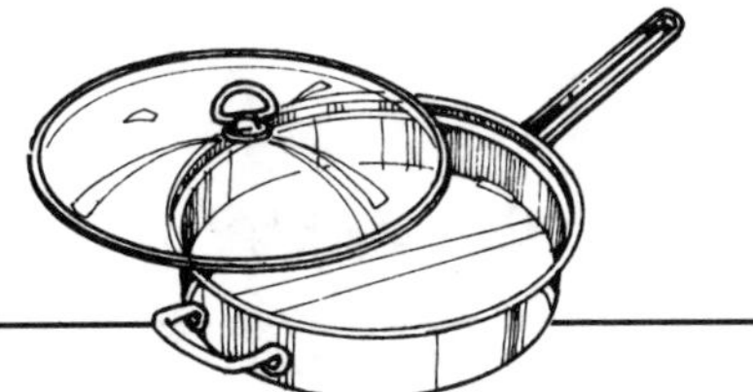

10-INCH SAUTÉ PAN

2 whole chicken breasts, about 1¼ pounds each
Salt
Freshly ground black pepper
4 tablespoons unsalted butter, clarified (page 182)
3 tablespoons chopped scallions
2 tablespoons raspberry vinegar (page 88)
¼ cup water

Remove skin from the whole chicken breasts and cut meat away from both sides of the breastbones, leaving 4 breast halves. On the underside of each you will see a long fillet of meat that can easily be pulled off with your fingers. Detach it, remove and discard the attached white tendon, and reserve the fillet. Lay the remaining piece of breast meat on a cutting board, skin side up. Hold flat with the palm of one hand and with a sharp knife slice the breast in two, parallel with the board. Repeat with the other breast halves. You will finish up with 8 thin oval slices plus 4 small fillets. Sprinkle pieces lightly with salt and pepper and set aside.

Heat butter in sauté pan and cook chicken pieces for 1 minute on each side, until opaque but not fully cooked. Do this in 2 batches to avoid overcrowding pan. Set aside and keep warm. Add scallions to pan, sauté for a few seconds and then add raspberry vinegar and water. Stir well to loosen all cooking residue. Return chicken to pan and cook for 1 minute, turning once. Check seasoning and serve immediately.

Serves 4.

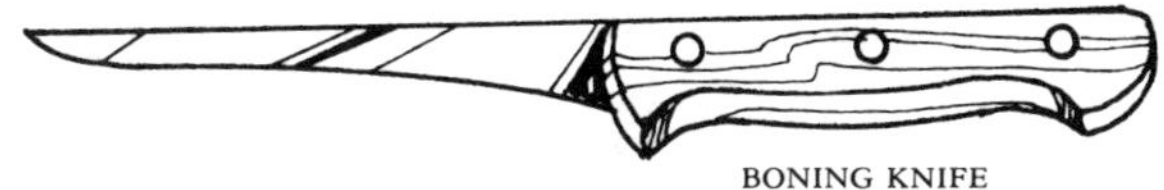

BONING KNIFE

Chicken Stew

10-INCH SAUTÉ PAN

This recipe makes a "stew" that is more like a soup. If you prefer a more traditional sauce, follow the optional instructions.

4 chicken thighs
4 chicken drumsticks
4 cups water
1 small onion, diced
½ stalk celery
Pinch dried thyme leaves
1 small bay leaf
½ teaspoon salt
2 sprigs parsley
2 medium tomatoes
6 small new potatoes, cut in half
2 medium carrots, diced
2 stalks celery, in 1-inch slices
¼ pound string beans, in 1½-inch pieces
2 medium zucchini, in ½-inch slices
Salt
Freshly ground black pepper
Chopped parsley for garnish
Hot noodles or rice

Optional Sauce Ingredients:

1 tablespoon unsalted butter
1 tablespoon flour
½ cup heavy cream
1 egg yolk

Wash and dry chicken pieces, removing any skin and fat from them. With a sharp knife, cut meat from the bones. Cut each piece of meat in two and set aside. Put bones and skin in saucepan with the water, bring to a boil and skim. Add the diced onion and celery, thyme, bay leaf, salt and parsley sprigs. Cover and simmer for 1 hour. Strain the broth, let stand for a few minutes and skim off fat. Cut core from tomatoes and make a small cross at the blossom end. Dip in boiling water for 5 seconds to loosen skin. Peel, cut in half crossways and gently squeeze out seeds. Chop tomatoes coarsely and set aside.

Pour broth into sauté pan. Bring to a boil and add chicken meat. Quickly return to simmering point and add potatoes, carrots and celery. Cover and simmer for 10 to 15 minutes. Lay string beans, zucchini and tomatoes on top of chicken and season with salt and pepper. Cover and simmer for 5 to 10 minutes more, until beans and zucchini are just cooked. Check seasoning and serve immediately, garnished with chopped parsley.

Accompany with crusty French bread. (It is best to serve this stew in soup plates, with the broth ladled over the chicken and vegetables.)

Serves 4.

If a thickened sauce is desired, remove chicken and vegetables to a serving platter and keep warm. In saucepan, melt butter, stir in flour and let cook for one minute. Add the hot chicken broth and stir until it boils and thickens slightly. Remove from heat.

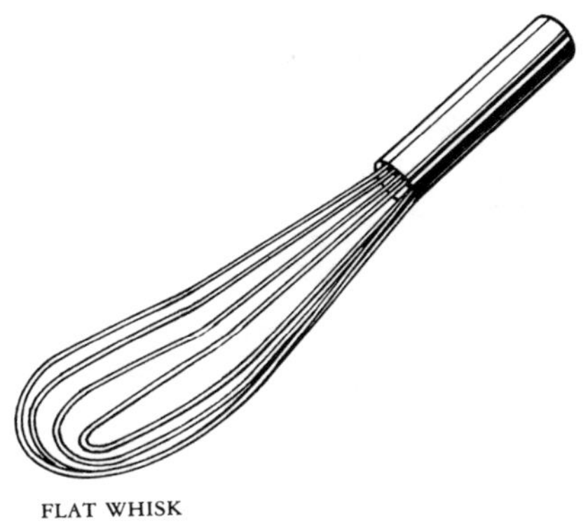
FLAT WHISK

Combine cream with egg yolk, stir in some of the broth, then stir this mixture into the pan of broth. Return to low heat and let cook, stirring, until thickened a little more: it should coat the spoon. Do not let boil.

Check seasoning, then pour over the chicken and vegetables, garnish with parsley and serve with noodles or rice.

Serves 4.

Chicken and Walnut Salad with Walnut Oil

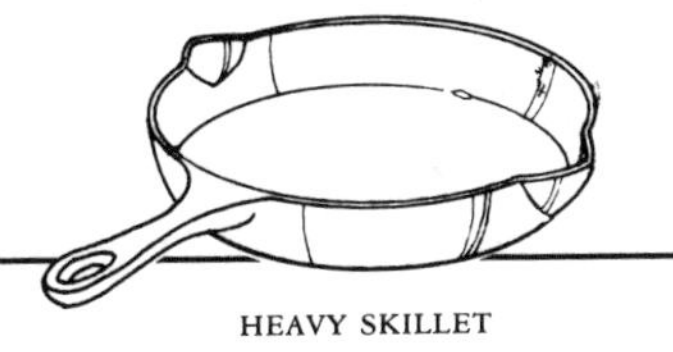
HEAVY SKILLET

¾ cups walnuts, coarsely chopped
3 cups poached or roasted chicken, in bite-sized pieces
1 cup celery, finely chopped
½ teaspoon salt
2 tablespoons mild white wine vinegar
3 tablespoons walnut oil (page 87)
3 tablespoons vegetable oil
Freshly ground black pepper
Lettuce leaves

In heavy skillet, over moderate heat, stir walnuts until lightly toasted, about 2 minutes. Set aside.

In bowl, combine chicken, celery and walnuts. Dissolve the salt in the vinegar and whisk in the walnut and vegetable oils. Season with pepper, whisking well. Pour over chicken mixture and toss together thoroughly. Let stand at room temperature for 15 minutes for flavors to blend and mellow. Divide between four plates lined with lettuce leaves.

Serves 4.

Clay Pot Chicken, Greek Style

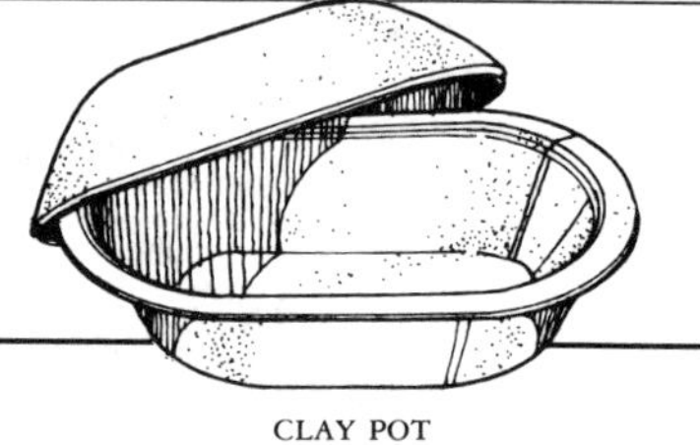

CLAY POT

This is a robust and savory country dish. Be sure to use brine- or dry-cured olives from Greece or Italy, not canned ripe olives.

3- to 3½-pound chicken
1 lemon, cut in half
1 piece cinnamon stick, 2½-inches long
2 medium potatoes, in 1½-inch chunks
2 stalks celery, in ¼- x 2-inch-long sticks
2 medium carrots, in ¼- x 2-inch-long sticks
1 medium onion, in small chunks
2 cloves garlic, minced
3 sprigs fresh oregano, or ½ teaspoon dried
Salt
Freshly ground black pepper
1 tablespoon olive oil
¼ cup dry white wine, heated
12 black olives, halved and pitted

Soak top and bottom of clay pot in cold water for 15 minutes. While pot is soaking, wash and dry chicken, remove any loose fat and cut off and discard wing tips. Rub bird inside and out with one of the lemon halves, squeezing out some of the juice as you do so. Place both lemon halves and the cinnamon stick inside chicken cavity.

In a bowl, combine potatoes, celery, carrots, onion and garlic. Season with the oregano, salt and pepper, and toss lightly.

Place vegetables in bottom of clay pot and lay chicken on top, breast side up. Rub bird with ½ tablespoon of the olive oil and sprinkle with salt and pepper. Cover pot and place in cold oven. Turn heat to 500° and bake for 45 minutes. Remove from oven, uncover and tip pot slightly so that the aromatic juices which will have collected inside the chicken can run out over the vegetables. Pour in wine and push the olives down among the vegetables. Drizzle remaining oil over chicken and bake uncovered for 15 minutes more, until nicely browned and crisp. Allow chicken to rest for 5 minutes on a warmed platter before carving. Pour any accumulated juices from casserole into a small bowl and remove fat. Pour over vegetables.

Serves 4.

Grilled Chicken with Paprika

BASTING BRUSH

This is a very simple grilled chicken recipe, and a very good one. Be careful not to place the chicken too close to the heat, or the yogurt coating will burn. Watch it carefully. If you like, you can line the broiler pan with aluminum foil, which makes clean-up easier. The chicken can also be done in the top section of a hot oven.

2½- to 3-pound chicken
½ cup unflavored yogurt
3 teaspoons paprika
1 clove garlic, finely chopped
Salt
Freshly ground black pepper

Heat broiler, and oil the grid or rack of broiler pan.

Wash and dry chicken. Cut into 8 serving pieces, discarding back and neck, or cut into 4 quarters. Trim off any fat. Combine yogurt, paprika and garlic in bowl and mix well.

Season the chicken pieces with salt and pepper and place on broiler rack, skin side down. Brush with a coating of the yogurt mixture. Place under broiler about 2 to 3 inches below heat and cook for 10 minutes, basting once or twice. Turn chicken pieces over and brush with yogurt mixture. Cook for 10 minutes more, basting twice with yogurt mixture. Turn again, baste and cook for another 5 to 6 minutes. Check for doneness by piercing thigh with a sharp knife: juice should run slightly pink or clear. Be sure chicken is done, but do not overcook. Serve at once.

Serves 4.

Oriental Chicken

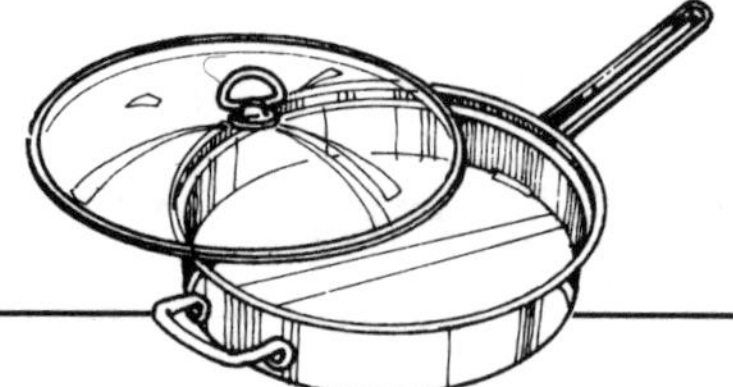

10-INCH SAUTÉ PAN

I had this dish in Canton recently, and when I got home I reproduced it as best I could from what I remembered. I was surprised to find sweet potatoes in China, but had them there several times.

2 pounds chicken thighs and breasts
1 large sweet potato
1 medium leek
1 tablespoon unsalted butter
2 cups chicken stock (page 107)
2 tablespoons dry sherry
1 red bell pepper, in strips
2 ounces smoked ham, in 1-inch strips
½-inch piece fresh ginger root, peeled and thinly sliced
Salt
Freshly ground black pepper

Remove skin and bones from chicken and trim off any fat. Cut thigh meat in half and breasts in 3 pieces. Set aside. Peel the sweet potato, cut into ¾-inch cubes and put in saucepan. Cover with water, bring to a boil and cook for 10 minutes. Drain and reserve. Clean leek thoroughly, discard green top and cut white part into ⅛-inch pieces. Melt butter in sauté pan. Add leek and sauté for 2 minutes. Do not let brown. Add the chicken stock and sherry and bring to a boil. Add chicken meat, sweet potato, bell pepper, ham and ginger. Season with salt and pepper. Cover and simmer for 20 minutes. Check seasoning and serve at once with rice.

Serves 4.

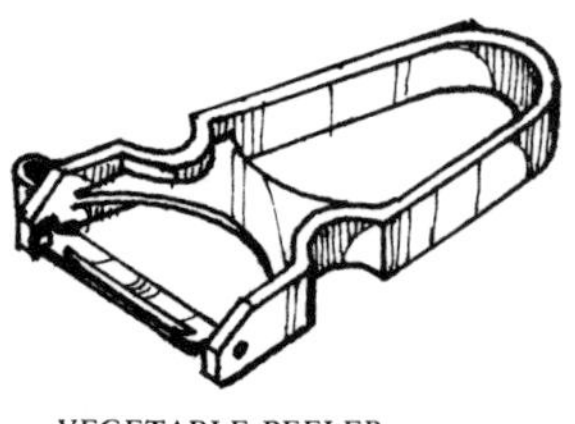

VEGETABLE PEELER

Pot-Roasted Chicken with Fennel Seeds

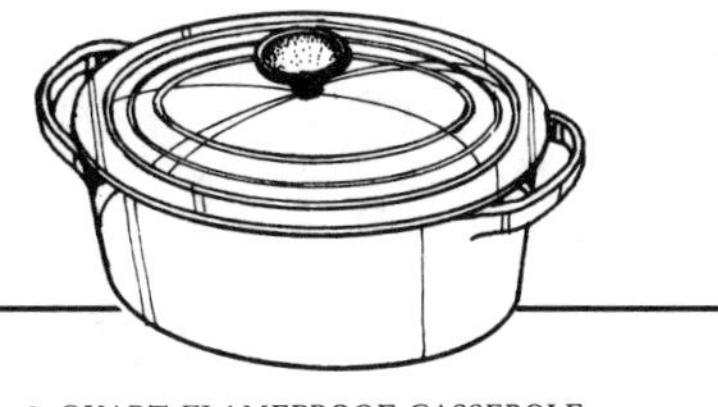

3-QUART FLAMEPROOF CASSEROLE

This is my version of a dish that is typical of those you'll find in good, unpretentious Tuscan restaurants. Pot roasting a whole chicken is an exceptionally successful idea. The dish really doesn't need precise timing; it won't matter if it stays a while longer than necessary in the oven. Don't discard any leftover cooking juices. When chilled, they turn into a very aromatic jelly that can be used to flavor and enrich another sauce, perhaps for plain sautéed breast of chicken.

2½- to 3-pound chicken
1 lemon, cut in half
12 black peppercorns, coarsely crushed
3 cloves garlic
1 teaspoon fennel seeds
1 tablespoon olive oil
Salt
4 bay leaves
4 tablespoons brandy

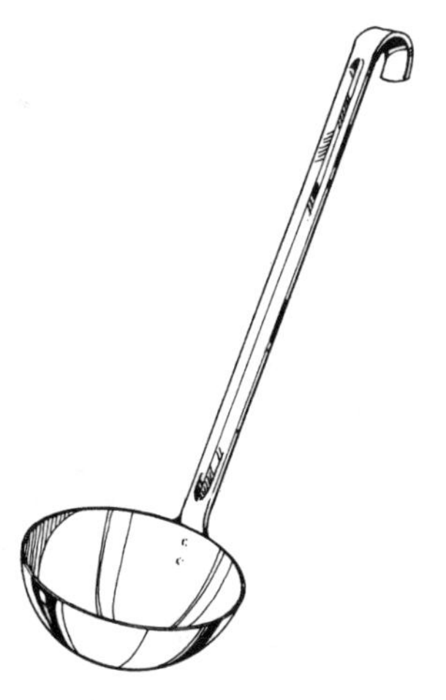

LADLE

Preheat oven to 400°. Wash and dry chicken, remove any loose fat and rub inside and out with one of the lemon halves. Place both lemon halves inside the chicken, together with peppercorns, garlic and ½ teaspoon of the fennel seeds.

Rub outside of chicken with olive oil and place on its side in the casserole. Sprinkle with salt and remaining fennel seeds, and tuck bay leaves under the bird. Cover, place in oven and bake for 30 minutes. Turn chicken over, basting with accumulated juices, and cook, covered, for 30 minutes more. Turn chicken breast side up, baste once again, and allow to roast uncovered for a further 15 minutes.

Transfer casserole to top of stove. Pour brandy into a ladle, warm it and ignite carefully. Pour the flaming brandy over the chicken. After flame has died down, put chicken on a serving platter and keep warm. Strain juices from casserole and skim off fat. Transfer this light sauce to a warmed sauceboat.

Serves 4.

Roast Duck with Parsnips

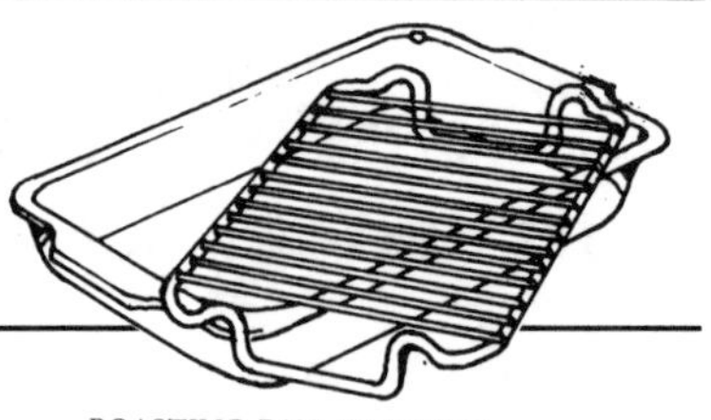
ROASTING PAN AND RACK

4- to 5-pound fresh duck, including neck, gizzard and heart
2 small onions, diced
1 whole clove
1 stalk celery
1 bay leaf
2 sprigs parsley
4 sprigs fresh marjoram or ¼ teaspoon dried
Salt
3 cups water
½ lemon
1 pound parsnips
2 tablespoons dark-brown sugar
¼ cup Marsala

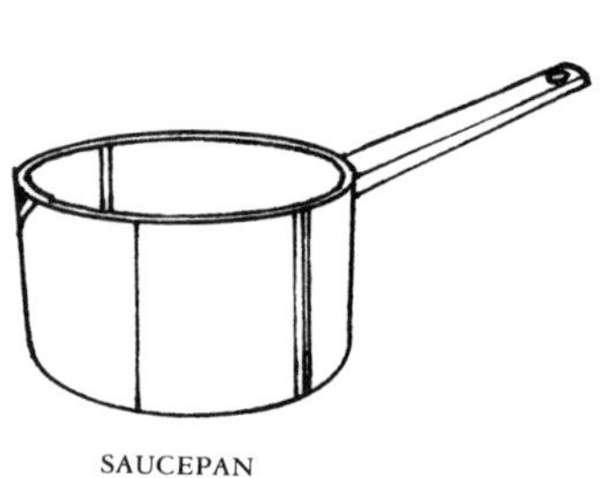
SAUCEPAN

Preheat oven to 350°. Remove wing tips from duck and place in saucepan, together with the neck, gizzard and heart. Add half the onion, the clove, celery, bay leaf, parsley and half the marjoram. Add ½ teaspoon salt and the water. Partially cover and simmer for 1½ hours. Strain, let stand for 5 minutes, remove fat and reserve.

Wash the duck thoroughly and dry well. Rub inside of cavity with the lemon half, squeezing out some of the juice. Leave lemon inside, together with remaining onion, marjoram and ½ teaspoon salt. Place duck on roasting rack breast side down, put rack in roasting pan, place in oven and roast for 45 minutes. Turn duck, prick the skin all over to let fat drain off and roast for another 45 minutes. Prick the skin several times during roasting.

While duck is cooking, peel and slice the parsnips into ¼-inch pieces. Place in saucepan, cover with water, add ½ teaspoon salt and partially cover. Let cook for 20 minutes, until just tender. Drain and set aside.

At end of roasting time, test to see if duck is done by wiggling a leg: it should be loose. Or pierce thigh with a knife tip: juice should run pink for medium rare. A meat thermometer inserted in the thigh should read 180°. If you like duck well done, roast for 10 to 20 minutes more. (Meat will be rather dry, be warned!) Remove duck, pouring off accumulated liquid from cavity into roasting pan, and place on warmed platter. Keep warm.

Remove fat from the juices in the roasting pan. Place pan on top of stove over moderate heat and loosen any brown particles stuck to the pan with a wooden spoon. Add 2 cups of the reserved duck stock,

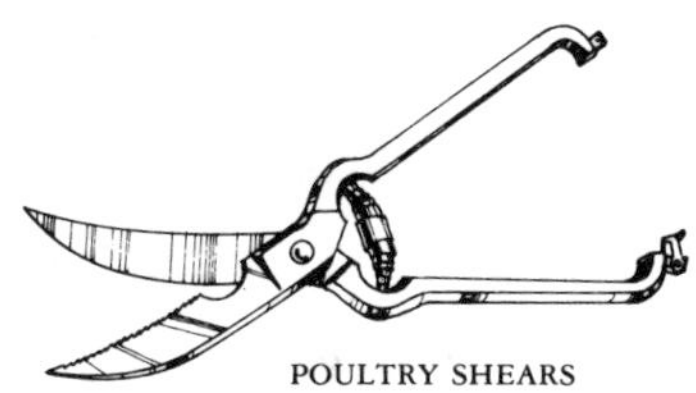
POULTRY SHEARS

the brown sugar and the Marsala. Let boil for 2 minutes to reduce and thicken slightly. Check seasoning. Add the parsnips and cook for another minute. Cut the duck into 4 pieces with poultry shears, discarding backbone. Add any accumulated juices to the roasting pan. Serve duck with parsnips and sauce.

Serves 4.

Roast Turkey with Herbes de Provence

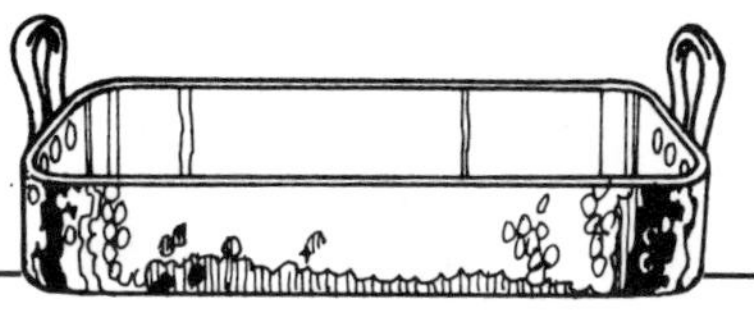
ROASTING PAN

10-pound turkey, at room temperature
1 lemon
3 stalks celery
2 medium onions
1 teaspoon salt
2 cloves garlic
3 sprigs parsley
4 teaspoons Herbes de Provence *(page 175)*
2 tablespoons olive oil
2 cups boiling water

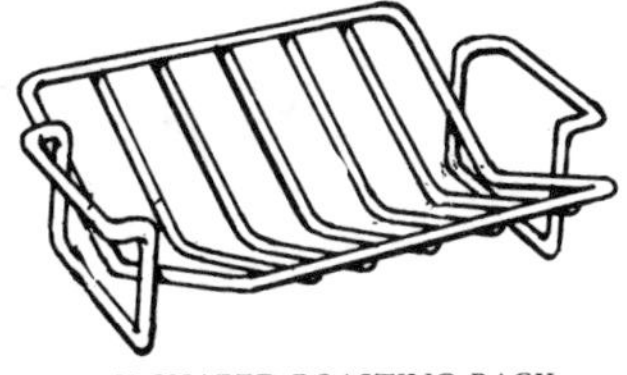
V-SHAPED ROASTING RACK

Preheat oven to 325°. Trim and remove any pin feathers from turkey. Wash and dry both inside and out.

Cut the lemon in half and rub inside of bird with one of the halves, squeezing out some of the juice as you do so. Place both halves inside the turkey. Cut one of the celery stalks into 1-inch pieces and quarter one of the onions. Combine with the salt, garlic, parsley and 2 teaspoons of the *Herbes de Provence.* Place inside the bird. Sprinkle half the remaining *Herbes* in the neck opening. Truss by tying the legs together and the wings close to the body. Rub the outside of the turkey with the olive oil and the remaining *Herbes.*

Lay turkey, breast side down, on a rack and place rack in roasting pan. Slice remaining celery and onion and add to pan. Add the boiling water. Transfer to oven and bake for 30 minutes. Turn turkey on its side, baste with pan juices and bake for another 45 minutes. Turn on its other side, baste and bake another 45 minutes. Turn turkey breast side up, baste and bake for a further 30 minutes, basting once or twice more. Check for doneness by wiggling one of the legs; when

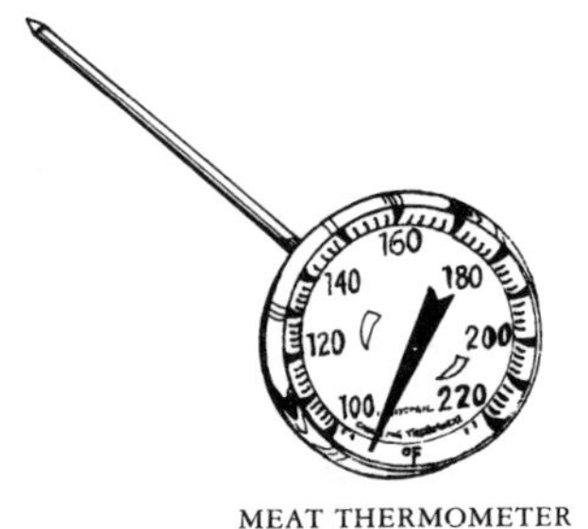

MEAT THERMOMETER

done it should move easily. Or pierce one thigh with a sharp knife—the juices will run clear when done. A meat thermometer inserted in the thickest part of the thigh, without touching bone, should register 170° to 175°.

Transfer turkey to hot platter, cover loosely with foil and let rest for 15 minutes before carving.

Serves 10 to 12 with leftovers.

Turkey Gravy

FLAT WHISK

While turkey is resting, make the gravy.

4 tablespoons fat from roasting pan
3 tablespoons all-purpose flour
2 cups chicken stock (page 105), heated
1 tablespoon brandy
Salt
Freshly ground black pepper

Place roasting pan on top of stove and remove all but 4 tablespoons of the fat. Heat pan, scraping up all the browned bits on the bottom, and stir in the flour. Let cook over moderate heat for 3 to 4 minutes, stirring, until flour is lightly browned. Slowly add the stock and stir until smooth. Add brandy and allow to simmer over low heat for 10 minutes. Taste for seasoning, adding salt and pepper if desired, and strain into warmed sauceboat.

Makes approximately 2 cups.

Herbes de Provence

SMALL BOWL

This is typical of the herb blends used in southern France. Some specialty food stores in this country import it in clay crocks; or you can make your own, using the most aromatic whole dried herbs (not powdered) you can find. You may have to look for dried lavender in a shop that sells soaps and body lotions.

I like to crumble a little of this mixture into the olive oil before I sauté vegetables such as zucchini or sliced potatoes, and it does great things for meats or poultry oven-roasted or cooked on a barbecue.

2 tablespoons dried thyme
2 tablespoons dried summer savory
2 tablespoons dried basil
1 teaspoon fennel seeds
½ teaspoon dried lavender

Combine all the herbs in a small bowl and store in an airtight container.

Makes about ¼ cup.

Chestnut and Sausage Dressing for Roast Turkey

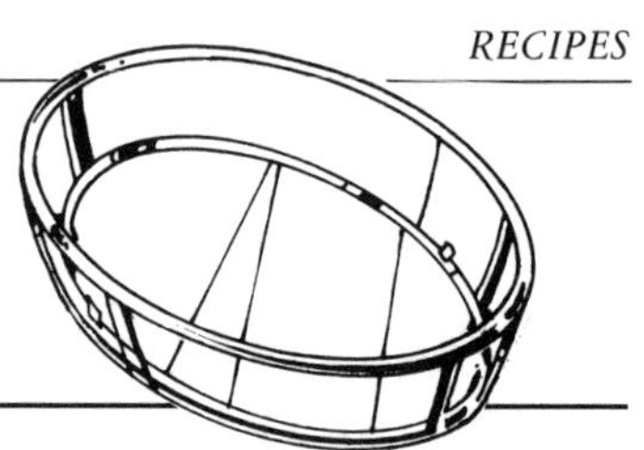

3-QUART BAKING DISH

I much prefer to bake poultry dressing in a separate dish. I think you get a better flavor and texture. I don't believe that stuffing does a thing for most birds; it just lengthens the cooking time. You can get far more flavor by putting a lemon, some celery, onion and aromatic herbs inside a turkey. You can, if you like, use ready-prepared chestnuts imported from France in this recipe. Remember to dry the bread chunks the night before the turkey is to be cooked.

1-pound loaf French bread
3 tablespoons unsalted butter
1 medium onion, chopped
1 stalk celery, chopped
½ pound fresh bulk pork sausage, crumbled
¼ pound ground beef
1 quart milk
1 pound roasted, shelled chestnuts, chopped (see below)
3 tablespoons parsley, chopped
Salt
Freshly ground black pepper
1 teaspoon fresh thyme, chopped, or ½ teaspoon dried, optional

Tear bread into small chunks, spread out on a baking sheet and leave to dry overnight.

Preheat oven to 375° and grease baking dish. In skillet, heat the butter and sauté onion and celery until transparent, about 2 minutes. Do not let brown. Remove with slotted spoon and reserve. In the same pan, sauté crumbled sausage meat and ground beef, stirring and mashing with a fork, until cooked through—about 10 minutes. Drain off fat.

Soak the bread in as much milk as it will absorb, using the whole quart if necessary. Add the onion and celery, meat mixture, chestnuts and parsley. Season with salt and pepper, adding thyme if sausage meat is bland. Mix well. Place in baking dish and bake for 1¼ to 1½ hours until nicely browned.

Serves 10 to 12.

Roast Chestnuts

Preheat oven to 450°. With a sharp paring knife or short-bladed chestnut knife, cut a ½-inch cross on the flat side of each chestnut, cutting through the shell. Spread nuts out on a cookie sheet and bake for 15 to 20 minutes, until shells open. When cool enough to handle, peel chestnuts. Be sure to do this while they are still warm. You will probably need 2 pounds of chestnuts for a pound of shelled meats.

Sautéed Turkey Breast, Kashmiri-Style

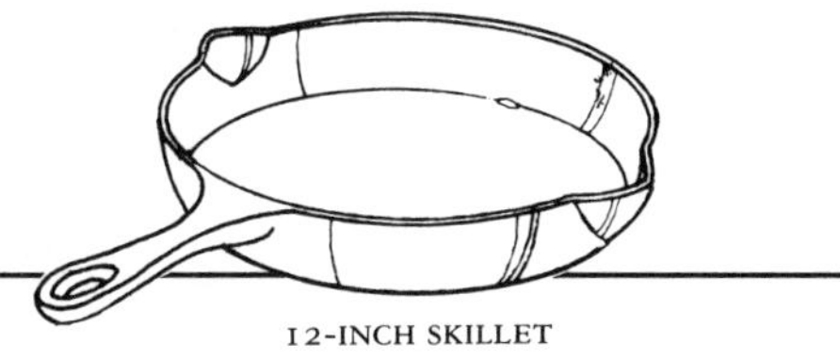
12-INCH SKILLET

Turkey scaloppine (thinly sliced breast meat) is fast to prepare and can be seasoned in many different ways. I sometimes use an Indian spice mixture, reminiscent of one I enjoyed forty years ago, when I lived there. This dish takes only a few minutes to cook, so be sure to prepare your rice ahead of time.

2 medium tomatoes
1 pound turkey breast meat, skinned and boned, in 1/4-inch slices
Flour
4 tablespoons (1/2 stick) unsalted butter
Salt
Freshly ground black pepper
1/4 teaspoon ground turmeric
1/4 teaspoon ground cumin
1/8 teaspoon ground cayenne
1/8 teaspoon ground cloves
1/4 teaspoon ground cinnamon
2 medium onions, finely chopped
1-inch piece of ginger root, peeled and thinly sliced
3/4 cup chicken stock (page 105)
Boiled rice
Curry condiments (optional)

SLOTTED SPOON

Core the tomatoes and make a small cross at the blossom end. Dip in boiling water for 5 seconds to loosen skin. Peel, cut in half crossways and gently squeeze out seeds. Chop tomatoes and reserve.

Dredge turkey slices lightly in flour, shaking off excess. Heat 2 tablespoons of the butter in skillet and cook the slices over medium high heat for 2 minutes, turning once. They should be only just cooked. Do this in 2 batches to avoid overcrowding pan. Remove with slotted spoon, sprinkle lightly with salt and black pepper and reserve.

In a small bowl, combine turmeric, cumin, cayenne, cloves and cinnamon. Add remaining butter to pan and stir in spice blend. Let cook over low heat for 1 minute. Add the onions and sauté until transparent, about 3 minutes. Stir in tomatoes, ginger root, chicken stock and a little salt. Let simmer for 10 minutes and taste for seasoning. Return turkey to pan and heat for 1 minute. Serve with boiled rice and, if you like, condiments such as Indian mango chutney, sliced banana, shredded coconut and chopped peanuts.

Serves 4.

MEATS

Braised Beef

9-INCH DEEP SAUTÉ PAN WITH COVER

This is one of the best beef dishes I know, because it's so honest. It tastes only of itself. I like to use boneless beef shoulder or chuck for the best flavor and texture. Don't think that you've made a mistake if when, at the end, there's only about ¾ cup of gravy—it's not meant to be soupy. Be sure to use a heavy pan with a tight-fitting cover.

2 pounds lean stewing beef
Flour
4 tablespoons olive oil
1 small onion, thinly sliced
1 clove garlic
1 bay leaf
3 sprigs fresh thyme or ¼ teaspoon dried
3 strips orange peel, colored part only, ½" x 2", stuck with 3 whole cloves
3 sprigs parsley
½ cup dry vermouth
1 medium carrot, very thinly sliced
1 stalk celery, very thinly sliced
1 medium leek, white part only, well washed and thinly sliced
1 teaspoon salt
Freshly ground black pepper
Freshly cooked noodles

Trim the meat of all fat and cut into 1-inch cubes. Dredge lightly in flour, shaking off excess. Heat the olive oil in sauté pan. Add meat and brown on all sides. Do this in 2 batches to avoid overcrowding pan. Remove with slotted spoon and set aside. Add onion and garlic to pan and let cook, stirring, until transparent, about 2 minutes. Remove with slotted spoon and set aside with the meat. Pour off any fat from pan. Return meat, onion and garlic to pan and add the bay leaf, thyme, orange peel and cloves, parsley and vermouth. Tightly cover and simmer very slowly for 1½ hours. Check liquid during cooking, and if it evaporates too much, add a little more vermouth. Add the carrot, celery and leek, season with salt and pepper and cook for 20 to 25 minutes more. Remove parsley, fresh thyme sprigs, bay leaf, garlic and orange peel. Check seasoning and serve with noodles.

Serves 4.

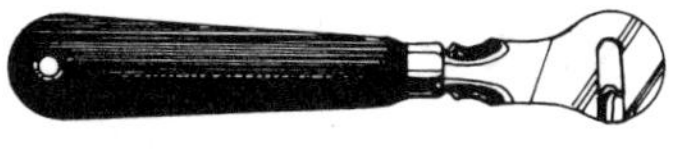

LEMON STRIPPER

Braised Loin of Pork with Orange

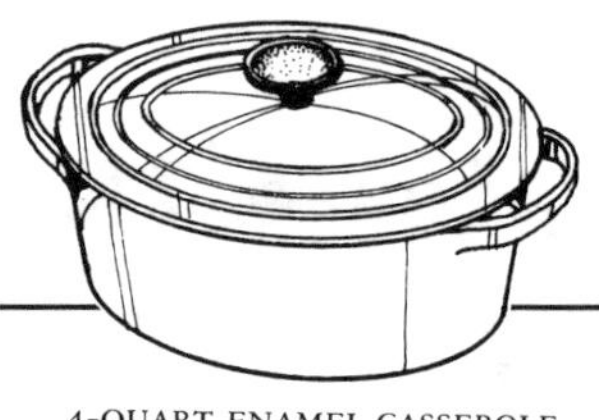

4-QUART ENAMEL CASSEROLE

In 1963 I brought home from Paris a copy of *Les Recettes de Mapie,* a collection of recipes by the Comtesse Guy de Toulouse-Lautrec. Inspired, I translated from the French and tried my own version of her pork loin with orange on a number of friends and pretty soon it seemed that everyone in the Bay Area was serving it. It's best to use clarified butter for browning the meat, otherwise the butter tends to burn.

4 ounces (1 stick) butter, in small cubes
2½- to 3-pound loin of pork, boneless, fat removed
4 medium carrots, thinly sliced
1 teaspoon fresh thyme, chopped, or ½ teaspoon dried
1 bay leaf
4 tablespoons Cognac
1 cup dry white wine, slightly warmed
½ teaspoon salt
Freshly ground black pepper
3 oranges

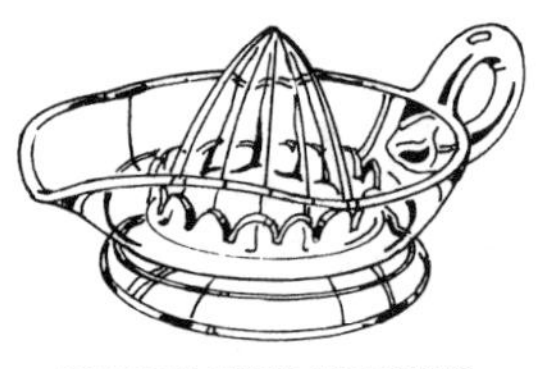

ORANGE JUICE SQUEEZER

Melt butter in saucepan over very low heat. Remove from heat and let set for a minute to settle, then skim foam off top and pour yellow liquid into a cup, leaving the milky solids in the pan. The clear yellow liquid is clarified butter.

Heat the clarified butter in the casserole, which should be just large enough to hold the meat easily. Brown pork on all sides, remove and reserve. Add carrots to casserole and toss until slightly browned. Add thyme and bay leaf. Return meat to casserole. Heat Cognac in a ladle, ignite carefully and pour over meat. When flame dies down, pour wine over meat and season with the salt and pepper to taste. Cover pan and simmer for about 2 hours or until meat is very tender. Remove meat and keep warm. Discard bay leaf.

Skim fat from meat juices and boil juices down to 1 cup. Pare the colored part of the peel from one of the oranges and cut into tiny strips. Blanch in boiling water for 2 minutes and drain. Squeeze juice from the orange and add to sauce, together with drained peel. Simmer for 10 minutes.

Cut the other oranges into ¼-inch slices and arrange around serving platter. Place pork in center and pour sauce over it.

Serves 4 to 6.

Braised Pork Chops with Capers

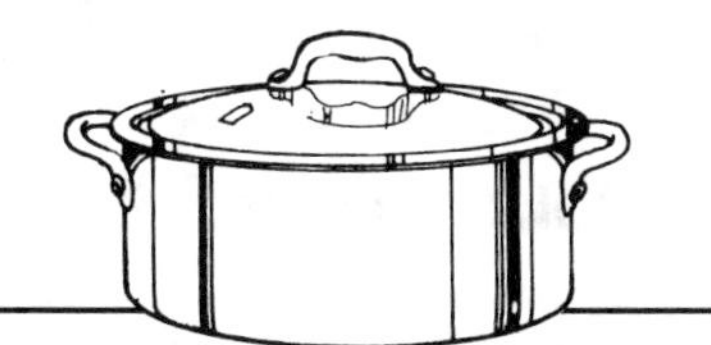

2-QUART SHALLOW CASSEROLE WITH COVER

4 tablespoons (½ stick) unsalted butter
4 double pork chops, 1½-inches thick
½ teaspoon salt
2 medium onions, thinly sliced
2 stalks celery, thinly sliced
1 cup dry white wine or vermouth
1 cup water
4 sprigs parsley
2 tablespoons Dijon mustard
4 teaspoons capers
4 tablespoons heavy cream

Preheat oven to 325°. Heat butter in skillet and brown the chops carefully on both sides. Do not let butter burn. Transfer to shallow casserole and season with salt. Sauté the onions and celery in the same skillet until softened but not browned, about 3 minutes. Add wine and water, bring to a boil and pour over chops. Place parsley on top. Cover and bake for 1 to 1¼ hours, until meat is tender. Remove chops and keep warm. Strain the juices into small pan and remove fat. Add mustard, capers and cream to juices and simmer for a few minutes. Pour over chops and serve at once.

Serves 4.

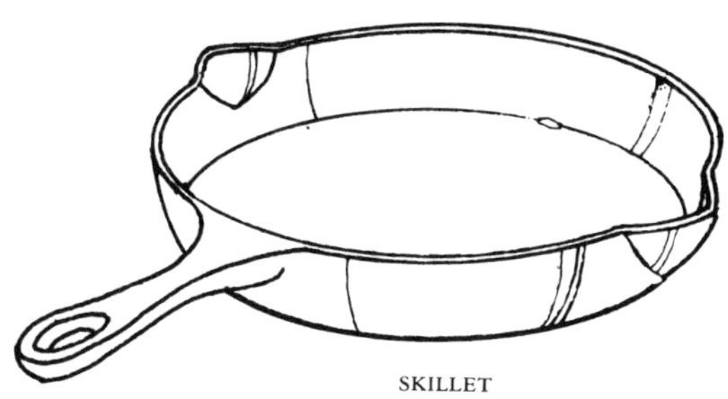

SKILLET

Choucroute Garnie

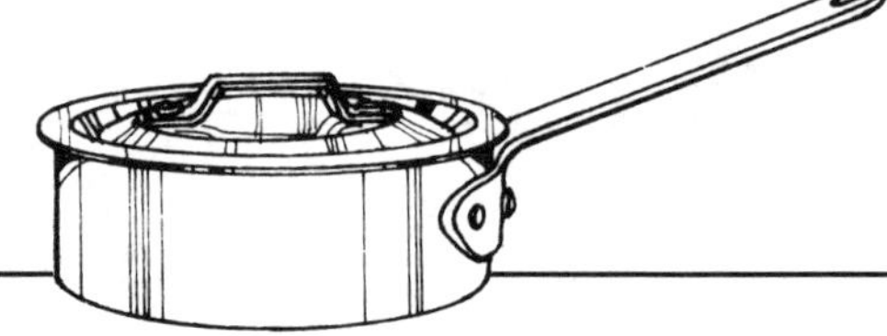
3-QUART SHALLOW SAUCEPAN

Serve this dish with a fruity white wine such as Gewurztraminer from Alsace.

3 pounds sauerkraut (bulk, canned or in a jar)
4 ounces (1 stick) unsalted butter
1 medium-sized onion, chopped fine
15 juniper berries
½ cup dry white wine
3 cups chicken stock (page 105)
2-pound piece of cooked ham
12 strips thick-cut lean bacon
12 best-quality veal frankfurters
12 small new potatoes, peeled

Rinse sauerkraut in 3 changes of water and squeeze dry. Heat butter in a large sauté pan or low wide saucepan and cook onion until transparent but not browned, about 2 minutes. Add sauerkraut, juniper berries, wine and ½ cup of the chicken stock. Stir with a wooden fork and then simmer very slowly, covered, for 1½ hours. There should never be more than about an inch of liquid in the pan; add more chicken stock if necessary.

Half an hour before the sauerkraut is ready, gently poach the ham and the bacon in the rest of the chicken stock for 20 to 30 minutes. Drain and cut ham into ¼-inch slices. In a separate pan, poach the frankfurters for 10 minutes, starting them in cold water and letting it come to a gentle simmer. In a third pan, boil potatoes in salted water until tender, about 20 minutes.

Heap the sauerkraut in the center of a large warmed platter, and surround with ham, bacon, frankfurters and potatoes.

Serves 6.

WOODEN FORK

Gigot de Sept Heures (Seven-hour leg of lamb)

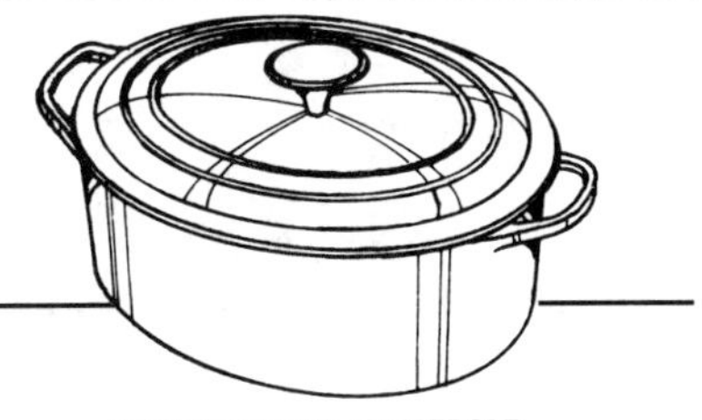
HEAVY ENAMEL CASSEROLE

I usually like rare lamb, but this old French country dish is extremely succulent; the meat just falls off the bone and in fact you "carve" it with a spoon. I find that the best pan to use is a heavy, oval, enameled cast-iron casserole, but you could also use an enameled steel one. In any event, measure your pan before buying the lamb and request a piece of meat that will just fit inside it; in other words have the butcher saw off the protruding shank bone. Glazed onions and poached tomatoes are good with this dish.

3 tablespoons unsalted butter
1 tablespoon cooking oil
2 onions, sliced
2 carrots, sliced
5- to 6-pound leg of lamb, all excess fat removed
3 to 4 cups white wine
2 cloves garlic, chopped
2 tablespoons tomato paste
Salt
Freshly ground black pepper

Heat butter and oil in the casserole. Sauté onions and carrots until onions are transparent but not browned, about 2 minutes. Remove vegetables and set aside. Brown meat on all sides. Draw off fat with a bulb baster. Return vegetables to casserole and pour in enough wine to reach halfway up the sides of the lamb. Add garlic, tomato paste and a little salt and freshly ground black pepper. Cover tightly and keep at a very low simmer for 5 to 6 hours, turning the lamb several times during cooking. Add more wine if necessary.

Transfer lamb to a serving dish and keep warm. Strain the juices, let rest for a few minutes and remove fat. Adjust seasoning if necessary and pour into a sauceboat.

Serves 6 to 8.

BULB BASTER

Lamb and Zucchini Moussaka

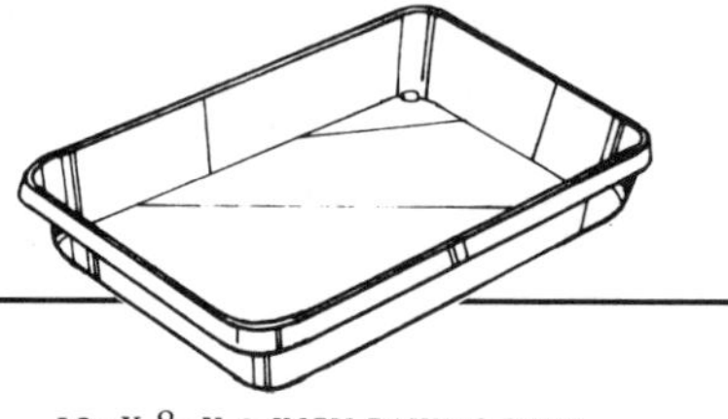

10- X 8- X 2-INCH BAKING DISH

One year, when I was trying to keep ahead of the zucchini vines that took over my modest vegetable garden in Sonoma, I invented this version of moussaka. Now I prefer this to the more traditional eggplant version.

4 to 5 medium zucchini
Salt
3 medium tomatoes
3 to 4 tablespoons olive oil
1 onion, chopped
1 clove garlic, chopped
1 pound ground lamb
1 teaspoon fresh oregano, chopped, or 1/2 teaspoon dried
2 eggs
1 cup fresh breadcrumbs
1/4 cup grated Parmesan or Romano cheese
1/4 cup chicken stock (page 105) or tomato juice

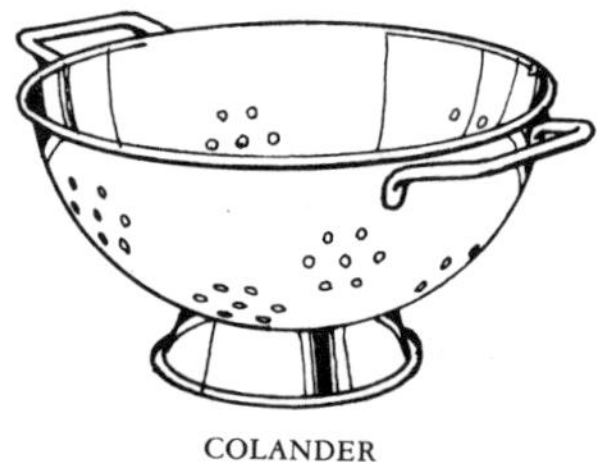

COLANDER

Cut zucchini lengthways into 1/4-inch thick slices. Arrange in a colander, overlapping as little as possible, sprinkle well with salt and let drain for 1 hour. Rinse and blot dry with paper towels.

Cut core from tomatoes and make a small cross at the blossom end. Dip in boiling water for 5 seconds to loosen skin. Peel, cut in half crossways and gently squeeze out seeds. Chop tomatoes finely.

Preheat oven to 375° and grease the baking dish. Heat the olive oil in sauté pan and sauté zucchini until lightly browned, about 5 minutes. Do this in 2 batches if necessary, adding more oil if needed. Remove with slotted spoon and set aside. In the same pan, sauté onion and garlic until transparent, about 3 minutes. Add ground lamb and let it brown slightly, breaking it up with a fork. Pour off any accumulated fat. Season with salt and the oregano. Remove from heat and let cool a little. Break eggs into a bowl, beat lightly and stir into meat mixture. Set aside.

Put half the prepared zucchini, in one layer and overlapping if necessary, in the baking dish. Cover with meat mixture, then the tomatoes and place the remaining zucchini in a layer on top. Mix breadcrumbs with cheese and sprinkle over zucchini. Moisten with stock or tomato juice. Bake for 35 minutes on middle rack of oven until mixture is cooked through and top is brown.

Serves 4.

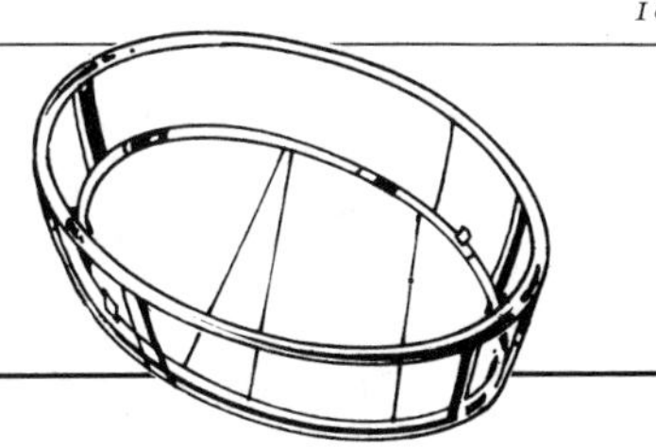

Leg of Lamb with Beans

BAKING DISH

1 pound dried white beans
1 stalk celery, cut in two
1 carrot, cut in two
1 medium onion, cut in two
1 bay leaf
4 ounces (1 stick) unsalted butter
2 pounds onions, sliced thin
2 pounds potatoes, sliced thin
Salt
Freshly ground black pepper
6- to 7-pound leg of lamb
1 cup chicken stock (page 105), warmed

Soak the beans overnight in plenty of water. Drain, place in pot, cover with fresh water and add celery, carrot, onion and bay leaf. Simmer until almost done but still firm, about 1 to 1¼ hours. Do not add salt at this stage as it makes the beans hard. Remove seasoning vegetables and bay leaf and discard. Drain the beans if there is too much liquid.

Preheat oven to 350°. Heat 2 ounces of the butter in sauté pan and cook sliced onions over moderate heat until transparent but not browned, about 2 minutes. Spread half the onions in baking dish. Top with half the beans and then a layer of half the potatoes, seasoning each layer lightly with salt and pepper. Repeat with other half of onions, beans and potatoes, in that order, seasoning lightly. Cover dish with brown paper or aluminum foil and bake for 15 minutes.

Remove fell (papery skin) and all but a very thin layer of fat from lamb. Take baking dish from oven and carefully place a small custard cup or ramekin down into the bean mixture, base upward. It should be a little lower than the level of the vegetables. Rest the meaty side of the leg on it. This prevents the lamb from sinking down into the dish. Spread the remaining butter on the meat and bake until a meat thermometer registers 140° for pink lamb; 160° for well done, 1½ to 1¾ hours. Baste from time to time with the chicken stock. Start testing temperature after 1 hour. Remove from oven and allow to rest for 10 minutes, covered with a tent of foil.

Serves 6 to 8.

3-QUART SAUCEPOT

Meat Loaf

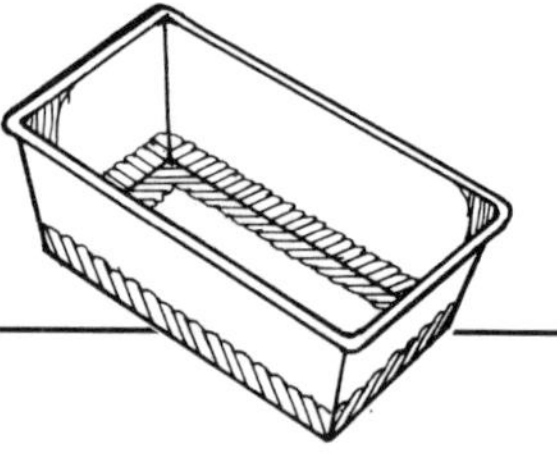

9- X 5-INCH LOAF PAN

Some people prefer a free-form meat loaf baked on a baking sheet with low sides, but I think you get a much jucier finished dish if it's baked in a loaf pan. Furthermore, any leftovers can be covered and weighted in the pan to compact the meat for slicing when cold.

1 tablespoon unsalted butter
1 medium onion, finely chopped
1 stalk celery, finely chopped
½ cup milk
1½ cups fairly fine breadcrumbs (day-old French bread is best)
1½ pounds lean ground beef, chuck or round
½ pound ground veal
½ pound ground pork
2 eggs
2 tablespoons parsley, chopped
1 teaspoon fresh thyme, chopped, or ½ teaspoon dried
1½ teaspoons salt
Freshly ground black pepper

Preheat oven to 350°. Grease pan. Heat butter in skillet and sauté onion and celery until transparent but not browned, about 2 minutes. Set aside. In bowl, dribble the milk over the breadcrumbs, stirring, and let stand until crumbs have absorbed liquid. Add all the other ingredients and mix well—with the hands is best.

Spoon meat mixture into prepared loaf pan. Do not pack down. Smooth and round off top. Bake for 1 to 1½ hours, or until internal temperature reaches 160°. Remove from oven and let rest for 5 minutes before slicing.

Serves 6 to 8.

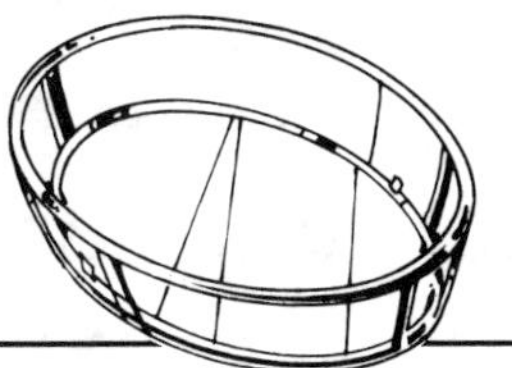

Potato, Onion and Ham au Gratin

4-QUART OVAL BAKING DISH

Because of the ham in this rich, old-fashioned dish, use salt sparingly.

3 tablespoons unsalted butter
5 medium onions (about 2 pounds), sliced thin
5 large potatoes (about 3 pounds)
Salt
Freshly ground black pepper
Freshly grated nutmeg
1 pound cooked ham, in 1/8-inch slices
1 1/2 cups heavy cream

Preheat oven to 375° and grease baking dish. Heat butter in sauté pan and cook onions over moderate heat until transparent but not browned, about 2 minutes. Peel and slice potatoes into thin rounds, rinse in cold water and dry very thoroughly with paper towels. Put half the potatoes in the prepared baking dish, laying them in overlapping rows. Top with half the onions. Season with a little salt, pepper and nutmeg. Cover the onion layer completely with the sliced ham and top with the remaining onions and potatoes, in an overlapping, even layer. Pour all but a quarter cup of the cream over the top, making sure that all the potato slices are moistened. Sprinkle with a little salt, pepper and nutmeg.

Bake for 1 1/2 hours, basting several times with the remaining cream until used up—then tip dish and baste with cream from bottom of dish. Keep potatoes moist on top. Potatoes should absorb most of the cream and be very tender, and the top should be golden brown.

Serves 6 as a main course.

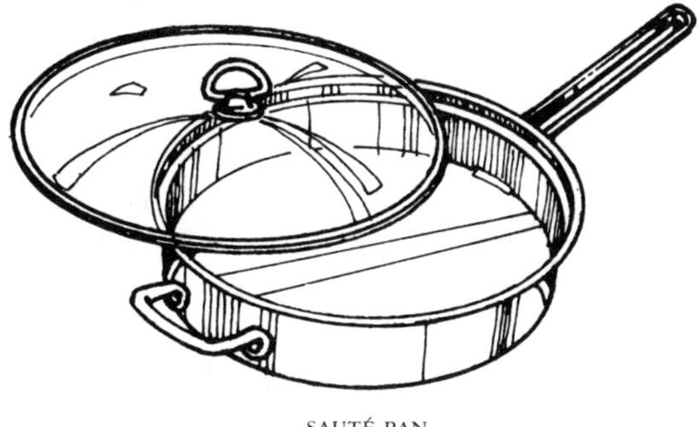

SAUTÉ PAN

Pot Roast of Beef with Aceto Balsamico

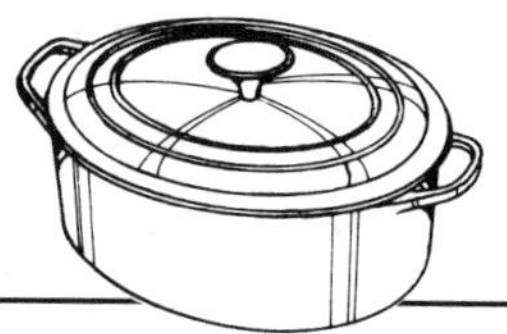

4-QUART DUTCH OVEN

4 tablespoons olive oil
4- to 5-pound piece of beef rump, chuck or round
1 medium onion, sliced
1 medium carrot, sliced
1 stalk celery, sliced
1 bay leaf
3 whole cloves
3 sprigs fresh thyme, or 1/4 teaspoon dried
3 sprigs parsley
2 tablespoons Aceto Balsamico (page 86)
1 cup water
2 teaspoons salt
Freshly ground black pepper
Boiled potatoes or noodles

Heat the olive oil in the Dutch oven. Brown meat on all sides. Remove and set aside. In the same pot, sauté onion, carrot and celery until onion is transparent but not browned, about 3 minutes. Add bay leaf, cloves, thyme and parsley. Return meat to pot, sprinkle with Aceto Balsamico and add water. Cover and cook at a very low simmer for 2 hours, turning once. Add salt and freshly ground pepper to taste. Cook for another half hour or more, until meat is tender.

When done, turn off heat and let rest for 5 minutes. Remove meat to a warm platter. Strain juices into saucepan and skim off fat. Bring to a boil and reduce liquid by one half. Taste for seasoning, and serve with meat. Serve with boiled potatoes or noodles.

Serves 8 to 10.

SAUCEPAN

Shoulder of Veal with Mushrooms

4-QUART SAUCEPOT

This dish is really too delicate to be called a stew. The veal becomes butter-tender and is served in a light lemon sauce that is made at the last minute. Don't discard the liquid when you drain the veal and vegetables. It's a flavorful veal stock that can be used another time.

2 pounds boneless shoulder of veal, in 1-inch cubes
12 small boiling onions
2 carrots, sliced thin
3 cloves garlic, chopped
3 sprigs fresh thyme, or 1/4 teaspoon dried
1 teaspoon salt
2 cups mushrooms, sliced thin
2 tablespoons unsalted butter
2 tablespoons flour
3 egg yolks
1 cup heavy cream
Juice of 1/2 lemon
White pepper, optional
Chopped parsley for garnish
Hot rice or noodles

DOUBLE BOILER

Place veal in pot, cover with cold water and bring to a boil. Lower heat to simmer, and skim off foam. Cover and simmer for 30 minutes. While the meat is cooking, put onions in a bowl and cover with boiling water. Let stand for 30 seconds, then drain. Cool under running water, then slip off skins. Cut a small cross in the root ends to prevent onions from coming apart while cooking. Add onions, carrots, garlic, thyme and salt to veal. Cover pot and keep at a low simmer for 30 minutes more. Add mushrooms and simmer for 15 minutes more. Keep warm while preparing sauce.

In the top of double boiler placed over direct heat, melt the butter and stir in the flour. Cook, stirring, for 1 minute but do not let brown. Remove from heat and stir in 1½ cups of liquid from the veal. Return to heat and cook, stirring, until thickened, 2 or 3 minutes. Set aside.

In a bowl, beat the egg yolks and cream together. Stir into the sauce, place pan over lower half of the double boiler, which should contain barely simmering water. Stir sauce until thickened and creamy, but do not let boil, or egg yolks will curdle. Add lemon juice and check for seasoning, adding pepper if desired.

Drain veal and vegetables, reserving liquid for another use. Transfer to heated serving dish. Cover with sauce and sprinkle with chopped parsley. Serve with rice or noodles.

Serves 4.

Steak and Kidney Pie

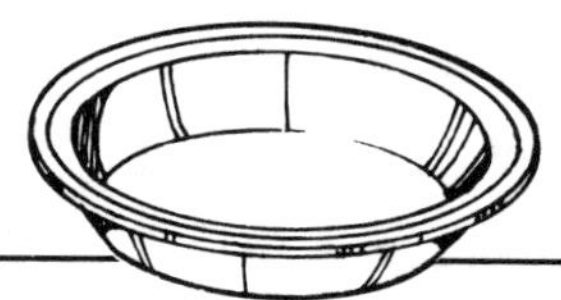

1½-QUART OVAL PIE DISH WITH RIM

It's hard to find this famous English dish well prepared in English restaurants any more. The stew should be baked under pastry, which then can absorb the good meat juices. It's not usual, but try marinating the kidneys in tarragon vinegar; they really hold the herb flavor.

1 tablespoon vegetable oil
2 tablespoons unsalted butter
2 medium onions, sliced
1½ pounds lean top round beef, in 1½-inch cubes
Flour
½ cup red wine
½ cup beef stock (page 105)
3 sprigs fresh thyme or ½ teaspoon dried
3 sprigs parsley
1 bay leaf
1 teaspoon salt
1 tablespoon Worcestershire sauce
6 lamb kidneys
½ cup tarragon-flavored wine vinegar
1 cup water
Freshly ground black pepper, optional

In skillet, heat oil and 1 tablespoon of the butter. Sauté onions until transparent but not browned, about 2 minutes. Remove with a slotted spoon and set aside. Dredge beef in flour, shaking off excess. In the same pan, sauté a few cubes at a time until browned. Place beef and onions in pot. Deglaze skillet with the wine and stock, scraping up the cooking residue. Add to meat and stir in thyme, parsley, bay leaf, salt and Worcestershire sauce. Simmer, covered, over very low heat until meat is tender, about 1½ hours. Discard parsley and bay leaf.

While beef is cooking, slice kidneys in half lengthways and remove membranes and core. Soak kidneys in the vinegar and water for 1 hour. Drain and pat dry.

SKILLET

Pastry:

1 3/4 cups all-purpose flour
1/4 teaspoon salt
4 ounces (1 stick) unsalted butter, cold
1 egg
2 tablespoons ice water
1 tablespoon lemon juice

4-QUART SAUCEPOT

To prepare pastry, sift flour and salt into a mixing bowl. Cut butter into small pieces and add to flour. With the fingertips, work butter quickly into flour until mixture resembles tiny peas. Separate egg and reserve the white. Beat yolk with the ice water and lemon juice and add to mixture. Blend together but do not overmix. Gather into a ball, enclose in plastic wrap and chill for 30 minutes.

Preheat oven to 350°. Heat remaining butter in skillet and sauté kidneys quickly for about 3 minutes, turning often. Combine with meat and check seasoning, adding pepper if desired.

On a lightly floured board, roll pastry out to 1/8-inch thick. Transfer meat to pie dish and top with pastry, tucking it under the rim. (There will be no bottom crust.) Cut slits in top for steam to escape. Beat egg white with 1 teaspoon water and brush over pastry. Place dish on middle shelf of oven and bake for about 20 minutes until pastry is golden brown.

Serves 4 to 6.

Veal Shanks

12-INCH DEEP SAUTÉ PAN WITH COVER

This recipe was given to me by Valentina, an Italian dressmaker who had a shop across the street from the Williams-Sonoma store on Sutter Street in San Francisco, years ago. She cooked on an electric hot plate, but managed to turn out marvelous food. She said it was important to really taste the veal in this dish, not a lot of extra seasonings, and to use the best Cognac you could afford. That's what makes it good! If possible, get small veal forelegs, which are meatier and more tender than the hind shanks. It is best to use a zester for the lemon peel, shredding it over the finished dish just before serving.

4 veal shanks, each cut in 3 pieces
Flour
3 tablespoons olive oil
3 tablespoons unsalted butter
¼ cup Cognac
1 to 1½ cups well-flavored beef, veal or chicken stock
1 medium onion
½ teaspoon salt
Freshly ground black pepper
1 teaspoon arrowroot or cornstarch (optional)
Finely shredded peel of 1 lemon, colored part only
Hot Arborio rice, noodles or orzo (rice-shaped pasta)

Dredge veal shanks lightly in flour, shaking off any excess. Heat oil and butter in sauté pan, which will hold the meat in one layer cut side up, and brown meat on all sides. Remove pan from heat.

Warm the Cognac in a ladle, ignite carefully and pour over veal. When the flame dies down, add enough of the stock to reach ¼ way up the meat. Add the onion. Make sure that the slices of veal shank are lying in the pan cut side up, not on their sides, or the marrow will tend to shrink and fall out. Cover tightly and barely simmer for 1½ hours, turning meat completely over once during cooking time. Season with salt and pepper and simmer for 15 minutes more.

Arrange the veal in a large warmed serving dish, discarding the onion. If there is too much juice, or it is too thin, reduce by rapid boiling or thicken by adding the arrowroot or cornstarch dissolved in water, and boil for 2 minutes. Pour sauce over meat and sprinkle with the lemon peel. Serve with rice, noodles or orzo.

Serves 4.

FISH

AND SEAFOOD

Baked Red Snapper

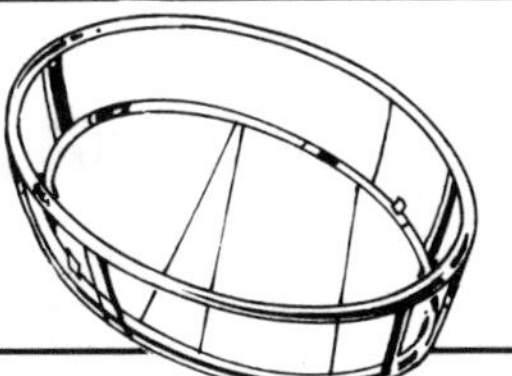
SHALLOW BAKING DISH

If you can't get red snapper, use any similar white-fleshed fish.

4 medium tomatoes
2 small leeks
2 stalks celery
6 tablespoons (3/4 stick) unsalted butter
1/2 cup (6 ounces) chopped ham
2 teaspoons fresh oregano, chopped or 1 teaspoon dried
Salt
Freshly ground black pepper
4 fillets red snapper, 6 to 8 ounces each
Chopped parsley for garnish
Hot rice, polenta or pasta

Preheat oven to 425°. Cut core from tomatoes and make a small cross at the blossom end. Dip in boiling water for 5 seconds to loosen skin. Peel, cut in half crossways and gently squeeze out seeds. Cut each half into quarters. Discard green part of leeks and wash remainder well. Cut into 1/2-inch pieces. Chop celery fine.

Melt 4 tablespoons of the butter in saucepan and sauté the leeks for 1 minute. Add tomatoes, celery, ham and oregano. Stir well, cover and cook over low heat for 10 to 15 minutes. Season with salt and pepper. Spread in baking dish and lay the fish fillets on top. Dot with remaining butter, sprinkle with salt and pepper and bake for 15 minutes. Garnish with parsley and serve with rice, polenta or pasta.

Serves 4.

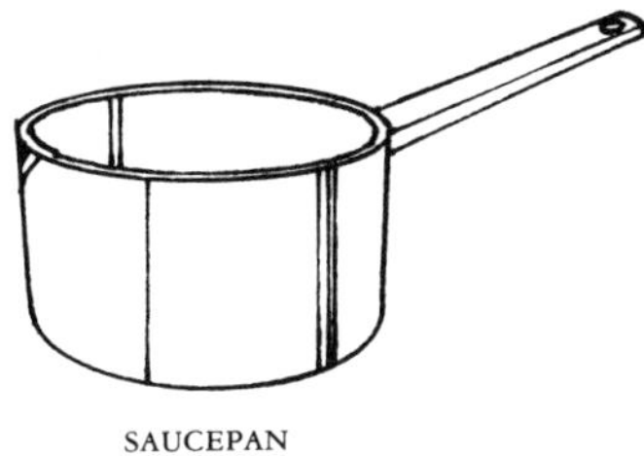
SAUCEPAN

Baked Salmon Stuffed with Mélange of Vegetables

SHALLOW BAKING DISH

This recipe works best with salmon from the tail end.

3- to 4-pound piece of salmon, at room temperature
4 tablespoons (1/2 stick) unsalted butter
1 small onion, finely chopped
1 carrot, finely chopped
1 stalk celery, finely chopped
1/2 green bell pepper, cored, seeded and finely chopped
2 teaspoons fresh dill, chopped, or 1 teaspoon dried
Salt
Freshly ground black pepper

Preheat oven to 425° and butter baking dish. Skin and bone salmon to give two large fillets, or have this done at the fish market. Heat 2 tablespoons of the butter in sauté pan and cook onion over very low heat for 1 or 2 minutes. Add carrot and celery and cook for 3 minutes. Stir in bell pepper and cook for 2 minutes more, until vegetables are tender. Do not let brown and do not overcook. Remove pan from heat, add dill and season with salt and pepper. Stir to blend well.

Lay one half of the fish in the prepared baking dish, skinned side down. Spread the warm vegetable mixture on top and cover with the other half of the fish, skinned side up. Dot with remaining butter and sprinkle with salt and pepper. Measure the fish at its thickest part (not across) and bake for 10 minutes for each inch, basting once. (If fish is 2 inches thick, it will be cooked in 20 minutes.)

Serves 6.

Deviled Crab

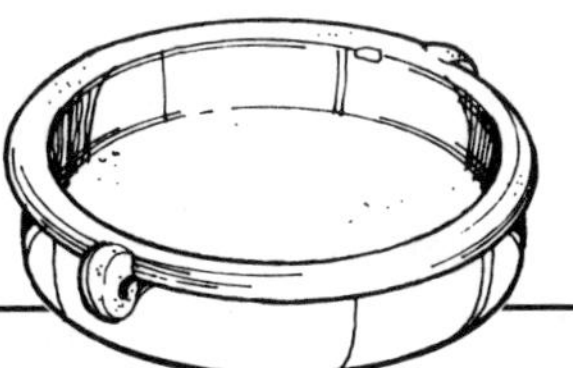

1 ½-QUART OVENPROOF BAKING DISH

One large whole crab should yield three quarters to one pound of meat. If you are buying crab meat in bulk, get one pound and pick it over carefully for bits of shell. I find that day-old French bread makes the best breadcrumbs for this recipe. Make the breadcrumbs 2 or 3 hours ahead and spread them out on paper towels to dry a little.

2 tablespoons unsalted butter
1 medium onion, diced
1 small green bell pepper, cored, seeded and diced
1 stalk celery, diced
1 ½ cups fresh breadcrumbs
⅓ to ½ cup milk
¾ to 1 pound fresh crabmeat
2 teaspoons fresh dill, chopped, or 1 teaspoon dried
1 tablespoon lemon juice
Pinch cayenne pepper
½ teaspoon salt
Freshly ground black pepper

Preheat oven to 375° and grease the baking dish. Melt the butter in the skillet, add the onion and let cook for 1 minute on low heat. Add the green pepper and celery and cook for 1 or 2 minutes more, stirring frequently. Remove from heat and set aside. Place the breadcrumbs in bowl and dribble the milk over them, while stirring. Let stand for 5 minutes. Add the crabmeat, vegetables, dill, lemon juice, cayenne, salt and pepper. Mix well and spoon into the baking dish. Place on middle rack of oven and bake for 20 to 25 minutes, until lightly browned.

Serves 4 to 6.

SKILLET

Fish and Vegetables in a Cataplana

CATAPLANA

You can use for this dish any kind of white fish—red snapper or sea bass, for example.

4 to 5 medium boiling potatoes
Olive oil
3 medium onions, sliced thin
2 garlic cloves
3 medium tomatoes
1 bay leaf
6 Swiss chard, cut into strips
1 red pepper, cut into ½-inch slices
⅓ cup chopped parsley
Salt
Freshly ground pepper
6 pieces (4 to 5 ounces each) boneless white fish
½ to 1 cup white wine
3 tablespoons butter

Parboil potatoes in salted water until just tender and cut into ¼-inch slices. In a covered pan, heat 3 tablespoons of the olive oil and sauté onions with the garlic until transparent. Set aside.

Cut core from tomatoes and make a small cross at the blossom end. Dip in boiling water for 5 seconds to loosen skin. Peel, cut in half crossways and gently squeeze out seeds. Cut into ¼-inch slices.

Coat the inside of both halves of the cataplana with oil. In the bottom half, place the bay leaf and one half the onions, potatoes, tomatoes, Swiss chard and pepper, arranged in layers. Sprinkle with parsley and season with a little salt and pepper. Add the fish in one layer and repeat the layers of vegetables, parsley and seasonings. Add wine and dot with butter. Tightly close the two halves of the cataplana, fastening clips down snugly. Place on a gas or electric burner and cook for 15 minutes over medium heat. Open and check fish for doneness, close and cook for another few minutes as needed. Serve immediately.

Serves 4 to 6.

José Wilson's Fillet of Sole Rockport

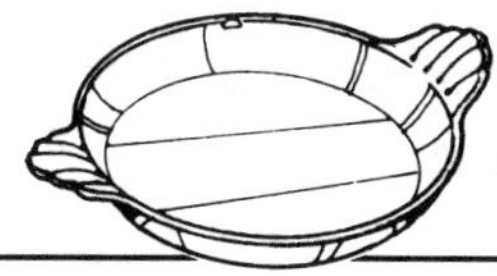
GRATIN DISH

4 tablespoons (½ stick) butter
4 tablespoons Dijon mustard
2 tablespoons prepared horseradish
4 tablespoons lemon juice
4 tablespoons grated Parmesan cheese
½ cup sour cream
4 fillets of sole, 6 to 8 ounces each

Preheat broiler and grease the gratin dish.

Melt butter in saucepan. Off heat, stir in the mustard, horseradish, lemon juice, 2 tablespoons of the Parmesan cheese and the sour cream. Sauce should be thick and pungent; taste for seasoning.

Place sole in prepared dish in one layer and spread thickly with the sauce. Sprinkle with remaining Parmesan. Broil until sauce is lightly browned and glazed and fish cooked *au point,* or just done, about 5 minutes.

Serves 4.

Marinated Cold Poached Fish

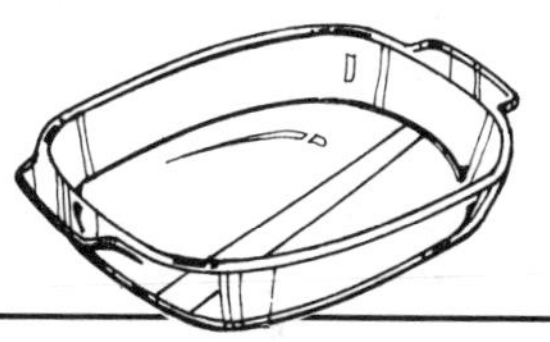
SHALLOW BAKING DISH

Jim Beard always maintained fish should be marinated in white cider vinegar, plus white wine or water. (I think the white wine is better.) The acid balance is superior, and the taste is cleaner and sharper than if you use wine vinegar.

2 pounds cold poached fillets of fish, such as salmon, halibut, bass or snapper
2 cups white wine
1 cup white cider vinegar
1 teaspoon sea salt (p. 64)
6 sprigs fresh dill or 1 teaspoon dried
1 bay leaf
½ red onion, sliced
1 small carrot, sliced thin
1 stalk celery, sliced thin
½ teaspoon cracked peppercorns

Remove any skin or bone from fish. Place in a deep dish large enough to hold the fish in one layer. Pour in wine and vinegar and add the other ingredients. Cover dish with plastic wrap and refrigerate for 24 hours.

Serves 4.

Oven-Broiled Shrimp and Vegetable Shish Kebab

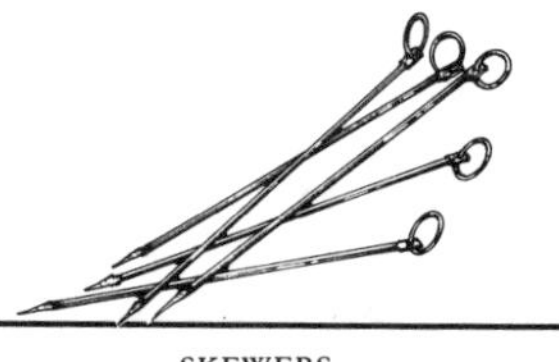
SKEWERS

This dish can be done under a broiler or on a barbecue if you prefer.

½ cup olive oil
1 to 1½ teaspoons fresh ginger root, finely chopped
1 clove garlic, finely chopped
½ teaspoon fresh oregano, chopped, or ¼ teaspoon dried
Grated peel of 1 lemon, colored part only
1 teaspoon salt
Freshly ground black pepper
32 medium uncooked shrimp (about 1 pound)
4 small summer squash
1 green bell pepper
1 sweet red Bermuda onion
1 small cucumber
2 tablespoons unsalted butter
1 small onion, finely chopped
1 cup long-grain rice
1¾ cups boiling water
¼ cup fresh lemon juice

SAUCEPAN

Preheat oven to 425°. In a bowl, combine the olive oil, ginger, garlic, oregano, lemon peel, ½ teaspoon of the salt and a pinch of pepper. Mix well and set aside.

Remove shells from shrimp, leaving last segment and tail intact. Devein if necessary. Set aside.

Trim and quarter summer squash. Remove core and seeds from bell pepper and peel onion. Cut sixteen 1½-inch pieces of each. Peel cucumber and cut sixteen ½-inch slices. Fill saucepan with water, heat to boiling, add the vegetables, quickly return to boil and cook for 1 minute only. Drain and immediately plunge into cold water to stop cooking.

Separate the shrimp and vegetables into 8 portions and arrange alternately on 9-inch skewers. Set aside.

Heat butter in saucepan, add the chopped onion and sauté for 1 minute. Add the rice, stir to coat the grains with butter and cook, stirring for 2 to 3 minutes over moderate heat until rice is transparent. Add the boiling water, lemon juice and remaining salt, and stir. Cover, reduce heat to a low simmer and cook for 5 minutes. Stir, and cook for 15 minutes more.

Place prepared skewers on a baking pan, resting the ends on the edges of the pan so that shrimp and vegetables do not touch the bottom. Stir the reserved olive oil and herb mixture and brush the shrimp and vegetables well. Place in top section of oven and bake for 5 minutes, basting with marinade once. Turn skewers over, baste and bake another 5 minutes, basting twice. Turn again, baste and cook for another 2 to 3 minutes. Shrimp should be pink.

BAKING PAN

To serve, spoon a bed of rice on each plate. Top each with 2 skewers. Brush again lightly with marinade and serve at once.

Serves 4.

Packets of Sole with Spinach

4-QUART SAUCEPOT

1 bunch spinach (about 1 pound)
1/4 cup water
4 fillets of sole, 5 to 6 ounces each
4 scallions, trimmed and sliced thin diagonally
8 mushrooms, thinly sliced
3 ounces (3/4 stick) unsalted butter
Salt
Freshly ground black pepper
1 lemon, thinly sliced

COOKIE SHEET

Preheat oven to 425°. Prepare spinach by removing stems and discarding any yellowed or torn outer leaves. Wash well. Place spinach in pot, add the water, cover and steam over medium high heat for 1 to 2 minutes until just wilted. Drain immediately and plunge into cold water to stop cooking. Drain again and press out excess liquid; spinach must be dry. Spread on paper towels.

Cut 4 pieces of heavy aluminum foil about 14 inches long. Butter the center of each piece, covering an area about 9 inches square. Spread one quarter of the spinach on each piece of foil and top with a fillet. Sprinkle with scallions and mushrooms. Dot each serving with small pieces of butter, season with salt and pepper and lay 2 slices of lemon on each.

Press together the sides of the foil along the length of the fish and fold over twice to seal. Close the ends of each packet and seal. Lay the packets on a baking sheet, place on middle shelf of the oven and bake for 15 minutes. Remove from oven, open packets carefully and transfer fillets to warm serving plates. Spoon a little of the cooking liquid over each and serve at once.

Serves 4.

Poached Salmon in Foil

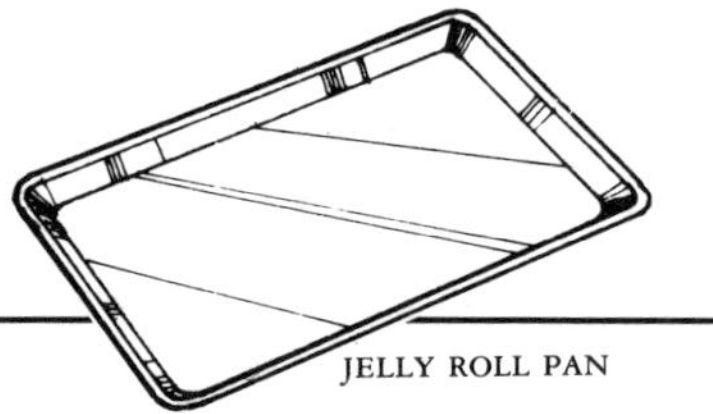
JELLY ROLL PAN

2 fillets fresh salmon, 12 to 16 ounces each
1 medium white onion, thinly sliced
1 medium carrot, thinly sliced
1 stalk celery, thinly sliced
1 lemon, thinly sliced
2 teaspoons fresh dill, chopped, or 1 teaspoon dried
2 sprigs parsley
Salt
Freshly ground black pepper

Preheat oven to 425°.

Cut two pieces of heavy aluminum foil large enough to completely enclose each salmon fillet. Lay out on a countertop and arrange in the center of each piece of foil 2 slices of the onion, 5 or 6 slices of the carrot, 5 to 6 slices of the celery, 2 slices of lemon, ½ of the dill and 1 sprig of parsley. Sprinkle with salt and pepper. Lay a salmon fillet on each arrangement of vegetables.

Pull the sides of the foil together and fold over twice. Then close the ends and fold over twice. This will make a tight seal, and prevent any liquid from running out. Place packets on a baking sheet, put on middle rack of the oven and bake for 20 to 25 minutes.

Remove packets from the oven and open carefully. Cut each fillet in half and serve fish with the vegetables as garnish, spooning the cooking liquid on top.

Serves 4.

Scallops with Mushrooms and Cream

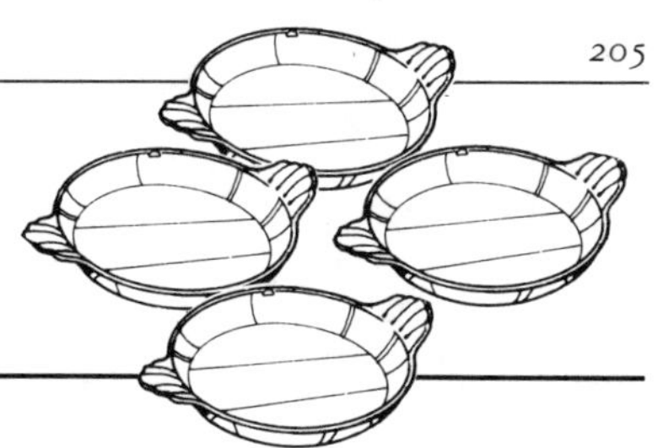
4 INDIVIDUAL GRATIN DISHES

1 carrot, sliced thinly
1 tablespoon shallots or scallions, chopped
¾ cup water
Salt
¾ cup white wine
4 to 6 mushrooms (2 ounces), sliced thinly
1 pound small bay scallops
1 tablespoon unsalted butter
1 tablespoon flour
½ cup heavy cream
Chopped parsley for garnish

Preheat oven to 400° and butter 4 scallop shells or 4 individual gratin dishes.

In saucepan, combine carrot, shallots or scallions, water and a little salt and simmer, covered, for 10 minutes. Add wine and return to simmer. Add mushrooms and poach for 2 minutes. Add scallops and poach for 1 to 2 minutes more. Drain vegetables and scallops, reserving liquid. Return liquid to saucepan and reduce to half by rapid boiling. Set aside.

In another saucepan, melt butter, stir in flour and cook for 30 seconds. Add reduced liquid and the cream and stir over low heat until smooth and thickened, about 3 minutes.

Arrange scallops and vegetables in shells or dishes. Pour sauce on top and bake for 5 minutes. Garnish with the chopped parsley.

Serves 4 as a first course.

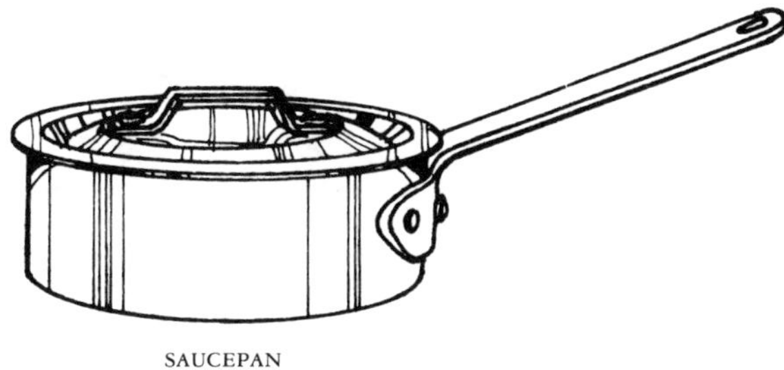
SAUCEPAN

Scampi

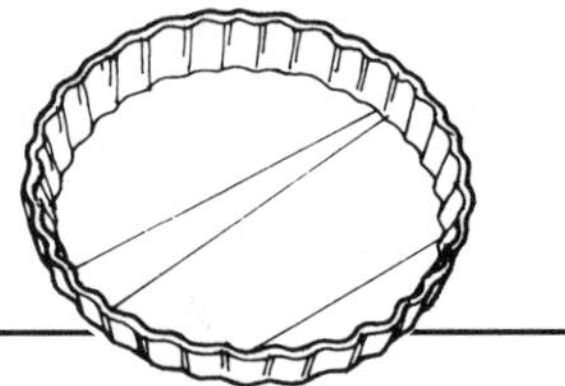
TWO 10-INCH ROUND LOW BAKING DISHES

I have listed fresh tarragon and shallots for flavoring the shrimp, but the dish is just as good with garlic, scallions and fresh oregano or marjoram. If you can't find fresh herbs, get the most flavor possible from dried leaves by heating them gently in the oven for a few minutes and then pulverizing with a mortar and pestle.

To butterfly shrimp, remove heads, hold by tail and cut along center of back without going all the way through. Spread shrimp out into a round shape.

2 pounds large shrimp or prawns
3 teaspoons fresh tarragon, chopped, or 1½ teaspoons dried
2 tablespoons parsley, chopped
2 shallots, chopped fine
Salt and pepper
3 to 4 tablespoons olive oil

Preheat oven to 400°. Peel, devein and butterfly shrimp, leaving on tail and last segment of shell.

Butter baking dish and arrange shrimp in a single layer, tails upward. Mix the tarragon, parsley and shallots together and sprinkle over the shrimp. Season with salt and pepper and drizzle with the olive oil. Place on middle rack of oven and bake for 8 to 10 minutes, until shrimp are pink and all is bubbly. Serve at once with French bread for mopping up the juices.

Serves 6 as a first course.

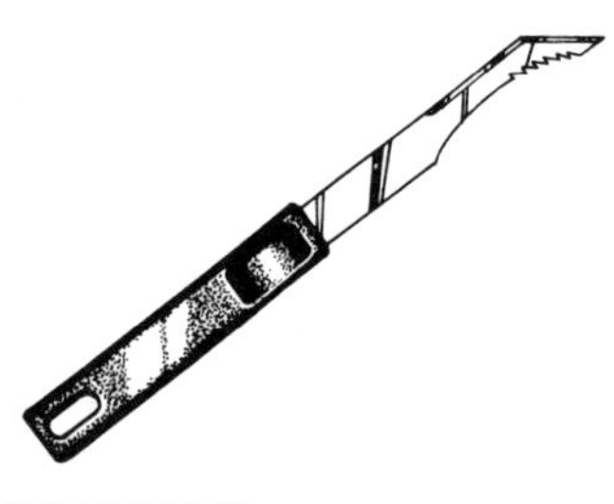
SHRIMP PEELER

Sole Fillets with Dill

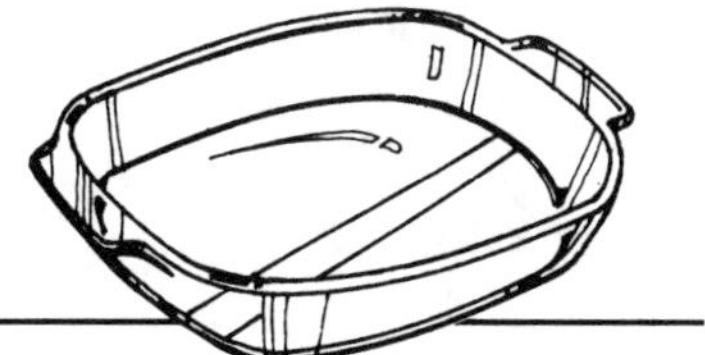

2-QUART SHALLOW BAKING DISH

3 ounces unsalted butter, melted
2 tablespoons onion, finely chopped
2 tablespoons celery, finely chopped
1 cup fresh breadcrumbs
2 teaspoons fresh dill, chopped, or 1 teaspoon dried
Juice of ½ lemon
Pinch salt
4 fillets of sole, 6 to 8 ounces each
Chopped parsley for garnish

Preheat oven to 400° and butter a shallow 2-quart baking dish.

Heat 1 tablespoon of the butter in skillet and sauté onion and celery until just transparent, about 2 minutes. Stir in breadcrumbs, dill, lemon juice and salt, and set aside.

Place sole in prepared baking dish in one layer and cover with breadcrumb mixture. Drizzle with remaining butter and bake for 8 to 10 minutes, until sole is just cooked. If necessary, slide under hot broiler very briefly to brown crumbs lightly. Sprinkle with chopped parsley and serve at once.

Serves 4.

SKILLET

Stir-Fried Shrimp and Snow Peas

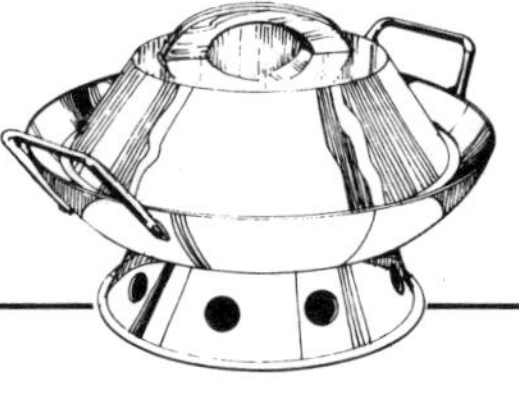
WOK

This is one of the few Chinese dishes I have attempted that can be done in a skillet as well as in a wok. If you can only get large shrimp, cut them in half before cooking.

¼ pound snow peas
½ pound medium-sized raw shrimp
5 tablespoons cornstarch
½ cup cold water
2 tablespoons cooking oil
1 scallion, finely chopped
1 tablespoon dry sherry
Salt

Snap off ends and remove strings from snow peas. Let pods soak in cold water for 15 minutes to crisp. Bring a pot of salted water to the boil and blanch snow peas for 1 minute. Drain and plunge into cold water to stop cooking. They should be bright green. Drain well and set aside.

Remove shells from shrimp and devein if necessary. Mix cornstarch with the water and dip each shrimp to coat. Add oil to skillet or wok and heat. When oil is hot, add shrimp and stir-fry for a few seconds. While stirring briskly, add scallions, sherry, snow peas and a pinch of salt. Stir-fry for 1 minute and serve immediately.

Serves 4 as a first course.

PASTA

Making your own pasta is very simple if you mix the dough in a food processor and then roll and cut it in a pasta machine. It takes about 10 minutes, and fresh pasta cooks in a few seconds. I'm sure I'd never make noodles at home if I had to knead, roll and cut the dough by hand. It's too much work, and it's very difficult unless you were taught how as a child by an Italian grandmother!

Homemade pasta isn't necessarily superior to good quality dried pasta, it's just different in texture. All-purpose flour, which is what most people use, makes a soft fresh pasta that cooks in seconds. Finely ground durum wheat flour—not the coarse granular semolina—makes a firmer fresh pasta that cooks in about 5 minutes. Dried, commercially made durum wheat flour pasta, which comes in lots of different shapes and sizes, can take up to 20 minutes to cook.

When using a roller-type pasta machine, electric or manual, I work with a small ball of dough made with 1 egg. I find that if you try working with more than that, the strip of rolled pasta becomes too long to handle easily. Running the dough through a pasta machine is a very rapid process (though it may *sound* complicated!) so even if you're making pasta for 8 people, it still doesn't take very long.

The rule of thumb is that 1 pound of pasta serves 4 people as a main course or 6 to 8 as an appetizer. My basic pasta recipe makes about 5 ounces of pasta.

Homemade pasta made with all-purpose flour doesn't really become *al dente* or resistant to the bite when cooked, as commercially dried pasta does. It just gets soft, so you have to watch it very carefully to make sure it doesn't overcook. Fresh pasta, dried for 10 minutes or so, will take 15 to 20 seconds to become tender in rapidly boiling water. If it has been allowed to dry out completely, it can take up to 60 seconds.

The Italians always add salt to water intended for cooking pasta *after* it comes to a boil, so I do too. There may be some scientific basis for this, or it may be just another kitchen superstition, I don't know! And another thing: The Italians say you should always put your drained pasta back into the pot or a warmed serving bowl with a little of the cooking water. The pasta will absorb it along with the sauce and it makes a better finished dish.

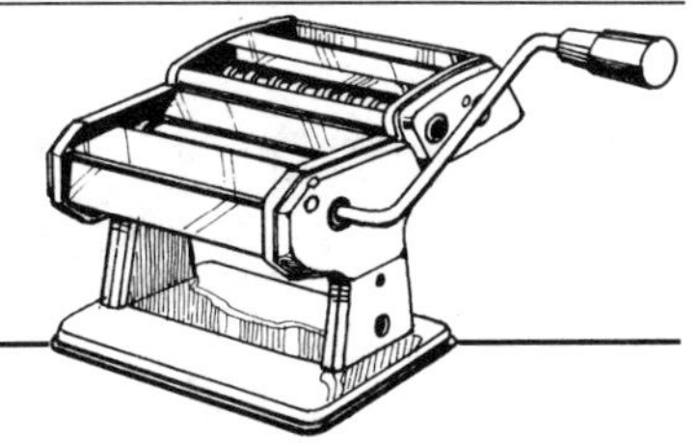

Egg Noodles (fettuccine)

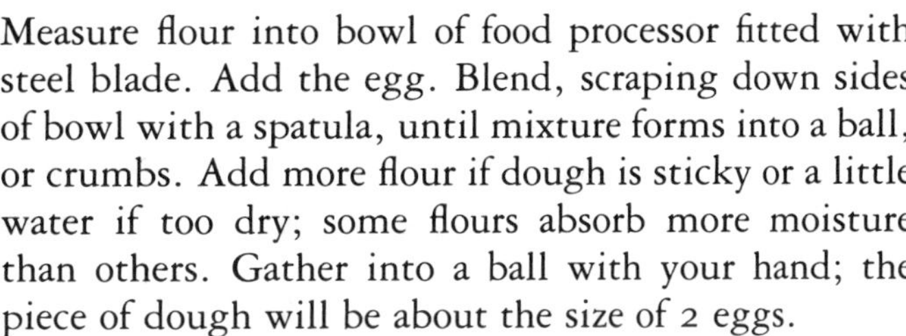

PASTA MACHINE

$2/3$ cup plus 1 tablespoon all-purpose flour, for pasta dough
1 large egg
$1/2$ cup additional flour, for rolling pasta

FOOD PROCESSOR

Measure flour into bowl of food processor fitted with steel blade. Add the egg. Blend, scraping down sides of bowl with a spatula, until mixture forms into a ball, or crumbs. Add more flour if dough is sticky or a little water if too dry; some flours absorb more moisture than others. Gather into a ball with your hand; the piece of dough will be about the size of 2 eggs.

Set rollers on pasta machine at their widest opening. (#6 on most machines.) Place the additional flour on work surface next to pasta machine. Flatten ball of dough with your hand and feed through rollers. Dust sheet of dough in the flour, coating each side, fold in half and run through rollers again. Repeat 8 or 10 times, dipping the dough in flour and folding in half each time, until dough is smooth and silky. It should be considerably drier than when you started, and pale in color. Don't be afraid of overhandling the dough—it benefits from lots of rolling. Cut dough into 2 equal lengths so it will be easier to manage.

Next, decrease the width of roller opening by one or two notches or numbers and run dough through twice. Repeat, reducing roller opening width one or two notches at a time, running dough through until desired thickness is obtained. Remember that pasta expands when cooked. I like to make mine thin. (Usually #1 on pasta machine.) Cut each strip of dough in half, resulting in 4 sheets about 12 inches long × 4 inches wide. Rub flour into both sides to prevent sticking and shake off any excess.

Now run each section of dough through the cutting rollers, either wide or narrow. Heap cut strands loosely in "nests" on a wooden board to dry a little. (They tend to stick on formica or tile.)

Makes about 5 ounces of fresh noodles; enough for 2 served with a salad.

Fresh Fettuccine with Chicken Liver and Lemon Sauce

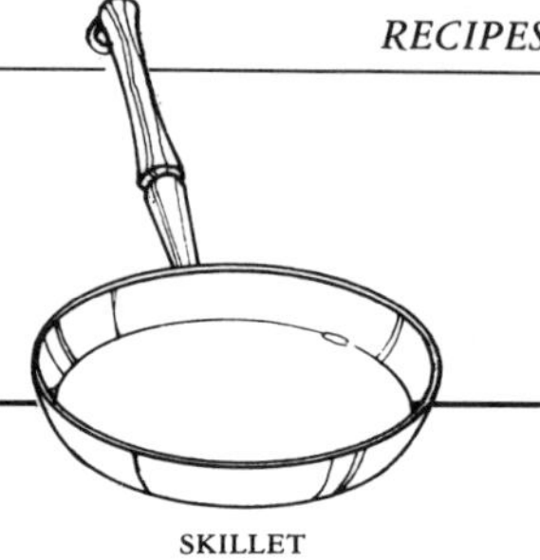

SKILLET

Elizabeth David included this recipe in a letter that she wrote me about ten years ago. She got it from a young Tuscan girl named Giovanna, who cooked it for her in a country restaurant (alas, now vanished), in a remote part of the Chianti region of Tuscany. This restaurant was so remote that it didn't even have a name, much less a telephone. Reservations were made by driving there the previous day to order a meal, or one simply took a chance and arrived at midday, hoping that food would be provided. As Elizabeth says, Giovanna was a most original and gifted pasta cook, and this recipe is a most unexpected and delicious combination of flavors and textures. It is very important that the chicken liver is not overcooked: the pieces should be creamy and still pink inside, and "melt" like pâté in the mouth. Naturally, you may substitute dried pasta for fresh if you prefer.

1/4 pound chicken livers
1/2 cup best quality olive oil, preferably Tuscan
2 cloves garlic, finely chopped
4 ounces prosciutto, in thin strips
Coarsely grated peel of 1 lemon (colored part only)
Salt
Freshly ground black pepper
1 whole egg
4 egg yolks
7 ounces freshly grated Parmesan or Pecorino cheese
Freshly grated nutmeg
15 ounces fettuccine (page 213)

Trim chicken livers of any tubes or membranes and cut into 1/2-inch pieces. Set aside.

Heat olive oil and add garlic, prosciutto and lemon peel. Cook for 1 minute, making sure that garlic does not brown. Add chicken livers, cook and toss for about 1 minute and remove pan from heat. Liver pieces should be pink inside, and will continue to cook in the hot pan. Season with salt and pepper.

In a bowl, beat egg and egg yolks lightly, add cheese and a sprinkling of nutmeg. Reserve.

Cook pasta in plenty of boiling salted water until just tender. Drain and pour into a big, deep, heated dish. Stir in egg and cheese mixture—the heat of the pasta will cook the eggs. Quickly add chicken liver mixture and toss together well. Serve immediately in heated bowls or on plates.

Serves 4 as a main course, 6 as a first course.

Fresh Fettuccine with Leek, Cream and Parmesan Sauce

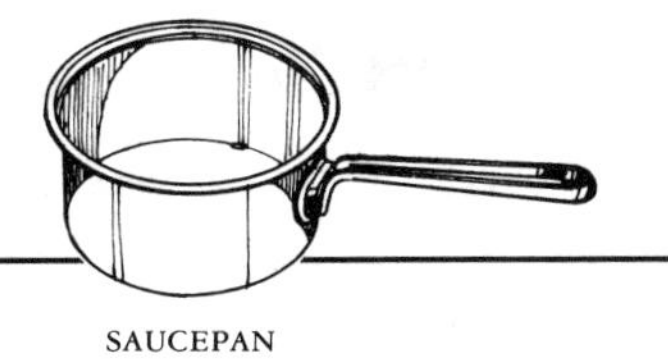
SAUCEPAN

You can, of course, substitute dried pasta if you wish.

2 medium-sized leeks
3 tablespoons unsalted butter
1 cup cream
1/4 cup freshly grated Parmesan cheese
Salt
Freshly grated nutmeg
10 ounces fettuccine (page 213)
Additional grated Parmesan cheese

Trim leeks, cutting off most of the green, wash well and slice thin. There should be about 2 cups. Heat butter in the saucepan and gently sauté leeks for 4 to 5 minutes until softened but not browned. Add cream, bring to a boil and let bubble for 1 minute. Stir in Parmesan cheese and season to taste with salt and nutmeg.

Cook fettuccine in plenty of boiling salted water until just tender—20 to 30 seconds. Drain and immediately combine with the sauce. Toss well and serve at once in heated bowls or plates. Serve with additional grated Parmesan cheese.

Serves 4 as a first course.

4-QUART SAUCEPOT

Fresh Fettuccine with Tomato and Shrimp

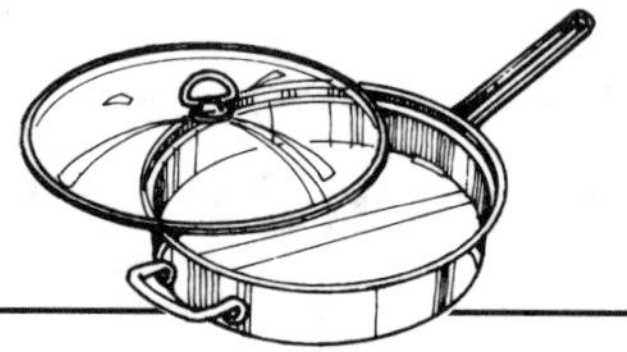
SAUTÉ PAN

3 medium tomatoes (about 1 pound)
5 tablespoons olive oil
1 medium onion, diced
1 clove garlic, finely chopped
1/4 pound cooked ham, in 1/4- × 1-inch strips
1/2 teaspoon fresh oregano, chopped, or 1/4 teaspoon dried
2 tablespoons Madeira
Salt
Freshly ground black pepper
1/2 pound medium raw shrimp, shelled, cut in half
1/4 pound small mushrooms, sliced
1/2 lemon
1 pound fresh fettuccine (page 213)
1/4 cup black olives, pitted
Parsley, chopped
1/4 cup fresh green peas, blanched (optional)

Fill saucepot with 5 quarts of water and heat to boiling. Cut core from tomatoes and make a small cross at the blossom end. Dip in boiling water for 5 seconds to loosen skin. Peel, cut in half crossways and gently squeeze out seeds. Chop tomatoes and set aside.

Heat 2 tablespoons of the olive oil in sauté pan. Add onion and garlic and sauté gently for 2 minutes until onion is wilted. Add the ham and cook for 20 seconds. Stir in the tomatoes, oregano and Madeira and season lightly with salt and pepper. Remove from heat. Heat remaining olive oil in a skillet. Add the shrimp and cook, stirring and tossing, for 1 or 2 minutes until they turn pink. Remove with slotted spoon and add to tomato mixture. Add mushrooms to olive oil in skillet and squeeze about 1 teaspoon of lemon juice over them to keep them white. Cook for 1 or 2 minutes, stirring and tossing constantly. Transfer to pan containing tomato mixture.

Add 2 tablespoons of salt to the pot of boiling water. Add the fettuccine and cook until just tender. Drain and combine with the sauce. Garnish with the black olives and parsley, and the peas if used.

Serves 4 to 6.

SLOTTED SPOON

Fusilli with Tomato Asparagus Sauce

SAUCEPAN

2 medium ripe tomatoes
2 tablespoons olive oil
1 small onion, chopped
1/4 cup cooked ham, diced
1/2 teaspoon fresh oregano, chopped, or 1/4 teaspoon dried
1/4 teaspoon salt
6 slender asparagus spears
10 ounces fusilli (spiral-shaped pasta)
Grated Parmesan or Romano cheese (optional)
Freshly grated black pepper (optional)

Core the tomatoes and make a small cross at the blossom end. Dip in boiling water for 5 seconds to loosen skin. Peel, cut in half crossways and gently squeeze out seeds. Chop coarsely and reserve. In saucepan, heat olive oil and sauté onion until transparent, about 2 minutes. Add tomatoes, ham, oregano and salt. Simmer for 3 or 4 minutes.

Discard any thick, woody ends of the asparagus stalks and slice spears diagonally into 1-inch pieces. Blanch in boiling water for 2 minutes. Drain and set aside. Cook pasta in plenty of boiling, salted water until *al dente* or just resistant to the bite, about 10 minutes. Drain and combine with sauce and asparagus. Toss together well and serve immediately in heated bowls or plates. Sprinkle with cheese and pepper if you like.

Serves 4 as a first course.

COLANDER

Linguine with Tomato, Basil and Lemon Sauce

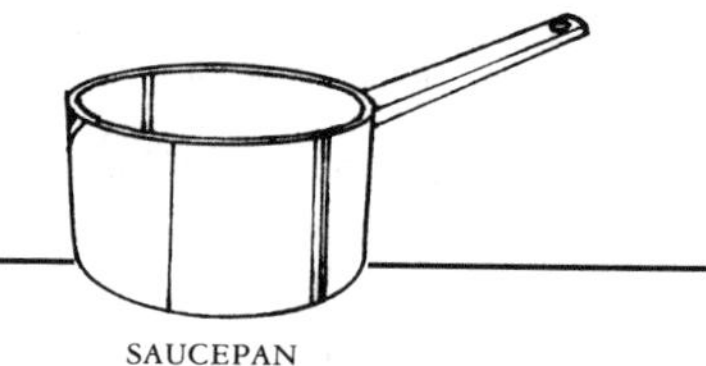

SAUCEPAN

1 pound ripe tomatoes
2 tablespoons chopped fresh basil
Juice of 1 lemon
4 tablespoons olive oil
Salt
Freshly ground black pepper
10 ounces dried imported linguine (thin oval spaghetti)

Core the tomatoes and make a small cross at the blossom end. Dip in boiling water for 5 seconds to loosen skin. Peel, cut in half crossways and gently squeeze out seeds. Chop tomatoes coarsely and place in saucepan. Warm through over low heat and add basil. In bowl, stir together lemon juice and oil, then season with salt and pepper.

Cook pasta in plenty of boiling salted water until *al dente* or just resistant to the bite. Drain and combine with lemon and oil mixture, and add tomatoes and basil. Toss all together well and serve immediately in heated bowls or plates.

Serves 4 as a first course.

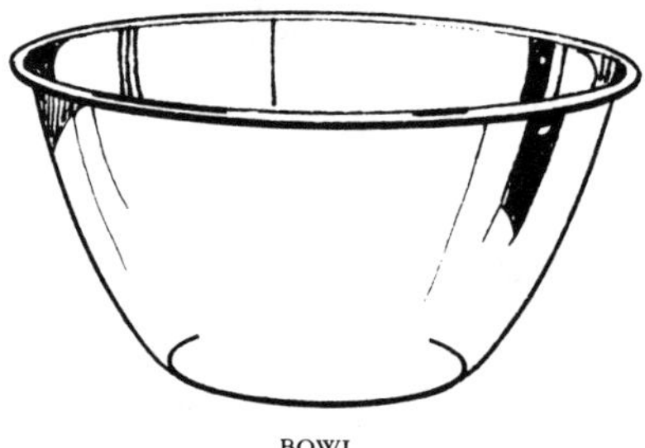

BOWL

Spaghetti with Fresh Tomato, Black Olives and Anchovy Sauce

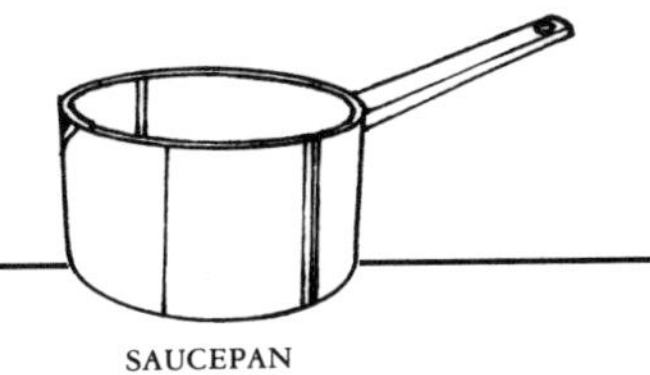
SAUCEPAN

For this recipe you can use olives from Italy or the dry, oil-cured type from California. Regular ripe black California olives are too bland.

2-ounce can anchovy fillets
1 pound ripe tomatoes
4 ounces (about 1/2 cup) black olives
4 tablespoons olive oil
2 cloves garlic, finely chopped
1 tablespoon capers
1 pound dried Italian durum wheat spaghetti
Freshly grated Parmesan cheese (optional)

Rinse anchovies under cold running water to get rid of salt and oil. Drain and set aside. Core the tomatoes and make a small cross at the blossom end. Dip in boiling water for 5 seconds to loosen skin. Peel, cut in half crossways and gently squeeze out seeds. Chop tomatoes coarsely and reserve. Pit and halve the olives.

Heat olive oil in saucepan, add garlic and cook over low heat for 1 minute. Do not let garlic brown. Add anchovies and mash with a wooden spoon to dissolve. Add tomatoes, olives and capers. Barely simmer sauce for 8 to 10 minutes.

Cook spaghetti in plenty of boiling salted water until *al dente* or just resistant to the bite, about 10 minutes. Drain and toss with sauce. Serve at once in heated bowls or on plates, with grated cheese if desired.

Serves 4 as a main course, 6 as a first course.

WOODEN SPOON

Spaghetti with Pine Nuts

SKILLET

For this dish to really "come off" you have to use the very best ingredients. I use durum wheat spaghetti from Italy, and premium quality Parmesan cheese: Parmigiano Reggiano.

1 pound spaghetti
6 ounces (1½ sticks) unsalted butter, softened
½ cup pine nuts (pignoli)
½ cup freshly grated Parmesan cheese
Salt
Freshly grated black pepper

Cook spaghetti in plenty of boiling salted water until *al dente* or just resistant to the bite, about 10 minutes.

While pasta is cooking, cut butter into small cubes and reserve. Place pine nuts in skillet and allow to brown to a light golden color, stirring constantly. This will take about 2 minutes or less. Set aside.

When pasta is ready, drain and immediately combine with the cheese and toss well. Add butter and pine nuts. Season to taste with salt and pepper and toss again. Serve at once in heated bowls or on plates.

Serves 4 as a main course, 6 as a first course.

BREADS

Breadmaking

I don't know of any more satisfying task in the kitchen than making bread. There's a little magic in turning yeast, flour and water into something that smells and tastes so good. I think that everyone interested in cooking should learn to make bread by hand, as it's the only way you can judge the "feel" of yeast dough. Granted, it's less tiring to use a powerful electric mixer equipped with a dough hook, but you should still knead for a minute or two by hand when the machine has done its work, to make sure that the dough feels silky and smooth. You can't judge that just by looking at it.

Kneading by hand is simple enough. Working on a floured surface, and with floured hands, push the mass of dough vigorously away from you with the heels of your hands. Pick up the far side of the dough with your fingers, fold it toward you, and make a quarter turn. Repeat this motion, adding a little more flour if necessary, and keep up a good rhythm for about 10 minutes, until the dough stops feeling sticky and becomes smooth and supple. To test if the dough has been sufficiently kneaded, stick two fingers in it. It should spring back. There's nothing mysterious about the rising period: as the well-distributed yeast expands, it makes the dough increase in volume, which happens slowly or quite quickly depending on the spot you've chosen to place your bowl of dough. An electric oven with the light left on is ideal. But even in a cool kitchen, dough will eventually rise. Softer bread doughs are baked in pans for support; firmer ones can be patted into rounds or ovals that can stand alone.

Baguettes (French bread)

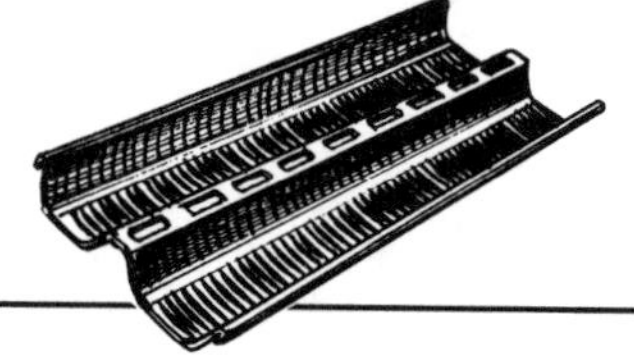

2 DOUBLE BAGUETTE PANS

With a little practice, you will be able to make very good, crisp-crusted loaves of French bread. They might not look too professional the first time, but they will taste good, and you will soon develop a "feel" for the dough and the timing. If you make this bread by hand rather than using an electric mixer with a dough hook, you'll discover that the dough is unusually sticky at the start. Use a pastry scraper to lift and turn the dough until it becomes firm enough to knead.

Curved black steel French bread pans are pretty standard equipment in U.S. kitchens today, but I can remember how surprised the French manufacturers were when I first asked them to make such a pan for the American home market. French home cooks don't make baguettes, and they simply couldn't imagine why Americans would do such a thing. Of course, the answer is we don't have French bakeries on every street corner!

1 package (1 tablespoon) active dry yeast
1 teaspoon sugar
2 cups warm water (110°)
4½ cups all-purpose flour
2 teaspoons salt
Cornmeal for baguette pans
1 egg white beaten with 1 teaspoon water for glaze

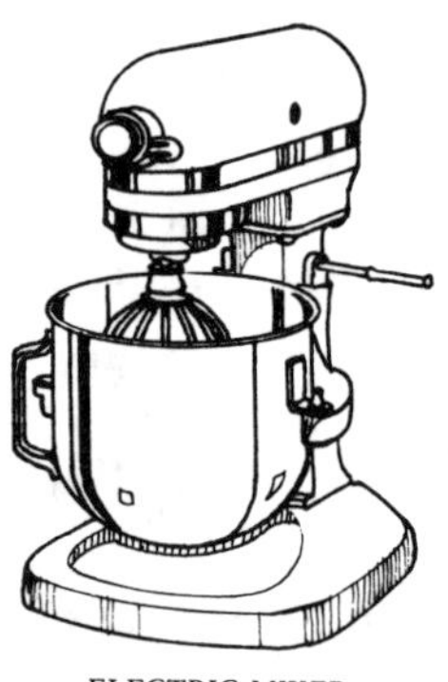

ELECTRIC MIXER

Dissolve yeast and sugar in ¼ cup of the water and let stand until foamy, about 3 minutes. In bowl of electric mixer, combine 4 cups of the flour and the salt. Add remaining water and yeast mixture and stir well with a wooden spoon. Fit bowl onto mixer stand and knead with dough hook at medium speed for 8 to 10 minutes, or until dough is smooth and elastic. Turn out onto a lightly floured surface and knead by hand for 2 minutes, adding remaining flour if too sticky. Transfer ball of dough to mixing bowl. Cover with greased plastic wrap and let rise in a warm place until dough is doubled in bulk, 1 to 1½ hours.

Dislodge dough from sides of bowl with a rubber spatula and turn out onto a lightly floured surface. Punch down, knead for a few seconds and return to bowl for a second rising, which helps develop flavor and a good airy "crumb." Cover and let rise until again doubled in bulk, 30 to 45 minutes.

Grease baguette pans and sprinkle with cornmeal; set aside. Turn dough out onto a lightly floured surface and pat flat. Cut into 4 equal pieces, form into balls and let rest for 5 minutes. Roll each ball into a long

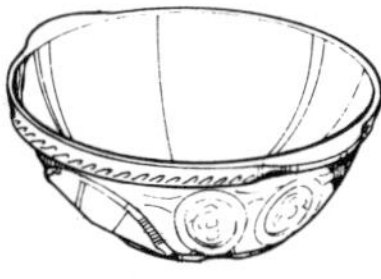
LARGE MIXING BOWL

rope almost the length of the pan, tapering the ends. Place in pans. Cover with a clean kitchen towel and let rise until almost double in bulk, about 30 minutes.

Preheat oven to 450°. Brush loaves with the beaten egg white mixture and, with a razor blade, slash each one three times, making deep ¼-inch diagonal cuts. Put on middle rack of oven and bake for 20 to 25 minutes, until brown and crusty. Unmold and cool on a rack.

Makes 4 baguettes.

"Beehive" Country Loaf

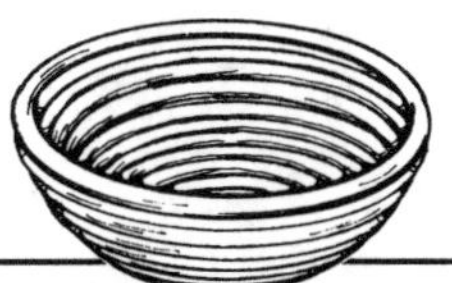
8-INCH BANNETON

I first saw the reed baskets which give this bread its distinctive shape in a bakery across the square from the Düsseldorf railway station. The shelves were stacked high with beehive-shaped loaves in all sizes, and they both looked and smelled marvelous. Soon afterward I found the baskets, or bannetons, at a bakery equipment manufacturer in France. The people were German-Swiss as I recall, and I think they got the baskets from Germany originally. The banneton should be well coated with flour so that the loaf will unmold easily. Do not disturb flour that sticks to the bread; it forms an interesting pattern when baked.

1 package (1 tablespoon) active dry yeast
1 teaspoon sugar
1¼ cups warm water (110°)
3 cups all-purpose white flour
1 cup whole-wheat flour
2 teaspoons salt
Cornmeal

Dissolve the yeast and sugar in ¼ cup of the water and let stand until foamy, about 3 minutes. Butter a large mixing bowl and set aside. In the bowl of electric mixer, combine the white flour, whole-wheat flour and salt. Add the yeast mixture and remaining water and stir well with a wooden spoon. Fit bowl onto mixer stand and knead with dough hook at medium speed for 10 minutes, until dough is smooth and elastic. Turn out onto floured surface and knead by hand for 1 minute, adding more flour if necessary. Dough should not be sticky. Place in prepared mixing bowl and turn dough to grease top. Cover with plastic wrap and let

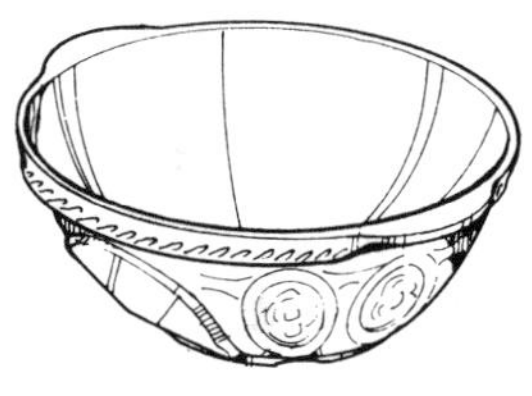

LARGE MIXING BOWL

rise in a warm place until doubled in bulk, 1 to 1½ hours.

Flour the inside of banneton well. Turn dough out, punch down and knead a few times to expel air. Form into a ball and carefully place in the banneton. Cover with greased plastic wrap and let rise until doubled in bulk, 45 minutes to 1 hour.

Preheat oven to 425° and sprinkle baking pan with cornmeal. Carefully turn risen dough out of banneton onto cornmeal. Place pan on middle shelf of oven and bake for 15 minutes. Reduce heat to 375° and bake for 30 minutes longer, until golden brown. Let loaf cool on rack.

Braided Buttermilk Loaf

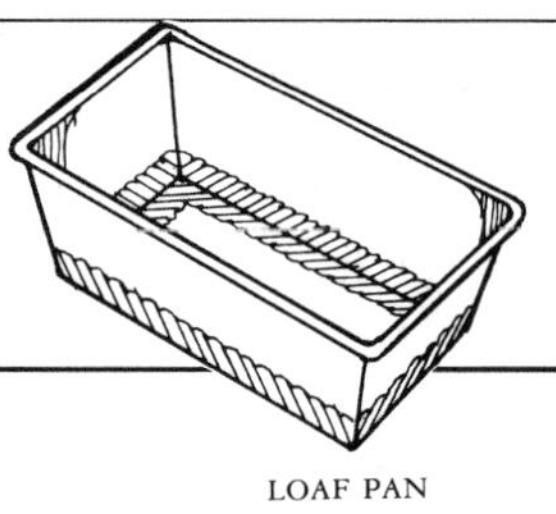

LOAF PAN

This is a very attractive loaf with good old-fashioned flavor.

1 package (1 tablespoon) active dry yeast
1 tablespoon sugar
½ cup warm water (110°)
2 tablespoons unsalted butter
1 cup buttermilk
3 cups all-purpose flour
½ teaspoon baking soda
1 teaspoon salt
1 egg yolk beaten with 1 teaspoon water
2 teaspoons sesame seeds

Dissolve yeast and sugar in the water and let stand until foamy, about 3 minutes. Melt butter in saucepan, add buttermilk and heat to lukewarm. In bowl of electric mixer, combine flour, soda and salt. Using a wooden spoon, stir in buttermilk mixture. Add yeast mixture and blend well. Fit bowl onto mixer stand and knead with dough hook at medium speed for 10 minutes, until dough is smooth and supple. Turn dough out onto floured surface and knead by hand for 1 minute, adding more flour if necessary. Dough should not be sticky. Place in mixing bowl and cover with greased plastic wrap. Let rise in a warm place until more than doubled in bulk, 1½ to 2 hours.

Butter loaf pan and set aside. Turn dough out onto

FEATHER BRUSH

lightly floured surface, punch down and knead for 1 minute to expel air. Form into 3 equal-sized balls and let rest for 5 minutes. Roll each ball into a 12-inch rope, lay side by side and plait the three pieces together into an 8½-inch-long braid. Pinch at both ends to seal. Place dough in prepared loaf pan, cover with greased plastic wrap and let rise until doubled in bulk, 45 minutes to 1 hour.

Preheat oven to 375°. Brush loaf with egg-yolk mixture and scatter with sesame seeds. Place on middle rack of oven and bake for 30 to 35 minutes, until golden brown. Loaf should sound hollow if tapped on underside; if not, return to oven for a few minutes without the pan. Cool on rack.

Brioche

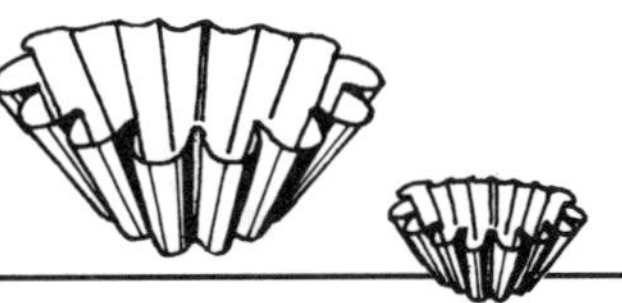

FLUTED 8-INCH BRIOCHE MOLD

This bread has to rise in the refrigerator overnight, but it's worth the wait.

1 package (1 tablespoon) active dry yeast
1 tablespoon sugar
½ cup warm water (110°)
3 cups all-purpose flour
1 teaspoon salt
4 eggs, slightly beaten
8 ounces (2 sticks) unsalted butter, at room temperature
1 egg yolk beaten with 1 teaspoon water for glaze

Dissolve the yeast and sugar in the water and let stand until foamy, about 3 minutes. Add ½ cup of the flour and mix until smooth. Cover with plastic wrap and let rise in a warm place until doubled in bulk, about 15 minutes. This is known as the "sponge."

In bowl of electric mixer, combine remaining flour, salt and eggs. Add sponge and mix with wooden spoon until flour is absorbed. Fit bowl onto mixer stand and knead with dough hook at medium speed for 10 minutes, until dough is smooth and elastic. Turn dough into mixing bowl, cover with greased plastic wrap and let rise in a warm place until doubled in bulk, about 2½ hours. (This dough is slow to rise.)

Return dough to clean electric mixer bowl. Cut

DRY MEASURE CUPS

butter into small pieces and gradually knead into dough with dough hook. Knead for 5 to 7 minutes after butter is incorporated. Transfer dough to clean mixing bowl, cover with greased plastic wrap and let rise in the refrigerator overnight.

Butter brioche mold. Turn dough out onto floured surface. It will be cold and firm, but quite easy to knead. Knead for 2 minutes, then cut off a piece of dough the size of a large lemon for the "topknot" or crown. Form this into a pear shape. Form the rest of the dough into a ball and place in the prepared mold. Make an indentation in the center with your finger and insert the smaller end of the pear-shaped crown. Cover loosely with greased plastic wrap and let rise in a warm place until doubled in bulk, about 1½ to 2 hours.

Preheat oven to 400°. Brush brioche with egg-yolk mixture and place on middle rack of oven. Bake for 20 minutes, then reduce heat to 350° and bake for 40 minutes more until golden brown. Cover loosely with aluminum foil if browning too fast. Unmold and cool on rack.

Chocolate Bread

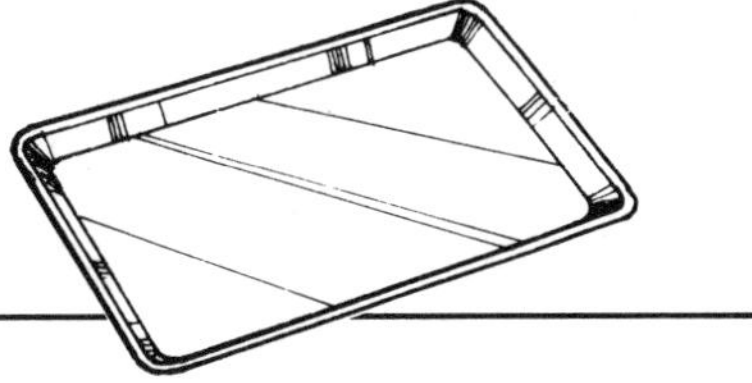

11- X 17-INCH BAKING PAN

This recipe is based on one that I got from IL FORNAIO, the Italian bakery chain that specializes in regional Italian breads and pastries. One of the owners of the chain once came to dinner at my house in San Francisco and was dumbfounded when I produced two large round loaves of bread that I'd made that afternoon. In Italy, that kind of bread is produced in bakeries, not at home! The original recipe listed 16 kilos of flour. Needless to say, I had to fiddle with it quite a bit. It's best to use the tiny-size chocolate morsels if you can get them.

1 package (1 tablespoon) active dry yeast
2 tablespoons sugar
1¼ cups warm water (110°)
4 cups all-purpose flour
⅓ cup Dutch process unsweetened cocoa
2 teaspoons salt
1 egg, lightly beaten
2 tablespoons (¼ stick) unsalted butter, at room temperature
1 cup chocolate morsels

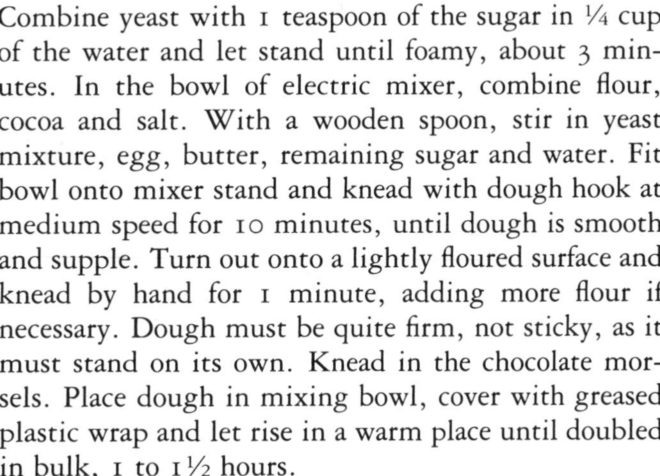

Combine yeast with 1 teaspoon of the sugar in ¼ cup of the water and let stand until foamy, about 3 minutes. In the bowl of electric mixer, combine flour, cocoa and salt. With a wooden spoon, stir in yeast mixture, egg, butter, remaining sugar and water. Fit bowl onto mixer stand and knead with dough hook at medium speed for 10 minutes, until dough is smooth and supple. Turn out onto a lightly floured surface and knead by hand for 1 minute, adding more flour if necessary. Dough must be quite firm, not sticky, as it must stand on its own. Knead in the chocolate morsels. Place dough in mixing bowl, cover with greased plastic wrap and let rise in a warm place until doubled in bulk, 1 to 1½ hours.

Grease baking pan. Turn dough out, punch down and knead for 1 minute to expel air. Let rest for 5 minutes. Form into an 8- x 4-inch oval and place on baking pan. Cover loosely with greased plastic wrap and let rise until doubled in bulk, about 1 hour.

Preheat oven to 450°. Place on middle rack of oven and bake for 15 minutes, then reduce heat to 375° and bake for 25 minutes more. Cool on rack and serve with sweet butter.

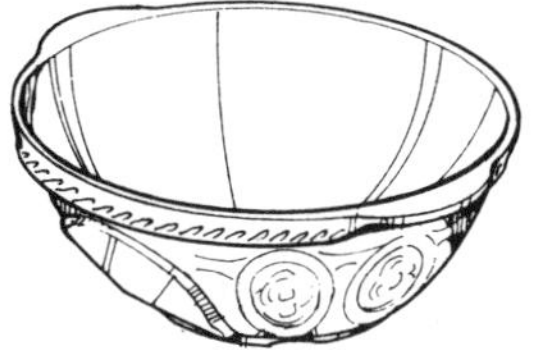

LARGE MIXING BOWL

Focaccia con Olio e Sale (Italian flat bread with olive oil and salt)

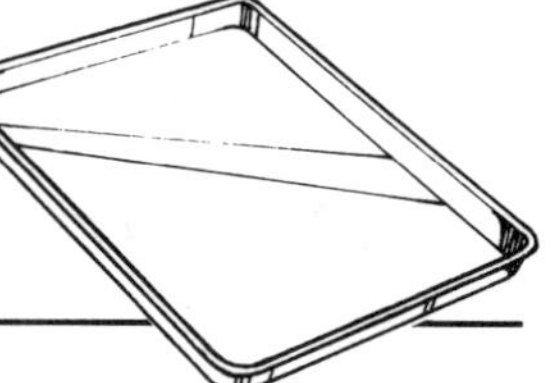
13- X 18-INCH BAKING SHEET

- *1 package (1 tablespoon) active dry yeast*
- *1½ cups warm water (110°)*
- *4 cups unbleached hardwheat or all-purpose flour*
- *2 teaspoons salt*
- *¼ cup Italian olive oil (page 87)*
- *Additional olive oil for brushing top of dough*
- *Coarse salt crystals for top of dough*

Dissolve yeast in ¼ cup of the water and let stand until foamy, about 3 minutes. In bowl of electric mixer, combine the flour and salt. Using a wooden spoon, stir in remaining water, yeast mixture and olive oil. Fit bowl onto mixer stand and knead with dough hook at medium speed for 8 to 10 minutes, until dough is smooth and elastic. Turn out onto lightly floured surface and knead by hand for 1 minute, adding more flour if necessary. Dough should not be sticky. Form into a ball, place in mixing bowl and cover with greased plastic wrap. Let rise in a warm place until doubled in bulk, 45 minutes to 1 hour.

Oil the baking sheet. Turn dough out, punch down, place on prepared pan and let rest for 5 minutes. Stretch dough so that it completely covers bottom of pan. Cover with greased plastic wrap and let rise for 30 minutes.

Preheat oven to 350°. Using fingertips, make a pattern of "dimples" over the entire surface of dough, at 2-inch intervals. Brush surface with oil and sprinkle lightly with coarse salt. Bake for 15 to 20 minutes or until golden brown. It is important to serve this bread hot.

WOODEN SPOON

Kugelhopf

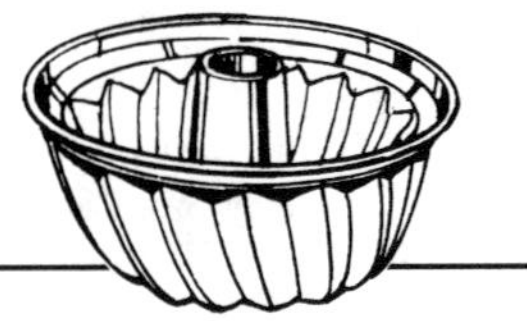

9-INCH, 2-QUART KUGELHOPF MOLD

This yeast-raised coffee cake is a regional specialty of Alsace. It's delicious when freshly made, but tends to go stale quickly. Years ago, Alsatian cooks got the idea of freshening up leftover slices of Kugelhopf by soaking them in a rum-flavored syrup. The result is a bit like *baba au rhum,* and it's a good way to make leftover Kugelhopf into a rich-tasting dessert. You'll find directions at the end of this recipe.

1 cup seedless raisins
2 tablespoons kirsch
2 tablespoons unsalted butter, melted
3 cups plus 2½ tablespoons all-purpose flour
1 package (1 tablespoon) active dry yeast
⅓ cup sugar
¼ cup warm water (110°)
Pinch salt
¾ cup milk, lukewarm
3 eggs, slightly beaten
¾ cup (1½ sticks) unsalted butter, at room temperature
Grated peel of 1 orange (colored part only)
Confectioners' sugar

In a bowl, combine raisins and kirsch and let soak for 30 minutes.

Prepare Kugelhopf mold: Stir the melted butter and 2½ tablespoons of the flour together and brush over entire inside surface of mold. Let stand upside down while preparing batter. (This coating prevents the baked Kugelhopf from sticking to the mold.)

Dissolve yeast and 1 teaspoon of the sugar in the water and let stand until foamy, about 3 minutes. Sift remaining flour into bowl of electric mixer. With a wooden spoon, stir in salt, remaining sugar, yeast mixture, milk and eggs. Mix well. Fit bowl onto mixer stand. Beat with flat beater on medium speed until smooth, about 5 minutes. Cut up butter and beat in, a little at a time, until batter is smooth and elastic—about 5 minutes. Add raisins and orange peel.

Spoon batter into prepared mold, cover with greased plastic wrap and let rise until it is doubled in bulk and comes to within 1 inch of the top of mold, 1 to 1½ hours.

Preheat oven to 350°. Bake Kugelhopf for 1 hour. Unmold immediately onto a rack and let cool. Dust with confectioners' sugar before serving.

Serves 10 to 12.

To use leftover Kugelhopf: Make a syrup by combining 1 cup water with ½ cup sugar. Let simmer for 10

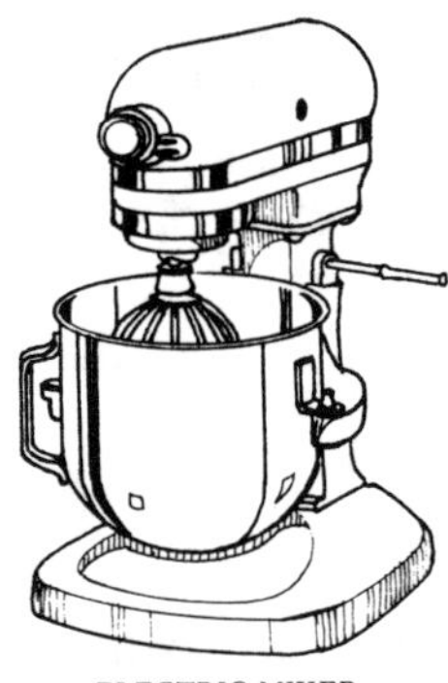
ELECTRIC MIXER

minutes. Cool slightly, then stir in ½ cup dark rum. Place a slice of Kugelhopf on each dessert plate and soak liberally with warm syrup. Top each serving with whipped cream. The syrup keeps indefinitely, but reheat before using since it is absorbed better when warm.

Lemon Tea Bread

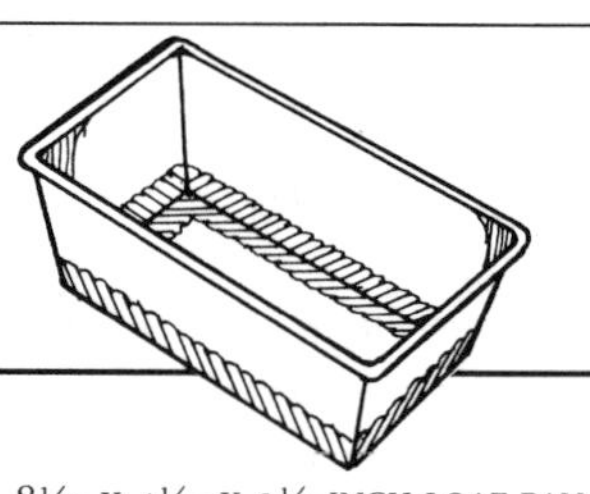
8½- X 4½- X 2½-INCH LOAF PAN

This recipe is based on one which took a prize in a contest I judged—it came from Mrs. John Edmond Sullivan, and it is very good indeed.

6 ounces (1½ sticks) unsalted butter, at warm room temperature
1 cup sugar
2 eggs
½ cup milk
Grated peel of 1 large lemon (colored part only)
1½ cups all-purpose flour
1 teaspoon baking powder
½ teaspoon salt

Glaze:

1 tablespoon lemon juice
2 tablespoons confectioners' sugar

Preheat oven to 350° and grease loaf pan.

In a bowl, cream butter and sugar together. Beat in eggs, then milk and lemon rind. Sift together flour, baking powder and salt, and quickly stir into other ingredients. Do not overmix. Spoon batter into prepared pan and bake for 1 hour, or until toothpick inserted in center of loaf comes out clean. Remove from pan and place on rack.

In a small bowl, mix lemon juice and confectioners' sugar to a smooth glaze. Brush over top of bread while it is still warm—glaze will be slightly opaque.

PASTRY BRUSH

Oatmeal and Molasses Bread

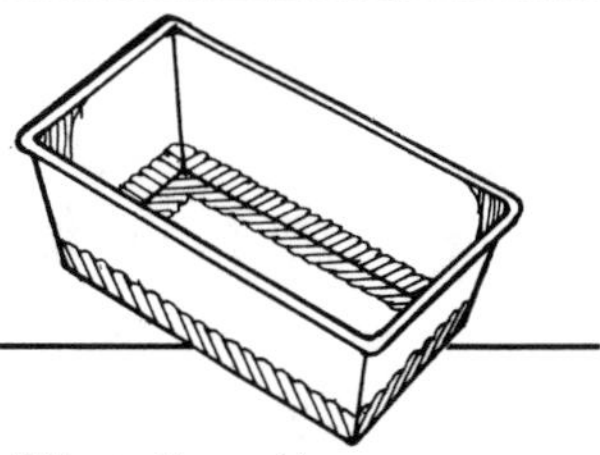

8½- x 4½- x 2½-INCH LOAF PAN

Use the old-fashioned type of oatmeal for this bread, not the instant kind.

1 package (1 tablespoon) active dry yeast
1 teaspoon sugar
¼ cup warm water (110°)
½ cup rolled oats
¾ cup boiling water
3 ounces (¾ stick) unsalted butter, cut up
¼ cup molasses
1 teaspoon salt
1 egg, slightly beaten
1½ cups all-purpose flour
1 cup whole-wheat flour
Additional rolled oats for top of loaf

Dissolve yeast and sugar in the water and let stand until foamy, about 3 minutes. Grease a loaf pan and set aside.

In a bowl, combine oats and boiling water. Stir in butter, molasses and salt. Add egg. Cool to 110°, then stir in the yeast mixture. Gradually beat in both flours, and beat for 3 minutes. Spoon batter into prepared pan, smooth top with spatula and sprinkle generously with rolled oats. Cover with greased plastic wrap and let rise in warm place until dough is doubled in bulk and reaches the top of the pan, about 1 hour.

Preheat oven to 375°. Place pan on middle rack of oven and bake for 1 hour, until brown and crusty. Unmold and cool on rack.

Orange Tea Bread

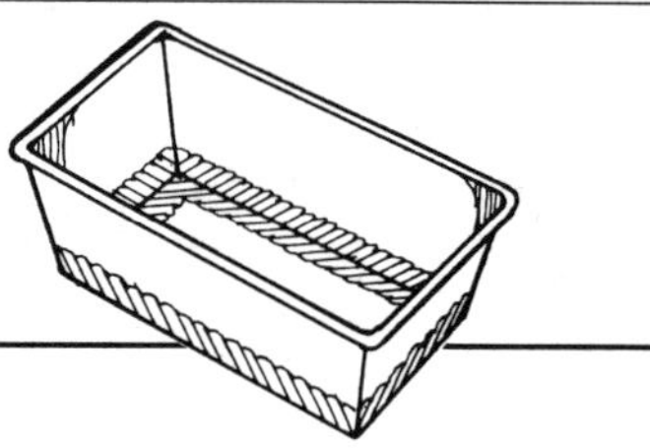

8½- x 4½- x 2½-INCH LOAF PAN

This excellent tea bread recipe came from Patrice Gunn, an award winner at a recipe contest I judged for United Western Newspapers a couple of years ago. It's worth making an extra batch of the candied orange peel that goes into it; it's delicious eaten by itself.

2 cups whole-wheat flour
¾ cup sugar
1 tablespoon baking powder
½ teaspoon salt
2 eggs
1 cup freshly squeezed orange juice
3 tablespoons vegetable oil
¾ to 1 cup candied orange peel, chopped (page 235)

Preheat oven to 350° and grease a loaf pan.

In a bowl, combine flour, sugar, baking powder and salt. In a separate bowl, beat the eggs. Stir in orange juice and oil. Add liquid ingredients to flour mixture and beat well. Stir in candied orange peel.

Turn mixture into prepared pan and bake for 1 hour, or until toothpick inserted in center of loaf comes out clean. Remove from pan and cool on rack. Wrap and store overnight before slicing.

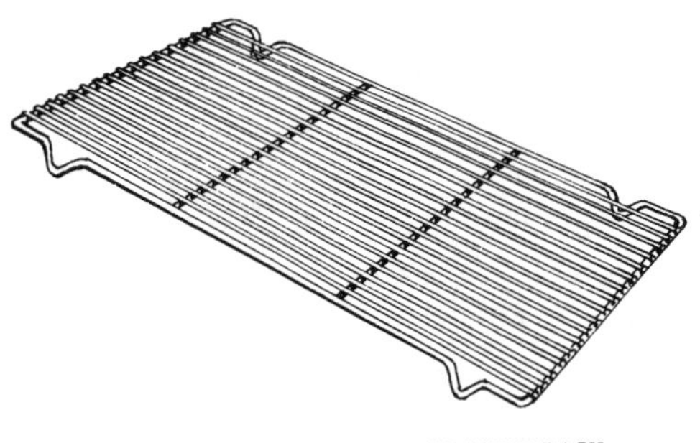

COOLING RACK

Candied Orange Peel

CANDY THERMOMETER

3 oranges
1 cup sugar
½ cup water
Granulated sugar for coating peel

With a sharp knife, cut around circumference of orange, going only through peel and not into fruit. Make a second cut at right angles to first, again going completely around orange. Now remove peel in 4 quarter segments. Repeat with other 2 oranges.

Put peel into a small pan, cover with cold water and bring to a boil. Cook slowly until soft, about 15 minutes. Drain and cool. Scrape off white membrane with the edge of a spoon. Cut peel into ¼-inch strips.

Combine sugar and water in a saucepan and bring to a boil; add the peel. Cook slowly until peel is almost transparent and the syrup measures 230° on a candy thermometer. Remove peel with slotted spoon and spread on cookie sheet to cool. Roll in granulated sugar and spread on waxed paper to dry.

Makes about 1 cup.

Panettone (Italian fruit bread)

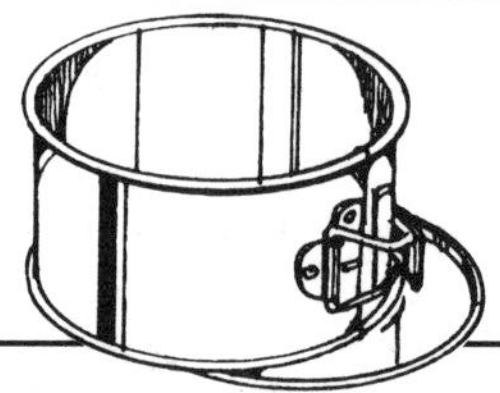
PANETTONE MOLD

1½ packages (1½ tablespoons) active dry yeast
⅓ cup sugar
1 cup warm water (110°)
5 egg yolks
1 teaspoon vanilla extract
Grated peel of 1 lemon, colored part only
1½ teaspoons salt
5 cups all-purpose flour
6 ounces (1½ sticks) unsalted butter, at room temperature
½ cup dark raisins
½ cup white raisins
½ cup chopped candied lemon or orange peel
2 ounces (½ stick) unsalted butter, melted, for brushing loaf

LARGE MIXING BOWL

Combine yeast and 1 teaspoon of the sugar in ½ cup of the water and let stand until foamy, about 3 minutes. In bowl of electric mixer, whisk together the egg yolks, vanilla, grated lemon peel, salt, remaining sugar and rest of water. Add the yeast mixture and, using a wooden spoon, stir in 3 cups of the flour.

Fit bowl onto mixer stand. Cut up the butter and gradually incorporate into the dough with the dough hook. When butter is all added, knead in remaining flour a little at a time. It is advisable to use spatter shield on mixer, if you have one. Knead for 10 minutes at medium speed. Turn dough out onto lightly floured surface and knead by hand for 1 minute. This is a soft dough; do not add extra flour unless absolutely necessary. Form dough into a ball, place in mixing bowl and cover with greased plastic wrap. Let rise in a warm place until doubled in bulk, about 1 to 1½ hours.

Butter panettone mold. Turn dough out onto a lightly floured surface and knead in raisins and candied peel. Form into a ball, flatten slightly to form a circle almost the diameter of mold. Place dough in mold, cover with greased plastic wrap and let rise in a warm place until doubled in bulk, 45 minutes to 1 hour.

Preheat oven to 400°. Brush top of loaf with melted butter, place on middle shelf of oven and bake for 15 minutes. Reduce heat to 350° and brush again with butter. Bake for 45 to 50 minutes more, brushing again with butter after 30 minutes. If top browns too fast, cover lightly with a sheet of aluminum foil. Unmold onto rack, brush top and sides of loaf with remaining butter and let cool. Cut in thin wedges to serve.

Pear Walnut Bread

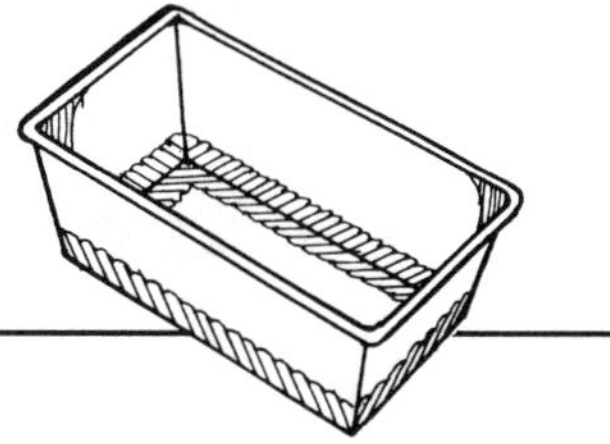

8½- X 4½- X 2½-INCH LOAF PAN

This batter bread is fast to prepare, and it's unusual in that it contains no shortening. The texture is very special.

1 cup all-purpose white flour
1 cup whole-wheat flour
½ cup sugar
½ teaspoon salt
1 tablespoon baking powder
1 cup (6 ounces) moist dried pears, chopped
½ cup chopped walnuts
1 egg
1 cup milk
1 tablespoon lemon juice

Preheat oven to 350° and butter and flour a loaf pan.

In a bowl, combine flours, sugar, salt and baking powder. Mix well. Stir in the pears and walnuts. In a separate bowl, beat the egg and stir in milk and lemon juice. Add the liquid ingredients to the flour mixture and mix well. Pour into prepared pan, and bake for 1 hour until golden brown and a toothpick inserted in the center of the loaf comes out clean. Remove from pan and cool on rack.

Pullman Loaf

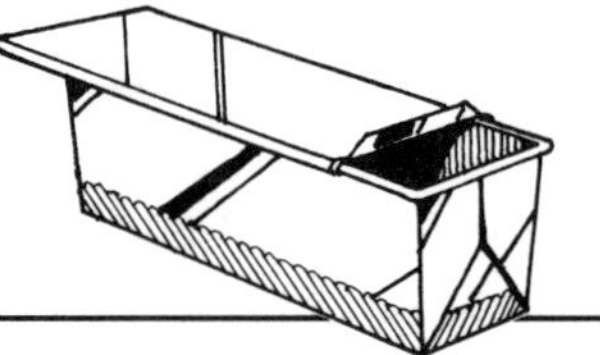
PULLMAN LOAF PAN

This is the bread that's always used for breakfast toast on French trains. I suppose that's why we call it a Pullman loaf; however it's called *pain de mie* in France. It's so good that it's worth catching the Paris–Bordeaux early train just to eat breakfast. Then you get off in Tours and return to Paris! Plan to start early when you make this bread. It needs about 2½ hours for the first rise, another 2 for the next.

1 package (1 tablespoon) active dry yeast
1 teaspoon sugar
¼ cup warm water (110°)
4 cups all-purpose flour
2 teaspoons salt
1½ cups warm milk (110°)
2 ounces (½ stick) unsalted butter, cool but not hard

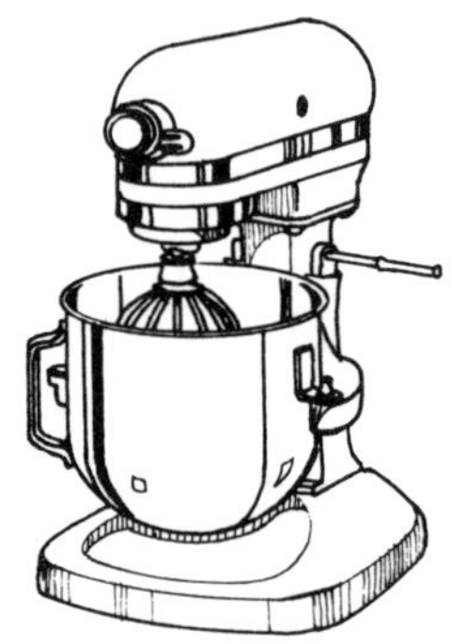
ELECTRIC MIXER

Dissolve yeast and sugar in the water and let stand until foamy, about 3 minutes. In the bowl of electric mixer, combine flour and salt. With a wooden spoon, stir in milk and the yeast mixture until all of the flour is absorbed. Fit bowl onto mixer stand and knead with dough hook at medium speed for 10 minutes, or until dough is smooth and elastic. Knead butter into dough 1 tablespoon at a time. Dough will become sticky, but will return to its former smoothness as it is kneaded.

Turn out onto a floured surface and knead by hand for 1 minute, adding more flour if necessary. Dough should not be sticky. Transfer to mixing bowl. Cover with greased plastic wrap and let stand in a warm place until tripled in bulk, 2 to 2½ hours. Turn dough out onto a lightly floured surface and pat flat into a 12- x 7-inch rectangle. Fold in three (like a letter) and make a quarter turn, rotating the dough toward you. Pat flat into a rectangle as before, and again fold in three. Return to bowl and let rise again, covered, for 1½ hours or until dough has more than doubled in volume.

Butter inside surface and underneath cover of Pullman loaf pan. Turn dough out, pat flat and form into a rectangle a little longer than the pan. Fold in half lengthways and press edges together to seal. Roll dough so that seam is uppermost and centered. Pat flat and again fold lengthways, sealing edges. (This helps eliminate air bubbles; a Pullman loaf is very close-textured.)

LARGE MIXING BOWL

Shape the dough gently into a rectangle and place in the pan, seam side down. Dough should fill pan about ⅓ full. Cover with plastic wrap and let rise until pan is ¾ full, about 30 minutes.

Preheat oven to 400°. Put cover on pan, discarding plastic wrap, and bake for 50 minutes. If loaf needs more browning, remove from pan and return to oven for a few minutes. Cool on rack. This bread slices best if wrapped and stored overnight.

Round Country Loaf Baked in an Instant Brick Oven

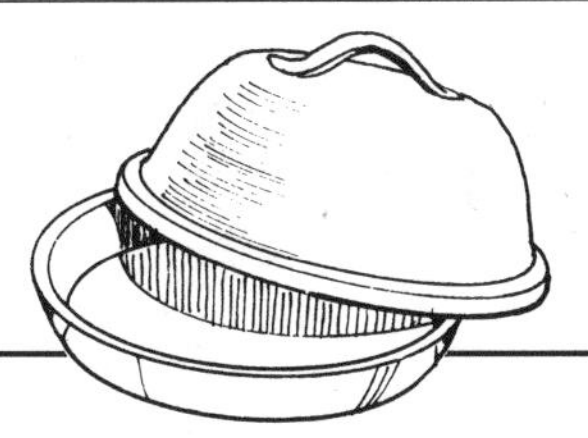
INSTANT BRICK OVEN

Baking a round loaf inside an Instant Brick Oven simulates using an old-fashioned brick-lined bread oven. You really do get spectacular results: The bread rises extremely well, and develops a thin, crisp, crackly crust. You can also use an old ovenproof earthenware mixing bowl turned upside down on a heavy baking sheet, which is what I used to do. If you can get unbleached hard-wheat flour, use it instead of all-purpose flour.

1 package (1 tablespoon) active dry yeast
1 teaspoon sugar
2 cups warm water (110°)
5 cups unbleached all-purpose flour
1 tablespoon salt
Cornmeal

Dissolve yeast and sugar in ¼ cup of water and let stand until foamy, about 3 minutes. In bowl of electric mixer, combine flour and salt. With a wooden spoon, stir in remaining water and the yeast mixture. Fit bowl onto mixer stand and knead with dough hook at medium speed for 10 minutes, or until dough is smooth and elastic. Turn out onto floured surface and knead by hand for 1 minute, adding more flour if necessary. Dough should not be sticky. Place in mixing bowl, cover with greased plastic wrap and let rise in a warm place until doubled in bulk, 1 to 1½ hours.

Sprinkle bottom surface of Instant Brick Oven with cornmeal.

Turn dough out, punch down and knead for 1 minute. Form into a ball, roll in flour and place in center of bottom part of Brick Oven. Cover with dome and let rise in a warm place until doubled in bulk, 1 to 1½ hours. Dough should fill dome ⅔ to ¾ full.

Preheat oven to 475°. Adjust racks if necessary to accommodate dome and bake for 15 minutes. Reduce heat to 400° and bake for 35 to 45 minutes more. Loaf should be crusty, golden brown and sound hollow if tapped on underside. Cool on a rack.

Rye Bread

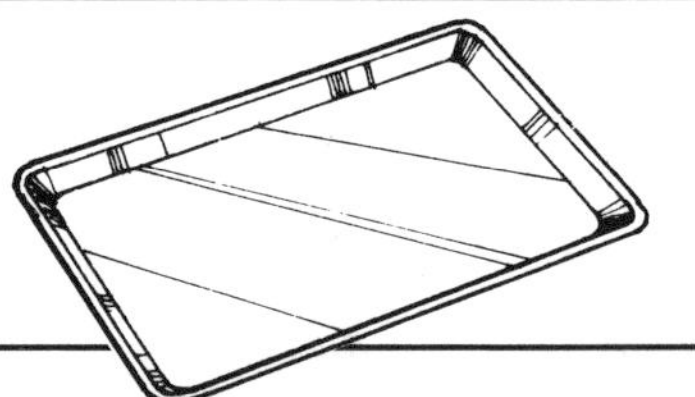

11- X 17-INCH BAKING SHEET

This recipe is based on one given to me years ago by Terry Shelton, a very talented baker who worked for me in our original San Francisco store. It has an excellent flavor and texture and keeps well.

1 package (1 tablespoon) active dry yeast
1 teaspoon sugar
1½ cups warm water (110°)
1 tablespoon vegetable oil
½ cup molasses
1½ teaspoons salt
1½ teaspoons caraway seeds
2½ cups rye flour
1 cup whole-wheat flour
1 cup all-purpose flour
1 egg yolk beaten with 1 teaspoon water

Combine the yeast and sugar in ¼ cup of the water and let stand until foamy, about 3 minutes. Grease mixing bowl and set aside. In bowl of electric mixer, combine remaining water, oil, molasses, salt, caraway seeds and yeast mixture. With a wooden spoon, stir in flours. Fit bowl onto mixer stand and knead with dough hook at medium speed for 10 minutes, until dough is smooth and elastic. Turn out onto lightly floured surface and knead by hand for 1 minute, adding more all-purpose flour if necessary. Dough should not be sticky. Place in prepared bowl and turn dough to grease top. Cover with greased plastic wrap and let rise in a warm place until doubled in bulk, 1 to 1½ hours.

Turn dough out, punch down and divide in half. Shape into 2 tapered loaves approximately 9- x 4-inches long. Place on baking sheet and cover with

Assortment of breads

Choucroute Garnie; Clay Pot Chicken, Greek Style; Pot Roast of Beef with Aceto Balsamico

CONTENTS:
BALSAMIC
VINEGAR
FINI

Oven Broiled Shrimp and Vegetable Shish Kebab

Opposite: Ginger Orange Steamed Pudding

Apple Charlotte

Opposite: Pizelle

Sliced apple, lemon and cucumber

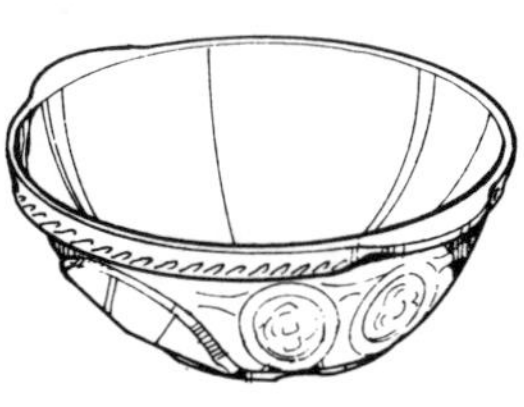

LARGE MIXING BOWL

greased plastic wrap or a clean kitchen towel. Let rise for 30 to 45 minutes, until doubled in bulk.

Preheat oven to 350°. Brush loaves with egg and water mixture and place on middle shelf of oven. Bake for 30 to 35 minutes until a shiny brown and well risen. Let cool on rack.

Tomato Pizza

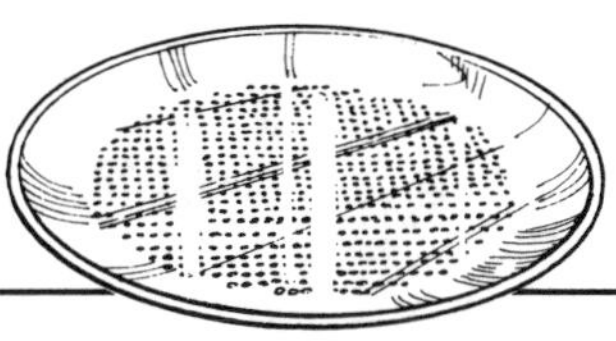

PIZZA PAN

Dough

2 teaspoons (⅔ package) active dry yeast
¾ cup warm water, 110°
2 cups all-purpose flour
1 teaspoon salt
2 tablespoons olive oil
Additional olive oil for top of pizza and pan

Topping

3 medium tomatoes
4 to 5 strips thick-cut lean bacon
1 tablespoon olive oil
1 medium Bermuda onion, sliced
1 cup coarsely grated mozzarella cheese
Additional olive oil for topping
2 to 3 teaspoons Herbes de Provence *(page 175)*
Salt
Freshly ground black pepper

Oil the baking pan. Dissolve the yeast in ¼ cup of the water and let stand until foamy, about 3 minutes. In bowl, combine the flour and salt and add the yeast mixture, remaining water and olive oil. Mix well, turn out on a floured surface and knead for 10 minutes, until dough is soft and silky and no longer sticky. Add more flour if necessary. (If preferred, dough may be kneaded with dough hook in an electric mixer.) Return dough to clean bowl, cover with greased plastic wrap, place in a warm spot and let rise until doubled in bulk, 1 to 1½ hours. Punch down, knead a couple of times and let rest for 5 minutes. On a well-floured surface, roll or stretch out to a 15-inch circle. Place on baking pan, cover with greased plastic wrap and let rise for 20 minutes.

Preheat oven to 475° and prepare topping. Core the tomatoes and make a small cross at the blossom end. Dip in boiling water for 5 seconds to loosen skin. Peel, cut in slices and reserve. Cut the bacon into ½-inch pieces and put in skillet. Let cook over moderate heat until most of the fat is rendered and bacon is lightly browned. Remove with slotted spoon and drain on paper towels. Drain fat from skillet, wipe out with

SKILLET

paper towel and add the olive oil. Heat, then add onion and sauté gently for 3 minutes until onion is transparent but not browned.

Make indentations in pizza dough with fingertips approximately 2 inches apart. Brush with olive oil and place in oven. Prebake for 5 to 7 minutes. Remove from oven and arrange onions evenly over the dough, then the tomato slices, bacon and cheese. Brush with olive oil, sprinkle with the *Herbes* and season with salt and pepper. Return to oven, reduce heat to 425° and bake for another 10 to 15 minutes until edges are brown, cheese is melted and all is bubbly.

Serves 4 to 6.

Walnut Ring Loaf

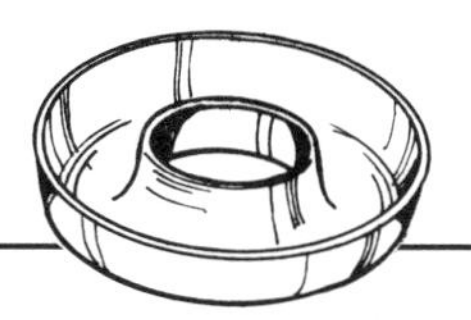
8-INCH DIAMETER SAVARIN MOLD

This firm-textured bread, usually baked in a savarin mold, is a regional Italian loaf that I first came across in Milan, at one of the famous IL FORNAIO bakeries. It's marvelous with cheese.

- *1 package (1 tablespoon) active dry yeast*
- *1 teaspoon sugar*
- *1 cup warm water (110°)*
- *2 cups whole-wheat flour*
- *1 cup all-purpose white flour*
- *2 teaspoons salt*
- *2 teaspoons walnut oil or olive oil*
- *1½ tablespoons honey*
- *½ to ¾ cups walnut halves and pieces*
- *1 egg yolk beaten with 1 teaspoon water*

Dissolve yeast and sugar in ¼ cup of the water and let stand until foamy, about 3 minutes. In bowl of electric mixer, combine flours and salt. Add remaining water, oil, honey and yeast mixture and mix well with a wooden spoon. Fit bowl onto mixer stand and knead with dough hook at medium speed for 10 minutes, or until dough is smooth and elastic. Turn out onto a floured surface and knead by hand for 1 minute adding more flour if necessary. Dough should not be sticky. Place in mixing bowl and cover with greased plastic wrap. Let rise in a warm place until doubled in bulk, 1 to 1½ hours.

Oil the savarin mold. Turn dough out, pat flat and divide into 10 equal pieces. Allow to rest for 5 min-

PASTRY BRUSH

utes. Flatten each piece of dough and put a few walnut pieces in the center. Gather edges, pinch together to seal and form into a ball. Place balls, seam side down and touching one another, into prepared mold. Place a walnut half on top of each ball and press in. Cover with greased plastic wrap and let rise until doubled in bulk, about 45 minutes.

Preheat oven to 400°. Brush top of dough with egg yolk mixture and bake for 15 minutes. Reduce heat to 350°, lay a sheet of foil loosely over bread to keep walnuts from over-browning, and bake for 20 to 25 minutes more. Unmold and cool on rack.

White Bread

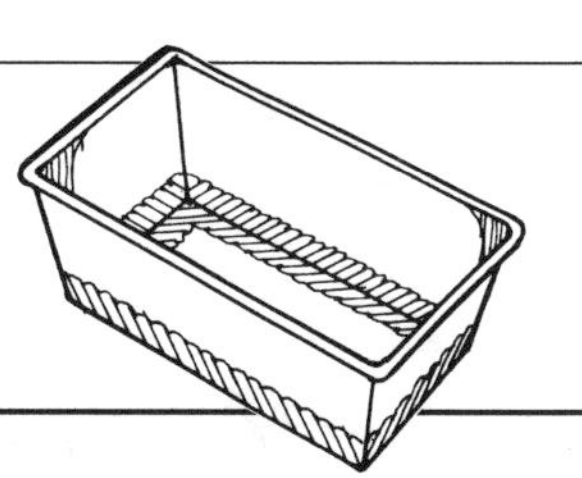
9- X 5- X 3-INCH BREAD PAN

1 package (1 tablespoon) active dry yeast
1 teaspoon sugar
¾ cup warm water (110°)
4 cups unbleached white flour
1½ teaspoons salt
¾ cup warm milk (110°)
3 tablespoons unsalted butter, melted
1 egg yolk beaten with 1 teaspoon water for glaze

Butter loaf pan and mixing bowl. Dissolve the yeast and sugar in ¼ cup of the water and let stand until foamy, about 3 minutes. In bowl of electric mixer, combine 3½ cups of the flour and the salt. Add the yeast mixture, the remaining water, the milk and the melted butter. Mix with a wooden spoon until flour is absorbed. Fit bowl onto mixer stand and knead with dough hook at medium speed for 5 minutes. Stop machine and add half the remaining flour. Mix in by hand until flour is absorbed. Turn machine on to medium speed and knead for another 5 minutes. Turn dough out onto floured surface and knead by hand for 1 minute, adding remaining flour if needed. Dough should be smooth and silky, not sticky. Place in prepared mixing bowl and cover with plastic wrap. Put in a warm place and let rise until doubled in bulk, 1 to 1½ hours.

Turn dough out onto floured surface, punch down and knead 3 or 4 times to expel air. Shape into an 8½-inch-long roll and place in prepared loaf pan. Cover

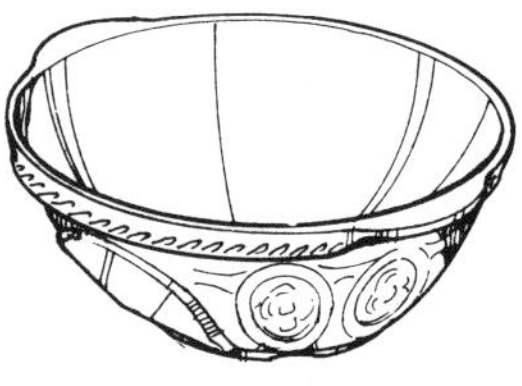
LARGE MIXING BOWL

loosely with greased plastic wrap or a clean kitchen towel and return to warm place. Let rise until doubled in bulk, about 45 minutes to 1 hour.

Preheat oven to 425°. Uncover loaf and make one or two ½-inch deep slashes in top with a sharp knife or razor blade. Brush with egg yolk mixture. Place on middle rack of oven and bake for 15 minutes. Turn heat down to 375° and cover top of loaf loosely with aluminum foil if top is browning too fast. Bake for 30 minutes more, until brown and crusty. Turn bread out and cool on rack.

Whole-Wheat Bread

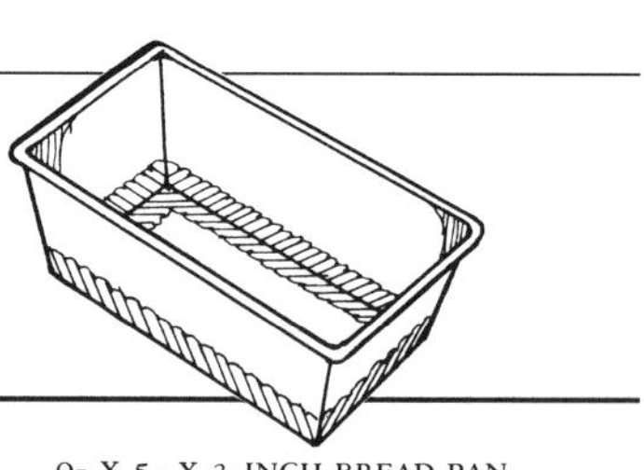
9- X 5- X 3-INCH BREAD PAN

If unbleached flour is not available, use all-purpose flour.

1 package (1 tablespoon) active dry yeast
1 teaspoon sugar
1½ cups warm water (110°)
1 cup unbleached white flour
3 cups unbleached whole-wheat flour
1½ teaspoons salt
2 tablespoons molasses
2 tablespoons (¼ stick) unsalted butter, melted

Butter bread pan and mixing bowl. Dissolve the yeast and sugar in ¼ cup of the water and let stand until foamy, about 3 minutes. In bowl of electric mixer, combine all the white flour, 2½ cups of the whole-wheat flour and the salt. Mix well. Add the yeast mixture, the remaining water, the molasses and the butter. Mix with a wooden spoon until flour is absorbed. Fit bowl onto mixer stand and knead with dough hook at medium speed for 5 minutes. Stop machine and add half the remaining flour. Mix in by hand until the flour is absorbed. Turn machine on to medium speed and knead for another 5 minutes. Turn dough out on to floured surface and knead by hand for 1 minute, adding remaining flour if needed. Dough should be smooth and silky, not sticky. Place in pre-

ELECTRIC MIXER

pared mixing bowl and cover with greased plastic wrap. Put in a warm place and let rise until doubled in bulk, 1 to 1½ hours.

Turn dough out on floured surface, punch down and knead 3 or 4 times to expel air. Shape into an 8½-inch-long roll and place in prepared bread pan. Cover loosely with greased plastic wrap or a clean kitchen towel and return to warm place. Let rise until doubled in bulk, about 1 to 1½ hours.

Preheat oven to 425°. Uncover loaf and slash top with a sharp knife or razor blade if desired. Place on middle rack of oven and bake for 15 minutes. Turn heat down to 375° and cover top of loaf loosely with aluminum foil if top is browning too fast. Bake for 30 minutes more, until brown and crusty. Turn bread out and cool on rack.

MUFFINS,

ETC.

Buttermilk Popovers

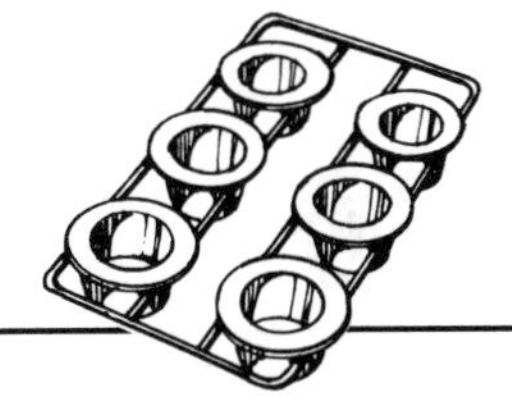

POPOVER PAN

As far as I'm concerned, the only "secret" to making great puffy popovers is to resist opening the oven door to check on whether the popovers are popping.

Oil for greasing popover pan
1 cup all-purpose flour
1/4 teaspoon salt
3 eggs
1 cup buttermilk
1 tablespoon unsalted butter, melted, for batter
6 to 9 teaspoons unsalted butter for bottom of popover cups

Preheat oven to 425°. Lightly oil cups of a popover pan and preheat for 2 minutes.

In a bowl, sift together flour and salt. Add eggs, buttermilk and melted butter. Beat vigorously for 2 minutes, until mixture is the consistency of heavy cream. Put approximately 1 teaspoon butter into each cup of popover pan. Heat in oven for a few minutes until butter is bubbling. Fill each cup half full of batter and bake for 20 minutes. Reduce heat to 325° and bake for 15 to 20 minutes more, until popovers are well risen.

Makes 6 to 9 popovers, depending on size of cups.

FLOUR SIFTER

Chocolate Muffins

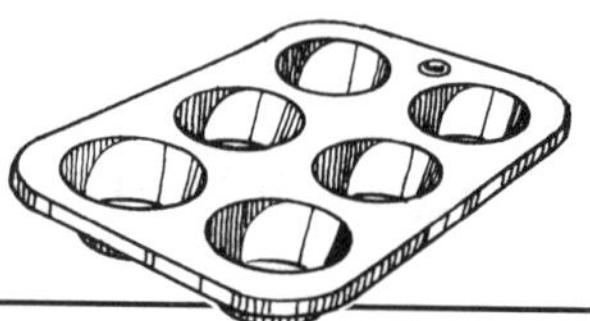
MUFFIN PAN

1 ½ cups all-purpose flour
½ cup unsweetened Dutch process cocoa
¼ teaspoon salt
⅓ cup sugar
3 teaspoons baking powder
2 eggs
¾ cup milk
1 teaspoon vanilla extract
2 ounces (½ stick) unsalted butter, melted

Preheat oven to 425° and butter molds of a muffin pan. In a bowl, sift together flour, cocoa, salt, sugar and baking powder. In a separate bowl, beat eggs lightly, then beat in milk, vanilla and butter. Add liquid to dry ingredients and stir quickly but thoroughly.

Fill molds ¾ full and bake for 15 to 20 minutes, or until a toothpick inserted in the center of a muffin comes out clean. Remove from molds immediately and serve warm with unsalted butter.

Makes approximately 2 cups batter; enough for 12 standard 2¾-inch muffins.

Orange Cornmeal Muffins

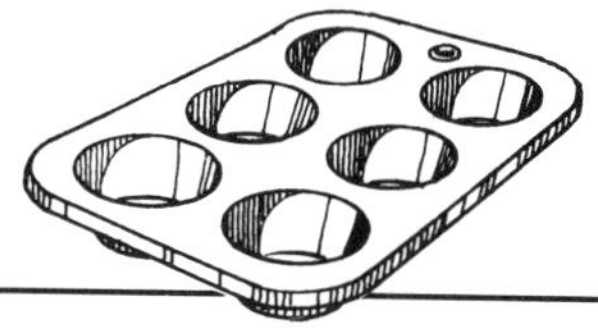
MUFFIN PAN

1 cup yellow cornmeal
1 cup all-purpose flour
1 teaspoon salt
3 teaspoons baking powder
⅓ cup orange marmalade
2 eggs
¾ cup milk
2 ounces (½ stick) unsalted butter, melted

Preheat oven to 450°. Butter molds of a muffin pan.

In a bowl, sift together the cornmeal, flour, salt and baking powder. Heat the marmalade until dissolved. In a separate bowl, beat the eggs and then stir in milk, marmalade and butter. Add the liquid to the dry ingredients and stir quickly but thoroughly.

Fill molds ¾ full and bake for 15 to 20 minutes. A toothpick inserted in the center of a muffin should come out clean. Remove from molds immediately and serve warm with unsalted butter.

Makes approximately 2 cups batter, enough for 12 standard 2¾-inch muffins or 14 cornsticks.

Peanut Butter Muffins

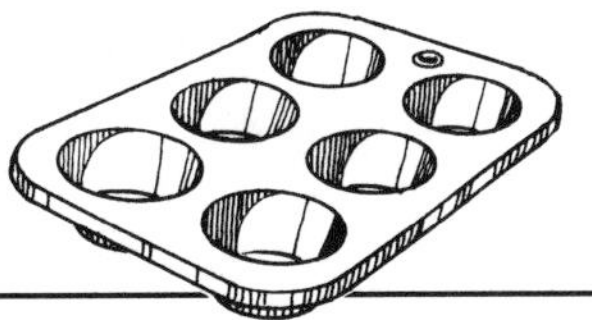
MUFFIN PAN

These are the best lunch-box muffins that I know of: they freeze beautifully and can be allowed to defrost whenever it's convenient. All-natural or old-fashioned-type peanut butter should be used for this recipe, and worth searching for.

½ cup yellow cornmeal
1½ cups all-purpose flour
5 tablespoons brown sugar
1 teaspoon salt
3 teaspoons baking powder
2 eggs
⅔ cup peanut butter
1⅓ cups milk
2 ounces (½ stick) unsalted butter, melted

Preheat oven to 425°. Butter molds or muffin pan.

In a bowl, sift together the cornmeal, flour, sugar, salt and baking powder. In a separate bowl, beat the eggs with a whisk. Mix peanut butter with part of the milk until smooth, then add to the eggs together with the rest of the milk and the butter. Beat well. Add the liquid to the dry ingredients and stir quickly but thoroughly.

Fill molds ¾ full and bake for 15 to 20 minutes. A toothpick inserted in the center of a muffin should come out clean. Remove from molds immediately and serve warm with unsalted butter.

Makes approximately 2 cups batter, enough for 12 standard 2¾-inch muffins or 14 cornsticks.

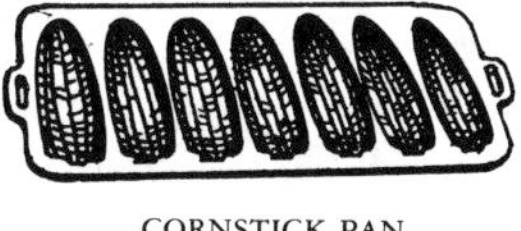
CORNSTICK PAN

DESSERTS

Apple Charlotte

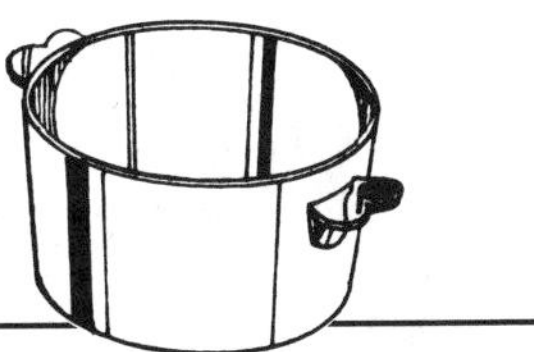

2-QUART CHARLOTTE MOLD

I find that Golden Delicious apples must be used in this recipe, as they hold their shape well. Be sure to cook the excess juice out of the apples before making the charlotte, or it won't unmold properly. Height of bread should be as high as sides of charlotte mold.

6 pounds Golden Delicious apples
2 ounces (1/2 stick) unsalted butter
1 1/2 cups sugar
3 teaspoons vanilla extract
1 loaf home-style sliced white bread
8 ounces (2 sticks) unsalted butter, clarified (page 182)
Powdered sugar
Heavy cream

Peel, quarter and core the apples and cut into thin slices. Melt the butter in the sauté pan and add the apples, sugar and vanilla. Cook over moderate heat for 20 to 25 minutes, stirring frequently, until apples are just cooked and transparent and any juice has evaporated. Do not let burn.

Cut ten 2-inch circles from the sliced bread, dip in the melted clarified butter and arrange in an overlapping pattern in bottom of charlotte mold. Remove crusts from nine slices of bread and cut each into two pieces lengthways. Dip each in the butter and vertically line the mold, overlapping the slices slightly. They should extend up to or slightly above top of mold.

Preheat oven to 425°.

Spoon the apple slices into the mold, packing well, and fill to top. Cover surface with additional slices of crustless bread, cut to fit and dipped in melted butter. Place mold on middle rack of oven and bake for 30 to 35 minutes, until golden brown. Let cool for 15 minutes and unmold onto a plate. Dust lightly with powdered sugar. Serve with slightly sweetened, vanilla-flavored whipped cream.

Serves 8 to 10.

12-INCH SAUTÉ PAN

Baked Applesauce

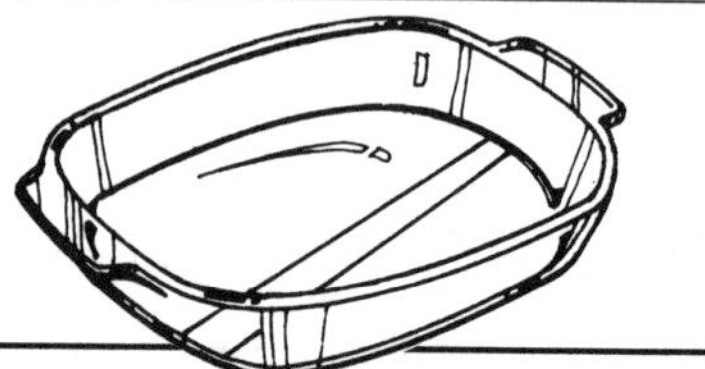

15- X 10½- X 3-INCH BAKING PAN

Cooked this way, the apples break down completely and the result is a smooth applesauce. I like to serve it at room temperature with sour cream or vanilla-flavored whipped cream.

3-inch piece of vanilla bean
6 or 7 Granny Smith apples (about 3 pounds)
½ cup sugar
Sour cream or heavy cream

Preheat oven to 350°. Place the piece of vanilla bean in the bottom of baking dish.

Peel and quarter apples, removing core. Cut each quarter into 5 or 6 thin slices. Spread evenly in the baking dish, filling it only halfway. Spoon sugar over top. Cover dish with aluminum foil and cut a 1-inch slit in center for steam to escape. Put a second sheet of foil on bottom rack of oven to catch any drippings should the apples boil up. Place dish on middle rack and bake for 40 minutes. Check to see if apples are cooked, and return to oven for a few minutes if necessary, stirring apples down if they have boiled up. Cool to room temperature and remove piece of vanilla bean. Serve with sour cream or heavy cream.

Makes 3½ to 4 cups.

Baked Pears with Maple-Ginger Cream

ROUND BAKING PAN

This simple, flavorful recipe for baked pears was created by Cheryl Schultz, the manager of one of our stores.

4 firm Bartlett pears, cored (unpeeled)
8 whole cloves
1/4 cup light-brown sugar, packed
1/4 cup walnuts, finely chopped
1/3 cup dried currants
3/4 cup maple syrup
1/2 cup water
1/3 cup preserved ginger in syrup, drained and chopped
1 orange
1 cup heavy cream

Preheat oven to 325°.

Place the pears standing up in the baking dish. Stick 2 cloves in each pear. In a bowl combine the brown sugar, walnuts and currants and fill the center of each pear. In the saucepan combine the maple syrup, water and ginger. Hold the orange over the saucepan and use a zester to remove the outer skin in thin strips. This allows the oil from the skin to spray over mixture. Bring to a boil and cook for 5 minutes while stirring.

Pour mixture over pears, put on center shelf of oven and bake for one hour until tender. Remove from oven and cool slightly. Stir the cream into the syrup. Serve immediately, spooning some of the syrup over the pears.

Serves 4.

LEMON ZESTER

Bread-and-Butter Custard

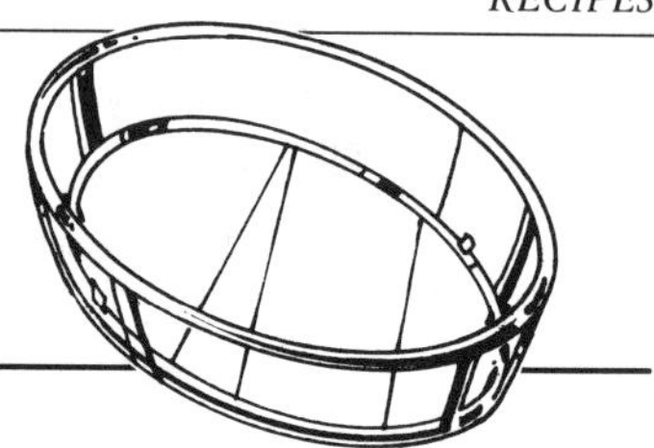
10- X 8- X 2-INCH OVAL BAKING DISH

Most bread-and-butter custard recipes instruct you to put the bread in the bottom of the dish, where it gets all soggy. I much prefer this version because it has such a crisp crust.

2 cups heavy cream
2 cups milk
3 strips orange peel, colored part only
6 egg yolks
3 whole eggs
½ cup sugar
3 tablespoons Galliano or Grand Marnier liqueur
3 to 4 slices day-old French bread (⅜" to ½" thick)
Unsalted butter, room temperature
Boiling water
Confectioners' sugar

Preheat oven to 325°. Place cream, milk and orange peel in a saucepan and bring just to a boil. Remove from heat and let cool for 5 minutes. Place egg yolks and whole eggs in a large bowl, add sugar and beat until a light lemon color. Add the liqueur and gradually stir in cream mixture, discarding orange peel. Pour into baking dish.

Assemble bread slices and trim them so that, without overlapping, they will cover top of custard. (You don't have to remove crusts.) Butter the bread slices and float on top of liquid, buttered side up. Do not submerge. Place dish in a larger baking pan and pour in enough boiling water to reach halfway up the sides. Bake for 40 to 50 minutes, until a knife blade inserted in the custard comes out clean. Remove from oven and let cool. (This dessert is best served slightly warm or at room temperature.) Dust with confectioners' sugar before serving.

Serves 6.

CONFECTIONERS' SUGAR DREDGER

Chocolate Orange Floating Island

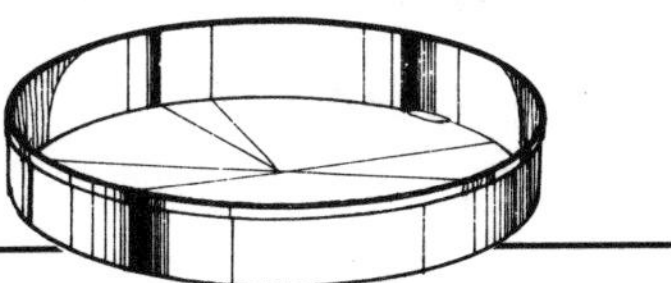

8½-INCH ROUND CAKE PAN

A floating island has gotten away from what it used to be, which was cake, probably leftover, floating in a sea of vanilla custard. The cake was gradually replaced by soft meringues. This version consists of slices of rich, moist, but not too sweet chocolate cake in a sea of orange custard. The flavor combination is outstanding. If you have a zester, use it instead of a grater for the orange peel in the sauce—it produces a less bitter flavor.

Cake

3 ounces bittersweet or semisweet chocolate
2 tablespoons milk
⅓ cup all-purpose flour
2 tablespoons cornstarch
1 teaspoon baking powder
2 egg whites
1 tablespoon cold water
⅓ cup sugar
2 egg yolks
1 teaspoon vanilla extract
Candied orange peel for garnish (page 235)

Orange Sauce

3 whole eggs
2 egg yolks
½ cup sugar
½ cup milk
1 cup fresh orange juice
Grated peel of 1 orange, colored part only

Preheat oven to 325°. Butter cake pan and cut a piece of baking parchment to fit bottom of pan. Place in pan and butter the paper.

Break the chocolate into small pieces and put in top of double boiler. Heat over barely simmering water, stirring, until melted. (Do not let water touch bottom of upper pan.) Remove from heat, stir in milk and set aside.

Combine the flour, cornstarch and baking powder. Sift and set aside.

In bowl of electric mixer, combine egg whites and the water. Beat at moderately high speed until soft peaks form, 40 to 50 seconds. Add the sugar gradually, and beat until stiff, 1 to 2 minutes. Put the egg yolks in a large bowl and beat vigorously with a whisk until light, thickened and foamy. Add the vanilla extract and beat in. Spoon the egg whites over the egg yolks and sift the flour mixture over the whites. Fold all carefully together, deflating mixture as little as possible. Add a couple of spoonfuls of the mixture to the chocolate and stir in, to thin it down. Add chocolate to egg mixture and carefully fold in, again being careful not to deflate batter. Pour mixture into prepared cake pan, level top surface and place on middle shelf of oven. Bake for 20 to 25 minutes until a toothpick stuck in the middle of the cake comes out clean. Remove from oven and let rest for 2 to 3 minutes. Run a sharp knife around edge of pan to loosen sides,

DOUBLE BOILER

place a round cooling rack or a plate on top of pan and turn upside down. Remove pan and peel off paper. Immediately place a second round cooling rack over cake and invert, so that cake is right side up. Let cool.

Heat a little water in bottom part of double boiler to a simmer. In top part of double boiler, combine the whole egg, egg yolks and sugar. Beat with a whisk until light and well blended. Add the milk, orange juice and grated peel. Stir well. Place over the simmering water (do not let water touch the underside of the pan) and cook gently, stirring, until mixture thickens and coats the spoon, 10 to 15 minutes. Do not cook too much or it will curdle. Remove from heat, immediately strain through a coarse sieve into a clean bowl, and chill.

To serve, spoon 2 or 3 spoonfuls of sauce onto dessert plates, using enough to cover the bottom of the plate. Cut cake in wedges and place a wedge in center of sauce on each plate. Decorate cake with pieces of candied orange peel and serve at once.

Serves 8.

Christmas Pudding

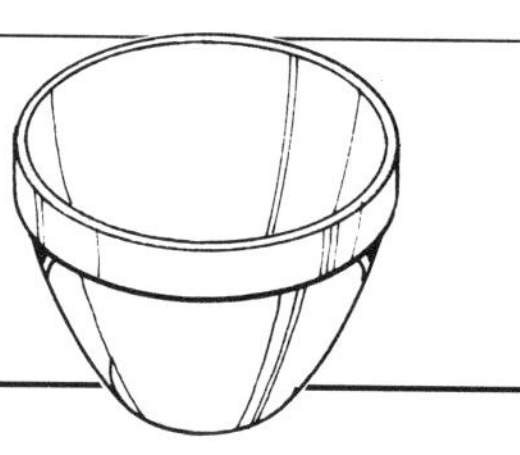
4-PINT PUDDING MOLD

Several friends have told me that this is the best Christmas pudding they have ever eaten—even people who say that they don't like Christmas pudding! It's based on an old recipe that I've fiddled with over the years. It's simple, easy, light, not too sweet, and you don't have to wait for six months to eat it. I'm not so sure that aging Christmas puddings does all that much for them, anyhow. Furthermore, this recipe doesn't make enough to feed the Russian army—you can make one family-sized pudding or 4 small ones, using 2-cup pudding molds.

1½ cups fresh suet, shredded
4½ cups breadcrumbs from home-style white loaf (approx. ¾ loaf)
1½ cups dark seedless raisins
1½ cups white seedless raisins
1½ cups currants
1 lemon
1 orange
½ cup blanched almonds, lightly toasted and chopped fine
½ teaspoon nutmeg, freshly grated
¼ teaspoon ground cloves
½ cup dark-brown sugar
¼ cup milk
3 eggs
½ cup plus 2 tablespoons brandy

Shred the suet finely by hand or on a medium shredder, discarding any stringy membranes. Make the breadcrumbs in a food processor.

Place the raisins and currants in a large mixing bowl. Using a zester, shred the colored part of the peel of half the lemon and one quarter of the orange directly over the dried fruit to catch all the released citrus oil. Add the suet, breadcrumbs, almonds, nutmeg, cloves and brown sugar. Mix well, making sure suet is well broken up and distributed.

In a separate bowl, combine the milk and eggs and beat well. Add to the fruit along with ½ cup brandy. Mix until all is well blended. Cover with plastic wrap and let stand overnight in refrigerator or cool larder.

Butter the pudding basin. Heat water to boiling in teakettle or large saucepan. Spoon mixture into pudding basin, leaving a little space for expansion. Cover with baking parchment or buttered waxed paper, then a piece of aluminum foil. Fit down tightly around rim of bowl and tie with string. Trim off excess paper. Put a small rack in bottom of stockpot and place basin on it. Pour boiling water into pot to reach ⅔ way up sides of basin. Cover and bring water to a simmer. Adjust heat so that water is just bubbling gently. Let steam for 7 hours. Maintain water level in pot, replenishing it as it evaporates. Do not let boil dry.

Remove pudding basin from pot and let cool on a rack. If keeping for later use, store in a cool place.

When ready to use, the next day or several weeks later, add another tablespoon of brandy before reheating. Steam pudding for 2 hours. Serve with foamy hard sauce (see page 262).

Serves 16.

TEA KETTLE

Foamy Hard Sauce

BALLOON WHISK

1 cup powdered sugar
2 ounces (½ stick) unsalted butter
1 egg, separated
Salt
½ pint heavy cream
Vanilla extract or rum

Blend sugar and butter together until creamy. Beat egg yolk and add to butter with a pinch of salt. Beat egg white until stiff and fold into mixture. Whip cream thoroughly and fold in. Flavor to taste with vanilla or rum.

Coffee Custard

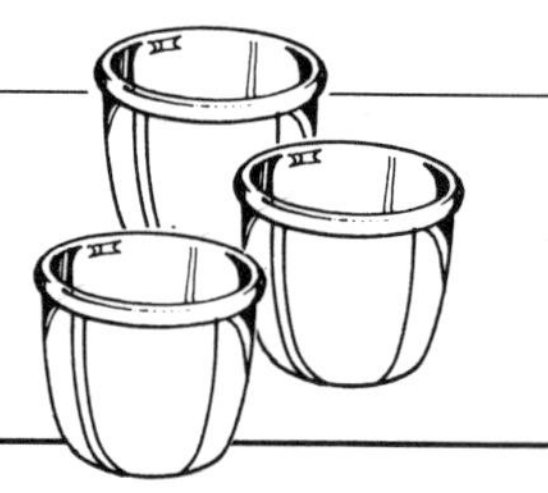
CUSTARD CUPS

I'm not a coffee drinker, though I like the flavor in desserts. The first time I made this recipe I used far too much espresso powder. I didn't sleep that night! But I corrected my mistake, and the custard now has a true coffee flavor without overdoing it.

2 cups milk
1 cup heavy cream
1½ tablespoons instant espresso coffee powder
4 whole eggs
2 egg yolks
½ cup sugar
2 tablespoons rum

Preheat oven to 350°, and heat a tea kettle full of water.

Pour milk and cream into saucepan and bring just to a boil. Add the instant espresso coffee and stir until dissolved. In a large bowl combine the whole eggs, egg yolks and sugar. Beat until light in color. Add the hot milk slowly while stirring. Add the rum. Pour into custard cups or baking dish. Place cups or dish in baking pan. Add boiling water to come ¾ way up sides of cups or dish. Place in oven, cover with a sheet of aluminum foil and bake for 30 minutes. Check for doneness: custard should be firm and a knife inserted

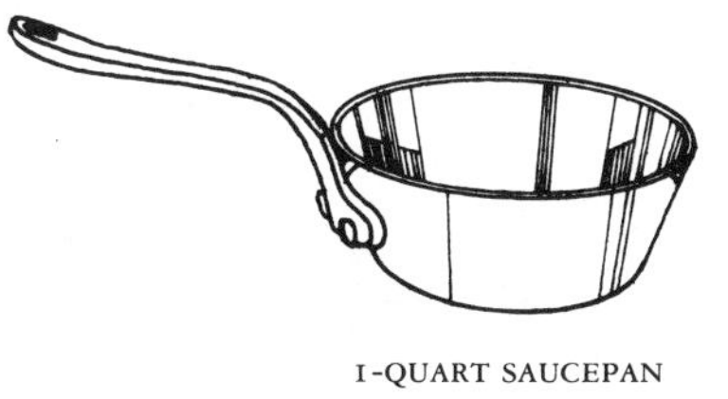

1-QUART SAUCEPAN

in it should come out clean. Bake from 5 to 20 minutes longer as needed—custard baked in a large dish will take longer to cook. Let cool and serve at room temperature.

Serves 8.

Ginger-Orange Steamed Pudding

2-QUART STEAMED PUDDING MOLD WITH COVER

There is quite a lot of ginger in this pudding, but it doesn't taste too strong.

8 ounces (2 sticks) unsalted butter
1 1/4 cups sugar
5 eggs
1 tablespoon brandy
Grated peel of 1 orange, colored part only
1/4 cup fresh orange juice
3 cups all-purpose flour
2 tablespoons ground ginger
1 1/4 teaspoons baking soda
1 cup crystallized ginger, finely chopped
Heavy cream

Butter mold and set aside. Heat a teakettle full of water. Cream butter and sugar together until light. Beat eggs lightly and add to mixture. Add brandy, orange peel and juice. Sift flour, ground ginger and soda together. Add crystallized ginger to flour and then combine with the butter-egg mixture. Beat until smooth and spoon into prepared mold. Cover, place in pot and pour in enough boiling water to reach 2/3 way up sides of mold. Cover pot and simmer for 1 1/2 hours. Turn pudding out onto plate and serve warm or cold with whipped cream, sweetened and flavored with vanilla, rum or liqueur.

Serves 8 to 10.

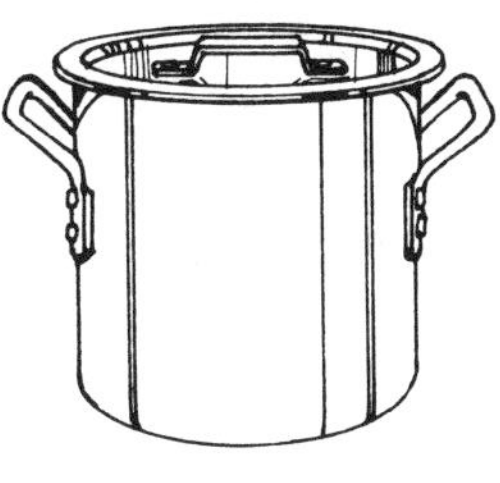

8-QUART STOCKPOT

Grapefruit Dessert, Circa 1930

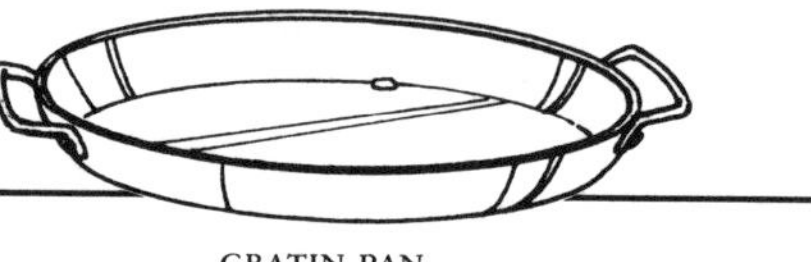
GRATIN PAN

This is a dessert that I had frequently as a child, only without the rum. I think it tastes better to me now than it did then.

2 grapefruit
4 to 8 tablespoons dark-brown sugar
4 teaspoons rum

Preheat broiler. Cut the grapefruit in half and remove any seeds. Carefully cut around perimeter of each grapefruit with serrated grapefruit knife, separating the fruit segments from their end membranes and outer skin. With a paring knife, cut each segment from its connecting side membranes. Drain off the accumulated juice. Spread 1 to 2 tablespoons brown sugar on surface of each grapefruit and moisten with 1 teaspoon rum. Put in baking pan and place under broiler for 5 to 7 minutes until sugar is melted and bubbly. Serve at once.

Serves 4.

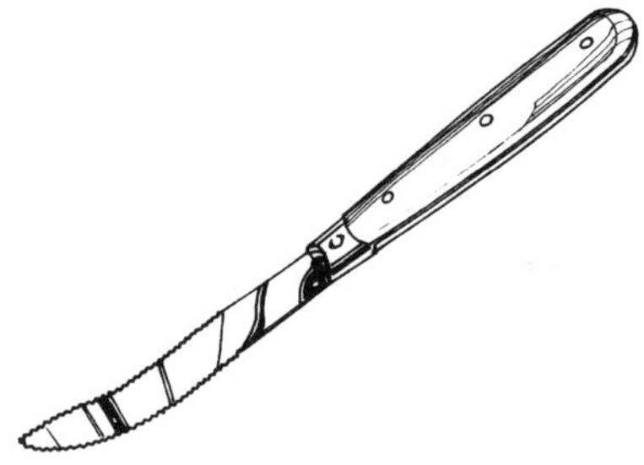
GRAPEFRUIT KNIFE

Hot Pear and Banana Compote

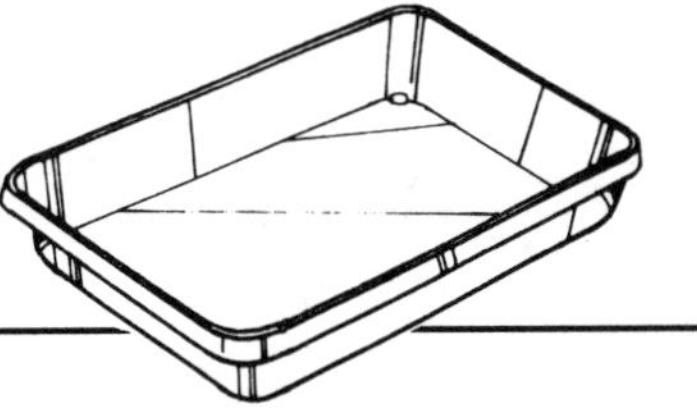

2-QUART BAKING DISH

1 ½ cups fresh orange juice
⅓ cup French cassis (black currant) syrup
2 ripe pears
2 large bananas
1 cup white seedless grapes

Preheat oven to 375°. In a bowl, combine orange juice with cassis syrup. Check for sweetness and add more syrup if desired. Pour juice into baking dish. Peel the pears, cut in half, scoop out seeds with a melon baller and cut out core. Immediately place in orange-juice mixture to keep from discoloring. Peel bananas, cut into thirds and arrange in dish with the pears. Spoon juice over the fruit, and scatter with grapes. Place on center rack of oven and bake for 30 to 40 minutes, until tender. Serve hot.

Serves 4.

MELON BALLER

Lemon Cream

CUSTARD CUPS

This dessert is like a light lemon mousse. Serve it with a fresh raspberry purée or tomato conserve (page 269).

1 package (1 tablespoon) plain gelatin
½ cup sugar
2 cups water
Peel of 2 large lemons, colored part only, in strips
4 egg yolks
4 tablespoons Madeira
½ cup fresh lemon juice
1 cup heavy cream

SAUCEPAN

Combine gelatin, sugar, water and lemon peel in saucepan. Let stand for 10 minutes, then heat slowly while stirring, without allowing to boil. Remove from heat and take peel from syrup with a slotted spoon and discard.

Whisk together the egg yolks, Madeira and lemon juice. Pour a little of the hot syrup into the egg-yolk mixture and combine well. Then slowly pour egg-yolk mixture into saucepan containing rest of syrup. Heat, stirring, until mixture thickens and coats the spoon, but remove from heat before it starts to boil. Transfer immediately to a bowl and refrigerate, stirring occasionally, until the mixture just begins to gel, about 2 hours.

Whip the cream until stiff and fold into partially gelled lemon custard. Spoon into 6 or 8 custard cups or pour into a serving bowl. (There will be 1 quart of lemon cream.) Chill until set.

Serves 6 to 8.

Poached Pears with French Bay Leaves

9-INCH SAUTÉ PAN

Only French bay (laurel) leaves will do for this dish. California bay leaves are too strong and pungent.

1 ½ cups sugar
2 cups water
2 small French laurel (bay) leaves
3 firm ripe pears, such as Anjou
Heavy cream

Combine sugar, water and bay leaves in sauté pan. Bring to a boil over moderate heat, stirring until all sugar is dissolved. Cook gently for 5 minutes. Remove from heat.

Peel pears and cut in half lengthways. Remove cores and stems. (A melon scoop is useful for taking out cores neatly.) Immediately submerge pear halves in the syrup. Return to heat, bring to simmer and cook gently for 20 to 25 minutes or until tender, turning fruit halfway through cooking time. Let cool in syrup. Remove with slotted spoon and serve with slightly sweetened whipped cream flavored with vanilla.

Serves 6.

SLOTTED SPOON

Rhubarb Compote

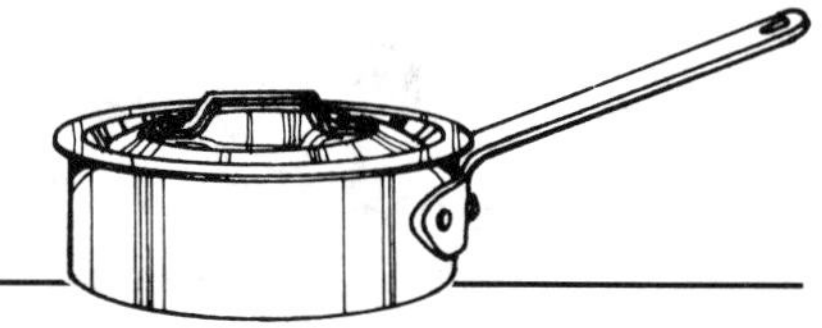

3-QUART SAUCEPAN WITH COVER

Rhubarb can be very good if you don't cook it for too long. I don't blame people for hating the gray mush that's often served under the name of stewed rhubarb.

3 pounds rhubarb
1 cup sugar
1/4 cup water
3-inch piece of vanilla bean, partially split
Sour cream

Trim, wash and then chop the rhubarb into 1-inch lengths. Place in the saucepan with the sugar, water and vanilla bean. Cover and bring to a simmer. Cook very slowly for 10 minutes, with the pan partially covered, occasionally turning the pieces of rhubarb over so that they cook evenly. Be careful not to stir too much or overcook, or the fruit will break down. Allow to cool and then refrigerate. Serve with sour cream.

Serves 6.

Tomato Conserve

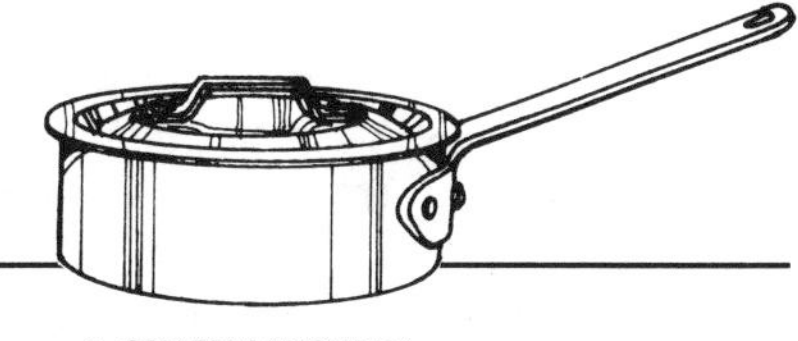

3-QUART SAUCEPAN

Because we usually treat the tomato as a vegetable, though technically it is a fruit, tomato conserve may sound odd. In fact, it makes a delicious, very clear red jam with a flavor somewhat reminiscent of quince. The French traditionally serve it with fresh cream cheese, crème fraîche or spooned into the cavities of poached pears. (It is also very good with the lemon cream on page 266.)

2½ to 2¾ pounds ripe tomatoes
5 cups sugar
1 cup water
4-inch piece of vanilla bean, partially split

Core the tomatoes, cut a cross in blossom end. Dip tomatoes in boiling water for 1 minute and slip off skins. Cut in half crossways, squeeze out the seeds, and cut into small pieces. There should be 4 cups. In the saucepan, combine the sugar and water. Boil for 5 minutes and then add the tomatoes. Boil steadily for 30 minutes, stirring frequently. Add the vanilla bean and continue cooking for 15 to 20 minutes more, until thickened and at jelling stage. Mixture should register 220–222° on a jelly thermometer. Skim and pour into jars.

Makes 5 cups, or enough to fill three 500-gram straight-sided French confiture jars.

CAKES,

COOKIES AND TARTS

Caramel Crunch Cake

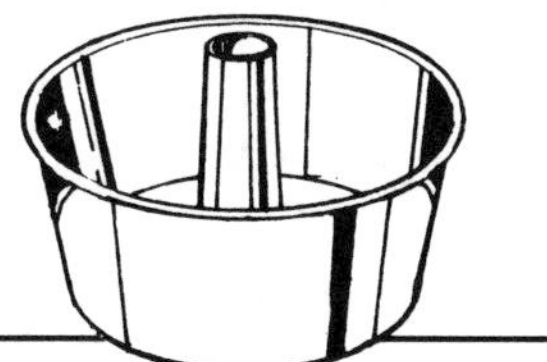

10-INCH ANGEL CAKE TUBE PAN

This is an old-fashioned, very American cake, a great favorite of my mother's thirty years ago in Sonoma. She used to make it for special occasions, to great applause. Blum's, the famous but unfortunately now defunct San Francisco pastry shop, practically built their reputation on a cake very similar to this one, and when I first put the recipe in the Williams-Sonoma catalog, we got nostalgic mail from all over the country. If you have an unlined copper bowl, by all means use it for beating the egg whites. You'll get more volume.

Cake

1 1/4 cups cake flour
1 1/2 cups sugar
6 egg yolks
1/4 cup water
1 tablespoon lemon juice
1 teaspoon vanilla extract
8 egg whites
1 teaspoon cream of tartar
1 teaspoon salt

Topping

1 1/2 cups sugar
1/4 cup strong brewed coffee
1/4 cup white corn syrup
3 teaspoons baking soda, sifted

Filling

2 cups heavy cream
2 tablespoons confectioners' sugar, sifted
2 teaspoons vanilla extract

Preheat oven to 350° but do *not* grease the pan. Sift flour into mixing bowl and add 3/4 cup of the sugar. Add egg yolks, water, lemon juice and vanilla and beat until a smooth batter is formed. In bowl of electric mixer, beat egg whites, cream of tartar and salt until a fine foam forms throughout. Gradually beat in remaining sugar and continue beating until meringue is firm and stands in stiff peaks. Remove bowl from mixer stand and pour batter gently over meringue. Fold in with a rubber spatula until just blended. Do not stir. Gently spoon batter into tube pan. Cut through batter with a knife to break up air bubbles and level mixture. Place on middle rack of oven and bake for 50 to 55 minutes or until top springs back when touched. Remove from oven and immediately turn pan upside down and rest tube over an inverted funnel or the neck of a bottle. Let cake cool, then loosen with a pastry spatula and place on plate.

To make topping: Combine sugar, coffee and corn syrup in saucepan. Stir, bring to a boil and cook to hard-crack stage, 310° F. on a candy thermometer. Remove from heat and immediately add baking soda. Stir vigorously until mixture thickens and pulls away from sides of pan. Do not destroy foam. Pour quickly into the ungreased baking pan. Do not stir or spread. Let cool without disturbing pan. Knock out of pan

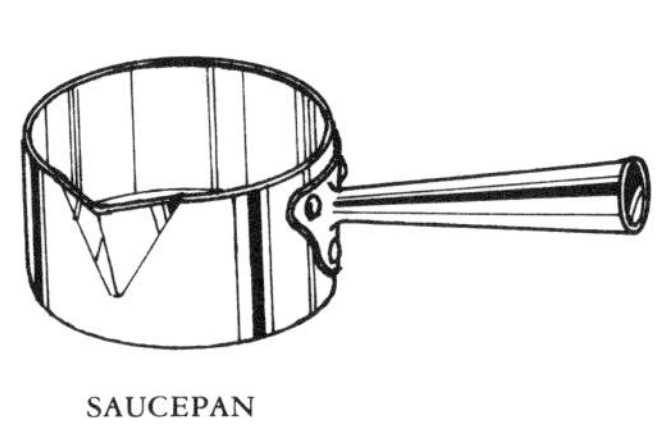
SAUCEPAN

and place between two sheets of waxed paper. Crush into coarse crumbs with a rolling pin.

To make filling: Whip cream, sugar and vanilla until stiff.

To assemble cake: Split cake evenly into 4 layers. Spread half of whipped cream filling between the layers and remainder on top and sides. Refrigerate until ready to serve. Just before serving, cover cake generously with the crushed caramel crisp topping.

Serves 10 to 12.

Chocolate Angel Cake

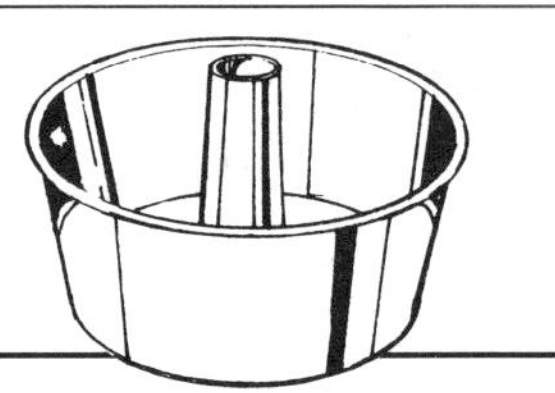
10-INCH ANGEL CAKE TUBE PAN

Every recipe that I've ever read for angel cake says you have to cut through the center of uncooked batter with a knife to break up air bubbles. I really don't know if this makes a bit of difference, but after using up 12 eggs, I've never dared omit the ritual. This reminds me of a friend in Sonoma of Armenian parentage who taught me to make yogurt thirty years ago. The final step was to make a sign of the cross in the milk with a silver knife, to ensure that it turned into yogurt. I always do that, too!

Angel cakes are cooled upside down in the pan. Some tube pans have three small feet around the rim so you can invert it and still get air circulation underneath, but I generally just rest the tube over an inverted funnel or the neck of a bottle. The cake won't fall out, believe me. It sticks to the side of the pan. If you have an unlined copper bowl, by all means use it for beating the egg whites. You'll get more volume.

¾ cup sifted cake flour
1 ½ cups sifted confectioners' sugar
⅓ cup Dutch process unsweetened cocoa
2 teaspoons powdered instant espresso coffee
1 ½ cups egg whites (from 10 to 12 eggs) at room temperature
¼ teaspoon salt
1 ½ teaspoons cream of tartar
1 cup sugar
Additional confectioners' sugar (optional)

Preheat oven to 375° but do *not* grease the pan. Combine the flour, confectioners' sugar, cocoa and coffee by sifting together 3 times. Place egg whites and salt in bowl of electric mixer. Beat until just foamy, sprinkle cream of tartar over surface and then beat at high speed until stiff peaks form. Using a rubber spatula, fold in the sugar a little at a time. Sift the flour mixture over the surface one quarter at a time, folding it in lightly but thoroughly. Do not overmix or stir, as this deflates the batter. Pour into tube pan and cut through center of batter in a circle with a knife to break up air bubbles. Place on middle rack of oven and bake for 35 to 40 minutes until cake springs back when lightly touched. Remove from oven and immediately turn pan over and rest tube over an inverted funnel or the neck of a bottle. Let cake hang upside down until cool, then loosen with a pastry spatula and place on plate.

Serve plain, or dust with confectioners' sugar.

Serves 10 to 12.

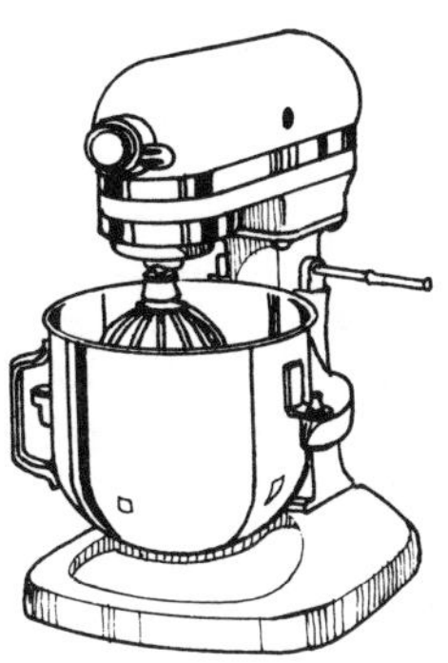

ELECTRIC MIXER

Chocolate Truffles

1-PINT SAUCEPAN

4 ounces (1 stick) unsalted butter
¼ cup heavy cream
3 strips orange peel (colored part only)
8 ounces bittersweet or semisweet chocolate
2 tablespoons Grand Marnier
½ cup Dutch process unsweetened cocoa

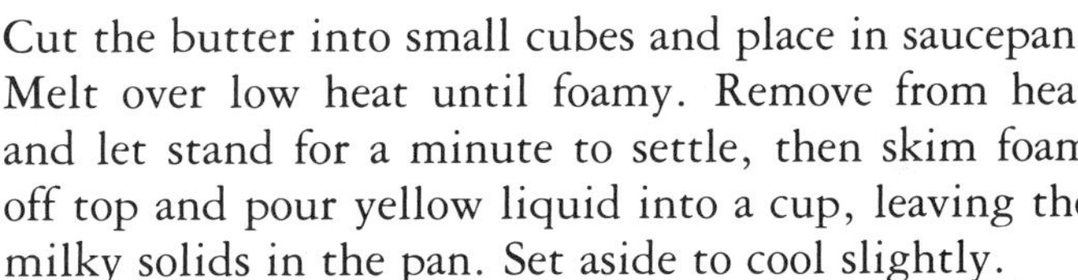

Cut the butter into small cubes and place in saucepan. Melt over low heat until foamy. Remove from heat and let stand for a minute to settle, then skim foam off top and pour yellow liquid into a cup, leaving the milky solids in the pan. Set aside to cool slightly.

Place cream in separate saucepan, add the orange peel, place over moderate heat and bring just to a boil. Set aside and let cool. Cut chocolate into small pieces and place in top of double boiler. Place over barely simmering water. (Do not let water touch underside of top pan.) Stir gently until melted, and remove from heat.

In bowl, combine melted butter and chocolate and stir until blended. Remove orange peel from cream and stir cream into chocolate mixture. Add the Grand Marnier and blend well. Place in refrigerator to thicken.

Put cocoa on large plate and spread out. After about 5 to 10 minutes, when chocolate has thickened, form into ¾-inch pieces with 2 teaspoons and drop onto the cocoa. Return to refrigerator to harden. When firm enough to handle, shape with the fingers into irregular balls like truffles, rolling in the cocoa until completely covered. Place in a storage container. Pour the remaining cocoa over them, shake to distribute it, cover and return the truffles to refrigerator. They will form a crust of cocoa and be easier to handle when eaten. Keep refrigerated, covered, removing them 10 minutes before serving. Chocolate truffles will keep for several weeks refrigerated.

Makes approximately 50 pieces.

DOUBLE BOILER

Cookie-Gun Butter Cookies

COOKIE GUN

This dough can be prepared in a food processor in seconds. Naturally you can mix it by hand if you prefer. In that case, use room-temperature butter, and cream it with the sugar before adding the flour and cornstarch. Chill the dough for 20 minutes, or it will be too soft to eject from the cookie gun. Fit gun with a star- or flower-shaped tip.

6 ounces (1 ½ sticks) unsalted butter, chilled
1 cup all-purpose flour
½ cup cornstarch
½ cup confectioners' sugar
½ teaspoon vanilla extract
Small pinch salt
¼ cup walnut pieces or candied peel (optional)

Preheat oven to 350°. Cut butter into cubes. Place flour, cornstarch, confectioners' sugar, vanilla and salt in bowl of food processor fitted with steel blade. Add butter and process for a few seconds until ball of dough forms; remove from bowl, wrap and chill for 20 minutes. Fill cookie gun with dough and eject cookies onto ungreased baking sheet. Repeat until dough is used up. If you like, decorate center of each cookie with a piece of walnut or candied peel. Place one sheet of cookies on middle rack of oven (refrigerate the other) and bake for 15 minutes, until cookies are golden brown at edges. Repeat with remaining baking sheet.

Makes approximately 4 dozen 1 ½-inch cookies.

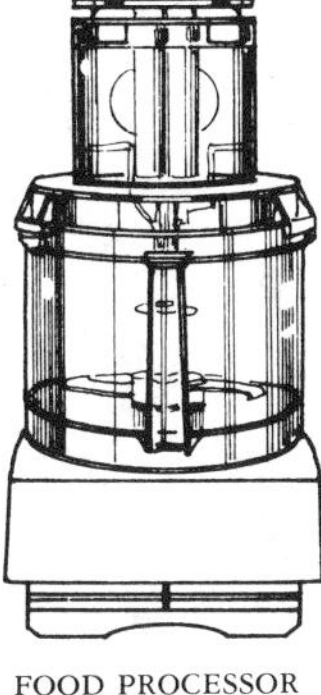
FOOD PROCESSOR

Gino Cofacci's Chocolate Rum Cheesecake

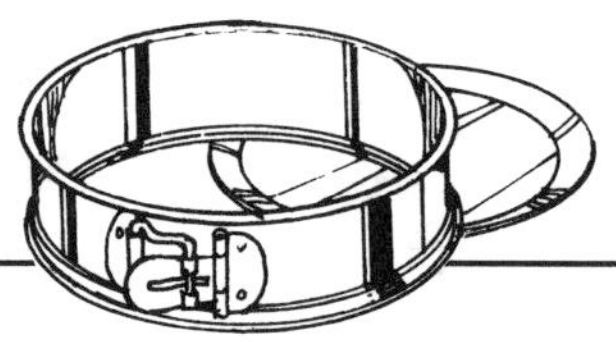
9-INCH SPRINGFORM PAN

Gino Cofacci is an old friend who lives in New York. He and Jim Beard used to cook up a storm together, and this cake was a great favorite of theirs. Gino has made it for years for several very good restaurants in New York. Don't worry if, after baking, the center of the cake appears underset. It will firm up as it cools.

1 1/4 cups graham cracker crumbs
3/4 cup plus 2 tablespoons sugar
2 ounces (1/2 stick) unsalted butter, melted
6 ounces semisweet chocolate
1/4 cup rum
1 pound cream cheese
1/2 cup sour cream
1 tablespoon vanilla extract
5 eggs

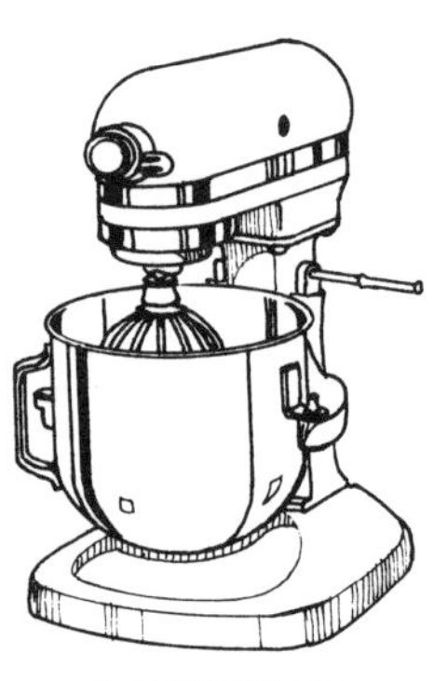
ELECTRIC MIXER

Preheat oven to 325°. Butter inside of springform pan well and cover the outside (bottom and sides) with a sheet of heavy-duty aluminum foil, *shiny side out.* This reflects heat away from cheesecake and prevents it from baking too fast and becoming overcooked. Mix graham cracker crumbs with 2 tablespoons of the sugar and add melted butter. Press evenly on bottom and sides of pan and refrigerate until ready to use.

Cut chocolate into small pieces. Combine with rum in top of double boiler and place over barely simmering water. (Do not let water touch underside of top pan.) Stir gently until chocolate is melted and smooth, and set aside.

In bowl of electric mixer, beat cream cheese until light and fluffy. Gradually beat in sugar, sour cream and vanilla. Add eggs, one at a time. Mix well, and remove bowl from mixer stand. Place bowl over a pan of hot water and mix until smooth (do not let water touch bottom of bowl). Pour about 1 1/4 cups of this batter into a separate bowl and set aside. Whisk remaining batter with the chocolate, then stir over hot water until smooth.

Take springform pan from refrigerator and fill with chocolate batter. Gently pour plain batter over top and make swirls down into the chocolate batter with a fork. Place on middle rack of oven and bake for 50 minutes. Cool to room temperature, remove foil and rim of pan and refrigerate overnight.

Serves 10 to 12.

Icebox Cookies

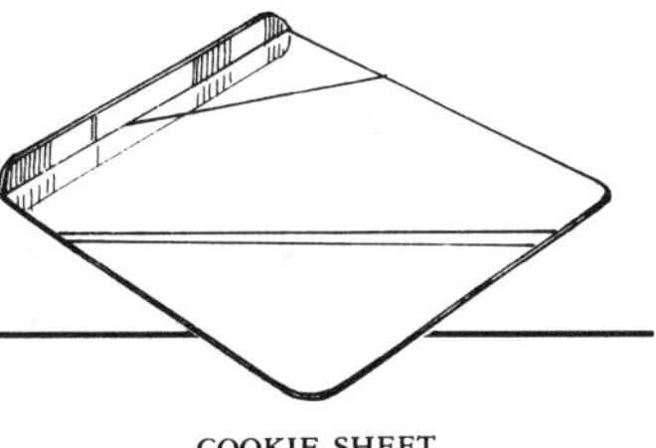
COOKIE SHEET

This wasn't an icebox cookie dough to start with, it was one to roll out and use with cutters, but I found it very convenient to have on hand in the refrigerator, as it keeps well, and you can slice off some dough and bake cookies as you need them. The recipe can make a tremendous number of cookies: up to 300 if you form dough into 4 rolls—1½ inches in diameter by 10 inches long. Chill the dough thoroughly before using, preferably overnight.

6 ounces (1½ sticks) unsalted butter
1½ cups sugar
1 egg
1 tablespoon lemon juice
1 tablespoon milk
1 teaspoon vanilla extract
3½ cups all-purpose flour
2 teaspoons baking powder
½ teaspoon salt

Cream together the butter and sugar until light and fluffy. Beat in the egg. Add lemon juice, milk and vanilla. Sift together the flour, baking powder and salt. Combine with butter mixture and blend well, kneading by hand if necessary to make a smooth, rather stiff dough.

Divide dough in half and form into two rolls approximately 2 inches in diameter by 10 inches long. Wrap tightly in waxed paper, place in refrigerator and chill overnight.

Preheat oven to 375° and butter baking sheet. Remove one roll of cookie dough from refrigerator and slice into rounds the thickness of a fifty-cent piece. Place on baking sheet and bake for 10 to 12 minutes

Lemon, Walnut and Chocolate Torte

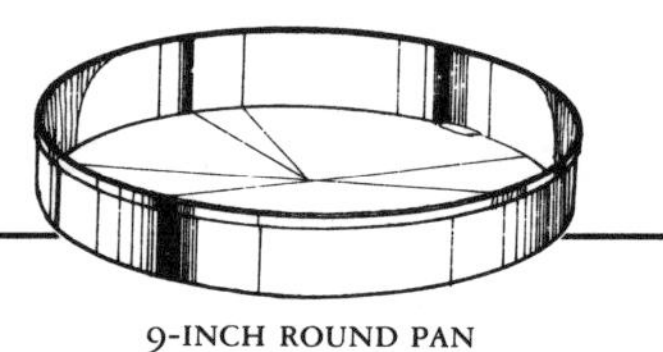

9-INCH ROUND PAN

This is the kind of cake that you pay an arm and a leg for in an exclusive pastry shop. It's not too sweet, has wonderful flavor and texture combinations, and it's easy to make.

Cake

1/2 cup all-purpose flour
1/3 cup cornstarch
1 teaspoon baking powder
3/4 cup walnuts, chopped
2 egg whites
1 tablespoon cold water
1/2 cup sugar
2 egg yolks
1 teaspoon vanilla extract

Lemon Filling

1/3 cup sugar
1 lemon
1 whole egg
1 egg yolk
2 tablespoons fresh lemon juice
3 tablespoons unsalted butter

Chocolate Glaze

4 ounces bittersweet or semisweet chocolate
1/3 cup heavy cream
3 teaspoons Grand Marnier

Preheat oven to 375°. Cut a circle of baking parchment to fit in bottom of pan. Butter pan, place parchment inside and butter it, too.

Cake

Sift the flour, cornstarch and baking powder together, combine with walnuts and set aside. Place the egg whites and water in bowl of electric mixer and beat until soft peaks form. Add 1/4 cup of the sugar and beat until stiff, 2 to 3 minutes. In mixing bowl, combine egg yolks and remaining sugar and whisk vigorously until light and creamy. Add the vanilla extract. Spoon the egg whites on top of the egg yolks, and sprinkle flour and walnut mixture on top. Fold all together carefully with a spatula. Pour into cake pan, level, and place on lower rack of oven. Bake for 20 to 25 minutes until golden on top and a toothpick inserted in center of cake comes out clean. Remove from oven and let rest for one minute. Run a sharp knife around sides of pan, turn cake out onto rack upside down, peel off paper and let cool.

Lemon Filling

Place sugar in top of double boiler. Using a zester, shred the peel off the lemon over the sugar. (The aromatic lemon oil will be released at the same time.) Add the whole egg, egg yolk and lemon juice. Beat well to blend. Cut the butter into small cubes and add to mixture. Place over barely simmering water. (Do not let water touch underside of top pan.) Cook, stirring, until mixture has thickened to consistency of a heavy cream sauce, 5 to 6 minutes. Using a coarse mesh strainer, immediately strain into a bowl and chill.

COARSE MESH STRAINER

Chocolate Glaze

Cut chocolate into small pieces. Combine with cream in top of double boiler and place over hot or barely simmering water. (Do not let water touch underside of top pan.) Stir gently until chocolate is melted and smooth. Remove from heat and place pan in a bowl filled with enough cold water to reach halfway up sides and let cool to room temperature, but still of pouring consistency. Stir in the Grand Marnier.

To assemble cake: Using a sharp knife, cut the cake horizontally and evenly into two layers. Remove top layer and set aside. Place bottom layer on a serving plate and spread the lemon filling evenly over the surface. Replace the top layer of cake. Pour the chocolate glaze over the cake, letting a little run over the edges. Run a spatula round the sides to form an even covering of chocolate glaze. Chill for 1 hour before cutting and serving. This torte is best eaten the same day, but will keep for several days if refrigerated.

Serves 10.

Madeleines

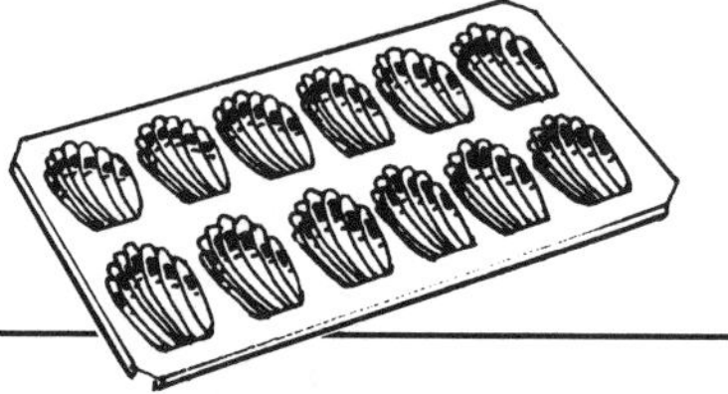

MADELEINE PLAQUE

I suspect that when Proust wrote about madeleines he was talking about these little cakes as they came fresh from the oven, still warm and a little crisp on the outside. This is when they are at their best. They've become very popular in recent years, probably due to the good marketing of the special pan in which they are baked. However, many madeleines I've seen and eaten in bakeries wouldn't prompt anyone to start writing a book. So do make them yourself and serve them within an hour or two; you can taste the difference. Orange-flower water from France is obtainable in specialty food shops.

2½ ounces (½ stick plus 1 tablespoon) unsalted butter
½ cup all-purpose flour
½ teaspoon baking powder
Pinch salt
1 egg
Grated peel of ½ lemon, colored part only
1 teaspoon orange-flower water
⅓ cup sugar
Confectioners' sugar

Preheat oven to 375°. Melt butter in saucepan over medium heat. Brush a little melted butter in the molds of the plaque. Reserve the remainder and let cool to lukewarm.

Sift flour, baking powder and salt into a bowl. Combine egg, lemon peel, orange-flower water and sugar and beat lightly. Stir into flour mixture and beat for a few seconds longer until well combined. Add reserved butter and beat just long enough to incorporate thoroughly without overmixing. Spoon into molds of prepared pan, filling each one half full. Place on middle shelf of oven and bake for 12 to 15 minutes, until golden and starting to brown at the edges. Unmold and place on rack. Dust with confectioners' sugar and serve while still slightly warm.

Makes twelve 3-inch madeleines.

CONFECTIONERS' SUGAR DREDGER

Marlborough Pie

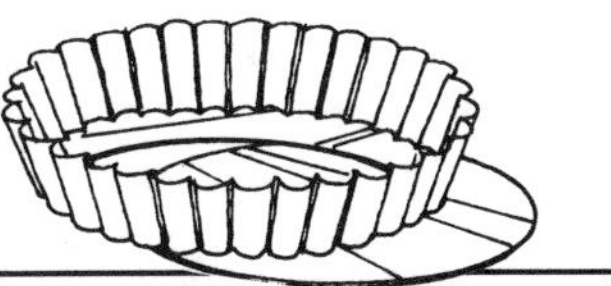

9- X 1-INCH FLUTED TART PAN WITH REMOVABLE BOTTOM

I have read at least six different recipes for this, and they are all unrelated! This is my version, a creamy custard tart with bits of apple in the filling. You'll need two large- or three medium-sized apples, and be sure to use Golden Delicious. Most other apples just go to pieces when cooked, and you get applesauce.

1 recipe sweet shortcrust pastry (page 287)
2 to 3 Golden Delicious apples
4 tablespoons (½ stick) unsalted butter
½ cup sugar
1 lemon
3 eggs
1 cup heavy cream
2 tablespoons Madeira

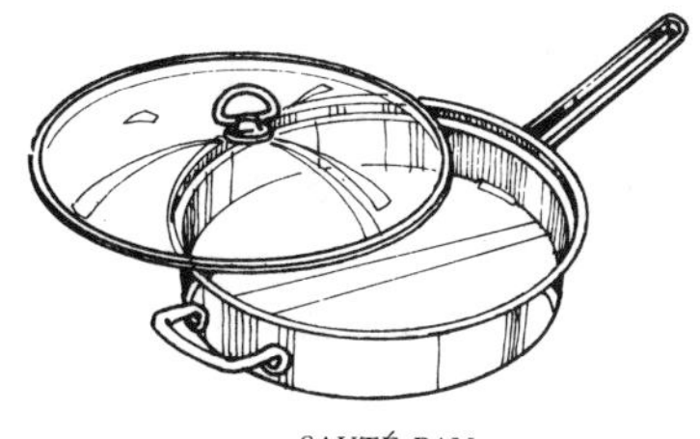

SAUTÉ PAN

Preheat oven to 400°. Roll shortcrust pastry dough out into a 12-inch circle, fit into tart pan, pressing carefully into sides without stretching dough and trim, leaving about ½ an inch above rim. Fold over, making a double thickness that is a little higher than the pan. Prick bottom of dough with a fork, and place in freezer for 10 minutes.

Fit a 12-inch square of heavy aluminum foil into frozen pastry shell. Push it down to fit smoothly over the bottom of the dough, then crimp it up the sides and over the top; this prevents the dough from shrinking down while baking. Place on middle rack of oven and bake for 15 minutes. Remove foil, reduce heat to 375° and bake for 10 minutes more, until light gold. Set aside, leaving pie shell in the pan. Let oven remain at 375°.

Peel, core and quarter apples. Cut each quarter in half and slice crossways into 4 pieces. There should be about 3 cups, no more.

Melt the butter in sauté pan. Add apples and sugar. Holding the lemon over the sauté pan and using a zester, remove the colored part of half the peel in small shreds. (This is much easier than using a grater, and you get the benefit of the lemon oil, which will be released into the apples.) Cut lemon in half and add 1 tablespoon of the juice to the pan. Cook apples rapidly, stirring, until they have absorbed most of the sugar and most of the accumulated liquid has evaporated. This should take about 10 to 15 minutes. Do not let apples brown. Let cool slightly.

LEMON ZESTER

In bowl, beat the eggs, add the cream and Madeira and beat until smooth. Add the apples and stir until blended. Pour into prepared pastry shell, which should remain in the tart pan, and place on middle rack of oven. Bake for 20 to 25 minutes until custard is set and slightly puffed. Serve lukewarm or at room temperature.

Serves 8.

Pizelle (Italian wafer cookies)

PIZELLE IRON

These wafer cookies are very thin and crisp. They can be left flat, or made into different shapes while still hot and pliable. You can roll each cookie into a cylinder or cone, or press into a small bowl or custard cup to form a basket for serving ice cream or fruit, but be sure to do this immediately after removing them from the iron.

3 eggs
¾ cup sugar
4 ounces (1 stick) unsalted butter, melted
2 teaspoons vanilla extract
Grated peel of ½ small lemon, colored part only
1¼ cups all-purpose flour
2 teaspoons baking powder
Additional melted butter for iron

RACK

In a bowl, combine eggs and sugar and beat until light and creamy. Add the butter, vanilla and lemon peel and stir until blended. Sift together the flour and baking powder and fold into mixture.

Heat the pizelle iron on both sides. Remove from heat. Brush lightly with butter and place about 1 tablespoon of batter on one side of the iron. Close it, and if the iron is hot enough, the batter will spread out inside the iron and any excess will ooze out. Cut excess off with a knife and return iron to heat. Cook for about 30 seconds on each side until pizelle are golden. Turn out on rack to cool. Repeat the process with the remaining batter. It should only be necessary to brush the iron with butter once, the batter should not stick after that.

Makes approximately 40 pizelle.

Raspberry and Almond Cookies

NUT MILL

Grind the almonds needed for this recipe in a nut mill or food processor; a nut mill is best, however. There is no need to remove the skins if the almonds are not blanched.

1 1/2 cups all-purpose flour
3/4 cup ground almonds
1/2 cup sugar
Grated peel of 1/2 lemon, colored part only
6 ounces (1 1/2 sticks) unsalted butter, chilled
1/2 cup raspberry jam

Preheat oven to 350°. Place flour, ground almonds, sugar and lemon peel in bowl of food processor fitted with steel blade. Cut butter into small cubes and add to bowl. Process for a few seconds until a ball of dough is formed.

Dough can also be mixed by hand, in which case mix the butter, sugar and grated lemon peel in a bowl until light and creamy; add the flour and ground almonds and blend well.

On a lightly floured surface, roll dough out to 1/8-inch thick. With a round, fluted cookie cutter, 2 inches in diameter, cut out as many cookies as possible and transfer to two large ungreased baking sheets. Reroll dough trimmings and use; this amount of dough should make approximately 60 cookies. Cut a hole in the center of half the cookies with a 1/2-inch round cutter. Place one of the baking sheets on the middle rack of oven and bake for 7 to 8 minutes, until cookies are lightly browned. (Refrigerate second sheet of cookies until ready to bake.)

Cool on rack. When cold, spread solid cookies with raspberry jam and top with pierced cookies.

Makes approximately 30 sandwich cookies.

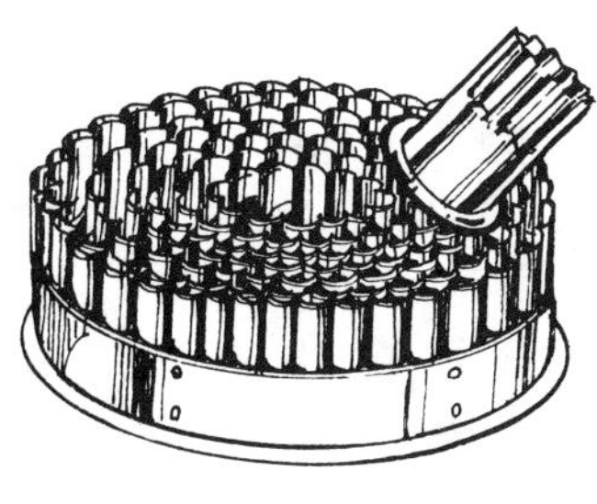
COOKIE CUTTERS

Scottish Mincemeat Tart

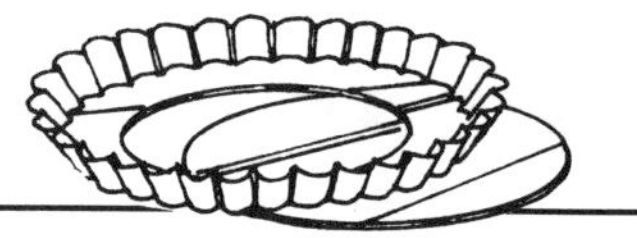

9-INCH FLUTED TART PAN WITH REMOVABLE BOTTOM

This recipe was given to me by Jackie Mallorca, who grew up in Scotland. We usually think of mincemeat as something you have at Christmas, but this tart is good at any time of year.

1 recipe sweet shortcrust pastry (page 287)
1 cup walnuts, coarsely chopped
1/3 cup currants
1/4 cup raisins
1/4 cup mixed candied peel, chopped
1/2 cup sugar
Grated peel of 1/2 lemon, colored part only
2 ounces (1/2 stick) unsalted butter, melted
1 egg, lightly beaten
1 to 2 tablespoons Scotch whisky
Confectioners' sugar

Preheat oven to 375°. Roll out shortcrust pastry dough into an 11-inch circle, fit into tart pan, pressing it carefully into fluted sides without stretching the pastry. Trim edges level with top of pan.

In a bowl, combine walnuts, currants, raisins, chopped peel, sugar, lemon peel, butter, egg and Scotch. Spoon evenly into tart shell and place on middle rack of oven. Bake for 30 to 35 minutes, until pastry is nicely browned and filling is golden brown. Unmold and cool on rack. Before serving, dust top of tart with confectioners' sugar.

Serves 8.

Sweet Shortcrust Pastry

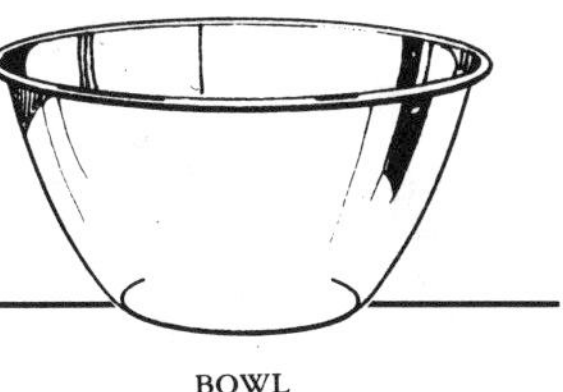
BOWL

I like pastry made with all butter. The less you handle it the better it will be, and everything should be cold, including the cook's hands!

1 cup plus 3 tablespoons all-purpose flour
1 tablespoon sugar
1/4 teaspoon salt
3 ounces (3/4 stick) unsalted butter, chilled
1 egg, beaten lightly

PASTRY BLENDER

By hand:
Sift flour into mixing bowl and stir in sugar and salt. Cut butter into small cubes and blend into flour with fingertips, a pastry blender or two knives until mixture resembles coarse crumbs. Make a well in the center and add the egg. Incorporate into flour and gather dough into a ball. Wrap and chill for 30 minutes before rolling out on a lightly floured surface, or between two sheets of plastic wrap.

By food processor:
Place flour, sugar and salt in bowl of food processor fitted with steel blade. Cut butter into small cubes and add to bowl. Process very briefly to blend evenly into coarse crumbs. With motor running, add egg. Do not overmix. The dough will form into a ball and can be used immediately. Roll out on a lightly floured surface, or between two sheets of plastic wrap.

Makes enough for one 9- x 1-inch tart shell.

"Professional" Shortcrust Pastry

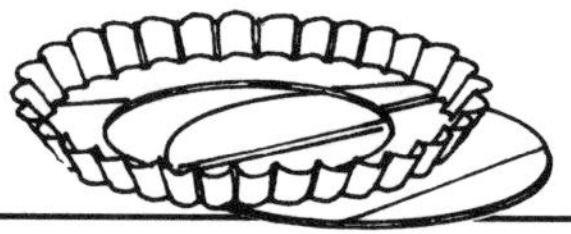

9-INCH FLUTED TART PAN WITH REMOVABLE BOTTOM

I get out my scale for this recipe, which I got from a professional chef in England some years ago and adapted for the food processor. Trained pastry chefs weigh most ingredients (even eggs!) for consistently good results, and I must say that this is a good plan. Use this exceptionally tender shortcrust pastry for savory or sweet tarts.

6 ounces all-purpose flour
1 teaspoon sugar
1/4 teaspoon salt
4 ounces (1 stick) unsalted butter, chilled
1 1/2 tablespoons ice water

Place flour, sugar and salt in bowl of food processor fitted with steel blade. Cut batter into small cubes and add to bowl. Using pulsing switch, process with 2 or 3 short pulses until mixture is crumbly, resembling coarse cornmeal. Again use pulsing switch and quickly add the water. Pulse 2 or 3 times. Dough will begin to form into a ball. Gather it together, flatten and immediately roll out onto a lightly floured surface or between 2 sheets of plastic wrap.

Makes one 9-inch tart shell.

Strawberry Tart

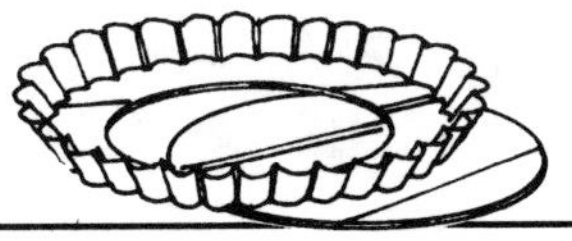

9-INCH FLUTED TART PAN WITH REMOVABLE BOTTOM

1 recipe sweet shortcrust pastry (page 287)
1/2 cup strawberry jam, heated
8 ounces (1 cup) sour cream
Grated peel of 1/2 lemon, colored part only
2 tablespoons honey
1/2 cup ground almonds
1 basket (12 ounces) small to medium strawberries

Preheat oven to 400°. Roll dough out into an 11-inch circle and fit into tart pan, pressing carefully into the fluted sides without stretching dough. Trim edges level with top of pan. Prick bottom of dough with a fork and place in freezer for 10 minutes. Fit a 12-inch square of heavy aluminum foil into frozen pastry shell and crimp it tightly over the sides to prevent them from shrinking down while baking.

Place on middle rack of oven and bake for 15 minutes. Remove foil, reduce heat to 375° and bake for 10 minutes more or until golden. Unmold and cool on rack. Brush bottom surface with 2 tablespoons of the jam.

In a bowl, combine sour cream, lemon peel, honey and ground almonds. Do not overmix, or cream will get thin. Refrigerate while preparing fruit.

Wash, hull and dry strawberries and cut in half. Spoon cream filling into prepared pastry shell. Arrange strawberries over cream, cut side down and touching each other. Brush berries with remaining melted glaze and refrigerate for 15 minutes before serving.

Serves 8.

Walnut Lace Cookies

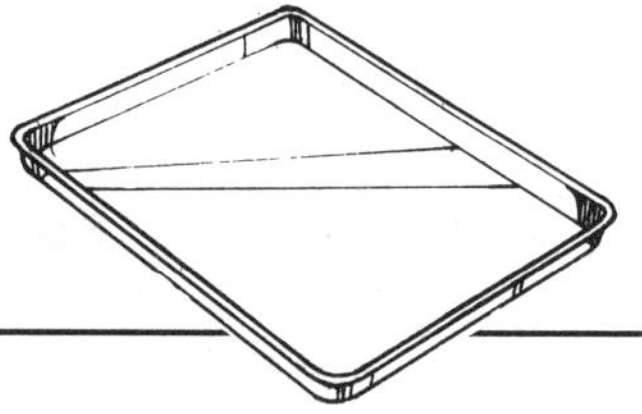

11- X 17-INCH HALF SHEET CAKE PAN

This recipe was given to me twenty-five years ago by Helen White, the manager of the Francisca Club in San Francisco at that time, which is right across the street from our Sutter Street shop. All she gave me was a list of ingredients—I had to guess how to make the cookies! I had to dig the first batch off the pan, but then I tried using baking parchment, and it worked fine. Mine are thinner and lacier than the originals I remember, and I think they are best eaten the day they are made.

4 ounces (1 stick) unsalted butter
1 cup sugar
2 eggs
1 teaspoon vanilla extract
2 tablespoons all-purpose flour
½ teaspoon baking soda
½ teaspoon salt
1½ cups walnuts, coarsely chopped

Preheat oven to 375°. Line baking pan with baking parchment. Cut butter into small cubes and combine with sugar in a mixing bowl. Cream well. Add eggs and vanilla and beat until smooth. Sift the flour, baking soda and salt together and fold into mixture. Add the walnuts. With a teaspoon place small mounds of the batter 4 inches apart on prepared pan. They spread out during baking. Place on middle rack of oven and bake for 10 to 12 minutes, until evenly browned. Remove from oven and slide baking parchment out of pan onto counter. Let cool for a minute or two until cookies have hardened. Remove with flat spatula and place on cooling rack. Wipe parchment off and repeat with remaining batter.

Makes approximately 60 cookies.

KITCHEN PARCHMENT

INDEX